DEVIANT BEHAVIOR

DEVIANT BEHAVIOR

Cliff Roberson
Emeritus Professor of Criminal Justice
Washburn University
Topeka, Kansas, USA

Elena Azaola
Senior Researcher
Center for Advanced Studies and Research
in Social Anthropology
Mexico City, Mexico

CRC Press
Taylor & Francis Group
Boca Raton London New York

CRC Press is an imprint of the
Taylor & Francis Group, an **informa** business

Reprint 2019

CRC Press
Taylor & Francis Group
6000 Broken Sound Parkway NW, Suite 300
Boca Raton, FL 33487-2742

ISBN: 978-0-367-24045-5

Visit the Taylor & Francis Web site at
http://www.taylorandfrancis.com

and the CRC Press Web site at
http://www.crcpress.com

Printed and bound in India

For sale in India, Pakistan, Nepal, Bhutan, Bangladesh and Sri Lanka only.

To my sons, Clif, Marshall, Kenneth, and Dwayne

—CR

To my daughter, Andrea, and my son, Pablo

—EA

Contents

Preface

Deviant Behavior is designed to provide both students and persons interested in deviant behavior and criminology with an easy-to-read and understand one-volume text on the key issues involved in social actions that are considered deviant. We have attempted to remove any indications of our political viewpoints or opinions. Some may have crept in, for which we apologize in advance.

Deviant behavior is a fascinating subject. It is about life and our everyday conduct. The issues of what constitutes deviant behavior are difficult, if not impossible, to explain or define. What may be deviant to one social group may be acceptable behavior to another group. In Chapter 1, we discuss why certain conduct is labeled as deviant and some is not. In the next chapter we examine the theoretical explanations of certain behaviors. In Chapter 3, we look at the constructionist approaches. In the remaining chapters, we discuss various categories of behavior and their causation.

While a good portion of the book may emphasize American theorists and theories, the book does have an international approach. Coauthor Cliff Roberson is educated in both law and human behavior. In addition, he has taught sociology, criminology, and deviant behavior for more than 30 years. Coauthor Elena Azaola of Mexico City is a social anthropologist who has taught and researched crime and prison issues for more than 30 years. She is presently a senior researcher at her institution.

While we are listed as the authors of the text, we have received outstanding assistance from many other professionals in the field and in the production process. One person in particular is Professor John Paul of Washburn University. He discussed his views on deviant behavior with us and contributed a section to Chapter 1. We also wish to thank our great editor at Taylor & Francis, Carolyn Spence, and very proficient project coordinator, Marsha Pronin.

Comments, recommended corrections, and suggestions for improvement are welcome. You may contact us via e-mail at cliff.roberson@washburn.edu.

About the Authors

Cliff Roberson is professor emeritus of criminal justice at Washburn University, Topeka, Kansas, and a retired professor of criminology at California State University, Fresno. He previously served as editor in chief of the international police journals *Police Practices and Research* and *Professional Issues in Criminal Justice Journal*. He is also an adjunct professor for Kaplan University.

He has authored or coauthored more than 60 books and texts on legal subjects. His previous academic experiences include associate vice president for academic affairs, Arkansas Tech University; dean of arts and sciences, University of Houston, Victoria; director of programs, National College of District Attorneys; professor of criminology and director of the Justice Center, California State University, Fresno; and assistant professor of criminal justice, St. Edwards University.

Dr. Roberson's nonacademic experience includes U.S. Marine Corps service as an infantry officer, trial and defense counsel and military judge as a marine judge advocate, and director of the military law branch, U.S. Marine Corps. Other legal employment experiences include trial supervisor, Office of State Counsel for Offenders, Texas Board of Criminal Justice, and judge pro tem in the California courts. He is admitted to practice before the U.S. Supreme Court, U.S. Court of Military Appeals, U.S. Tax Court, Federal Courts in California and Texas, Supreme Court of Texas, and Supreme Court of California.

Dr. Roberson's educational background includes earning a PhD in human behavior, U.S. International University; LLM in criminal law, criminology, and psychiatry, George Washington University; JD, American University; BA in political science, University of Missouri; and one year of postgraduate study at the University of Virginia School of Law.

Elena Azaola is professor emeritus at the Center for Advanced Studies and Research in Social Anthropology located in Mexico City. She earned a PhD in anthropology and did her postgraduate study on deviant behavior at Columbia University. She is also a psychoanalyst.

Dr. Azaola is presently Mexico's representative to the Human Rights Commission. In addition, she was an advisor with the National Commission of Human Rights and a council member at the Federal District Commission of Human Rights. She coordinated the European Commission project for street children in Mexico (1999–2003).

She has published more than 125 journal articles and numerous books on human behavior, crime, and human rights. Her research on the commercial sexual exploitation of children was sponsored by the United Nations Children Fund. She cocoordinated a national report on violence sponsored by the World Health Organization. Dr. Azaola was the board chair of the Institute for Security and Democracy, which created the first center for police accreditation in Mexico and won the MacArthur Foundation Award for Creative and Effective Institutions.

chapter one

What Is Deviant Behavior?

Chapter Objectives

What you should know and understand after studying this chapter:

- Have a working definition of what constitutes deviant behavior
- What is the process that labels a person as a deviant
- Why crime and deviant behavior are not interchangeable terms
- The difficulties in defining deviant behavior
- What constituted deviant behavior 10 years ago may not be deviant behavior today or tomorrow
- The dimensions of deviant behavior
- How social groups use sanctions to control group behavior
- The importance of social norms
- The various types of social norms
- Categories of deviance

Introduction

Deviance is behavior that is unusual in a society. Deviance implies nonconformity.

Is selling a body organ deviant behavior? We have two kidneys. We need only one. Suppose that you are unemployed and in danger of losing your home because you are behind on your mortgage payments. Would selling one of your kidneys to the highest bidder be considered deviant behavior? The answer to this question may depend on your definition of deviant behavior. Is your moral sense affected by how much the kidney is worth? Would your answer be different if an impoverished donor received only $500 or if he or she received $100,000?

In a post on a blog, one writer wrote that the most common objection to the practice of selling kidneys by individuals who are under financial pressures is that the act of selling a kidney is "exploiting the poor." Supporters of the right to sell one's kidney contend that the risks of donating a kidney are actually very small. In addition, the supporters contend that if allowing individuals to sell a kidney is in fact exploitation of impoverished individuals, then is the saving of lives justification for

SOCIETY IN ACTION

HOW WOULD THE LATE U.S. SUPREME COURT JUSTICE POTTER STEWART DEFINE DEVIANT BEHAVIOR?

Justice Potter Stewart, in attempting to define hard-core pornography, once stated:

> I shall not today attempt further to define the kinds of material I understand to be embraced within that shorthand description; and perhaps I could never succeed in intelligibly doing so. But I know it when I see it.[1]

"I know deviant behavior when I see it." Is that an acceptable approach to use in defining deviant behavior?

FOCUS ON PEOPLE

DANIEL GLASER

The focus of the interactionist perspective is on variable definitions of conduct as deviant and on the causes and consequences of this variability. It is not surprising, therefore, that proponents of this approach illustrate deviance as crime primarily by citing types of behavior toward which enactment of criminal law is most controversial.[2]

the exploitation? The supporters also contend that kidney markets may benefit poor donors far more than conceivably harming them.

Deviant behavior is not a subject that you study in school and then file away. Deviant behavior is a study of life—it is about life and is ever changing. It is also about how we live in a social relationship. Does deviance in essence mean being different? If everything was the same and there were no differences, our lives would be boring.

This chapter starts with an exploration of the nature and definition of deviance. What do we mean when we talk of deviance and deviant behavior?

Defining Deviance and Deviant Behavior

Defining the concept of deviant behavior is one of the most difficult tasks to overcome when studying the subject. Sociologists probably disagree more over the meaning of *deviant* and *deviant behavior* than any other subject. Simply defining deviant behavior as bizarre, unexpected, predatory, or self-destructive acts only requires us to attempt to define what we mean by bizarre, unexpected, and so on. Some sociologists conceive deviance to be those conditions, persons, or acts that are disvalued by society.[3] If we accept this definition, can there be positive deviant behavior?

One of the few areas where sociologists tend to agree is that deviant behavior does not automatically imply criminal behavior. Too often, we think of the study of deviant behavior as an extension of the study of criminology or a criminal justice subject. While the commission of crimes probably constitutes deviant behavior, deviant behavior is much broader and not entirely overlapping. A deviant act is not necessarily a crime, and as will be discussed later, a criminal act may not be a deviant act.

To many people, deviant behavior is a violation of the social rules of accepted behavior. These rules may be in the form of criminal laws or other types of social rules. Many individuals contend that behavior may be deviant without violating any social rules.

If we use the term *deviance* as a variation of the norm, then we can argue that deviance does not have to be negative; deviant behavior can be good or positive as long as it deviates from the norm. For example, handing out $100 bills on a street corner to passersby might be considered deviant by some sociologists because it certainly is not the norm, although the recipients of the bills will certainly say it is good behavior. However, many sociologists contend that the phrase "positive deviance" is an oxymoron (Figure 1.1).

Working Solution

In most perspectives, certain acts are always considered deviant, such as murder and forcible rape. It is the acts in the fringe areas that present the most trouble in determining deviance. One solution may be to use the positivist perspective when looking at acts that are clearly deviant, such as murder and forcible rape, and to use the constructionist perspective when assessing those acts that are on the fringes of acceptable or unacceptable conduct. The next section discusses the constructionist and positivist perspectives.

Faces of Deviance

The two major perspectives on what constitutes deviance and a deviant are the positivist and constructionist perspectives. The positive perspective tends to consider deviance as intrinsically objective, determined behavior that is observable empirically. The constructionists see deviance as a societal label and a subjective experience. Positivists see the deviant as a person who is not normal; constructionists see deviant behavior as a societal label.

Figure 1.1 Is the graffiti in this photo a form of art and self-expression, or is it social deviance? In the beginning, graffiti was a form of expression that was not supported by mainstream culture; that is, defacing public property was not an acceptable art form, and anyone caught doing so was depicted as a deviant. It presently appears that many in society are now accepting graffiti as a form of art. (Photo by Cliff Roberson.)

Positivist Perspective

The positivist perspective is based on the assumptions that deviance is

- Absolutism
- Objectivism
- Determinism

Prior to the emergence of the sociology of deviance, deviant behavior was studied and written about by the early criminologists, many who believed that individuals who committed deviant acts were biologically different from those who did not. When deviance emerged as a separate branch of sociology, the positivist criminologists' concepts and beliefs were carried over to the study of deviance.

The positivist perspective holds that deviant persons differ from nondeviant individuals, and deviant behavior resides within the deviant individual. According to the positivists, deviants were born deviant. Originally deviant behavior was thought to be caused by biological factors such as defective genes, body build, bumps on the head, and shapes of the jaw; later positivists tended to base the causation on inherent psychological traits.

Current positivist sociologists have generally abandoned the concept that deviance is caused solely by biological or psychological traits and recognize that social factors do play a major role in determining a person's status as a deviant. But generally, they still consider deviance as real and emphasize the study of deviance and deviants rather than the study of nondeviant acts and those who are not classified as deviant.

Using the psychological causation approach, positivist sociologists believe that deviants have different mental characteristics from nondeviants. The differences include psychotic, neurotic, psychopathic, and otherwise mentally defective or disturbed. According to this approach, the different mental characteristics are permanent, and once a deviant, always a deviant. The positivist perspective was noted in a widely quoted statement by Gwynn Nettler: "Some people are crazier than others; we can tell the differences; and calling lunacy a name does not cause it."[4]

The absolutism's assumption holds that deviance has intrinsically real and observable qualities that distinguish it from nondeviance. Accordingly, deviance is an attribute that resides in the individual, and the deviant person will always be a deviant person.

The objectivism's assumption is based on the concept that deviant behavior is an observable act that can be studied, and the study of deviants should focus on studying deviants as objects of study rather than persons. According to the positivists, when studying deviants as objects, the researcher should not pass moral judgment on the subjects or empathize with the feelings of the deviants. By studying deviants as objects in a scientific manner, the researchers' findings are open to be replicated by other researchers.

The final positivist assumption, determinism, is based on the concept that deviance is determined or caused by forces beyond an individual's control. Accordingly, there is a lack of free will in the deviant's conduct. To hold that the individual made a decision to act in a deviant manner would undermine the principle of determinism. Carrying this concept to an illogical extreme, why should we punish the mother who kills her baby if she had no choice in committing the act of killing her baby?

Generally, the positivist sociologists of today have abandoned the concept of hard determinism and instead stress the concept of soft determinism. Most recognize that the deviant person has some limited degree of freedom of choice. They see causation factors as the reason the individual chooses to commit the conduct in question. The causation factors may include coming from a broken home, spousal abuse, social disorganization, differential association, and lack of social controls.

Constructionist Perspective

The constructionist perspective evolved in the late 1950s and early 1960s as a direct challenge to the positivist perspective. According to the constructionist perspective, an act is considered deviant only because some societal group has so labeled it as deviant. Deviance is only:

- A mental construct
- Socially constructed
- By a societal group

Constructionists are interested in how society defines certain acts. They use the phrase "social construction of deviance" to refer to conditions, processes, and effects of social interactions and the culture, which results in the classification of an act as deviant and an actor as a deviant. According to the constructionist perspective, deviance is not an object that is tangible and real. It is a subjective concept that is created through human interaction. The deviant is not a type of person identifiable by a checklist; instead, the deviant is a person to whom the deviant label has been successfully applied.[5]

Howard S. Becker provides this definition of deviant behavior in his book *Outsiders*: "The deviant is one to whom that label has been successfully applied; deviant behavior is behavior that people have so labeled."[6] By this definition, Becker indicates that deviant behavior is a socially constructed concept. The term *socially constructed* means a concept constructed by society and dependent on definitional processes for, as Becker points out, the definition is not a static one but one that changes over time and varies from place to place.

Becker notes that all social groups make rules and attempt to enforce them. Those social rules define situations and the kinds of behavior that are not considered appropriate. Becker notes that society has many different kinds of rules, ranging from those formally enacted into law to those that represent informal agreements among the people in the society. Becker also notes that we do not ordinarily question the label "deviant" once it has been applied to particular acts or people, but rather take it as it is applied. According to him, in doing so, we accept the values of the group making the judgment.

Becker notes that the simplest view of deviance is based on statistics: simply defining anything that varies too widely from the average. Using this definition, one of the authors could be considered deviant because he is left-handed. Becker's definition of deviance is divorced from the concept that deviance is rule-breaking behavior. According to Becker, deviance is anything that is not normal behavior.

A more common constructionist view of deviance identifies deviance as the failure to obey group rules. The problem with this view is that it fails to provide us with guidance as to which rules to use as a yardstick to measure behavior. As Becker recognized, a society has many groups, each with its own rules. This definition of deviance also means that society creates deviance by making rules that can be broken to constitute deviant behavior.

Deconstruction of Deviance

Frequently, sociologists use the phrase "the deconstruction of deviance." As Konty notes in his article on the deconstruction of deviance, one can become dizzy when considering the voluminous debate over what the phrase really means. Konty suggests that in its broadest sense, deconstruction is the analytical process that examines how assumptions and experiences shape meaning. He then contends that the phrase "deconstruction of deviance" calls attention to or examines the conditions, processes, and effects that are used to construct deviance. Konty concluded that deconstruction of deviance is the process that takes apart the building materials of deviance and examines each independently.[7]

Borrowing from Konty's example, consider an unmarried woman who is labeled as a deviant because she has an active sex life. If we exam each element used in the labeling process, most of us in today's world would probably conclude that an active sex life is insufficient behavior to be labeled a deviant, especially as a similar label would probably not be applied to an unmarried male with a comparable sex life.

Normative and Situational Perspectives

Additional attempts to find a workable definition of deviant behavior include defining the concept from either the normative or the situational perspective. The normative perspective views deviant behavior as behavior that violates existing and generally accepted social norms. The situational perspective looks at the social situation surrounding the behavior in question. The situational perspective is relativistic because it defines deviant behavior primarily in terms of when and where the act in question occurs.

The situational perspective views behaviors as essentially neutral; they take on meaning only when defined by some social entity.[8] This perspective uses a three-step approach in assessing whether certain acts or behaviors are deviant:

1. Define the behavior.
2. Label the actors.
3. Respond to the label attached to the actors.

The social behavior may be assessed as good or bad, moral or immoral, or admired or condemned. Individuals are then labeled based on this assessment of the behavior. An individual who commits an act that is assessed as immoral would, under the situational perspective, be labeled as a deviant.

If a young male appears at the local high school wearing no clothes, the overwhelming number of people who observe him would be shocked and consider his conduct to be inherently wrong or deviant. In this scenario, the nude man would be judged by the norms of the community. This conduct, under the normative viewpoint, would undoubtedly be considered deviant behavior.

If instead of going to the local high school, the nude man went to Black's Beach, which is a "clothes optional" beach, would his conduct be considered deviant? Probably not. Persons who frequent a clothes-optional beach expect to see some nude individuals. In this scenario, the focus shifts from the conduct of the individual to the social situation. In the first scenario at the high school, the individual would be judged deviant because he violated generally accepted norms of behavior of persons in a high school. In the second scenario at the beach, the individual would not generally be judged as deviant because of the situational viewpoint of accepted behavior.

One could argue that in both scenarios, one could view the behavior from either a normative or situational viewpoint based on the fact that nudity at a high school is a violation of the norm because of the location of the incident, and nudity at the clothes-optional beach is not a violation of the norm because of the location. So this behavior would probably be viewed the same way in both viewpoints. Accordingly, it appears that many behaviors will be defined as deviant regardless of which viewpoint or perspective is used. There are some behaviors, however, that may be unacceptable using one assessment and acceptable using the other, depending on the perspective used for assessment that cause issues in society.

Under both perspectives, the societal responses the behavior generates dictate the extent of the deviance. While the nude man appearing at the local high school may generate a strong response and create a high degree of public condemnation, the same person appearing at the high school barefooted would not. Therefore, it would appear that appearing barefoot is not as deviant as appearing nude.

SOCIETY IN ACTION

SUMMARY OF THE COMMON PERSPECTIVES OF DEVIANCE

Statistical deviance: What the majority of people do is normal; behavior that is not within a certain norm is deviant.

Positivist view of deviance (or absolutist view): Deviance is taken for granted, and the basic rules of society are obvious. The deviant is physically or mentally different from the nondeviant.

Constructionist view of deviance (or reactivist view): Deviance is behavior that social groups label as such. It is subjective. A deviant person is one whom society has labeled as such.

Normative: The designation of deviance depends on a group's notion of what one ought or ought not to do. It is a situational conception and is ever changing as society changes. Deviance is the violation of a group norm or standard of behavior and constitutes only those deviations from the norm in a disapproved direction.

Situational perspective: This perspective views behavior as essentially neutral and it takes on meaning, including the label of deviant, only when defined by some social entity. This perspective uses a three-step approach in assessing whether the behavior is deviant: (1) define the behavior, (2) label the actors, and (3) respond to the label attached to the actors.

FOCUS ON PEOPLE

DR. JOHN PAUL

Dr. John Paul is a different type of professor. He has a joint tenure in the sociology and art departments at Washburn University in Topeka, Kansas. Each year he teaches courses in both deviant behavior and art.

Q: John, art and deviant behavior seem two vastly different disciplines. Is there any connection between the two disciplines?

There is a strong connection between art and the study of deviance. Art is often an act of deviance, in that the making of art often breaks established rules and accepted societal patterns of thought. In this way, movements in the history of art are particularly associated with rule breaking, as they challenge tradition and force new ways of seeing and experiencing the world around us.

Q: Are there any similarities between the two disciplines, deviance and art?

Scholars who teach deviance are generally fascinated with rules: what are the rules that guide a certain practice or human activity, how are rules established and enforced, and what happens when rules are violated. Similarly, the history and practice of art is an exploration of rule makers and breakers. Thus, both art and deviance are disciplines that explore, and routinely challenge, the rules and their makers. The study of art and deviance reminds us that rules and accepted concepts of conventional behavior are situational and fluid, and it is often the "powers that be" (not logic, fairness, or sensibility) that define what is "normal" and what is not.

Q: If an art student asked you "What is deviant behavior?" how would you answer?

Generally, deviance is defined as actions that violate accepted norms of behavior and thought. However, I would caution students to note that not all deviance is "bad." Sometimes deviance is simply difference, and in fact, no positive social change ever occurs without the deviant. In the end, I would say that deviance for an art student is something that is generally positive and something that should be encouraged; deviance is about creating new techniques that push the boundaries of how art should be made and finding new ways of depicting what art should look like.

Q: I am curious as to why you elected to teach in both disciplines.

My parents are artists and I learned from them that art was a way to study society and record (and make) social change. Thus, as a result of socialization and as a way to honor my parents, I studied art. However, along my academic path I also discovered the discipline of sociology and, like art, fell in love with its theoretical and methodological approaches to the study of society. I've elected to teach in both disciplines because I feel they complement and give growth to each other—I feel that art has made my teaching and research in the social sciences more innovative and creative, while the study of deviance has proven to be a vehicle for artistic growth and development in my own and my students' work. As a scholar of deviance and a practitioner of art I have multiple interdisciplinary tools at my disposal from which to study and make commentary upon society.

Q: Any special tips that you can provide for individuals studying deviance and behavior?

Deviance tends to vary on three major levels: across time, across cultures, and from group to group. Thus, when studying deviance, please resist the tendency of ethnocentric thinking and remember that deviance is neither inherently good nor bad—it may be (depending upon the context of its application) a label of social control and harassment or a tool of social change.

Positive Deviance

Can there be positive deviance? The answer to this question depends on your definition of deviant behavior. If you define deviance as a variation from the medium, then you could consider conduct that is above the standard norm as positive deviant behavior. If, however, you look at deviance as a labeling process, then you probably consider the concept of positive deviance an oxymoron. Edward Sagarin sees the concept of positive deviance as a contradiction in terms.[9] He notes that the two ends of the putative dimension are very different. He rejects the concept that the positive tail of a bell curve of human behavior should be considered positive behavior. Sagarin does note that sometimes negative deviant behavior may have positive consequences, such as when a crime brings a community together.

At the start of this chapter, we discussed the selling of one's kidneys. In recent news was the story of a charitable individual who gave money to the poor every Christmas. Later he decided that as he had two kidneys and needed only one, he would give one of his kidneys to a stranger who needed a transplant. The actions of this individual may clearly be considered as different and unusual. Is this an example of positive deviance?

Social Rules

Any discussion of deviant behavior includes the concept of rule breaking. Who makes the rules that result in the characterization of deviance? As Becker notes, social rules are the creation of social groups. Many theorists contend that society creates deviance. If there were no rules, there would be no rule breaking and no societal reaction to rule breaking, and therefore no deviance.[10] Taking this a step further, if there were no criminal laws, then there would be no crime in a society because there would be no laws to violate.

Our present-day society comprises many groups of complex organizations. The societal groups are highly differentiated along social class lines, ethnic lines, occupational lines, and cultural lines. Each has its own set of rules. The social rules of one group often conflict with the social rules of other groups. Accordingly, a person may break the social rule of one group while complying with the rules of another group. As deviance is created by responses of people to the rule-breaking activity, a person may be seen as a deviant by one group but not by other social groups.

Frequently one group will impose or try to impose its rules on another group. Whether a group is successful in doing so depends generally on the group's political, cultural, and economic powers. For example, parents impose their rules on their children. The middle class is frequently accused of imposing its rules on the lower socioeconomic class. An employer, to a limited extent, can generally impose its rules on its employees. Differences in the power to make rules may be referred to as power differentials. The strength of a power differential most likely determines whether one group or individual can impose rules on another group or individual.

Social Controls

Social controls are generally considered as either informal or formal. Researchers study why some people obey social rules and others do not. Those who do not are usually labeled as deviants. But even the most deviant individual obeys social rules the majority of the time. It has been reported that Charles Manson, who is serving a life sentence in the California prison system for leading a gang that committed the murder of movie star Sharon Tate and others in the 1960s, stated that he did not like to drive in the city of Los Angeles because the majority of drivers did not obey the traffic laws.

Generally, social groups use sanctions to deal with rule-breaking behavior. The method social groups use is called social control. Social control is a deliberate attempt to change human behaviors. In some situations people conform to social rules because they know of no other alternative. In some situations they conform because it is to their benefit to conform. In other situations, people conform because of inducements to conform.

Norms

Norms may be defined as the generally agreed on guidelines or rules for behavior that provide boundaries for interpersonal relations. Because the concept of deviance is defined in terms of societal norms, as norms change, so do the definitions of deviance. Some norms are fairly stable and do not change, while other norms are transitory.[11] Certain types of deviance are almost universally considered as deviance, such as murder, incest, and violent rapes. Many other types of deviance, however, are not universally accepted, and the norms may vary according to the social group.

Norms take two parallel forms: behavioral and expectational. Behavioral norms are the patterns of actual behavior that individuals typically follow when interacting under certain conditions. For example, we go to a diner for breakfast. The waitress hands us menus. The handing of the menus is the conduct that we anticipate from the waitress. This pattern of behavior is considered a behavioral norm. It is also an expectational norm. Expectational norms are what people typically expect others to do under given conditions. Because we expect the waitress to hand us menus, our expectations in this regard constitute an expectational norm.

The key difference between the two norms is that with behavioral norms, we are looking at conduct that has occurred and comparing it with what we expected. With expectational norms, we are anticipating certain behavior to occur. Both of these norms provide predictability regarding conduct.

It is this need for predictability in the actions of people that serves as a basis for any social organization or group.[12] Any deviation threatens the organization or group. For example, if we go to the diner for breakfast and take a seat and the waitress ignores us, this conduct would cause consternation.

Norms may be classified in many different ways, including their degree of acceptance by group members, the mode of their enforcement in the group, the manner in which a norm is transmitted, and the amount of conformity the norm requires of group members. Norms are considered crucial to the maintenance of order. They are also regarded as cultural ideals and conduct that we expect in certain conditions. Proscriptive norms tell us what we should do, and prescriptive norms tell us what we should not do. In general, norms are social or group standards for conduct and provide us with a means to interpret our experiences.

William Graham Sumner developed three categories of norms. Among their characteristics are the differences in individuals' reactions to violating them.[13] He categorized the three norms as mores, customs, and folkways.

- Mores are acts that when broken arouse intense feelings and lead to extreme consequences. Rape is a violation of a more.
- Customs are practices common to a people or place. A violation of custom usually generates a less severe reaction than the violation of a more. Usually people react with disgust, repulsion, or shock to

the violation of a custom. An example of the violation of a custom is filing one's nails during a luncheon.

- Folkways are thoughts, behaviors, or actions common to a social group. Often folkways relate to manner of dress, use of good manners, politeness, and speech. Folkways may be considered as trivial conventions by members of the group or by outsiders.

Laws enacted by federal and state governments are formal proscriptive norms, and their violation is normally punishable with criminal sanctions. To constitute a criminal act, a statute must exist that criminalizes the act in question, and the rule breaker must have committed the act in a manner that violates each element of the statute. Criminal laws merely describe those violations of social norms at the minimal level. The criminal laws do not pretend to describe what most of society considers as acceptable conduct.

While most criminal acts are also considered as violations of societal norms, some criminal acts are not. For example, state statutes in many states require that homeowners have a permit or license for their home security system, and the failure to have the required permit is a minor crime. If a state has such a statute and a homeowner violates it, that homeowner has violated the law but not necessarily a social norm.

Most deviant acts are not criminal acts. Most are violations of informal rules of social behavior. Generally norms are enforced by either formal or informal sanctions. The next section discusses these two sanctions and social control.

Socialization

Socialization is the label for the process a person goes through when learning the socially approved ways of a social group. It consists of learning the social rules. For example, the mother demonstrates to her daughter how a "young lady" should act. The daughter's process in learning what is expected of a "lady" is a form of socialization. During recruit training, the marine or soldier learns how to be a marine or a soldier and is thus undergoing the process of socialization during recruit training. A similar situation occurs in a police academy, where the recruit is involved in the socialization process of becoming a police officer.

While in most cases, the socialization process occurs with the use of role models, it can occur without any role models. A common example of socialization without a role model is the learning of social roles of a specific social group by formal study or formal education. For example, I want to become an airplane pilot, so I study and practice the skills necessary to become a pilot. If I wanted to be a baseball player like the great Stan

Musial, I could use him as a role model and study how he plays baseball and try to play like he does. In the latter example, I am using a role model.

Sanctions

Sanctions are the actions people take in response to behavior. Sanctions may be either negative or positive. A positive sanction is a reward meant to encourage rule compliance, whereas a negative sanction is a punishment designed to discourage rule breaking. More importantly, sanctions are classified as informal or formal according to the source of the sanction, or who is doing the sanctioning. Informal sanctions are the unofficial actions of groups or individuals, and formal sanctions are official group expressions. An informal sanction may be gossip, ostracism, or merely shaming.

When a child brings home a good report card from school, many parents give him or her a positive reward that may be money, a special treat, or just praise. But if the child's report card is not so good, the child may be hesitant to bring it home because he or she anticipates a negative sanction from the parents.

The most widely known formal sanction is the use of criminal sanctions. Frequently, individuals consider formal sanction as solely governmental action or criminal punishment. However, when an employer raises the pay of an employee, the employer is using a positive sanction, and when the employer reduces an employee's pay or fires an employee, the employer administers a negative sanction. Formal sanctions are incorporated into institutional systems of society and are administered by individuals who occupy particular roles within those institutions.

Generally most sanctions used in a societal group are of an informal nature. For example, if you wore blue jeans to a formal dinner, most people at the dinner would disapprove of your behavior but not take any formal sanctions. The fact that they appear to disapprove of your attire is generally sufficient for you to get the message that your manner of dress is unacceptable. Their demonstrated disapproval would be an informal sanction, whereas a pay cut by your employer would be a formal type.

Deviance as a Shifting Concept

What we consider as deviant today may not be deviant tomorrow. An excellent example of this movement or shift is demonstrated by the actions of the American Psychiatric Association (APA). At one time the APA's *Diagnostic and Statistical Manual* (DSM) listed homosexuality as a form of mental disease. The APA's members, in 1973, voted to remove homosexuality from the category of mental illness and reclassified it as an alternative form of sexual behavior. Today same-gender marriages are accepted in many states.

SOCIETY IN ACTION

THE CHANGING STATUS OF OBESITY

Obesity is generally defined as a medical condition in which excess body fat has accumulated to the extent that it may have an adverse effect on health, leading to reduced life expectancy or increased health problems. A person is considered obese when his or her body mass index (BMI) exceeds 30 kg/m^2. (The BMI measurement is obtained by dividing a person's weight in kilograms by the square of the person's height in meters.) Obesity increases the likelihood of various diseases and is considered as one of the leading preventable causes of death worldwide.

In recent years, obesity has become stigmatized in most of the world, though it was once widely perceived as a symbol of wealth and fertility and still is in some parts of the world.[14] Presently many members of society consider it a significant health problem, and many companies are making large profits off of selling weight reducing products. Why are Americans buying those products? Probably because individuals want to be accepted by their social groups as beautiful or healthy and do not want to be looked down upon because of their weight (an informal negative sanction).

Most of the early textbooks on deviant behavior discussed the question of whether or not homosexuality was deviant behavior. Because of the recent changes in societal acceptance of homosexuality and how the legal system currently looks at the issue, the authors decided not to discuss homosexuality as a separate issue. This does not mean that all groups or individuals accept the conduct as normal, but that societal rules are in a state of flux regarding homosexuality.

Utility of Deviant Behavior

Does deviant behavior play a useful function in our society? According to some scholars, the reaction to deviant behavior enhances the stability of our society by reaffirming our moral boundaries.[15] Jack Douglas notes, "Deviance is the mutation that is generally destructive of society, but it is also the only major source of creative adaptations of rules to new life situations." Douglas suggests that entire cultures and societies can change through deviance.

The scholars who suggest that deviance plays a functional role in society frequently cite Emile Durkheim and his discussions of the utility of crime.[16] Durkheim used similar arguments in his statements about how boring a society without crime would be. If we accept the fact that deviant behavior is behavior that challenges the morality of our society, think how boring it would be if all our conduct was clearly within the accepted behavioral range of societal norms. The authors wonder what movies and books would be about if there were no crime. Most television shows today are based on or concerned with crime. If society had no crime, then there would be no movies or books about it.

A society without deviance would probably be a society in which everyone had the same thoughts and beliefs and adhered to the same types of conduct. Imagine a society in which no one ever commits murder, rape, thefts, or other crimes. The most serious discretion in that unlikely society would probably be some minor infraction such as jaywalking. And as jaywalking would then be the most serious discretion, it would be dealt with by inflicting the most serious punishment.

Deviance can be a major source of creative adaptation of social rules and norms. In the 1950s, most states had state or local laws that prevented merchants from opening their stores on Sundays. These so-called blue laws thus prohibited the sale of many items on Sundays. As society changed and more merchants began ignoring and then challenging the laws and people began to shop on the day of rest, states were pressured to change or eliminate the Sunday closure laws. One could argue that societal noncompliance with these laws was the major factor in states eliminating the laws.

Frequently individuals are sanctioned in some manner for rules violation. The use of sanctions helps us draw the boundaries of acceptable conduct. A sanction does not need to be a criminal punishment to be effective. It may only be the neighborhood casting aspersions against the violating individuals or shaming them. Not sanctioning the individuals or ignoring the violations sends the message that the rule or norm may need to be reconsidered.

Politics and Deviance

According to Schur, the very process of defining a particular behavior pattern as deviant is inherently political.[17] Schur notes that the process of deviantization is a key element in the social stratification order because it intervenes in the process of resource allocation. And actors in the societal centers who negotiate power and morality in an attempt to define certain patterns of behavior as deviant or nondeviant construct the boundaries of acceptable societal conduct and affect the processes of change or stability.

Ben-Yehuda contends that all forms of deviance can be classified according to the three areas of society from which they emerge and at which they aim[18]:

- The periphery of society, aimed at the center
- The center of society, aimed at the periphery
- Either the center or the periphery, aimed at the same level, that is, center to center or periphery to periphery

The center that he refers to is the power group of a particular society, and the periphery refers to those individuals who are on the edge of society as far as power is concerned. Ben-Yehuda examined the issues of power and morality. To him, those who define deviance are the ones in society who have the power to enforce the definitions.

Behavior Assessment

Generally in determining whether certain conduct is deviant, the sociological concepts of culture and social organization are used. Palmer and Humphrey define culture as "a body of widely held shared customs and values which provide general orientations toward life and specific ways of achieving common goals."[19] Social organization is the organization of society that provides the means for carrying out the complex network of social interactions between individuals, social groups, and institutions.

Undetected Deviance

Taking the positivist's view, it would appear that a person who commits a deviant but undiscovered act is nonetheless a deviant. Under the constructionist perspective, the answer is probably different. Remember, the constructionist looks at how people react to an act to determine whether the act is deviant.

If a person commits a deviant act that is undetected, does the rule violation make the person a deviant? If the answer is yes, then probably a large segment of society should be labeled deviant. If the act does not make one deviant, but society labels the person deviant, then it is not the act that labels one a deviant, but the act of labeling. If the societal reaction to behavior results in the deviant label, it would stand to reason that if society was unaware of the behavior, there would be no reaction and thus no labeling.

Tolerable and Acceptable

Is there such a concept as tolerable or acceptable deviance? The concept of tolerable deviance is used sometimes to describe those conditions where an individual's conduct violates the rules of social norm, but the individual is not labeled as a deviant. Stebbins defines tolerance as an attitude or orientation that individuals hold toward certain activities or thoughts of others that differ substantially from their activities or thoughts.[20] When something is tolerated, it is accorded legitimacy, although perhaps grudgingly. The activities or thoughts are tolerated because they are not seen as threats to society.

College basketball fans eagerly look forward each year to March Madness. March Madness refers to the annual national basketball tournament to determine a national champion in college basketball. Most universities—in fact, most midsized and larger business establishments—organize a "bracket pool" where staff can submit their picks on the tournament games and the winner receives a jackpot. A popular ESPN morning talk sports show even has a "sheet of integrity" bet between the cohosts based on March Madness.

Gambling is one of those criminal laws that most members of society agree is a deviant act. Yet, the employees and others who participate in these pools are not considered deviants by society. This is the type of deviance that Robert Stebbins labels acceptable deviance. Stebbins indicates that it is acceptable to bend the rules of society as long as it is clear that the rule bender has limits to his or her conduct.[21] The rule bending in these gambling pools is not a threat to the society, and the individuals who engage in the pools still demonstrate their commitment to the group. Taking this to its logical conclusion, you could opine that while society sees gambling as a threat to society, society in general sees no threat to society by the numerous basketball pools.

Dimensions of Deviance

Deviance varies in a number of dimensions, by the degree in which it is socially patterned, the extent to which it is innovative, and possibly to the degree to which it is socially evaluated as either positive deviance or negative deviance. By the degree in which it is socially patterned refers mainly to whether the deviance is institutionalized or individualistic.

According to Palmer and Humphrey, all deviant behavior ranges between individualistic and institutionalized deviance.[22] They give the example that during the early part of the 20th century, wearing a scanty bathing suit was considered deviant behavior. In this situation, the deviant was individualistic and not generally accepted by society. Later, as values changed and more and more people began wearing scanty bathing suits, the deviant behavior became institutionalized. Currently, wearing a bathing suit that is very scanty is no longer considered deviance. This changing of attitude is another example of the fluid nature of our concept of deviance.

SOCIETY IN ACTION

BECKER'S SEQUENTIAL MODEL OF DEVIANCE

Howard Becker contends that to understand deviance better, we should examine a dimension of deviance with other dimensions of the concept.[23] Keep in mind that to Becker, deviance is the result of a labeling process.

Becker's Types of Deviant Behavior

	Obedient Behavior	Rule-Breaking Behavior
Perceived as Deviant	Falsely accused	Pure deviant
Not Perceived as Deviant	Conforming	Secret deviant

The falsely accused individual is one whose conduct did not constitute rule-breaking behavior, but the labeling social group perceived that he or she did break the rule or rules. The conforming category is where the individual conforms to the rules and the social group perceives the person as not deviant. The pure deviant is the individual who breaks the rules and is perceived by the social group as doing so. The final category is the secret deviant. The secret deviant is one who does rule-breaking behavior but is for some reason not considered a deviant. The failure to perceive the secret deviant as a deviant may be because his or her behavior is not known to others or others tend to overlook the behavior.

Innovation is the process of creating something or some new process. So the extent to which deviance is innovative refers to the fact that often social groups consider innovative ways or forms of conduct as deviance. The innovation is typically considered individualistic at first. As more members of the group adopt the innovative conduct, it becomes institutionalized and may finally be accepted as acceptable behavior.

Overview of Deviance Theories

The deviant-related theories are examined in greater depth in later chapters. This chapter presents only a brief introduction to deviance theories. Deviance theories are grouped as explanatory theories or constructionist theories. The theories are also generally divided into structured/functional, conflict/critical, and interactionist groups.

Explanatory theories are concerned with trying to explain why deviance does or does not occur. The explanatory theorists assume that a wide variety of factors determine deviant behavior, such as biological, sociological, or psychological makeup of the individual. These theorists assume that deviant behavior is real and can be studied empirically. Conversely, the constructionists are more interested in obtaining a better understanding of the process by which certain behavior is considered deviant and why certain individuals are classified as deviant. While the explanatory theorists take for granted that those who are in power have the authority to create and define deviance, the constructionists question the definitions of deviance and those who define it. The constructionists do not see deviance as real, but as subjective and as a social construction.

The structural/functional and conflict/critical theories are considered explanatory theories, and interactionist theories are considered constructionist. The structural/functional approach is generally credited to Emile Durkheim. Durkheim focused on crime, but his thinking can be expanded to include all forms of deviance. His basic theme was that because deviance and crime have existed in all societies at all times, they must be normal. He also assumed that deviance and crime have positive functions and would not exist if they were not functional. Durkheim considered that the most important function of deviance is that it allows groups to define and clarify their collective beliefs—their norms and values. According to Durkheim, without periodic violations of standards of conduct, the standards would become less clear to all members of the society, and thus less strongly held and less popular.[24]

One structural/functional theory is the strain theory. The strain theory contends that there is a discrepancy between societal values and the structural means available to individuals to obtain the desired societal values. The discrepancy is that the structural relationships between the desired goals and the institutionalized means to attain those goals are not equally available to all in society. For example, socially acceptable goals in the United States are for an individual to own a home and have a good profession. The legitimate means to obtain those goals are to attend college, get a good job, and accumulate the needed wealth to pay the down payment on a home mortgage. The legitimate means to obtain these goals are generally available to the upper and middle socioeconomic segments of the population, but are not generally available to those living in poor and minority areas of the nation. Hence, those individuals may use illegitimate means to obtain the social goals, such as being involved in trafficking illegal drugs.

Social control theories are also grouped under the structural/functional group. Social control theories contend that when social constraints on antisocial behavior are weakened or absent, delinquent behavior emerges.

The conflict/critical groups trace the source of deviance to the larger structures of society and the strains that they produce or the fact that they do not exercise adequate social control over people. The conflict/critical theorists are concerned with the structure of society and how the structure affects the members of society. According to the conflict theorists, inequality in societies causes less powerful individuals to engage in deviant behavior. According to the conflict perspective, conflict is a fundamental aspect of social life and can never be fully resolved. Modern conflict theorists were influenced by Marxist theory and considered deviance as a creation of the capitalist economic system. Conflict theorists contend the laws created by societal elites single out and sanction the actions of the have-nots.

The interactionist theories, also considered the social process theories, consider that deviance is learned in the interaction with others, and the socialization process that occurs as the result of group membership is the primary route through which the learning occurs. The labeling theory, one of the interactionist theories, sees continued deviance as a consequence of limited opportunities for acceptable behavior, which result from the negative responses of society to those defined as deviant.

Another interactionist theory, differential association, holds that individuals pursue deviant behavior to the extent that they identify themselves with real or imaginary people who consider their deviant behavior acceptable. According to the differential association theories, individuals learn to commit deviant acts similar to the manner in which they learn to play baseball.

Are Deviants Different?

In this section, we will explore the question: Are deviants difference from us? An interesting place to start this study is with Timothy Brezina's research on academic cheating.[25] According to many researchers, seeing the deviant as a different kind of person bolsters our self-esteem and helps us repress the fear that under certain circumstances, we too might commit the same deviant acts.

According to Brezina, academic cheating has been described as epidemic in schools, and there appears to be general agreement that it is endemic to education in the secondary schools as well as at the college level. Among school officials, if not students, academic cheating is viewed with disapproval and is thus socially defined as deviant. Brezina viewed academic cheating as a useful example of deviance since it is familiar to most students. He developed a cheating exercise. He asked students to reflect on their own cheating behavior and then to relate their behaviors and motives to various theories of deviance. He then asked students to write brief and anonymous responses to three questions:

- Have you ever cheated in high school?
- Have you ever cheated in college?
- If you answered yes to the above questions, explain your behavior.

The vast majority of the students admitted that they have cheated at some point in their educational careers. Students generally justified their behavior on the intense competition for or pressure to obtain high grades and unfair exams or assignments. For example, one student explained that he or she cheated because the professor gave an unreasonable assignment and he or she had no choice but to cheat to obtain a decent grade.

Brezina opined that students who engaged in academic dishonesty may tend to excuse their behavior with the aid of various rationalizations, including the belief that they were forced into cheating by intense pressure and competition for grades by so-called unfair exams and alleged time constraints. They may also justify cheating by dismissing its significance (e.g., "everybody does it") or by discounting the legitimacy of standard testing procedures).

Brezina considered that the excuses provided by the students for cheating related to the strain theory. The students were under pressure to perform and therefore took an unacceptable method to obtain the desired results. Brezina noted that while the student accounts of cheating behaviors can be interpreted from a variety of theoretical perspectives, he contended that it helps to establish that the majority of us would probably cheat in academic endeavors if confronted with sufficient motivation.

Brezina noted that while the rationalizations employed by academic cheaters and violent offenders may differ in substance and form, they serve essentially the same function or goal: to justify deviant acts and to neutralize moral prohibitions.

Study of Deviance as a Separate Discipline

While the study of deviance dates back to the 18th century or earlier with the works of the early criminologists, the study of deviant behavior as a separate subdivision of sociology from criminology dates back only to the 1950s. Still today many educated people equate deviant behavior with criminal behavior. The pioneers in the sociology of deviant behavior include Edwin Lemert[26] (1912–1996), Marshall Clinard[27] (1911–2010), and Howard Becker[28] (1928–).

Practicum

Study the following list of acts, and then answer the questions that appear at the end.

1. Plagiarizing a term paper
2. Borrowing a classmate's notes and using them to study for the final
3. Violating a traffic control signal
4. Using a friend's identification to purchase alcoholic beverages

FOCUS ON PEOPLE

EDWIN M. LEMERT

Edwin M. Lemert was born in Cincinnati, Ohio, in 1912. His parents wanted their son to be a lawyer; however, to his father's dismay, Lemert studied sociology instead of law, receiving a degree in sociology from Miami University of Ohio in 1934. After graduation, he worked as a caseworker in Cincinnati before pursuing graduate studies in sociology at Ohio State University, where he received his PhD. Lemert taught briefly at Kent State University and Western Michigan University before teaching at the University of California, Los Angeles.

Edwin Lemert advocated the labeling theory when studying social deviance. He preferred to use the term *societal reaction* rather than *deviant behavior.* He was a maverick in many areas, beginning with this important theory he first developed in his classic 1951 work *Social Pathology: A Systematic Approach to the Theory of Sociopathic Behavior,* the first textbook devoted to the sociology of deviance. Lemert's text used the constructionist approach to the study of deviance. To Lemert, the labeling process did not follow an exclusive social psychological path. He insisted on examining the wider social forces involved in the individuation of socially imposed identities.

FOCUS ON PEOPLE

MARSHALL CLINARD

Marshall Clinard was born in Boston, Massachusetts, in 1911 and died in 2010 at the age of 98. He studied at Stanford University and the University of Chicago. During World War II, he worked as chief criminal statistician for the U.S. Census Bureau. He taught at the University of Iowa, at Vanderbilt University, and, for 34 years, at the University of Wisconsin, Madison. He was widely recognized for his work on corporate crime, in addition to his work in the sociology of deviant behavior. In 1957, he published *Sociology of Deviant Behavior.* Clinard's text used the more traditional positivistic approach to the study of deviance.

5. Borrowing your brother's automobile without his permission
6. Failing to notify a cashier that he has given you an excess amount of change
7. Finding a book on the street and keeping it without trying to find its owner

FOCUS ON PEOPLE

HOWARD BECKER

Howard Saul Becker was born in 1928. He was educated at the University of Chicago. Becker began playing piano at an early age, and by age 15 he worked as a pianist in bars and strip joints, and later with a campus band at Northwestern University. Becker noted that he was able to work as a musician because of World War II and the fact that most musicians over the age of 18 were drafted into the military. It was during his work as a musician that Becker first became exposed to the drug culture, which he would later study.

In 1965, he was appointed a professor of sociology at Northwestern University, where he taught until his retirement in 1991. Becker wrote extensively on sociological writing styles and methodologies. Becker's 1963 book *Outsiders* provided the foundations for labeling theory. Becker is often called a symbolic interactionist or a social constructionist; however, he does not align himself with either method. Becker is considered part of the second Chicago School of Sociology, which also includes individuals such as Erving Goffman and Anselm Strauss. After retirement, he taught as an adjunct professor at the University of Washington until 1998.

The classic work in the study of deviant behavior is Becker's 1963 book *Outsiders: Studies in the Sociology of Deviance*. *Outsiders* is credited as one of the first books on labeling theory and its application to studies of deviance.

8. Driving in excess of posted speed limit
9. Shoplifting
10. Failing to report taxable income to the government

Questions:

How many of the above acts do you consider deviant?

Should someone who committed any of those acts be considered a deviant?

Would it make a difference to you if the individual's conduct was not detected?

How many of the acts do you also consider criminal?

Did you list any acts that were noncriminal but deviant?

Summary

- Defining the concept of deviant behavior is one of the most difficult tasks to overcome when studying the subject. Sociologists probably disagree more over the meaning of deviant and deviant behavior than any other subject.

- Deviant behavior does not automatically imply criminal behavior. Too often, we think of the study of deviant behavior as an extension of the study of criminology or a criminal justice subject.
- To many people, deviant behavior is a violation of the social rules of accepted behavior.
- If we use the term *deviance* as a variation of the norm, then we can argue that deviance does not have to be negative; deviant behavior can be good or positive as long as it deviates from the norm.
- The two major perspectives on what constitutes deviance and a deviant are the positivist and the constructionist perspectives.
- The positive perspective tends to consider deviance as intrinsically objective, determined behavior that is observable empirically.
- The constructionists see deviance as a societal label and a subjective experience.
- Positivists see the deviant as a person who is not normal; constructionists see deviant behavior as a societal label.
- The constructionist perspective evolved in the late 1950s and early 1960s as a direct challenge to the positivist perspective. According to the constructionist perspective, an act is considered deviant only because some societal group has so labeled it as deviant.
- Howard Becker notes that the simplest view of deviance is based on statistics, simply defining anything that varies too widely from the average.
- The normative perspective views deviant behavior as behavior that violates existing and generally accepted social norms.
- The situational perspective looks at the social situation surrounding the behavior in question. The situational perspective is relativistic because it defines deviant behavior primarily in terms of when and where the act in question occurs.
- Can there be positive deviance? The answer to this question depends on your definition of deviant behavior.
- Any discussion of deviant behavior includes the concept of rule breaking. Who makes the rules that result in the characterization of deviance?
- Social rules are the creation of social groups. Many theorists contend that society creates deviance. If there were no rules, there would be no rule breaking and no societal reaction to rule breaking, and therefore no deviance.
- Social controls are generally considered either informal or formal. Researchers study why some people obey social rules and others do not. Those who do not are usually labeled as deviants. But even the most deviant individual obeys social rules the majority of the time.

- Norms may be defined as the generally agreed on guidelines or rules for behaviors that provide boundaries for interpersonal relations. Because the concept of deviance is defined in terms of societal norms, as norms change, so do the definitions of deviance.
- Norms take two parallel forms: behavioral and expectational. Behavioral norms are the patterns of actual behavior that individuals typically follow when interacting under certain conditions.
- Socialization is the label for the process a person goes through when learning the socially approved ways of a social group. It consists of learning the social rules.
- Does deviant behavior play a useful function in our society? According to some scholars, the reaction to deviant behavior enhances the stability of our society by reaffirming our moral boundaries.
- The very process of defining a particular behavior pattern as deviant is inherently political.
- Explanatory theories are concerned with trying to explain why deviance does or does not occur.
- The constructionists are more interested in obtaining a better understanding of the process by which certain behavior is considered deviant behavior and why certain individuals are classified as deviant.
- The strain theory contends that there is a discrepancy between societal values and the structural means available to individuals to obtain the desired societal values.
- Social control theories are also grouped under the structural/functional group. Social control theories contend that when social constraints on antisocial behavior are weakened or absent, delinquent behavior emerges.
- The conflict/critical theorists are concerned with the structure of society and how the structure affects the members of society.
- The interactionist theories, also considered the social process theories, consider that deviance is learned in the interaction with others, and the socialization process that occurs as the result of group membership is the primary route through which the learning occurs.
- The first textbook devoted to the sociology of deviance was Edwin Lemert's *Social Pathology: A Systematic Approach to the Theory of Sociopathic Behavior*, which was published in 1951.

Questions in Review

1. How would you define deviant behavior?
2. Why is it difficult to define deviant behavior?
3. Explain how a social group exercises controls to keep its members from violating its rules?
4. How does Becker view the concept of deviance?

5. What roles do social norms play in controlling deviant behavior?
6. What is the difference between a formal sanction and an informal one?
7. Explain why not all criminal acts are considered deviant acts.
8. What is the difference between customs and mores?
9. What is the difference between informal controls and formal controls? Give an example of each.

Key Terms

Behavioral norms: These social norms refer to what people do normally when occupying a particular social role or in a given social situation.

Conflict/critical theories: The theories that trace the source of deviance to the larger structures of society and the strains that they produce, or the fact that they do not exercise adequate social control over people. The conflict/critical theorists are concerned with the structure of society and how the structure affects the members of society.

Constructionist theorists: Theorists who are more interested in obtaining a better understanding of why certain behavior is considered deviant and why certain individuals are classified as deviant.

Culture: A body of widely held shared customs and values that provide general orientations toward life and specific ways of achieving common goals.

Differential association: A theory that holds that individuals pursue deviant behavior to the extent that they identify with real or imaginary people who consider their deviant behavior acceptable. According to the differential association theories, individuals learn to commit deviant acts similar to the manner that we learned to play baseball.

Expectational norms: The behaviors that are ideal or expected of individuals in specific social situations.

Explanatory theories: Theories that try to explain why deviance does or does not occur.

Folkways: Norms that when violated carry with them the least intense feelings. They may be considered trivial conventions and are not generally taken as moral imperatives.

Interactionist theories (also considered the social process theories): Theories that consider that deviance is learned in the interaction with others, and the socialization processes that occur as the result of group membership are the primary route through which the learning occurs.

Labeling theory: One of the interactionist theories, it sees continued deviance as a consequence of limited opportunities for acceptable behavior, which result from the negative responses of society to those defined as deviant.

Mores: Rules that when violated arouse intense feelings and are subject to extreme consequences when they are broken. Forcible rape would be considered in this class.

Social control theories: Theories that contend that when social constraints on antisocial behavior are weakened or absent, delinquent behavior emerges.

Social norms: The generally agreed on guidelines or rules for behaviors that provide boundaries for interpersonal relations.

Social organization: The organization of society that provides the means for carrying out the complex network of social interactions between individuals, social groups, and institutions.

Social roles: A set of social norms for the behavior of individuals who occupy given statuses in a society.

Strain theory: A theory that contends that there is a discrepancy between societal values and the structural means available to individuals to obtain desired societal values.

Organizations and Websites of Interest

American Sociological Association (ASA): http://www.asanet.org.

The ASA is a nonprofit membership association based in Washington, DC, dedicated to advancing sociology as a scientific discipline and profession serving the public good. It was founded in 1905 and is an association of over 14,000 members. The ASA has 44 special interest sections with more than 21,000 members, including the Section on Crime, Law, and Deviance.

The Section on Crime, Law, and Deviance fosters the development of this aspect of sociology through the organized interchange of ideas and research results. The section examines matters of sociological interest related to the study and understanding of juvenile or adult law violating behavior and the organization and operation of law enforcement, judicial, and correctional processes.

Deviant Behavior (a journal): Information on this journal may be obtained by accessing http://www.tandf.co.uk/journals or http://www.tandfonline.com/toc/udbh20/current.

According to the publisher, Taylor & Francis, this is the only journal that addresses social deviance specifically and exclusively. International and interdisciplinary in scope, it publishes refereed theoretical, descriptive, methodological, and applied papers. All aspects of deviant behavior are discussed, including crime, juvenile delinquency, alcohol abuse and narcotic addiction, sexual deviance, societal reaction to handicap and disfigurement, mental illness, and socially inappropriate behavior. In addition, *Deviant Behavior* frequently includes articles that address contemporary theoretical and conceptual controversies, allowing the specialist in deviance to stay informed of ongoing debates.

Endnotes

1. *Jacobellis v. Ohio*. 378 U.S. 184 (1964) (concurring opinion).
2. Daniel Glaser. (1971, June). Criminology and public policy. *American Sociologist*, *6*(Suppl.), 30–37.
3. Edwin Sagarin. (1975). *Deviants and deviance: An introduction to the study of disvalued people and behavior*. New York: Holt, Rinehart, and Winston.
4. Gwynn Nettler. (1974). *Explaining crime*. New York: McGraw-Hill.
5. Howard S. Becker. (1963). *Outsiders: Studies in the sociology of deviance*. New York: Free Press.
6. Becker, 1963, p. 9.
7. Mark Konty. (2011). The deconstruction of deviance. In C. Bryant (Ed.), *The Routledge handbook of deviant behavior* (pp. 31–37). London: Routledge.
8. Becker, 1963.
9. Sagarin, 1975.
10. Becker, 1963.
11. Jack P. Gibbs. (1994). *A theory about control*. Boulder, CO: Westview Press.
12. Stuart Palmer & John A. Humphrey. (1990). *Deviant behavior*. New York: Springer.
13. William Graham Summer. (1906). *Folkways: A study of the sociological importance of usages, manners, customs, mores, and morals*. Boston: Ginn.
14. Robert F. Kushner & Daniel H. Bessesen. (2007). *Treatment of the obese patient*. Louisville, KY: Humana Press.
15. Jack D. Douglas. (1977). Shame and deceit in creative deviance. In Edwin Sagarin (Ed.), *Deviance and social change* (pp. 59–86). Beverly Hills, CA: Sage.
16. Emile Durkheim. (1938). *The rules of sociological method*. New York: Free Press.
17. Edwin Schur. (1980). *The politics of deviance*. Englewood Cliffs, NJ: Prentice-Hall.
18. Nadava Ben-Yehuda. (2011). Social change and deviance. In C. Bryant (Ed.), *The Routledge handbook of deviant behavior* (pp. 38–45). London: Routledge.
19. Palmer & Humphrey, 1990, pp. 2–3.
20. Robert A. Stebbins. (1996). *Tolerable differences: Living with deviance* (2nd ed.). Toronto: McGraw-Hill.
21. Stebbins, 1996.
22. Palmer & Humphrey, 1990.
23. Becker, 1963.
24. Robert A. Dentler & Kai Erickson. (1959). The functions of deviance in small groups. *Social Problems*, *7*, 98–107.
25. Timothy Brezina. (2000, January). Are deviants different from the rest of us? *Teaching Sociology*, *28*(1), 71–78.
26. Edwin Lemert. (1951). *Social pathology: A systematic approach to the theory of sociopathic behavior*. New York: McGraw-Hill.
27. Marshall Clinard. (1957). *Sociology of deviant behavior*. Belmont, CA: Wadsworth.
28. Becker, 1963.

chapter two

Theoretical Explanations

Chapter Objectives

What you should know and understand after studying this chapter:

- The importance of free will or lack of free will in explaining deviant behavior
- The concepts involved in the rational choice explanations of deviant behavior
- The issues examined by social control theories
- How social disorganization may contribute to deviant behavior
- The symbolic interactionism theories
- How strain theorists explain deviant behavior
- The different biological explanations of deviant behavior
- The psychological explanations of deviant behavior

Free Will or Lack of Free Will

Since the ancient Greeks, one of the most oft-discussed human behavior questions has been whether we have free will in determining the course of our actions, or whether our actions are determined by forces beyond our control.

Among the criminological theories, the first formal school is generally called the classical or free will school. According to this school of thought, we commit deviant behavior by voluntarily choosing a course of action. We tend to choose to commit acts that bring pleasure or are positive to our views and refrain from choosing those acts that bring less pleasure or more pain.

The classical or free will school is an outgrowth of the Age of Enlightenment, which dominated Europe for most of the 18th century. During the earlier Age of Science, scientists and mathematicians such as Copernicus, Descartes, Newton, Galileo, Locke, Rousseau, and others discovered new ideas that revolutionized human thinking. The Age of Enlightenment promoted optimism, certainty, reason, toleration, humanitarianism, the belief that all human problems could be solved, and finally, a belief in human progress. The period prior to the Age of Enlightenment was known as the period as the Age of Science.

It was during this Age of Enlightenment that the North American continent was settled. Those who settled the colonies were strongly influenced by the social thinking of this age. The influence of the Age of Enlightenment is clearly noted in the U.S. Constitution, especially the Bill of Rights, and in the Declaration of Independence.

As noted, the influence of the Age of Enlightenment is clearly present in the Declaration of Independence. The Declaration of Independence is the popular name of a resolution adopted by the Continental Congress on July 4, 1776. The declaration announced that the 13 American colonies, then at war with Great Britain, regarded themselves as 13 newly independent sovereign states, and no longer a part of the British Empire. Instead, they formed the United States of America. John Adams was one of the leaders in pushing for independence, which the Continental Congress unanimously approved on July 2. The formal declaration was drafted by a committee of five to be issued when Congress voted on independence. The term *Declaration of Independence* is not used in the document. Examine the second sentence of the declaration to see the influence of the Age of Enlightenment thinking. The famous second sentence declares:

> We hold these truths to be self-evident, that all men are created equal, that they are endowed by their Creator with certain unalienable Rights that among these are Life, Liberty and the pursuit of Happiness.

The leaders of the Age of Science were scientists and mathematicians, whereas the leaders in the Age of Enlightenment were philosophers. The second sentence of the Declaration of Independence referred to above clearly indicates a philosophical statement of a philosopher rather than the analytical statement of a scientist or mathematician. While the scientists and mathematicians were unable to solve the human problems at the time with analytical measures, the philosophers proceeded with mandates to solve them.

Cesare Beccaria and Jeremy Bentham were strongly influenced and adapted the ideas of the Age of Enlightenment to theories regarding human behavior and crime causation. Beccaria and Bentham were the leaders in the classical or free will movement.

In the study of deviant behavior like the study of crime causation, the key consideration is: Do we have free will? In other words, are we free to choose or do we lack the ability because of some reason or body makeup to make that choice? The classical school and its leaders, Beccaria and Bentham, were advocates of the position that we have free will and that we choose to become criminals or deviants.

FOCUS ON PEOPLE

CESARE BONESANA, MARCHESE DE BECCARIA (GENERALLY REFERRED TO AS CESARE BECCARIA), 1738–1794

Cesare Beccaria is credited with the founding of the classical school of criminological thought. He was the son of a rich family and considered by many as lazy and easily discouraged. He was born in Milan, Italy, in 1738. His parents were members of the aristocracy, and both had very distinguished academic careers. Cesare attended Jesuit College in Parma and studied economics. Next, he studied law at the University of Pavia. Except for a brief interest in mathematics, he was uninterested in academia.

After his studies were completed, Beccaria returned to Milan. There he developed an interest in philosophy and became an avid reader. He also joined a discussion group that met and discussed world problems or issues. The group contained two brothers, Pietro and Allessandro Verri. Allessandro was a creative writer and Pietro was a distinguished economist. The brothers assigned Beccaria the task of analyzing the Italian penal system. At the time, Beccaria knew little about the penal system. After studying and analyzing the system, Beccaria presented his arguments for reforming the system at one of their group meetings.

The brothers encouraged Beccaria to publish his thoughts. In July 1764, Beccaria published his now famous essay "On Crime and Punishments." He originally published the essay anonymously because of its criticism of the present system of justice in Italy. The essay became an immediate success and was quickly supported by public opinion. While during his lifetime he published several other documents, the 17-page essay was his only publishing success.[1]

Free Will Concept of the Classical School

At the time the classical school developed, there was a shift in thinking regarding the powers of the government. Prior to that time it was the common theory that governance was the divine right of kings. Followers of the classical school accepted the concept of governance by social contract. Social contract governance theory is based on the concept that by forming social groups, the citizens are agreeing on the moral and political obligations. These obligations are based upon a contract or agreement among the people for them to form the society in which they live. While Socrates used something quite like a social contract argument to explain why he must remain in prison and accept the death penalty, the contract theory is generally associated with the moral and political theories of Thomas Hobbes, John Locke, and Jean-Jacques Rousseau.

According to the classical theorists[2]:

- Human beings freely choose either criminal paths or noncriminal paths based on which paths they think will benefit them the most or will cause the least pain.
- Criminals, like noncriminals, will avoid behaviors that will bring pain and engage in behaviors that will bring pleasure.
- Before deciding what actions to take, individuals will weigh the expected benefits against the expected pain.
- People are responsible for their behaviors. They are human beings who are able to interpret, analyze, and dissect the situations in which they find themselves.
- Criminals are not victims of their environments.

SOCIETY IN ACTION

WHICH ACTION WOULD YOU TAKE?

What if this coming summer you and your family planned to take a vacation and visit Hawaii? You and your family had looked forward to this vacation for most of the year. However, prior to your vacation you needed to complete last year's income tax forms. As you complete the forms, you realize that your tax liability or the amount of taxes that you need to pay is significantly higher than you had anticipated. Paying the taxes due will require you to use the money that the family had saved for the vacation—thus no vacation if the taxes are paid. What would you do?

1. Obey the law, pay the taxes, and cancel the vacation
2. Cheat on the taxes and take the vacation to Hawaii

In making your decision, you consider the chances that the Internal Revenue Service will examine your return and the consequences if the IRS finds problems with your return. You also consider the probable enjoyment that your family will have if you take the vacation. Under the classical free will concept, you will weigh the pleasure of the vacation against the likelihood of being detected and the consequences of the detection in determining your course of action. Thus, you would make a conscious decision after examining the pluses and minuses of your choices of action.

FOCUS ON PEOPLE

JEREMY BENTHAM, 1748–1832

Unlike Cesare Beccaria, Jeremy Bentham was a prolific writer and was described as an armchair philosopher. His writings were on a multiple number of subjects, including law and prison building. Many researchers conclude that he was the greatest legal philosopher and reformer that the world has ever seen. He was one of the founders of the classical school.

Bentham's great grandfather was a wealthy pawnbroker in London. His father and grandfather were attorneys. Bentham also studied law and was a member of the bar. But, he apparently had ill feelings toward the legal profession. He once commented, "Only the lawyer escapes punishment for his ignorance of the law."

Bentham was uncomfortable with social groups and preferred books to being with people. His mother died when he was very young. He had problems with his stepmother. It appears that his only serious relationship with a woman was when he was 57. When she refused his offer of marriage, he had nothing further to do with women.[3]

Bentham died in 1832. In his will, Bentham directed his friend take charge of his body and have his skeleton "put together in such a manner as that the whole figure may be seated in a chair usually occupied by me when living, in the attitude in which I am sitting when engaged in thought in the course of time employed in writing." The skeleton, padded out with straw and cloth and clad in his own clothes, with a wax head, was placed in a cabinet and later given to University College in London. It was first housed in the anatomical museum there, and eventually put on display in the South Cloisters. At first, Bentham's mummified head was kept at his feet, but it was later removed for safekeeping. On one occasion it was kidnapped by King's College students; a small sum was paid to charity to secure its return.[4]

Bentham formulated the utilitarian principle that holds that an act had utility if it produced happiness or prevented pain. He advocated working for the greatest happiness for the greatest number of people in a society. According to him, people act rationally and deliberately—that people are motivated by the pursuit of pleasure and the avoidance of pain. To Bentham, people are hedonistic and criminal behavior is learned.

- Individuals act willfully and freely; therefore, criminals are totally responsible for their behavior.
- Criminals should be held responsible for their behaviors.
- Punishment should be only slightly harsher than the advantages that were derived from the crime.
- Prompt punishment is the most useful to society.
- Certainty of punishment is an absolute necessity.

Lack of Free Will

In the latter half of the 19th century, the positivist school was the leading school on crime causation. The school or concept was a product of the realism movement and a reaction to the harshness of the classical school.

Realism was a movement that began in France in the 1850s, after the 1848 French Revolution. It was originally primarily an artistic movement. The movement rejected the concepts of the Age of Enlightenment that had existed during the late 18th century. Realism sought to portray real and typical contemporary people and situations with truth and accuracy, and not avoiding unpleasant or sordid aspects of life. Realism also reverted to the concepts that problems could be solved by science.

To the followers of the positivist school, science was considered supreme. Crime could be studied and the causes of crime could be determined by the use of science. One of the leading positivist theorists was Cesare Lombroso, who many consider the father of modern criminology. Lombroso considered the criminal a subhuman.

In determining the causes of crime, the positivists would examine the criminal and not the crime, whereas the followers of the classical school would examine the crime. The basic difference between the positivists and the classical school followers is whether or not humans have free will. The classical school is based on the concept of free will, and the positivist school on the fact that humans lack free will.

Social Determinism

Social determinism is based on the hypothesis that social interactions and constructs alone determine individual behavior, as opposed to biological or objective factors. A social determinism when studying certain human behaviors, such as committing murder, would look only at social phenomena, such as customs and expectations, education, interpersonal interactions, and memes, to decide whether or not a given person would exhibit any of these behaviors. Social determinism is the opposite of biological determinism. And the followers would discount biological and other nonsocial factors, such as genetic makeup and the physical environment. Even ideas about nature and biology are considered by them to be socially constructed.

Rational Choice Explanations

The rational choice theory is based on the utilitarian belief that humans are reasoning persons who weigh means and ends, costs and benefits, and make a rational choice. This concept was designed by Cornish and Clarke to assist in thinking about situational crime prevention. It is assumed that crime is purposive behavior designed to meet the offender's commonplace needs for such things as money, status, sex, and excitement, and that meeting these needs involves the making of decisions and choices. The decisions and choices are often constrained by limits, ability, and the availability of relevant information.[5]

Rational choice is based on the following assumptions:

- Individualism—offenders sees themselves as individuals
- Individuals have to maximize their goals
- Individuals are self-interested—they are thinking about themselves and how to advance their personal goals

The basic concepts of rational choice theorists are the following[6]:

- The human being is a rational actor.
- People choose behaviors, both conforming and deviant, based on their rational calculations.
- Their choices involve cost-benefit analyses: pleasure versus pain or hedonistic calculus.
- With all other conditions equal, the choice will be directed toward the maximization of individual pleasure.
- Choice can be controlled through the perception and understanding of the potential pain or punishment that will follow an act judged to be in violation of the social good.
- The state is responsible for maintaining order and preserving the common good through a system of laws.
- The swiftness, severity, and certainty of punishment are the key elements in understanding a law's ability to control human behavior.

Social Control Theories

Social control theories propose that people's relationships, commitments, values, norms, and beliefs encourage them not to break the law. If moral codes are internalized and individuals are tied into and have a stake in their community, they will limit their propensity to commit deviant acts.[7]

While most theories involving crime causation try to explain why individuals deviate from expected behavior, the social control theories focus on why people do not deviate or why they do not commit crime.

The theories examine the external factors and processes that affect behavior. In other words, we commit deviant behavior because of inadequate constraints. That is, we have free will and choose to commit the behavior because the constraints are not effective in preventing us from choosing the deviant path.

Consider the following scenario: You were raised in a small community. Everyone knows your family and your conduct will reflect on your family's reputation in the community. But after graduation you move to a large city. No one knows you. If you get drunk and disorderly in the city, you will not harm your family's reputation. Whereas if you were still in your hometown, your conduct would reflect badly on your parents. Accordingly, one of the behavior controls is not present in your new location.

According to these theorists, even lawbreakers are likely to share the belief that social rules or laws should be obeyed. The social control theories contend that the absence of close relationships with conventional others frees individuals from the usual social constraints. And this allows them to engage in deviant behavior.

The social control theories emerged during the era of Enlightenment and the development of classical school of criminology. Thomas Hobbes, a 17th-century English philosopher, wrote about how humans have an inherent tendency toward self-indulgence and evil. He stated that individuals require external restraint in order not to commit deviant behavior. In other words, we are basically bad.

Often the theories are traced to Emile Durkheim, a prolific French writer who is considered the founder of sociology. To Durkheim, anomie results from the breakdown of social norms. He contended that crime and deviance were present in all societies. Durkheim said, "We are moral beings to the extent that we are social beings." Durkheim stated that crime serves the function of identifying boundaries for behavior, which are recognized collectively in communities and reinforced by negative societal reactions. Durkheim's view of social control is summarized as follows: The more weakened the groups to which the individual belongs, the less he or she depends on them, and the more he or she consequently depends only on himself or herself and recognizes no other rules of conduct than what are founded on his or her private interests.[8]

The social control theories propose that social learning develops with the help of social controls. Some of the more important types of social control include the following[9]:

- Direct social control via punitive action for wrongful behavior administered by the family or state authority
- Indirect social control with identification of wrong influences on behavior by family or state authority

- Internal social control developed by conscience questioning
- Control by the need to satisfy basic human needs

Social Disorganization

Social disorganization is an ecological theory that was developed by the Chicago School. The theory looks directly to neighborhood ecological characteristics to explain crime causation. According to this theory, youths from disadvantaged and disorganized neighborhoods are part of a subculture that approves of delinquency and acquires criminality in social and cultural settings. A basic principle of this theory is that one's residential location determines more than one's individual characteristics, such as age, gender, and race, in determining the likelihood that a person will become involved in illegal activities.[10]

SOCIETY IN ACTION

CHICAGO SCHOOL

The University of Chicago established the first department of sociology in 1892 and was the leader in American sociological thought from then until the mid-20th century. The diverse group of scholars who were collected at the University of Chicago became known as the Chicago School. The one recurring theme of the Chicago School is that human behavior is developed and changed by the social and physical environment of the person rather than simply by genetic structure (Figure 2.1).

The school made two major methodological contributions to criminology. The first was by the use of official data (crime figures, census reports, and housing and welfare reports). The second contribution was the use of the case study or life history approach to analyze the criminal behavior of an individual (ethnography). Borrowing the idea of studying plants and animals in their natural habitat, researchers attempted to present the human ecology to explain criminal behavior in certain individuals. For this reason, the Chicago School became known as the ecological school.[11]

From 1945 to about 1960, the University of Chicago was home to a group of faculty and graduate students whose work has come to define what is called the second Chicago School of sociology. Like its predecessor earlier in the century, the sociology department was again the center for qualitative social research on everything from mapping the nuances of human behavior in small groups to seeking solutions to problems of race, crime, and poverty.

Figure 2.1 The University of Chicago in 1901. The university produced many of the theorists that developed the disciplines of deviant behavior and criminology. (Photo from Library of Congress Collection.)

The key assumptions of the social disorganization theory include[12]:

- Crime and delinquency are caused primarily by social factors, that is, environmental determinism.
- The facts speak imperfectly for themselves.
- While official statistics are okay, fieldwork is better.
- A city is a perfect natural laboratory because it reflects society as a whole.
- If the components of the neighborhood social structure are unstable, more likely the individual will be encouraged to engage in anti-social conduct.
- Instabilities and their effects are worse for the lower classes.
- Human nature is basically good, but it is subject to vulnerability and an inability to resist temptation.

Concentric Zone Theory

Robert Park and Ernest Burgess, two Chicago School professors, developed the concentric zone theory.[13] Park and Burgess divided the city of Chicago into five zones: central business district, transition, workingman, residential, and commuter. According to them, each zone gradually invaded and dominated the adjacent zones, with an overall growth outward. The natural process was one of invasion, dominance, and succession—like the way a new species of plant takes control of an ecosystem. They stated that delinquency is greatest in the zone of transition. At the time, their findings were quite radical for the idea that cities grow from the inside out. Park and Burgess defined social disorganization as "the inability of a group to engage in self-regulation," which is a social control theoretic formulation.

Under their theory, as a city is formed and grows, people and their activities cluster in a particular area, that is, the process of concentration. Gradually, this central area becomes highly populated, so there is a scattering of people and their activities away from the central city to establish the suburbs, that is, dispersion. Eventually the competition for land and other scarce urban resources leads to the division of the urban space into distinctive ecological niches or natural zones in which people share similar social characteristics because they are subject to the same pressures. As a zone becomes more prosperous and desirable, property values and rents rise, and people and businesses migrate into that zone, usually moving outward from the city center. Park and Burgess labeled this process as succession and new residents take their place. At both a micro and macro level, society was of thought to operate as a super organism, where change is a natural aspect of the process of growth and neither chaotic nor disorderly. This movement creates competition. In the early stages of competition, there will be some level of disorganization caused by the disruption or breakdowns in the normative structure of the community. This disruption may lead to deviant behavior. During this transition the social and moral structures of the community are generally disorganized.

Cultural Transmission Theory

Clifford Shaw and Henry McKay, researchers from the Chicago School, built on the concepts of Park and Burgess. They studied and noticed that the same neighborhoods in Chicago seemed to have about the same delinquency rates regardless of which ethnic group moved in. Both Shaw and McKay contended that delinquent behavior was a form of group behavior. Shaw once noted that he had never met a delinquent who acted alone.[14]

Their cultural transmission theory contends that traditions of delinquency are transmitted through successive generations of the same zone in the same way language, roles, and attitudes are transmitted. To them, social disorganization was really an inability of local communities to realize the common values of their residents or solve commonly

FOCUS ON PEOPLE

EMILE DURKHEIM (1858–1917)

Emile Durkheim, like Lombroso, rejected the classical concepts that humans had free will were rational in a contractual society. Durkheim focused on society and its organization and development for explanations of criminal behavior. Durkheim's theories were complex and overlapping with different social approaches to criminal behavior.

Emile Durkheim was considered one of the best known and least understood major social thinkers. He was born of Jewish parents in a small French town near the German border. He was schooled in Paris and taught philosophy at various secondary schools in France. Later, he spent a year in Germany studying under the famed experimental psychologist Wilhelm Wundt. After the publication of two articles, he obtained a professorship at the University of Bordeaux. At the university, he taught the first course in a French university on sociology. Later, he received the first doctor's degree awarded by the University of Paris in sociology and an appointment to the faculty at the University of Paris, and he taught there until his death in 1917.

Durkheim's first major publication was *De la Division du Travail Social* (The Division of Labor in Society), which was his doctoral dissertation and was published in 1893. In this publication, he describes the processes of social change involved in the industrialization of societies. According to him, the processes are part of the development from a primitive society, which he labeled mechanical, to the more advanced form, called organic. In the mechanical society, each social group is relatively isolated from all other social groups, and each group is basically self-sufficient. In the mechanical society, individuals live largely under identical circumstances, do identical work, and have identical values. There is little division of labor since only a few persons in the clan or village have specialized functions. Accordingly, there is little need for individual talents, and because of the uniformity of its members, there is social solidarity among the clan or village members.

In the organic society, however, different segments of the society depend on each other in a highly organized division of labor. Since individuals are no longer working and living under identical circumstances, social solidarity is no longer based on these circumstances. Durkheim indicated that all societies are in some stage between the mechanical and the organic structures, with no society being totally one or the other.

According to Durkheim, law plays different roles in maintaining the social solidarity of each of the two types of societies. In the mechanical society, law functions to enforce uniformity of the members of the group and is oriented toward repressing deviations from the norm. In the organic society, however, law functions to regulate the interactions of the various groups in society and provides restitution in cases of wrongful transactions. Crime is also different in the two forms of society. In the mechanical society, crime is normal. And a mechanical society without crime would be pathologically overcontrolled. As society develops toward the organic form, it is possible for the pathological state of anomie to occur, and such a state would produce a variety of social maladies. In his later works, *The Rules of the Sociological Method* and his most famous publication, *Suicide,* Durkheim develops the concept that crime is normal in both types of societies.

Durkheim used the concept of anomie to describe modern society. Anomie (a Greek term defined as "lawlessness") is a state or a condition that exists within people when a society evolves from a mechanical to an organic entity. Anomie occurs as a result of wide-sweeping scientific, technological, and social changes. Anomie is a condition of normlessness, not a lack of norms, but the condition whereby norms have lost their meaning and become inoperative for large numbers of people. Anomie may also be described as the fragmentation or disassociation of one's center; the feeling of being a number, not a person; social isolation; or social loneliness. Durkheim believed that anomie was the product of societal transition. When society is in transition and anomie is high, institutions and laws become meaningless to people, and crime results.[15]

Durkheim also used his concept of anomie to explain the phenomenon of suicide. According to him, the degree of integration of a society was inversely related to its rate of suicide. He noted that there were low suicide rates in predominantly Catholic countries where religion provided a unifying theme. He also noted that there is increased social solidarity during wartime and in prolonged economic depressions. Whenever there is unification and high social solidarity within a society, anomie is low and suicide rates (and crime rates) are lower.

Durkheim took a broad approach to crime. He looked to the very nature of society to explain crime. He concluded that crime was imminent in society, and that it was a normal and necessary phenomenon in any society. According to Durkheim, all the uniformity that exists in a society is the "totality of social likenesses" or the "collective conscience." The collective conscience may be found in every culture; every society has a degree of diversity in that there are many individual differences among its members. He contended that there cannot be a society in which the individuals do not differ more or less from the collective type. Pressure is exerted in varying degrees for uniformity within the society.

Durkheim contended that even punishment plays a role in the maintenance of social solidarity. When the rules of the collective conscience are violated, society responds with repressive sanctions, not for retribution or deterrence, but because those of us who conform will be demoralized. When a criminal is punished, those of us who are not punished receive the award of "not being punished" because of our "good" behavior.[16]

experienced problems. The three sources of social disorganization in social disorganization theory are

- Residential instability
- Racial/ethnic heterogeneity
- Poverty

These are ways in which criminal traditions become part of the communities.

Symbolic Interactionism

A lasting perspective from the Chicago School was the social-psychological theory of symbolic interactionism. Symbolic interactionism is a sociological perspective that is influential in many sociological areas. It is particularly important in social psychology. From symbolic interactionism two theories of crime causation developed: differential association and labeling. The labeling theory is discussed in Chapter 3.

While Herbert Mead originated the concept, the term *symbolic interaction* was coined by his student in 1937. The concept developed from the belief that human behavior is the product of purely social symbols communicated between individuals. Accordingly, the mind and the self are not innate but are products of the social environment.

Mead contended that people's selves are social products. And the selves are also purposive and creative. He believed that the true test of any theory was that "it was useful in solving complex social problems." Mead's influence on symbolic interactionism was said to be so powerful that other sociologists regard him as the one true founder of symbolic interactionism tradition. Although Mead taught in a philosophy department, he is best known by sociologists as the teacher who trained a generation of the best minds in their field. He never, however, set forth his wide-ranging ideas in a book or systematic treatise. After his death in 1931, his students used his class notes and conversations with him to published *Mind, Self and Society* under his name.[17]

While John Dewey is considered by many as the leader of this sociological theory, Mead was the individual who transformed the inner structure of the theory, moving it to a higher level of theoretical complexity.[18]

Herbert Blumer, a student and interpreter of Mead, coined the term *symbolic interactionism* and put forward an influential summary of the perspective: People act toward things based on the meaning those things have for them, and these meanings are derived from social interaction and modified through interpretation.

Symbolic interaction is based on the concept that people act toward things on the basis of meanings that those things have for them. The meaning that a thing has is derived from, or arises out of, the social interaction that one has with others. The meaning that a thing has is handled in, and modified through, an interpretative process used by a person in dealing with the things that he or she encounters. Herbert Blumer summarizes symbolic interactionism as follows:

> The meaning of a thing for a person grows out of the ways in which other persons act toward the person with regard to the thing.... Symbolic interactionism sees meanings as social products, as creations that are formed in and through the defining activities of people as they interact.[19]

Differential Association

Edwin H. Sutherland originated the differential association theory to explain criminal behavior. He published his first version of differential association in 1939 and his final version in 1947. Sutherland considered that all behaviors are learned in an individual's social environment. Sutherland stated that the major difference between conforming behavior and criminal behavior is in what is learned rather than how it is learned, because he considered that individuals learn both criminal and noncriminal behavior in much the same way. According to him, criminal behavior is not necessarily different from noncriminal behavior. He stated that values are important in determining behavior, and that certain locations and people are more crime-prone than others. A statement out of his 1934 text, *Principles of Criminology*, became the basis for criminological theory. Sutherland stated in the text:

> First, any person can be trained to adopt and follow any pattern of behavior which he is able to execute. Second, failure to follow a prescribed pattern of behavior is due to the inconsistencies and lack of harmony in the influences which direct the individual. Third, the conflict of culture is therefore the fundamental principle in the explanation of crime.[20]

By the term *differential association*, Sutherland contended that the content of the patterns presented in association would differ from individual to individual. He does not, as some claim, indicate that mere association with criminals would cause one to commit criminal behavior. He apparently intended to imply that the content of the communications received from others is given different degrees of significance depending on the relationship between the person making the verbal or nonverbal communication and the person receiving the communication. According to Sutherland, a communication from a close personal friend would have more significance in affecting a person's behavior than communications from a stranger, such as a radio newscaster. Note: The communication referred to by Sutherland may be oral, written, behavioral, or any actions that imply a message.

In his 1947 version, Sutherland expressed his belief that all behavior is learned. With this concept he discounted the concept of social disorganization. Since all types of behavior are learned under his theory, the learning process may be applied to a broader range of societal behaviors. In his final version he summarized his theory with nine points, with number 6 being the heart of the theory:

1. Criminal behavior is learned.
2. Criminal behavior is learned in interaction with other persons in a process of communications.
3. The principal part of the learning of criminal behavior occurs within intimate personal groups.
4. When criminal behavior is learned, the learning includes
   a. Techniques of committing the crime, which are sometimes very complicated, sometimes very simple
   b. The specific direction of motives, drives, rationalizations, and attitudes
5. The specific direction of motives and drives is learned from definitions of the legal codes as favorable or unfavorable.

6. A person becomes delinquent because of an excess of definitions favorable to violation of the law over definitions unfavorable to violation of the law.
7. Differential associations may vary in frequency, duration, priority, and intensity.
8. The process of learning criminal behavior by association with criminal and noncriminal patterns involves all of the mechanisms that are involved in any other learning.
9. While criminal behavior is an expression of general needs and values, it is not explained by those general needs and values, since noncriminal behavior is an expression of the same needs and values.[21]

Differential association theory contends that criminal behavior is learned in association with intimate others by interacting and communicating with those others. Two things are learned: the techniques for committing the criminal behavior and the definitions of values, motives, drives, rationalizations, and attitudes to support such behavior. The techniques may be considered as the how and the definitions as the whys.[22]

Criminal behavior occurs, according to the theory, when there is an excess of definitions favoring criminal behavior. The excess of definitions does not mean a simple number of excesses, but the weight of the definitions as determined by the quality and intimacy of interaction with others. The theory holds that one learns to commit criminal behavior the same way one learns to play baseball. Note: The resulting behavior is often determined by not only the persons to whom one has been exposed, but also the absence of alternative patterns to fall back on.

To Sutherland, the real question regarding criminal behavior was not how certain conduct came to be criminal, but why the individual chose to commit the behavior. Differential association theory is a process theory.

Differential association has been criticized as being too general in nature and does not account for the fact that for most people, involvement in crime decreases as they grow older. It does not explain crimes of violence, and it fails to consider the role of free will in criminal behavior. Differential association theory contends that criminal behavior is learned in association with intimate others by interacting and communicating with those others. They borrow some of their concepts from the culture conflict theories, which hold that the definition of crime changes from time to time and from place to place.

Differential Association Reinforcement Theory

Robert Burgess and Ronald Akers attempted to provide a more adequate specification of the learning process. They formulated the differential association reinforcement theory. Their purpose was to merge

Sutherland's theory with the more general theory of behaviorism and the works of B. F. Skinner. The key points of their theory are as follows:

1. The primary learning mechanism in social behavior is operant conditioning, in which behavior is shaped by the stimuli that follow, or are consequences of, the behavior.
2. Direct conditioning and imitation of others are important in determining behavior.
3. Rewards, or positive reinforcement, as well as avoidance of punishment, strengthen this behavior.
4. The determination of whether the behavior is deviant or conforming depends on differential reinforcement.
5. People learn norms, attitudes, and so on, from those who are important to them; that is, our associations with the people who are important to us provide the stimuli for shaping our behavior.[23]

Strain Theories

According to the strain theories, the social structures within society pressure individuals to commit deviant behavior. The theories consider two different types of pressures: structural and individual. The structural pressure refers to the processes at the societal level that filter down and affect how the individual perceives his or her needs. And if particular social structures are inherently inadequate or there is inadequate regulation, this changes an individual's perceptions as to his or her means and opportunities. Individual pressures are caused by the frictions and pains experienced by an individual as he or she looks for ways to satisfy his or her needs. And if the goals of a society become significant to an individual, actually achieving them may become more important than the means adopted. For example, if individual pressure results in a goal to achieve academic success, then achieving the success may be more important than the means used to obtain that success. Accordingly, if an individual cheats for exams rather than preparing for them the legitimate way (by studying), the individual attains the goals but does not use socially approved means.

The strain theories use the following assumptions:

- If an individual fails to conform to social norms and laws, it is because there is excessive pressure or strain that propels the individual to commit criminal behavior.
- Lawbreaking and deviance are not normal.
- Misconduct or deviance is caused by immense pressures on the individual.
- People are basically moral and innately desire to conform to society's laws.

The critical question for strain theorists is what is the nature of the strains (pressures) that cause an individual to commit criminal behavior?

Robert Merton

Robert Merton revised Durkheim's conception of anomie and applied it directly to American society. Merton's research in *American Sociological Review* is probably the most frequently quoted article in modern sociology.[24] In the article, Merton examined the question of how malintegration in society related to deviance. Using the value of economic success as an example, and relating this example to institutional ways of achieving economic success, he applied his concepts to the United States using the premise that anomie is the greatest in societies where certain ends or goals are elevated but there are no means or limited means (access) to attain those goals.

Merton opined that the culture of any society defines certain goals it deems worth striving for, and that there are many such goals in every society. He stated the desire to acquire wealth as one of the most prominent cultural goals in American society. Merton noted that accumulated wealth is generally equated with personal value, which is associated with a high degree of prestige and social status. Accordingly, our culture encourages all individuals to seek the greatest amount of wealth.

Cultures also have approved norms or institutionalized means that individuals are expected to follow in pursuing the culture's goals. The American culture is also based on the egalitarian ideology in which it is maintained that all people have an equal chance to achieve wealth. The ideology is often illustrated by fictional literature in which a poor kid makes it big. To Merton, the American culture has adopted the approved goal of acquiring wealth, and the institutionalized means of obtaining that goal by a work ethic can be identified as middle-class values, and the use of force or fraud to obtain this wealth is not acceptable. He noted that only the most talented and most hard-working individuals in the lower socioeconomic class will be able to obtain the goal using the accepted means.

Merton noted that attaining the goal is much easier for individuals in the upper social economic class. For the majority of individuals in the lower socioeconomic class, attaining the goal through accepted means is not realistic. This inability to attain places severe cultural strains (pressures) on the lower-class individuals.

Merton referred to the person's acceptance of society's goals and the blocked access to achieving those goals as the goals-means dysfunction. This dysfunction is the essence of his theory. When there is a dysfunction between the culture's goals and the means to achieve those goals, Merton contended that specific and predictable adaptations would develop.

		Institutional means	
		Accept	Reject
Cultural goals	Accept	Conformity	Innovation
	Reject	Ritualism	Retreatism
Rebellion	Rejects both cultural goals and institutional means Adopts new goals and new means		

Figure 2.2 Robert Merton's typology of deviant behavior.

Merton theorized that there were five adaptations or ways that a person could deal with anomie (Figure 2.2). The five adaptations are listed below.

- **Conformity:** The individual accepts both the culture's goals and the institutionalized means for attaining those goals. Conformity generally does not lead to deviance and is considered the typical middle-class response. For example, with the cultural goal of getting a good job, one attends school and obtains an education (an acceptable institutionalized means for attaining the goal).
- **Innovation:** The individual accepts the culture's goals, but rejects the institutionalized means to achieve them. Innovation is like taking a shortcut. Merton believes that this adaptation was greater among the lower socioeconomic status groups, and that most crime that exists in society will be in the form of innovation by individuals who accept the goal of acquiring wealth but find they cannot succeed through the institutionalized means. Therefore, they look for new methods to acquire wealth.
- **Ritualism:** Ritualists reject the culture's goals and accept the institutionalized means to achieve goals; however, they believe the goals to be of little importance. The maintenance of a strict set of customs and manners that serve no purpose characterizes ritualism. College fraternities, clubs, and some religious practices are examples of ritualism. Merton believed that this was a lower-middle socioeconomic status group response.
- **Retreatism:** This individual rejects both the culture's goals and the institutionalized means to achieve them. Retreatism is an escape response. Addicts, alcoholics, psychotics, and vagrants could be viewed as retreating. These individuals are dropouts from society.
- **Rebellion:** This individual rejects the culture's goals and institutionalized means of obtaining those goals and replaces them with his or her own goals and means. He or she is angry and revolutionary.

> This individual differs from retreatism in that goals are not secretly desired by the rebel. Rebels, however, generally do care and have strong feelings about their own goals.

Merton notes that the modes of adaptation are designed to account for some, but not all, forms of criminal behavior.

Durkheim contended that the driving forces of criminal behavior can be traced to appetites and impulses toward cultural goals that are inherent in human nature. Since human nature does not change, differences in the amount of crime cannot be explained by differences in the forces driving people to commit criminal behavior. Accordingly, the differences in the amount of criminal behavior can only be explained by differences in the restraining forces. He argued that societies restrain human nature either through culture (consensus of values) or through structure (the interrelationships among the different functions in societies), and that these restraints break down during periods of rapid social change, resulting in higher levels of crime. Merton, in contrast to Durkheim, contended that the drive to commit crime was cultural in nature and not human nature, and that the forces restraining individuals from committing crime were also cultural. Merton maintained that the high level of crime in American society was caused by a cultural imbalance—the imbalance between the cultural forces that drive the individual toward criminal behavior and the cultural forces restraining the individual from criminal behavior. He believed that the distribution of criminal behavior is inversely related to the distribution of legitimate opportunities.

Biological Explanations

Franz Gall in 1791 developed the theory of phrenology. Gall was an anatomist who believed that each section of the brain was responsible for a different aspect of human functioning. He believed that areas of the brain were friendliness, destructiveness, benevolence, and acquisitiveness. Within the brain itself, these functions were grouped together into regions. Each of the brain's three regions controlled a major aspect of human behavior: Activity or the lower functions were controlled by one section, another controlled moral sentiments, and the third housed the intellectual faculties.

In determining whether an individual suffered from brain dysfunction, it was not necessary to do an internal examination of brain tissue, although phrenologists performed brain dissections when given the opportunity. However, external examinations were believed to be an accurate predictor of internal brain development. In particular, it was thought that enlarged or unusually undersized brain sections produced bumps or depressions in the skull, respectively. This belief made it possible for

FOCUS ON PEOPLE

ROBERT K. MERTON (1910–2003)

Robert King Merton, who was named Meyer R. Scholnick at birth, was born in Philadelphia, Pennsylvania. His parents were Eastern European immigrants. Merton is best known for coining expressions such as the "self-fulfilling prophecy" and the "San Matteo effect," and for the scientific use of the term *serendipity*. He taught at Columbia University for most of his academic career.

His main contributions were the functionalist work on medium-range theories, the clarification and reregulated functionalist analysis, the theory of deviance, and his work on the set of roles. In opposition to the idea of functionalists to construct a comprehensive theory and pure empiricism, Merton proposed middle-range theories. They were considered middle range because the theories were restricted to specific phenomena and problems.

Merton used the term *anomie,* derived from Emile Durkheim, with a new meaning. To Merton, anomie was used to refer to the discontinuity between cultural goals and the legitimate means to achieve them. He saw the American dream as an emphasis of economic success, as a cultural purpose, but there is not an adequate emphasis on the legitimate means to achieve it. According to him, this contradiction leads to a considerable increase of deviance.

Merton believed that all individuals subscribe to the American dream, but the ways in which people go about obtaining the dream are not the same because not everyone has the same opportunities and advantages as the next person. When a person accepts both the cultural goals and institutional means of obtaining those goals, then the individual is considered to be in conformity with society, that is, a nondeviant. If the individual accepts the means but tries to obtain them by unacceptable means, the individual would fit in the innovation square. This would describe the student who, rather than studies for an exam, cheats. If an individual rejects both the means and the goals, he or she is considered in the retreatism square. This is probably how the drug addict would be classified. Whereas the individual who establishes his or her own goals and means to obtain those goals would be considered in the rebellion square. A member of an outlaw motorcycle gang may fit in this category. In Figure 2.2, only those who accept both the goals and means would be considered a nondeviant.

nearly any doctor to perform phrenological examinations and describe the origins of a person's problematic behavior.

Generally the biological explanations focus on genetic predisposition toward deviance. In the 1870s, Cesare Lombroso, an Italian physician, compared 400 prisoners with 400 army soldiers. He proposed that criminals had distinctive physical features—low foreheads, prominent jaws and cheekbones, protruding ears, excessive hairiness, and unusually long arms. All these features taken together, the criminals resemble apelike ancestors of humans. He concluded that they are genetically abnormal.

His study was criticized because his sample was not representative of the general population. His focus was on comparing the declared criminals with the army soldiers. How about those criminals who committed crime but have never been caught? Also, criminals may have abnormality because of poverty and malnutrition.

The three major biological explanations are as follows:

- **Body type:** People with squarish, muscular bodies are more likely to commit street crime (mugging, rape, burglary).
- **XYY theory:** An extra Y chromosome in males leads to crime.
- **Intelligence:** Low intelligence leads to crime.

Body Type Theories

The body type theories have always been popular with the general public. We seem to believe that fat people are always jolly and redheads are hot tempered. The criminal, therefore, should be hard in appearance with a malformation in general facial structure or have a scar. Who were the criminals in the Superman comics? They were all deformed.

Ernst Kretschmer (1888–1964) studied the relationship between physique and mental illness. After researching 4,417 cases, he concluded that bodies could be divided into three distinct body types:

- **Asthenic type:** The asthenic person has a thin and narrow build, with long arms and delicate bone structure and appearance. He concluded that this type of person tended to be idealistic, introverted, and withdrawn. This body type he also associated with schizophrenia. He concluded that this type of person is generally associated with violent crimes.
- **Pyknic type:** The pyknic type person has a round body and is fat and fleshy. This body type is associated with manic depressiveness. He concluded that the pyknic type person tended to exhibit moodiness, extroversion, joviality, and realism. He concluded that pyknic types are generally associated with the crimes of larceny and fraud.

- **Dyplastic type:** The dyplastic type person has a body type that is part pyknic and part asthenic. He did not indicate an identifiable mental illness for this type of person.[25]

Earnest A. Hooton, a Harvard physical anthropologist, studied 17,000 people, including 13,873 prisoners. He was attempting to corroborate Lombroso's biological theories. Hooton concluded that there were differences between criminals and noncriminals. Criminals were more likely to have long thin necks, thinner beards and body hair, more red-brown hair, and thinner lips than noncriminals. Criminals also had low foreheads, compressed faces, and narrow jaws. Criminals were physically inferior to noncriminals, and differences were due to hereditary factors. His theories were often criticized because his famous book was published in 1939 and supported the Nazi belief of a "superior race."[26]

In 1949, William H. Sheldon studied delinquent male youths between the ages of 15 and 21. He concluded that delinquents had greater mesomorphy (tendency to be big-boned and muscular) than did nondelinquents. He developed his own method of body typing. He attempted to isolate three poles of physique, which he called somatotypes, and devised three classes of them:

- **Endomorph:** A person who is fat, round, and fleshy with short tapering limbs and small bones.
- **Ectomorph:** A person who is thin, small, and bony with a small face, sharp nose, fine hair, and relatively little body mass and relatively great surface area.
- **Mesomorph:** A person who is big-boned and muscular and tends to have a large trunk, heavy chest, and large wrists and hands.[27]

William Sheldon suggested that body type may predict criminality. He cross-checked hundreds of young men for body type and criminal history, and concluded that criminality was most likely among boys with a muscular, athletic build.[28] Later, in his text on delinquent youths, he listed both physique and temperament types. He then concluded that each person possesses the characteristics of the three types of physique and temperament. Sheldon used three numbers, each between 1 and 7, to indicate the extent to which the characteristics of the various types were present in a given individual. For example, an individual whose physique is 7-1-4 would have many characteristics of an endomorph, almost none of the ectomorph, and some of the mesomorph. He also concluded that most delinquent youths were significantly more mesomorphic than those least involved in delinquent behavior.[29]

Sheldon and Eleanor Gluecks, a husband and wife research team, studied the association between physical body types and delinquency.

They concluded that strength, physical ability, and activity level of mesomorphy can, under certain circumstances, be a factor in whether a juvenile becomes antisocial and criminal.[30]

The body type theories have been criticized for the following reasons:

- The theories have not actually demonstrated the relationship between physique and behavior.
- In most studies on body types, cultural factors were not considered.
- Most body type tests were conducted exclusively on males.
- Most body type theories were conducted on confined individuals and probably do not represent a normal sample.
- The test may really indicate which body types are more likely to be detected when involved in criminal behavior.

Chromosomal Abnormality

In a normal person, there are 23 pairs of chromosomes in each cell, including a pair of sex chromosomes, XY for men and XX for women. A relatively small number of males have an extra Y chromosome (XYY individuals). Over 200 research studies have failed to support the thesis that XYY men are more aggressive and violent than XY men. In addition, the XYY condition is so rare in the population that it cannot be a major factor in criminality.

In the 1960s, a team of British researchers reported that a disproportionate number of male inmates in a Scottish hospital for the criminally insane had an extra Y chromosome accompanying the normal male complement of one X and one Y chromosome. Next, attorneys for Richard Speck, the notorious Chicago multiple murderer, announced that they planned to appeal his case based on the fact that he was XYY, and therefore not responsible for his actions. It was later determined that Speck was not XYY. Several popular novels, including *The XYY Man* and *The Mosley Receipt*, came out in the late 1960s, which featured XYY characters who struggled against their compulsion for violence.

It has been determined that most criminals have the normal XY chromosome combination. So they are not different from those who do not commit crime. Therefore, this could not be the reason. Similarly, most men with the XYY combination do not commit crime. Hence, having an extra Y does not necessarily lead a person to criminal activity. Furthermore, no women have this combination of genes, so there should be no women criminals. But that is not true. Such an explanation based on the XYY chromosome combination has been discounted.

The intelligence theory has its own flaws because some criminals are highly intelligent. Also, their intelligent acts may have been declared as crime. How about breaking a computer code for national purposes? Will

SOCIETY IN ACTION

TENDENCY TO COMMIT VIOLENT CRIME—NOW WHAT?

The use of biological factors to predict an individual's tendency to commit violent crimes causes difficult problems for our society. Suppose it was determined that males with certain biological factors were twice as likely to commit a violent crime as males without this factor. Would this give us the right to take precautionary measures against someone discovered with this factor? Should this fact be made public and violate the individual's right of privacy? What about the concept of self-fulfilling prophecy?

we call it a crime or a patriotic service to the nation? Furthermore, most people with low intelligence do not commit crime.

Psychological Explanations

Psychological explanations of deviant behavior are generally based on either those that focus on intelligence or those that focus on personality. The most frequent psychological justifications are based on low intelligence.

Intelligence

Richard Herrnstein and Charles Murray, in their book *Bell Curve*, stressed that criminals consistently score between 91 and 93 on IQ tests, while the average IQ of the general population is around 100. According to them, someone with an IQ of over 125 is less likely to commit crime.[31] Researchers have discounted their findings. Many contend that IQ tests are not a very good indicator of intelligence since they are culturally biased. Other researchers contend that intelligence level and education does not predict whether or not one will commit criminal behavior, but probably predicts the types of crimes one will commit. According to them, criminals with low intelligence generally commit street crime, and criminals with higher intelligence generally commit white-collar crime.

Personality

Generally we use the term *personality* to refer to a complex set of emotional and behavioral attributes that tend to remain relatively constant. Frequently, words such as *aggressive, belligerent, suspicious, timid, argumentative*, and *likable* are used to describe a person's personality.

SOCIETY IN ACTION

MURDER IN THE UNITED STATES

The FBI's Uniform Crime Reporting (UCR) Program defines murder and nonnegligent manslaughter as the willful (nonnegligent) killing of one human being by another.

The classification of the offense is based solely on police investigation as opposed to the determination of a court, medical examiner, coroner, jury, or other judicial body.

- In 2011, an estimated 14,612 persons were murdered in the United States. This was a 0.7% decrease from the 2010 estimate, a 14.7% decline from the 2007 figure, and a 10.0% decrease from the 2002 estimate.
- There were 4.7 murders per 100,000 inhabitants, a 1.5% decrease from the 2010 rate. Compared with the 2007 rate, the murder rate declined 17.4%, and compared with the 2002 rate, the murder rate decreased 16.8%.
- Nearly 44% (43.6) of murders were reported in the South, the most populous region, 21.0% were reported in the West, 20.6% were reported in the Midwest, and 14.8% were reported in the Northeast.

Source: FBI homicide website, http://www.fbi.gov/about-us/cjis/ucr/crime-in-the-u.s/2011/crime-in-the-u.s.-2011/violent-crime/murder, retrieved May 1, 2014.

Psychologist Hans Eysenck contended that criminal behavior could be linked to three personality traits: extroversion, neuroticism, and psychoticism.[32] According to him, extroverts need more stimulation than typical people. Neurotics are unstable. Psychotics are aggressive and egocentric. Eysenck believed these three types could be difficult to condition to follow rules through typical punishment/reward systems in family and society. As a result, certain situations would lead to criminal behavior. Eysenck provided convincing studies that proved criminals scored higher as extroverts, neurotics, or psychotics than a control group of the general population.

Eysenck's critics have argued against the notion of a fixed personality. According to many researchers, personality type is an illusion created by an environment. For instance, prisoners who live in cramped, unpleasant conditions clearly will display stronger antisocial tendencies in a standardized test than everyday people. Other critics claim that Eysenck's system is too general because it does not explain how certain personality traits lead people to commit specific crimes. For example, Eysenck does not explain how neuroticism inclines a subject to steal as opposed to murder. All crimes appear to be generated by the same personality traits.

Impulse Control Disorder

Individuals with impulsive personality traits have been linked to criminal tendencies. Individuals who suffer from impulse control disorder (ICD) cannot resist committing acts that may hurt themselves or others. ICD involves crimes with lack of premeditation, such as a bar brawl or shoplifting. An individual with ICD probably would not commit more sophisticated crimes such as embezzlement.

Aggression

Many psychologists have linked aggressive personalities to crime. Aggressive personalities seek positions of dominance, abhor submission, display egocentrism, and lack impulse control. They look at every interaction as a win-lose situation. Individuals with aggressive personalities do not fit well with our systems of laws or rules.

Antisocial Personality Disorder

Antisocial personality disorder (APD) is identified by DSM-IV as a mental disorder with biological and environmental roots. A majority of criminals can be classified as suffering from APD; however, most criminologists tend to dismiss the illness as too broad a diagnostic category. The major symptoms of ADP involve refusal to observe social norms, disregard for the safety of others, and lack of remorse. In some ways, ADP combines ICD and aggression into one catchall personality type. (Note: DSM-IV codes are the classification found in the *Diagnostic and Statistical Manual of Mental Disorders*, 4th Edition, Text Revision, a manual published by the American Psychiatric Association that includes all currently recognized mental health disorders. The DSM-IV codes are thus used by mental health professionals to describe the features of a given mental disorder and indicate how the disorder can be distinguished from other, similar problems.)

Routine Activity

Routine activity theory focuses on situations of crimes (e.g., you are more likely to be robbed or a victim of assault in the park than in your locked home). It was developed by Marcus Felson and Lawrence E. Cohen. The premise of routine activity theory is that crime is relatively unaffected by social causes such as poverty, inequality, and unemployment.

Martha Smith and Ronald V. Clark use the routine activities approach of Cohen and Felson to examine crime on subways in large cities in the United States.[33] Cohen and Felson had contended that the absence of a capable guardian was a precondition of crime.[34] The researchers looked at opportunities for crimes facilitated by lack of supervision and noted that those crimes can also be blocked in other ways. For example, automatic ticketing may remove opportunities for passengers to avoid paying fares and for staff to pocket fare money. Their conclusion included the following:

- Robbery of passengers on mass transit is a rare event, even in systems with relatively high numbers of incidents such as New York City.
- Detailed analyses of passenger robbery incidents suggest that most robberies occur in one of the following three situations:
  - First, offenders prey on passengers in the deserted parts of large subway station complexes or at times when there are few other passengers around.
  - Second, offenders target passengers waiting at isolated rail stations in off-hours periods, particularly at elevated platforms and in high crime neighborhoods. Off-hours waiting areas are used to provide waiting passengers with the benefits of surveillance provided by transit employees, such as token clerks or ticket sellers, and other passengers.
  - Third, offenders appear to lie in wait for passengers leaving public transport. Prevention techniques focusing on target removal or surveillance may be useful against this type of robbery.
- A number of studies of the location of crime on subway systems have found that robbery is more likely to occur in the station than on the train.

Practicum

The earliest known U.S. shooting to happen on school property was the Pontiac's Rebellion school massacre on July 26, 1764, when four Lenape American Indians entered a schoolhouse near present-day Greencastle, Pennsylvania, and shot and killed the schoolmaster and either 9 or 10 children (reports vary).

April 20, 1999, in Littleton, Colorado, 14 students (including shooters) and 1 teacher were killed and 27 others wounded at Columbine High School in one of the nation's deadliest school shootings. The shooters had plotted for a year to kill at least 500 and blow up their school. At the end of their hour-long rampage, they turned their guns on themselves.

December 14, 2012, a killer armed with an assault rifle and two semi-automatic pistols entered Sandy Hook Elementary School in Newtown, Connecticut, and started shooting teachers and students. At the end of the massacre, 28 people had lost their lives. Six employees, the gunman's mother, and 20 children under the age of 7 were killed.

The deadliest school massacre occurred on May 18, 1927, in Bath, Michigan. Thirty-eight schoolchildren, aged 7–14, were killed when a series of bombs went off in the school. The bombs also killed 2 teachers, 4 adults, and another 58 people were wounded. The bomber, a school board member, was also killed during the deadliest school massacre in U.S. history.

Question: Which of the crime causation theories discussed in this chapter would best describe the reasons or rationale for the above listed school shootings?

Summary

- Among the criminological theories, the first formal school is generally called the classical or free will school. According to this school of thought, we commit deviant behavior by voluntarily choosing a course of action.
- The classical or free will school is an outgrowth of the Age of Enlightenment that dominated Europe for most of the 18th century.
- Cesare Beccaria and Jeremy Bentham were strongly influenced and adapted the ideas of the Age of Enlightenment to theories regarding human behavior and crime causation. Beccaria and Bentham were the leaders in the classical or free will movement.
- Social contract governance theory is based on the concept that by forming social groups, the citizens are agreeing on the moral and political obligations. These obligations are based upon a contract or agreement among the people for them to form the society in which they live.
- In the latter half of the 19th century, the positivist school was the leading school on crime causation. The school or concept was a product of the realism movement and a reaction to the harshness of the classical school.
- In determining the causes of crime, the positivists would examine the criminal and not the crime, whereas the followers of the classical school would examine the crime. The basic difference between the positivists and the classical school followers is whether or not humans have free will.
- The classical school is based on the concept of free will, and the positivist school on the fact that humans lack free will.
- Social determinism is based on the hypothesis that social interactions and constructs alone determine individual behavior, as opposed to biological or objective factors.

- A social determinism when studying certain human behaviors, such as committing murder, would look only at social phenomena, such as customs and expectations, education, interpersonal interactions, and memes, to decide whether or not a given person would exhibit any of these behaviors.
- The rational choice theory is based on the utilitarian belief that humans are reasoning persons who weighs means and ends, costs and benefits, and make a rational choice.
- Social control theories propose that people's relationships, commitments, values, norms, and beliefs encourage them not to break the law. If moral codes are internalized and individuals are tied into and have a stake in their community, they will limit their propensity to commit deviant acts.
- The social disorganization theory is an ecological theory that was developed by the Chicago School. The theory looks directly to neighborhood ecological characteristics to explain crime causation.
- A lasting perspective from the Chicago School was the social-psychological theory of symbolic interactionism. From symbolic interactionism two theories of crime causation developed: differential association and labeling.
- Edwin H. Sutherland originated differential association theory to explain criminal behavior. He published his first version of differential association in 1939 and his final version in 1947.
- Sutherland considered that all behaviors are learned in an individual's social environment. Sutherland stated that the major difference between conforming behavior and criminal behavior is in what is learned rather than how it is learned, because he considered that individuals learn both criminal and noncriminal behavior in much the same way.
- Differential association theory contends that criminal behavior is learned in association with intimate others by interacting and communicating with those others.
- According to the strain theories, the social structures within society pressure individuals to commit deviant behavior. The theories consider two different types of pressures: structural and individual.
- Generally the biological explanations focus on genetic predisposition toward deviance.
- Psychological explanations of deviant behavior are generally based on either those that focus on intelligence or those that focus on personality. The most frequent psychological justifications are based on low intelligence.

Questions in Review

1. Explain the basic differences between people who believe in determinism and those who advocate libertarianism.
2. How did Durkheim explain the causes of deviant behavior?
3. What is meant by the term *anomie*?
4. How do control theories differ from strain theories?
5. Explain the differential association theory of crime causation.

Key Terms

Anomie: A Greek term defined as lawlessness. It describes a state or a condition that exists within people when a society evolves from a mechanical to an organic entity.

Classical or free will theory of crime causation: The first formal school of thought on the causes of criminal behavior and based on the concept of free will. The school was called the classical school because it was the first formal school of criminological thought.

Determinism: The philosophical belief that for every event, including human action, there exist conditions that could cause no other event. That our actions are predetermined and we have no real choice.

***Diagnostic and Statistical Manual of Mental Disorders* (DSM):** A manual published by the American Psychiatric Association that includes all currently recognized mental health disorders. The DSM-IV codes are thus used by mental health professionals to describe the features of a given mental disorder and indicate how the disorder can be distinguished from other, similar problems.

Ectomorph: A person who is thin, small, and bony with a small face, sharp nose, fine hair, and relatively little body mass and relatively great surface area.

Endomorph: A person who is fat, round, and fleshy with short tapering limbs and small bones.

Impulse control disorder (ICD): A disorder in which individuals who suffer from it cannot resist committing acts that may hurt themselves or others.

Libertarianism: In a philosophical sense, a term that was first used by late Enlightenment free thinkers to refer to those who believed in free will, as opposed to determinism. Libertarianism is based on the concept of free will and holds that we are able to take more than one possible course of action under a given set of circumstances.

Mesomorph: A person who is big-boned and muscular and tends to have a large trunk, heavy chest, and large wrists and hands.

Routine activity: Routine activity theory focuses on situations of crimes (e.g., you are more likely to be robbed or a victim of assault in the park than in your locked home).

Endnotes

1. Coleman Philipson. (1923). *Three criminal law reformers.* London: Dutton.
2. Cesare Beccaria. (1963). *On crimes and punishments* (Henry Paolucci, Trans.). Library of Liberal Arts Series. New York: Bobbs-Merrill. (Original work published 1776)
3. Charles Milner. (2009). *Jeremy Bentham: His life and work.* Ithaca, NY: Cornell University Library. (Original work published 1905)
4. Negley Harte. (2005). Radical pants and the pursuit of happiness. Retrieved April 7, 2014, from http://www.utilitarianism.com/jeremy-bentham/jb.html
5. Ronald R. Clarke (Ed.). (1997). *Situational crime prevention: Successful case studies.* New York: Harrow and Heston.
6. S. Gul. (2009). An evaluation of rational choice theory in criminology. *Sociology and Applied Science*, 4(8), 36–44.
7. Travis Hirschi & Michael R. Gottfredson. (2005). Punishment of children from the perspective of control theory. In Michael Donnelly & Murray A. Straus (Eds.), *Corporal punishment of children in theoretical perspective* (pp. 134–156). New Haven, CT: Yale University Press.
8. Emile Durkheim. (1938). *Rules of the sociological method* (Sarah A. Solovay & John H. Mueller, Trans., George E. G. Catlin, Ed.). Chicago: University of Chicago Press.
9. Travis Hirschi. (2002). *Causes of delinquency.* New Brunswick, NJ: Transaction Publishers.
10. Charis Kubrin & Ronald Weitzer. (2003). New directions in social disorganization theory. *Journal of Research in Crime and Delinquency*, 40, 374–402.
11. Martin Bulmer. (1984). *The Chicago School of Sociology: Institutionalization, diversity, and the rise of sociological research.* Chicago: University of Chicago Press.
12. Robert Faris. (1967). *Chicago sociology: 1920–1932.* San Francisco: Chandler.
13. Robert E. Park, Ernest Burgess, & R. D. McKenzie. (1925). *The city: Suggestions for investigation of human behavior in the urban environment.* Chicago: University of Chicago Press.
14. Clifford Shaw & Henry McKay. (1942). *Juvenile delinquency in urban areas.* Chicago: University of Chicago Press.
15. Robert K. Merton. (1938). *Social structure and anomie.* New York: Free Press.
16. Ruth Masters & Cliff Roberson. (1990). *Inside criminology.* Englewood Cliffs, NJ: Prentice-Hall.
17. George Herbert Mead. (1934). *Mind, self and society from the standpoint of a social behaviorist* (Charles W. Morris, Ed.). Chicago: University of Chicago.
18. Nancy Herman-Kinney & Larry Reynolds. (2003). *Handbook of symbolic interactionism.* New York: Alta-Mira.
19. Herbert Blume. (1969). *Symbolic interaction: Perspective and method* (pp. 4–5). Englewood Cliffs, NJ: Prentice-Hall.
20. Edwin H. Sutherland & Donald R. Cressy. (1978). *Principles of criminology* (10th ed., pp. 80–82). Philadelphia: Lippincott.

21. Ruth Masters & Cliff Roberson. (1990). *Inside criminology* (pp. 209–210). Englewood Cliffs, NJ: Prentice Hall.
22. Frank P. Williams III & Marilyn D. McShane. (1994). *Criminological theory* (2nd ed.). Englewood Cliffs, NJ: Prentice Hall.
23. Ruth Masters & Cliff Roberson. (1990). *Inside criminology* (pp. 209–210). Englewood Cliffs, NJ: Prentice Hall.
24. Robert K. Merton. (October 1938). Social structure and anomie. *American Sociological Review*, 3(5): 672–682.
25. Ernst Kretschmer. (1925). *Physique and character* (W. J. H. Sprott, Trans.). London: Trubner.
26. Earnest A. Hooten. (1939). *The American criminal: An anthropological study*. Cambridge, MA: Harvard University Press.
27. W. H. Sheldon. (1949). *Varieties of delinquent youths*. New York: Harper.
28. George B. Vold & Thomas J. Bernard. (1986). *Theoretical criminology* (3rd ed.). New York: Oxford University.
29. Sheldon, 1949.
30. S. Glueck & E. Glueck. (1950). *Unraveling juvenile delinquency*. New York: Commonwealth Fund.
31. Richard J. Herrnstein & Charles Murray. (1994). *Bell curve: Intelligence and class structure in American life*. New York: Free Press.
32. H. J. Eysenck & S. B. G. Eysenck. (1969). *Personality structure and measurement*. London: Routledge.
33. Martha J. Smith & Ronald V. Clarke. (2000). Crime and public transport. *Crime and Justice*, *27*, 169–233.
34. Lawrence E. Cohen & Marcus Felson. (1979). Social change and crime rate trends: A routine activity approach. *American Sociological Review*, *44*, 588–608.

chapter three

Constructionist Approaches

Chapter Objectives

What you should know and understand after studying this chapter:

- How the constructionists look at deviant behavior
- The concepts involved with the labeling theory
- The effects of labeling a person a deviant
- How the concept of new criminology developed
- The general assumptions of the conflict theorists
- How the conflict theorists look at criminal laws

Constructionist Perspectives

> The constructionist looks not at the deviant act, but how deviance is defined and how these definitions are enforced.

Chapter 2 discussed the general theories of crime causation. In this chapter, we will examine in detail the constructionist approaches used to explain deviant behavior. The constructionist approach questions the conventionalization of behaviors, beliefs, and traits; definitions of deviance; the enforcement of societal rules; and the consequences of enforcement. Constructionists view deviance not as an action, but an infraction of societal rules. They tend to question what makes certain conduct deviant and what groups in society make and enforce the rules.

In this chapter, formal and informal social controls are examined along with perspectives that focus on defining deviance and the constructionist theories. The constructionist theories discussed in the chapter include labeling, conflict theories, and controlology or new sociology of social control. The basic premise of a constructionist is best explained by the statement of Herbert Becker in his classic book *Outsiders: Studies in the Sociology of Deviance*. He stated that "the deviant is one to whom the label has successfully been applied; deviant behavior is behavior that people so label."[1]

Labeling Theory

The labeling theory was developed in the early 1960s. It was first called the societal reaction school. The theorists, who supported the concept, contended that earlier theories of crime causation placed too much emphasis on individual deviance and neglected the reactions of people to this deviance.

Most scholars attribute the development of the labeling perspective to the works of Frank Tannenbaum and his 1938 book *Crime and the Community*.[2] He formalized the "dramatization of evil," which suggested that deviant behavior was not so much a product of the deviant's lack of adjustment to society as it was the fact that he or she had adjusted to a special group, and that criminal behavior was a product of the conflict between his group and the community. The conflict results in two opposing views of appropriate behavior. The community then places a "tag" on the child that identifies the child as a delinquent. This causes the child to change his or her self-image and causes people to react to the tag, not the child. Accordingly, it is the process of tagging criminals or delinquents that creates crime.

The labeling perspective was very popular in the 1960s. In the 1960s, as our society was becoming more conscious of racial inequality and civil rights, the issues of the underprivileged members of society became one of the topics of concern. The social atmosphere promoted by the Great Society of Presidents Kennedy and Johnson increased the popularity of the labeling theory. Labeling was accepted as the answer to the question of why certain groups of people were more frequently involved in the criminal justice system.

Labeling theory can be traced to Emile Durkheim's book *Suicide*. Durkheim opined that crime is not so much a violation of a penal code as it is an act that outrages society. He was the first to suggest that deviant labeling satisfies that function and society's need to control the behavior. As noted in Chapter 2, symbolic interactionism argues that human actions are best understood in terms of the meanings that those actions have for the actors. Under this concept, one of the most important meanings is the meaning that people give to themselves—their self-image. If people define themselves as worthless, they then tend to act toward themselves according to the meanings that has for them. As will be discussed later, a person's self-image is constructed primarily through social interactions with other people in what Mead called the self as a social construct and Cooley called a "looking-glass self."

Labeling theory is generally not concerned with the normal roles that define our behavior, but with those roles that society provides for deviant behavior, called deviant roles, stigmatic roles, or social stigma. A social role contains a set of expectations we have about a behavior. Social roles are necessary for the organization and functioning of any society or group. Deviance for a sociologist does not mean morally wrong, but rather behavior that is condemned by society. Deviant behavior can include both criminal and noncriminal activities.

According to the label theorists, most of the rules that define deviance and the contexts in which deviant behavior is labeled as deviant are framed by the wealthy for the poor, by men for women, by older people for younger people, and by ethnic minorities for minority groups. Under these concepts, those in the more powerful and dominant groups create and apply deviant labels to the subordinate or weaker groups. For example, many children engage in activities such as breaking windows, stealing fruit from other people's trees, climbing into other people's yards, or playing hooky from school. In affluent neighborhoods, these acts may be regarded by parents, teachers, and police as innocent aspects of the process of growing up. In poor areas, on the other hand, these same activities might be seen as tendencies toward juvenile delinquency.

Once the individual is labeled as deviant, it is extremely difficult to remove that label. He or she becomes stigmatized as a criminal or deviant and is likely to be considered, and treated, as untrustworthy by others. After the deviant individual accepts the deviant label and sees himself or herself as deviant, then the individual acts in a way that meet the expectations of that label. Even if the labeled individual does not commit any further deviant acts than the one that caused him or her to be labeled, getting rid of that label can be very difficult. For example, an ex-criminal who never commits another crime is still treated with suspicion.

Looking-Glass Self

> The mind is mental … because … the human mind is social. Beginning as children, humans begin to define themselves within the context of their socializations.[3]

Charles Cooley developed the social psychological concept of looking-glass self. He stated that a person's self grows out of society's interpersonal interactions and the perceptions of others. The term refers to people shaping their self-concepts based on their understanding of how others perceive them. Because people conform to how they think others think them to be, it's difficult, or arguably impossible, to act differently from how a person thinks he or she is perpetually perceived. To Cooley, society is an interweaving and interworking of mental selves.[4]

Cooley's looking-glass self has three major components and is unique to humans.[5] Those components are as follows:

- We imagine how we must appear to others.
- We imagine and react to what we feel their judgment of that appearance must be.
- We develop our self through the judgments of others.

In the looking-glass self a person views himself or herself through others perceptions in society and in turn gains identity. Identity, or self, is the result of the concept in which we learn to see ourselves as others do. The looking-glass self begins at an early age and continues throughout the entirety of a person's life, as one will never stop modifying his or her self unless all social interactions are ceased. Note: Some sociologists contend that the concept wanes over time, while others note that only a few studies have been conducted with a large number of subjects in natural settings.

Critics argue that the looking-glass self-conceptualization of the social self is critically incomplete in that it overlooks the divergent roles of in-groups and out-groups in self-definition. That is, while individuals will converge upon the attitudes and behaviors of in-group members, they will also diverge from the attitudes and behaviors of out-group members. The neglect of the latter scenario is attributed to the looking glass approach's implicit focus on in-group member appraisals. It is also argued that the looking-glass self metaphor fails to reflect the fact that influence derives from the self-categorization of other individuals as part of the self. By this latter reference the critics state that people are not shaped by the reflections from "others," but rather are shaped by the creation of a collective social identity that contrasts "us" against relevant "others."[6]

Frank Tannenbaum

Frank Tannenbaum is considered the father of labeling theory. In his book *Crime and the Community*, Tannenbaum described the social interactions involved in crime. He contended that the criminal differs little or none at all from others in the original impulse to first commit deviant behavior. He blamed societal reactions for continued deviant acts that develop patterns of interest to sociologists.[7] In other words, the deviant commits additional deviant behavior because we have labeled him or her a deviant.

Tannenbaum used the concept of tagging to explain the labeling process. He contended that a negative tag or label often contributed to further involvement in delinquent activities. This initial tagging may cause the individual to adopt it as part of his or her identity. According to Tannenbaum, the greater the emphasis or attention placed on the tag or label, the more likely the individual is to identify himself or herself as a person who fits within the label. Under this concept, if we label a youth as good and the youth accepts that label, he or she will act accordingly. If, however, we label a youth as delinquent and the youth accepts that label, he or she will act as a delinquent is expected to act (Figure 3.1).

Tannenbaum labeled his theoretical model as the dramatization of evil or labeling theory. The labeling theory developed in the mid

Figure 3.1 Photo of Frank Tannenbaum taken around 1915. Tannenbaum led the refinery workers in the Bayonne, New Jersey, refinery strikes of 1915–1916. The workers, mostly Polish Americans, struck Standard Oil of New Jersey and Tidewater Petroleum plants beginning in mid-July 1915. (Photo from the Library of Congress Prints and Photographs Division, Washington, DC.)

to late 1930s. During this time the nation was suffering under the Great Depression. The social climate was one of disillusionment with the government. The class structure was one of cultural isolationism. There was a general feeling that class structures caused many economic hardships. This was also the time that the communist party was the strongest in the United States. During the early 1930s, the positivist school of criminology was still dominant, and the emphasis on biological determinism and internal explanations of crime was the preeminent force in the theories. The dominance of the positivist school waned in the late 1930s with the introduction of conflict and social explanations of crime and criminality.

Tannenbaum contended that one of the central tenets of the labeling theory was to refuse to dramatize the evil. During that period, the growth of the labeling theory and its application, both practical and theoretical, provided a solid foundation for continued popularity. The practice of avoiding the labeling process encouraged the justice system to begin using diversion programs.

Edwin Lemert

Following the concepts noted earlier by Frank Tannenbaum, sociologist Edwin Lemert introduced the concept of secondary deviance. The primary deviance is the first experience connected to deviant behavior or the first offense by an individual. Secondary deviation is the role created to deal with society's condemnation of and reaction to the behavior.[8]

Lemert noted that deviant acts are social acts, a result of the cooperation of society. In studying drug addiction, Lemert observed a very powerful and subtle force at work. Besides the physical addiction to the drug and all the economic and social disruptions it caused, there was an intensely intellectual process at work concerning one's own identity and the justification for the behavior: "I do these things because I am this way."

While there may be certain subjective and personal motives that first lead a person to commit deviant behavior. This original activity itself tells us little about the person's self-image or its relationship to the activity. When an individual's acts are repeated and organized subjectively and transformed into active roles and become the social criteria for assigning status as the individual accepts his or her role and status, the individual begins to employ the deviant behavior or a role based on it as a means of defense, attack, or adjustment to the overt and covert problems created by the consequent societal reaction to him or her. This later deviation is secondary deviance.

Howard Becker

Howard Becker, picking up where Lemert left off, became the voice of the labeling theorists. He described the process of how a person accepted the deviant role in a study of dance musicians, with whom he once worked. He also studied the identity formation of marijuana smokers. His book *Outsiders* became their bible when it was published in 1963. As one researcher noted, his book became the manifesto of the labeling theory movement among sociologists.

In *Outsiders* Becker noted:

> Social groups create deviance by making rules whose infraction creates deviance, and by applying those roles to particular people and labeling them as outsiders. From this point of view, deviance is *not* a quality of the act the person commits, but rather a consequence of the application by other of rules and sanctions to an offender. The deviant is one to whom that label has been successfully applied; deviant behavior is behavior that people so label.[9]

Becker noted that while society uses the stigmatic label to justify its condemnation, and that the deviant actor uses it to justify his or her actions, instead of deviant motives leading to deviant behavior, it is the other way around: Deviant behavior in time causes deviant motivation.

Erving Goffman

Erving Goffman, former president of the American Sociological Association and one of most cited sociologists, was a leading contributor to labeling theory. In his book *The Presentation of Self in Everyday Life*, he discussed the concept of stigma.[10] Whereas other authors examined the process of adopting a deviant identity, Goffman researched the ways in which people managed that identity and controlled information about it.

Goffman's key points include the following:

- In the modern states there is a heightened demand for normalcy. The stigmas that are attached to individuals are the result of the demand for normalcy.
- Deviants, who are living in a divided world, divide their worlds into forbidden places where discovery means exposure and danger, places where people of that kind are painfully tolerated, and places where one's kind is exposed without need to dissimulate or conceal.
- Society's demands are filled with contradictions. On the one hand, a stigmatized person may be told that he is no different from others. On the other hand, he must declare his status as a resident alien who stands for his group. The demands require that the stigmatized individual cheerfully and unselfconsciously accept himself as essentially the same as normals, while at the same time he voluntarily withholds himself from those situations in which normals would find it difficult to give lip service to their similar acceptance of him.
- Familiarity may not reduce contempt. In spite of the common belief that openness and exposure will decrease stereotypes and repression, the opposite is true. Whether we interact with strangers or intimates, we will still find that the fingertips of society have reached bluntly into the contact, even here putting us in our place.[11]

David Matza

Sociologist David Matza, in his book *On Becoming Deviant*, noted that the acts of authorities in outlawing a proscribed behavior can not only control the proscribed behavior, but also provide new opportunities for creating deviant identities.[12] According to Matza, the concept of affinity does little to explain the dedication to the behavior. He states that it may be considered a natural biographical tendency born of personal and social circumstances that suggests but hardly compels a direction or movement. What gives force to that movement is the development of a new identity.

Matza notes that some offenses, including the use of violence, are universally recognized as wrong. Therefore, labeling either habitual criminals or those who have caused serious harm as criminals is not constructive. Society may use more specific labels, such as murderer or child abuser, to demonstrate more clearly after the event the extent of society's disapproval. The act of labeling invariably modifies the behavior of the one so labeled. In addition, applying a label that will last may cause prejudice against the offender, resulting in the inability to maintain employment and social relationships, and thus increasing recidivism.

Labeling Process in Nondeviant Behavior Situations

While the social construction of deviant behavior label plays an important role in the labeling process that occurs in society, this process involves not only the labeling of deviant behavior, which is behavior that does not fit socially constructed norms, but also labeling that reflects stereotyped or stigmatized behavior of other individuals, such as the mentally ill. Labeling theory was first applied to the term *mentally ill* in 1966 by Thomas Scheff.[13]

Scheff challenged common perceptions of mental illness by claiming that mental illness is manifested solely as a result of societal influence. He opined that society views certain actions as unacceptable or deviant. Society often places the label of mental illness on those who exhibit the unacceptable behaviors. Once the label is applied, certain expectations are placed on these individuals, and those so labeled change their behavior to fulfill the expectations. Criteria for different mental illnesses are not consistently fulfilled by those who are diagnosed with them because all of these people suffer from the same disorder; they are simply fulfilled because the mentally ill believe they are supposed to act a certain way, so over time, they come to do so.

Process of Labeling Behavior

The process of making the criminal is a process of tagging, defining, identifying, segregating, describing, emphasizing, and making conscious and self-conscious; it becomes a way of stimulating, suggesting, emphasizing, and evoking the very traits that are complained of. The person becomes the thing he is described as being. Nor does it seem to matter whether the valuation is made by those who would punish or by those who would reform. In either case, the emphasis is upon conduct that is disapproved of. The parents or the policeman, the older brother or the court, the probation officer or the juvenile institution, insofar as they rest on the thing complained of, rest upon a false ground. Their very enthusiasm defeats their aim. The harder they work to reform the evil, the greater the evil grows under their hands. The persistent suggestion, with whatever good intentions, works mischief because it leads to bring out the bad behavior it would suppress. The way out is through a refusal to dramatize the evil. The less said about it, the better.[14]

The basic points of the labeling theory are as follows:

- Society has multiple values with differing degrees of overlap.
- The quality of behavior is determined by the application of values to that individual's behavior. The identification of that behavior as deviant occurs through a reaction to that behavior.
- Deviance exists only when there is a reaction to the behavior.
- Once behavior is perceived and labeled deviant by a social audience, the individual who is responsible for the behavior is also labeled as deviant.
- The reaction to behavior and the labeling process is more likely to occur when the actor is a member of the less socially powerful class.
- Society tends to observe more closely those who have been identified as deviant, and therefore finds even more deviance in those persons. Subsequent acts are reacted to more quickly and the label more firmly affixed.
- Depending on the strength of an individual's original self-concept, once a person is labeled as deviant, the person may accept that label as self-identity.
- A person labeled as criminal is perceived to be first and foremost a criminal; other attributes are generally ignored.
- Further deviant behavior (secondary deviance) is a product of living and acting within the deviant label.

Critiques of Labeling Theory

The labeling theory has had a great influence on the study of crime causation. It has caused us to reexamine our basic concepts regarding crime and criminals. It has also had its critics. One of the most serious criticisms is that it is not a theory, but a perspective, and that it has no systemic theoretical basis. In addition, empirical testing of the labeling theory is impossible.

Another criticism of labeling theory is that it emphasizes the interactive process of labeling and ignores the processes that lead to the deviant acts. Such processes might include differences in socialization, attitudes, and opportunities. In addition, there is no explanation of the causation of the first deviant act—the one that results in the deviant label. Another critique of labeling theory is that it is still not clear whether or not labeling actually has the effect of increasing deviant behavior. Delinquent behavior tends to increase following conviction, but is this the result of labeling itself, as the theory suggests?

The effects of labeling theory on criminology have been substantial, according to Williams and McShane. It has caused criminologists to question the middle-class values, which they were using in their descriptions of deviance and criminality. In addition, researchers take a more critical examination of criminal justice agencies and the way in which those agencies process individuals.[15]

The labeling theory has influenced the study of crime causation. It has resulted in a reexamination of the basic concepts regarding crime and criminals.

Modified Labeling Theory

Bruce Link has developed a modified labeling theory based on the studies that point to the influence that labeling can have on mental patients. In his modified labeling theory he indicates that expectations of labeling can have a negative effect, that the expectations often cause patients to withdraw from society, and that those who are labeled as having a mental disorder are constantly being rejected from society in seemingly minor ways. When these rejections are taken as a whole, the small slights can drastically alter the self-concepts of those so labeled. They come to both anticipate and perceive negative societal reactions to them, and this can damage the quality of their life.[16] Critics have described the modified labeling theory as a sophisticated social-psychological model of why labels matter.

Efforts to cope with effects of labeling include not telling anyone, educating people about mental distress/disorder, and withdrawing from stigmatizing situations. These actions can result in further social isolation and reinforce negative self-concepts.

Hard and Soft Labeling

Advocates who believe in hard labeling contend that mental illness does not exist. It is merely deviance from the norms of society that cause people to believe in mental illness. Thus, mental illnesses are socially constructed illnesses and psychotic disorders that do not exist. Those who advocate soft labeling contend that while mental illness does exist, the labeling process aggravates the illness.

Conflict and Critical Theories

Conflict and critical theories examine the social, political, or material inequality of social groups. The theories focus on the power differentials, such as class conflict, and generally contrast historically dominant ideologies with a macro level analysis of society. Karl Marx is the

SOCIETY IN ACTION

SELF-AWARENESS AND TRANSGRESSION IN CHILDREN

Researchers conducted two field studies to explore the relationship between self-awareness and transgressive behavior. In one study, the participants were 363 children who arrived to trick-or-treat between 5:00 and 8:00 p.m. on Halloween, 1976, at any of 18 selected homes. Children were used only if they were not with a parent. Thus, all were old enough to be able to state their name and some description of where they lived. Furthermore, only children who came disguised by a costume, mask, or painted face were used. When too many children appeared at one time (more than seven), or if a second group of children arrived before the experimenter could leave the room, these children were not included as subjects.

The 18 homes were arranged in the same basic pattern. Inside a room near the front door was a low table approximately 5 ft (1.5 m) long. On the table was a large bowl full of wrapped, bite-sized candy bars that was replenished frequently during the evening. A large mirror was used in the self-awareness condition. The mirror rose above the table to a height of at least 5 ft from the floor.

The mirror was placed directly behind the table at a 90° angle such that the children would always see themselves while reaching for the candy. Within full view of the bowl was a decorative backdrop with a peephole that camouflaged an unobtrusive observer.

Procedure

A female experimenter greeted all children who came trick-or-treating, and an assistant served as the unobtrusive observer who recorded the data. Whenever a child or children arrived, the experimenter would greet them amicably and would comment on their costumes. The experimenter then told each child, "You (or each of you) may take one of the candies. I have to go back to my work in another room." The purpose of this, as in past studies, was to make the standard of taking only one candy clearly salient. If any child had any questions about what was supposed to be done, the experimenter repeated the instructions to take one candy. She then exited and made sure she was out of sight of the children.

The observer recorded the number of children who entered the house, the number of candies taken by each child, and the estimated age and sex of each of the children. In past research and pilot studies, estimates of number of candies taken have been found to be highly reliable. With regard to age estimations, any inaccuracies would tend to obscure real differences between the age groups. If observers tend consistently to overestimate or underestimate ages, then the age data would just be shifted consistently up or down and would be less specific but would not obscure the trends present.

Since the experimenters in each house knew whether or not a mirror was present and at least the greeter knew whether or not children were individuated (see below), experimental bias was possible. However, a number of controls minimized this concern. Both mirror and no mirror conditions were run at each home, and a large number of homes and experimenters were used.

Although all experimenters were carefully trained and rehearsed in the procedures, most were not on the research team involved in designing the study, and hence were blind to the predictions made. Also, due to the relatively large number of conditions, systematic inaccurate recording of the data was less likely. Additionally, since the mean number of subjects per house was 26, trends in the various conditions should not have been apparent to any group of experimenters at a particular home.

Self-Awareness Manipulation

In this condition a large mirror was placed behind the table. Half of the homes were randomly assigned to the self-awareness condition from 5:00 to 6:30 p.m. At 6:30 p.m. mirrors were removed in these homes, whereas in the remaining homes, mirrors were placed behind the tables and the self-awareness conditions were run from 6:30 to 8:00 p.m.

Individuation Manipulation

There was a concern prior to the experiment that the mirror manipulation of self-awareness might be ineffective for costumed (anonymous) children. The mirror might focus their attention on their costumes, not upon themselves as individuals. Thus, it might be more difficult to make anonymous children self-aware. It was therefore considered important to shift the focus of attention from examining and appreciating one's costume to reflection upon oneself. To do this, after greeting the children and commenting on their costumes, the experimenter explicitly asked each child in the individuated condition what his or her name was and where he or she lived. The experimenter carefully repeated each child's name and address to make it salient that she knew this information about each of them. She then continued with the rest of the basic procedure by telling each child to take one candy and excusing herself to work in another room while the child(ren) entered the room where the candy was. These procedures have been used several times before and require relatively little time.

Because the children are asked their names at many other homes on Halloween, they do not seem to find the request strange. No attempt was made to identify any of the costumed children in the anonymous condition. The children were assigned to the anonymous and individuated conditions alternately by groups in each home.

Results

Of the 363 children, 70 (19.3%) transgressed by taking more than one candy. Children arriving alone (n = 39) transgressed somewhat less frequently than groups of children did, 10.3% versus 20.4%. Since the distribution among all the various conditions of the few children who arrived alone resulted in sample sizes much too small for statistical analysis, and since the children who arrived alone seemed to transgress less often, the subsequent analyses of self-awareness effects are based upon the 324 children who arrived in groups.

Self-Awareness and Deindividuation

The overall rate of transgression can be computed for each relevant condition and contrasted with other conditions. One might just examine the behavior of the first child in each group, reasoning that those individuals will be less influenced by the group than the following children would be, and hence a more conservative analysis will emerge. One could instead assign a value to each group (such as the proportion of the group transgressing) and make groups, not individuals, the unit of observation. Since the group members certainly could influence each other, a group-as-unit analysis could be preferred. However, three important considerations argue for the use of the data from all individuals. First, past research employing the Halloween paradigm has found group and individual data to provide identical statistical outcomes. Second, since groups are comprised of mixed ages and sexes, hypotheses made concerning these variables could not be examined using groups as units. Third, the potential modeling effects (which work against independence of group members) require investigating each member's behavior, and this was one intent of the present design. Nevertheless, the analyses were performed when possible using the first child and also the proportion-per-group data. In almost every case the conclusions remained the same.

Children in the no mirror condition transgressed significantly more than those in the mirror condition, 28.5% versus 14.4%. The self-awareness effect seemed only to occur in the individuation condition, where each child's identity was made salient. In the individuated no mirror condition, 37.7% of the children transgressed compared to 8.9% in the individuated mirror condition. However, in the anonymous no mirror condition, 19.1% transgressed, compared to 19.6% in the anonymous mirror condition.

Deindividuation theory would not only predict lower stealing rates for children who arrive alone (as was found), but would also predict that groups of children who are anonymous would steal more than groups consisting of individuated children. However, the data indicated that overall the anonymous groups actually produced a transgression rate, 19.4%, about equal to that for the individuated conditions, 21.4%. In the no mirror condition, the anonymous children stole significantly less often, 19.1% versus 37.7%, than individuated children did. However, in the mirror condition the individuated groups' norm violations were reduced below those of the anonymous groups, 8.9% versus 19.6%. The unexpectedly low transgression rates among anonymous subjects have also occurred in several laboratory studies.

The results for the amount of candy taken per child replicated the earlier research of Diener, Eraser, Beaman, and Kelem in obtaining a mean of roughly three candies (two extra) for each transgressing child. They tend to take the amount their hands can hold easily. However, children in the condition with the reduced stealing rate, the individuated mirror condition, did take fewer candies than those in the individuated no mirror condition, 2.68 versus 2.0. It appears that self-awareness reduced both the rates and the amount of candy taken when children were individuated.

Discussion

As the theory of objective self-awareness predicts, standard consistent behavior was increased in a naturalistic setting by focusing children's attention upon themselves. This occurred only when children had first been individuated by being asked their name and address. This reduction in transgression seems to reflect an increase in compliance to a salient behavioral standard. The standard instituted in the present study was the instruction given by the experimenter to "take one candy only." The children in the present study altered their behavior to be more consistent with the standard of correctness when they were self-aware. Thus, the present findings add external validity to the earlier research showing greater adherence to standard appropriate behaviors.

Anonymity

In cases where the children remained anonymous, the presence of the mirror had no impact on behavior. We interpret this as an indication that the child's focus of attention was directed to aspects of his or her costume rather than to the self. Hence, no state of self-awareness seemed to develop. Although these findings are consistent with the contention that anonymity may inhibit self-awareness, this may occur only in the presence of a disguise, not as a general function of anonymity.

Future research in which self-awareness is induced and anonymity is experimentally manipulated in several different ways should help clarify the way in which anonymity affects self-awareness. It may be that when one is disguised and a group member, anonymity inhibits feelings of self-awareness. If one were alone in a costume on a downtown street at noon, the disguise might enhance self-awareness. Both the manner in which one is made anonymous and the situational context in which the anonymity occurs probably influence the effect this variable has on self-awareness. Data from the anonymous conditions were not what one would predict from the deindividuation theory. It was hoped that the present study might, in addition to assessing various self-awareness effects, shed light on the interaction of the two theories.

Earlier research has shown that group presence, and also anonymity, increases transgressions. Although some weak support for increasing transgressions among groups compared to children arriving alone was found in the present study, no overall effects were found for anonymity. In fact, anonymous children actually transgressed significantly less in the no mirror condition than individuated children did. One possible explanation for this is that in the present study the individuated no mirror condition may have had high rates of transgression due to some artifact introduced by the procedures used.

Source: Beaman, A. L., Klentz, B., Diener, E., and Svanum, S., Self-Awareness and Transgression in Children: Two Field Studies, *Journal of Personality and Social Psychology*, 37(10), 1835–1846, 1979.

generally considered as the founder of the social conflict theories. The conflict theories do not refer to any unified school of thought, and therefore should not be confused with peace and conflict studies. While the conflict theory is more commonly associated with Marxism, it is a reaction to functionalism and the positivist method. Other conflict perspectives include the following:

- Feminist theory, which advocates social equality for women and men, in opposition to patriarchy and sexism
- Postmodern theory, an approach that is critical of modernism, with a mistrust of grand theories and ideologies
- Poststructural theory
- Race conflict approach, which focuses on inequality and conflict between people of different racial and ethnic categories

Karl Marx

As early as the 16th century, theorists examining crime causation have linked deviant behavior with economic status. Karl Marx and Friedrich Engels are credited with originating the concept that crime or deviant behavior is a potential of capitalism. To them, a criminal or deviant individual was an individual who had been brutalized and demoralized by capitalism.[17]

Marxist criminology theories are difficult to summarize for several reasons. First, they are based on complex theories of society and social change. The complexity has led to profound disagreements among different Marxist theorists. In addition, the theories have changed significantly since they were first developed. Karl Marx (1818–1883) linked economic development to social, political, and historical change. He based his theory on the conflict between the material forces of production and the social relations of production. He used the term *material forces of production* to refer to a society's capacity to produce material goods, including technological equipment and the knowledge, skill, and organization to use that equipment. The term *social relations of production* refers to relationships between people and includes property relationships. The term also includes the distribution of goods and who gets what.

Marx argued that capitalist societies would inevitably tend to polarize into two groups, one growing smaller and smaller while getting richer and richer, and the other growing larger and larger while getting poorer and poorer. The tendency toward polarization is what Marx called the contradiction in capitalism. While Marx himself did not discuss crime causation or its relation to the economic system at length, he did address it. He believed that it was essential to human nature that people be productive in life and in work. Marx saw crime as the struggle of the isolated individual against the prevailing conditions that are dictated by those in power who represent only their own interests. He also believed that in industrialized capitalist societies there are large numbers of people unemployed and underemployed, and that these individuals become demoralized and are subject to all forms of crime and vice.[18]

Willem Bonger, an early Marxist criminologist, argued that the capitalist economic system encouraged all people to be greedy and selfish and to pursue their own benefits without regard to the welfare of others in society. Since the justice system criminalizes the greed of the poor while it allows legal opportunities for the rich to pursue their selfish desires, crime is concentrated in the lower classes. Bonger argued that a socialist society would ultimately eliminate crime since it would promote a concern for all in society, not just the rich. In addition, a socialist society would remove the present legal bias that favors the rich.

Marxist criminology is based on four propositions:

- Crime is best understood under the perspective of the scarcity of resources and the historical inequality in the distribution of those resources.
- Crime constitutes more than the state definition of crime.
- The state version of crime and other social harms are a product of the class struggle.
- Crime represents the alienation of individuals by capitalist social structures and institutions.

After Willem Bonger advocated Marxist criminology in the 1920s, it virtually disappeared. In the 1970s, many of the concepts reappeared in the form of critical criminology advocated by Richard Quinney and in Great Britain as new criminology with the works of Taylor, Walton, and Young.[19]

C. Wright Mills

Charles Wright Mills was an American sociologist and a professor of sociology at Columbia University from 1946 until his death in 1962. His book *White Collar: American Middle Classes* provided a historical account of the middle classes in the United States and contended that bureaucracies have overwhelmed middle-class workers, robbing them of their independent thoughts and turning them into near automatons.[20] And the bureaucracies have left them oppressed but cheerful. Mills noted three types of power within the workplace:

- Coercion or physical force
- Authority
- Manipulation

In the article Mills expressed his belief that Western society was trapped within the iron cage of bureaucratic rationality, which would eventually lead society to focus more on rationality and less on reason. Mills stated that the middle class was becoming politically emasculated and culturally stultified, which allows a shift in power from the middle class to the strong social elite. Mills believed that the middle-class workers receive an adequate salary but have become alienated from the world because of their inability to affect or change it.

Before he died at the age of 46 of a heart attack, Mills's major emphasis in his writings were on social inequality, the power of elites, the declining middle class, the relationship between individuals and society, and the importance of a historical perspective as a key part of sociological thinking.

Mills's most influential and famous work was his book *The Sociological Imagination*.[21] The book described a mindset for doing sociology that stressed being able to connect individual experiences and societal relationships. Mills noted that there are three components that form the sociological imagination:

- History (how a society came to be and how it is changing)
- Biography (what kind of people inhabit a particular society)
- Social structure (how the institutional orders in a society operate, which ones are dominant, how they are held together)

Mills advocated that one must look inside oneself to help important research problems because social scientists often translate private troubles into public issues. Mills claimed that if one has "sociological imagination," it gives the one possessing it the ability to look beyond his or her local environment and personality to wider social structures and a relationship between history, biography, and social structure. He wrote that every individual cannot simply be fully integrated into society and internalize all its cultural forms. Such domination may be seen as a further extension of power and social stratification.

According to Mills, there are "power elites" in society.[22] By that he is referring to those individuals that occupy the dominant positions in the dominant institutions (military, economic, and political) of a dominant country, and their decisions (or lack of decisions) have enormous consequences, not only for the U.S. population but "the underlying populations of the world." The institutions that the power elites head are a triumvirate of groups that have succeeded weaker predecessors:

- Two or three hundred giant corporations that have replaced the traditional agrarian and craft economy

- Strong federal political order that has inherited power from "a decentralized set of several dozen states" and "now enters into each and every cranny of the social structure"
- The military establishment, formerly an object of "distrust fed by state militia," but now an entity with "all the grim and clumsy efficiency of a sprawling bureaucratic domain"

Alan Sears

Alan Sears, a Canadian sociologist, provides a modern overview of the conflict theories.[23] According to Sears, societies are defined by inequality that produces conflict, rather than those that produce order and consensus. The conflict based on inequality can only be overcome through a fundamental transformation of the existing relations in the society. The disadvantaged have structural interests that run counter to the status quo. The disadvantages, when recognized, may lead to social change.

Sears noted that human potential or the capacity for creativity is suppressed by conditions of exploitation and oppression. These conditions of exploitation and oppression are a necessary part of any society that experiences an unequal division of labor. Sears saw the role of theory is to promote the realization of human potential and transformation of society, and not maintaining the unequal power structure. Consensus is a euphemism for ideology. Genuine consensus is not achieved; rather, the more powerful in societies are able to impose their conceptions on others and have them accept their discourses. Consensus does not preserve social order; it entrenches existing stratification with the myth of the American dream.

The state serves the interests of the most powerful while at the same time claiming to represent the interests of all. The notion of full participation by all in society is an illusion. He notes that inequality on a global level is characterized by the purposeful underdevelopment of Third World countries, both during colonization and after national independence. While Sears associates the conflict theory approach with Marxism, he argues that it is the foundation for much feminist, postmodernist, and antiracist theories.

Critical Theories

Critical criminology may be considered a mixture of the labeling and radical theories. These theories evolved from the social turbulence of the 1960s caused by the reaction to the American involvement in the Vietnam War, the development of the drug counterculture, and the war on drugs. This period of social turbulence caused many individuals to question the traditional assumptions of the criminal justice system and society's definitions of deviant behavior. There are three major themes to critical criminology:

- Criminologists should focus on why some people and not others are labeled as criminals, rather than focusing on the characteristics that distinguish criminals from noncriminals. Under this theme, the critical criminologists take issue with theories that view crime as a result of biological and psychological maladjustments and with sociological theories that rely on such factors as inadequate socialization and peer group pressures.
- The criminal justice system is a tool used for the purpose of maintaining the status quo and serves the interests only of those powerful members of society.
- Criminal laws reflect not our morality, but the desires and interests of only a small segment of our society. Law is, in reality, the rules imposed on society by the ruling class.

William Chambliss

William Chambliss looked at the questions of why some acts are defined by law as criminal or deviant, and others are not, and why crime or deviance is distributed as it is by social class, race, and gender. Chambliss also wondered why given the definition of certain acts as criminal or deviant, some people are arrested, prosecuted, convicted, and sentenced, whereas others are not.

Chambliss contended that criminal behavior is generated because of the contradictions and conflicts that inevitably arise in the course of life. These contradictions lead to conflicts between groups, classes, and strata, and the contradictions tend to intensify with time and cannot be resolved within the existing social framework.

He maintained that the amount and type of crime depend on the nature of existing contradictions, the conflicts that develop as people respond to the contradictions, and the mechanisms institutionalized for handling the conflicts and dilemmas produced by the contradictions.

Chambliss opined that criminal laws reflect not the morality of our society, but the desires and interests of only a small segment of our society. They reject the concept that criminal law is the collective moral judgment of the society and contend that law should be considered as rules imposed by the ruling regime.

Chambliss's theory may summarized as follows:

- In every historical era, societies and human groups in the struggle to survive invariably create contradictory forces and tendencies that serve as unseen forces moving the groups toward new social, political, and economic relations.

- In the movement, contradictions tend to intensify with time and cannot be resolved within the existing social framework. The contradictions lead to conflicts between groups, classes, and strata.
- Criminal behavior is generated because of the contradictions and conflicts that inevitably arise in the course of life. The type of crime and the amount depend on the nature of existing contradictions, the conflicts that develop as people respond to the contradictions, and the mechanisms institutionalized for handling the conflicts and dilemmas produced by the contradictions.

Chambliss contends that criminologists should be critical of traditional concepts and ask questions regarding them. He stated that the questions we ask will shape our knowledge far more than the theories we propose. According to Chambliss, the questions that we ask should include[24]

- Why are some acts defined by law as criminal, whereas others are not?
- Why, given the definition of certain acts as criminal, are some people arrested, prosecuted, convicted, and sentenced, whereas others are not?
- Why is crime distributed as it is by social class, race, and gender?

George Vold

Using conflict theorists' precepts, George Vold developed a group conflict theory of criminal causation.[25] The group conflict theory may also be considered a cultural deviance theory. The key points of the theory are as follows:

- The conditions of one's life determine the "schedules of reinforcement" that one experiences.
- Schedules of reinforcement include a person's values and interests.
- Complex societies are composed of groups with widely different life conditions and widely different schedules of reinforcement.
- Behavior is acquired and persists to the extent that it is reinforced over alternative behavior. Behavior is also evaluated as desirable or undesirable, depending on our schedules of reinforcement.
- Since individuals' values and interests tend to remain stable, groups tend to develop relatively stable behavior patterns that differ in varying degrees from the behavior patterns of other groups.

New Criminology

The new criminology approach to explaining crime, which became popular in the 1960s, rejected the established paradigms and considered the paradigms as incompatible with acceptable social and humanistic views of crime and deviance control. The theory asserts that crime is a political phenomenon. New criminology apparently offered a distinctive conceptual framework within which to conduct its work. Critics of new criminology argue that rather than presenting criminology with a novel theoretical alternative, the theory has taken some of the discipline's more established notions and rephrased them in political terms. The critics point out that the new criminology elements of a social pathological view are only extensions of the early Chicago School criminology.

New criminologists assert that crime is a political phenomenon. While this is a simple assertion, in one manner the statement is tautological. Laws are passed by political bodies, and these bodies are largely committed to the present social system.

New criminology can be best understood by the sociohistorical forces that were at work in the 1960s when the theories developed. Those forces include the following[26]:

- An increased cynicism concerning the motives of those in power, the creditability of official pronouncements, and the institution of government itself
- The growth of a counterculture that altered popular images of deviance
- An increasing politicalization of certain groups in American society that had accumulated enough power to dispute institutionalized discrimination and coercion

The critics note that new criminology came forward incrementally, and there was never a time when there was not a new criminology, and then a time when there was. The critics further assert that new criminology can only be understood as the result of the sociohistorical forces that were at work in the 1960s. These forces include the following:

- An increased cynicism concerning the motives of those in power, the credibility of official pronouncements, and the institution of government itself
- The growth of a counterculture that began to alter popular images of deviance and take more skeptical stances toward traditional bases of authority

Controlology

The theories that we have already examined in this chapter have focused on the meaning of deviance but have ended up focusing on the issue of power in society. The controlologists directly focus on the

SOCIETY IN ACTION

IS NEW CRIMINOLOGY A NEW THEORY?

According to researcher Jackson Toby, the new criminology is neither new nor criminology. He considers it a merely sentimental overidentification with the underdog masquerading as science. He contends that the popularity is because students of crime have traditionally been sympathetic to the underdog, and that new criminology uses the hypotheses of discriminatory law enforcement and white-collar immorality to gain sympathy for its concepts. To Toby, the hopes of the approach are illusory. Toby recognizes that justice is imperfect even in relatively decent societies, and he contends that this is no excuse for embracing nihilism or for giving up the attempt to maintain social order.

Source: Toby, J., The New Criminology Is the Old Sentimentality, *Criminology*, 16(4), 516–526, 1979.

relative power of deviance and the groups that define deviance. They do so with a Marxist context and orientation that looks into the state and its subservience to economically powerful groups.[27] They no longer attempt to explain deviance, but instead focus their attention on who defines it. To them, the criminal justice system is a segment of a broader range of social control mechanisms that are used by the state to control "problem" populations.

The term *controlology* was first introduced by Jason Ditton in 1979 to describe these theories.[28] It was probably Michael Foucault who first developed the foundation for the theories. Foucault opined in his book *Madness and Civilization* that it appeared that the more humane mental institutions had replaced prisons as the central instrument of state control.[29] Foucault noted that prisons became popular in the 1700s to replace the former systems of torture and execution. According to him, prisons were not designed to punish criminals or deter them. Prisons were designed to manifest state power.

The earlier use of torture and execution was generally performed in public in order to demonstrate the power of the state. But instead of making the crowds more docile and afraid, the public displays became the occasions for riots against the injustice by the state. With the use of prisons, except for executions, punishments were moved behind hidden walls. Later, the state began to look into the soul of the prisoners and discovered evil and sickness. Using the concept of mental illness, the state began to root out the evil and sickness.

SOCIETY IN ACTION

THE POLITICIZING OF CRIME, THE CRIMINAL AND THE CRIMINOLOGIST

Charles E. Reasons

This 1974 article from the *Journal of Criminal Law and Criminology* provides an excellent discussion and a distinctive viewpoint on how crime is politicized.

The substantive area of criminology has increasingly become politicized, with new paradigms arising to challenge the traditional perspectives. Ideology has been very important in the rise of, and subsequent changing focus in, the study of crime. In a well presented socio-historical analysis, Radzinowicz described the rise of the "liberal" position in criminology as a concomitant of the enlightenment, typified by growing scientism, emphasis upon reason and the revolt against unquestioning acceptance of tradition and authority. The system of criminal justice was subjected to a great deal of attack. Montesquieu, Voltaire and Beccaria, among others, condemned the legal institutions of the time for their arbitrariness, secrecy and cruel and oppressive nature. This Classical School of criminology arose as a reaction to the abuses of the time, and its leaders called for reform.

Unlike the Classical School, the Positive School was committed to the thesis that any measure necessary to protect society (from which the accused and, of course, the convicted person were automatically excluded) is justifiable. The belief in the ability to use laws and other techniques of social control to make a better society led to much legislation for the purposes of guiding man's morals. Instead of serving as a panacea for man's ills, however, Positivists' approach led to increasing "overcriminalization" and the belief in the perfectability of "deviants" through the use of the social sciences and law.

Most criminologists today continue to maintain the Positivist focus upon the "causes of criminal behavior." Their efforts have ranged from the measurement of skulls, to measurement of psychic conflict, self-concept, anomia, etc., with essentially the same results: the lack of a definitive answer to the question of "cause". The law has remained rather un-scrutinized, either in its formulation, enforcement or administration.

The increasing divisiveness of the 1960's (war protest, riots, Civil Rights Movement) magnified the fact that different perceptions of criminality were vying for public attention. The validity and efficacy of the law and legal institutions were brought into question. The consciousness of the younger generation may have precipitated a shift in perspective of societal wrongdoing. In recent years, this new perspective has led to attacks upon the legitimacy of the State. Such attacks have stemmed from several causes:

(1) a belief that the law and legal institutions are not only unresponsive but illegitimate,
(2) a condemnation of the bureaucratic delays, judicial indifference and overt racism of courts,
(3) a rejection, and in many instances, a contempt for Establishment officials—police, judges, and lawyers and
(4) an affirmation of individual rights and an identification with group, class, racial and sexual liberation.

Adding to this eroding legitimacy of the state is the view held by certain segments of our society that crimes are being committed in the form of the brutal destruction wrought upon IndoChina; the fraudulent dealing of large manufacturers and corporations; the prosecution and persecution of political criminals, e.g., war protestors; the lawlessness of the law, e.g., riots of 1967, Chicago, 1968, Kent State, Jackson State, and Southern University; and the lawlessness of political leaders and their accomplices, e.g., ITT, Watergate, and surveillance of political deviants. This divisiveness and conflict brought about changing perspectives of crime and society among segments of the general public. There was a growing realization among some criminologists of the importance of interest groups in determining what crime is, and which type of crime will be of major concern to law enforcement and administration of justice personnel, and thus to criminologists. Thus, the politics of crime, including the making of laws and their enforcement, and the administration of justice took on increased relevance and significance.

Demystifying the Law

Important in the sociological analysis of the law is the demystification of legal institutions. There is a mystique and sacredness attached to the law and legal bodies which is in part due to the general public's lack of knowledge concerning the law. This was not always the case. Blackstone's Commentaries were lectures given at Oxford University to liberal arts students. American colonists also acquired legal education in order to establish control systems in their new land. Edmund Burke's comment on the influence of Blackstone reflects this emphasis:

> In no country perhaps in this world is the law so general a study. The profession itself is numerous and powerful, and in most provinces it takes the lead. The greater number of deputies sent to congress were lawyers.... I have been told by an eminent bookseller that in no branch of his business, after tracts of popular devotion, were so many books as those on the law exported to the plantations. The basic fact is that law and legal education are powerful. They have been principally in the hands of those making policy. With the professionalization of law and its institutionalization in the form of law schools, a professional monopoly was established concerning the diffusion of legal education.

As our society has grown more urbanized and our law ways more complex, young men have had progressively fewer opportunities to learn about the workings of our legal system; at the same time the United States has become probably the most law-run and lawyer-run country in the history of mankind.

This professional monopoly has concentrated a great deal of power in the hands of the legal profession. The equating of legal knowledge and power is verified by the estimate that since the Civil War well over fifty percent of all elected or government officials have been lawyers.

While American criminologists have long been concerned with the control of human behavior, questioning the validity of laws has not been of major importance. The laws were a given, and the focus of attention was upon those who violated the law. Philosophies of law reflect the degree to which laws are considered reflecting the "common good" and subsequently, the degree of attention which should be paid to legal institutions versus the criminal by the student of crime. As Mills persuasively argues, students of "deviance" and "pathology" have assumed that legal institutions reflect the interests of all, including the "sick" deviant. Such a perspective has increasingly been eroded within recent years.

A number of schools of jurisprudence have denied that lawmakers have value-choices in the creation of laws. These schools suggest that the law and its agents, e.g., enforcers and administrators, stand alone and apart from society, comprising a neutral framework within which social struggle and conflict take place. This consensus perspective views the State as a value-neutral organ for the resolution of conflict. Thus, although the adversary proceedings pits the State against the accused, the confrontation occurs within the "neutral" framework of the court. The judge epitomizes the even-handed, non-biased, neutral arbitrator of institutionalized conflict. This perspective is still largely held among many segments of our society. The presumed non-political and unbiased nature of the judicial system has obscured the basically political nature of law, its enforcement and administration. In order to understand the law, its enforcement and its administration, it is necessary to demystify the conceptions of the nature and function of law and its operation, and to place it in the context of power, politics, and people.

Some schools of jurisprudence which have attempted this demystification begin with the assumption that law is a legitimizing weapon of the highest order, and those making, enforcing and administering laws are merely attempting to perpetrate the existing state. These schools have demystified the nature of laws by emphasizing that they are manmade and State-given, not found in some natural state of things beyond the influence and control of man. Rather than the State and its legal actors being value-free, these perspectives invest participants in the legal system with values, feelings and bias which influence their actions. The law, therefore, is not seen as a neutral framework for the collective interests of society. It is rather an instrument of those in power used to maintain their position and privilege.

A generally increased awareness regarding the political nature of crime has resulted in heightened conflict between traditionally powerless groups; students and youth, poor and nonwhite—and those in power. As a result, the criminologist, traditionally submerged in a consensus perspective of society, has begun to recognize the need to critically investigate the origin, enforcement, and administration of laws within the context of interests, power and conflict.

The viewing of law as an instrument of interests has become a growing area of concern among American criminologists. Quinney articulates what many dissident leaders of the 1960's suggested, namely, that criminal law is made, enforced and administered by interest groups largely for their own gains. A conflict perspective has become a paradigm of increasing usefulness in criminological study. Under this model, crime may be viewed as phenomena created by individuals in concerted action to have their definitions of rightness win out and become legitimated in public policy, i.e., laws and regulations.

Political Crime and Political Criminals

Although political crime may be the oldest and most recurring criminal phenomenon in history, criminologists nonetheless have in large part failed to investigate this area of criminal activity. One possible "inhibiting" factor is that criminologists are generally part of the dominant political and moral order, and such a focus may connote political problems rather than criminal ones. To suggest that political crimes should be recognized as an area of criminological focus portends the analysis of political trials and the influence of politics upon the legal order.

To acknowledge that political trials exist is unsettling to those steeped in the belief that the law is above politics. With the "demystification" of the law through more recent events and writings, some criminologists have taken stock of their relationship vis a vis political crime. While all crime is basically political, political crime has been designated a special type of criminal definition.

According to Quinney, political crime refers to the violation of laws created to protect the state. This strictly legalistic definition identifies such offenses against the state to include conduct threatening the existence of government, e.g., treason, insurrection, rebellion, sedition, criminal anarchy, criminal syndicalism and conduct interfering with government functions e.g., perjury, bribery, corruption, criminal libel by publication.

The greater proportion of writing and societal attention has been upon the first category of offenses, those "threatening the very existence of the state." In contemporary American society this "threat" has included, among others, the Black Panthers, Students for a Democratic Society, liberal/radical political activists, Communists, and anarchists.

The history of attempts to outlaw certain groups and ideas is the history of the use of the law to protect the viability of those in power. All nations have such laws and use them at various times to prevent attempts to change the distribution of power in society. These laws are by their very nature repressive of free communication and have often been the product of times of "national crisis." American examples of such efforts include the Sedition Act of 1798, the criminal anarchy laws and the criminal syndicalism laws enacted in the early twentieth century, the Smith Act of 1940, the McCaren Act of 1950, the "Rap Brown" portion of the 1968 Omnibus Bill and the more recent conspiracy trials of anti-war activists and political radicals.

Political criminals are characterized as being quite different from conventional criminals: they often announce their intentions publicly, challenge the very legitimacy of laws and/or their application in specific situations, attempt to change the norms they are denying, lack personal gain as a goal and appeal to a higher morality, pointing out the void between professed beliefs and actual practices.

Given this distinction, the "political criminal," e.g., draft-resister, sit-in demonstrator, conspirator, may be difficult to "explain" according to traditional criminological theories. Social scientists, including criminologists, have already begun to study these "new deviants," and will undoubtedly attempt to explain their behavior according to modifications of traditional paradigms. The study of the "new" criminal is obviously of concern to those in power because they are "enemy deviants" who represent a threat to those in political power. While all violators of political crime statutes may be regarded as political criminals, such a narrow definition fails to consider a number of significant issues. The analysis of the political prisoner suggests that the concept of the political criminal is undergoing much change among certain segments of society.

Political Prisoners

Of particular concern to penologists is how to deal with the political criminal and the politicizing of criminals. While our legal system does not officially recognize political crime or criminals, they have been differentially treated in the correctional setting. There is apparently a great fear of the political criminal infecting the "common" criminal. In fact, the politicization of prisoners has been increasing rapidly. The dissent and rebellion at San Quentin, The Tombs, Folsom, Soledad, Attica has given notice to the public and correctional officials that prisoners are organizing for their collective goals.

Bettina Aptheker has delineated a typology of four groupings of prisoners based upon their political views and activities. Each is specially victimized on the basis of class, racial or national oppression, which portends large increases in the number of political prisoners. Aptheker first points out that one group of prisoners include those who became effective political leaders and who found themselves victims of politically inspired frameups. While the proportion of prisoners under this category is undoubtedly small, evidence suggests such cases do exist.

A second group consists of those who have committed various acts of civil disobedience, including draft resistance. These violations are clearly political acts. This category also includes acts of resistance or self-defense, both within and outside prisons, which violate the law. As a result of the Civil Rights Movement, draft resistance, anti-war protests, student activism and other militant protest in the 1960's and 1970's, this category has greatly increased.

A third group is composed of those who have been arrested and convicted of crimes which they did not commit, this due to a lack of legal knowledge and political power. Finally, there is the large bulk of prisoners who committed a variety of non-political offenses but who have begun to develop a political consciousness while incarcerated, e.g., Soledad Brothers and Russell Magee. How has this occurred? According to Davis, this politicization has resulted from the increasing influx of political criminals in prisons who have organized their activities around the problems of the institution. In assessing the causes of politicization, Davis notes the changing conceptions of the causes of criminal behavior:

> Prisoners—especially Black, Chicanos, and Puerto Ricans—are increasingly advancing the proposition that they are political prisoners. They contend that they are political prisoners in the sense that they are largely victims of an oppressive politico-economic order, swiftly becoming conscious of the causes underlying their victimization.

The politicization of prisoners can only be understood within the context of the attempts at democratization of major social institutions. For example, universities, which have been traditionally characterized as apolitical, became the brunt of a rapid politicizing and conflict during the 1960's.

The Civil Rights Movement, anti-war movement, poor people's movement, welfare rights movement, among others, challenged the legitimacy of power distribution in our society. The law and legal institutions increasingly came under fire as they were exposed as being highly political. Youth, nonwhites, the poor and other, previously powerless groups were increasingly politically sensitized, and since they are the prime "recruits" for correctional institutions, this undoubtedly has had many ramifications for the prisons. As Fox has noted: "The same civil rights issues, religious issues, and other social issues appear in prison as appear in the city. The prison reflects the society it serves."

Thus, the politicizing of previously powerless and apolitical segments of society, e.g., poor, non-white and youth, has had tremendous ramifications upon the penal system.

Source: Reasons, C. E., The Politicizing of Crime, the Criminal and the Criminologist, *Journal of Criminal Law and Criminology*, 64(4), 471–479, 1974. Excerpts reprinted with permission from the *Journal of Criminal Law and Criminology*.

References and footnotes in the article have been omitted.

Foucault was criticized because of factual errors in his analysis, but his themes have been researched and discussed in many research analyses of deviant behavior, most notably by Erich Goode. Goode noted that the themes developed by Foucault include[30]

- The relationship between social control and state control is an important topic to research.
- The state attempts to maintain its legitimacy by presenting its control efforts in a manner so that they appear to be reasonable, humane, and necessary.
- The broad range of social control activities are all directed and manipulated by the state, even though some may seem to be independent of state control.
- The various types of state control have a general unity despite the fact that they may seem to be diverse.
- Ultimately all the state control methods work in a coherent way to achieve state control.

Practicum

In July 1977, New York City suffered a general electrical failure starting at 9:34 p.m. and continuing until the next day. Widespread looting occurred, and sympathetic note was taken of the fact that the looting occurred mainly in ghetto communities, presumably by the most deprived New Yorkers. However, the looting occurred in appliance, furniture, and jewelry stores and food stores. Of those arrested for looting, it appears that the looters were more likely to be employed and not on welfare (facts as reported in *New York Times*, August 14, 1977, p. 32).

Questions: Using one of the theories examined in this chapter, how would you explain the conduct of the looters? Is the fact that most of them were employed and not on welfare significant?

Summary

- The constructionist approach questions the conventionalization of behaviors, beliefs, and traits; definitions of deviance; the enforcement of societal rules; and the consequences of enforcement.
- Constructionists view deviance not as an action, but an infraction of societal rules. They tend to question what makes certain conduct deviant and what groups in society make and enforce the rules.
- The basic premise of a constructionist is best explained by the statement of Herbert Becker in his classic book *Outsiders: Studies in the Sociology of Deviance.* He stated that "the deviant is one to whom the label has successfully been applied; deviant behavior is behavior that people so label."
- Labeling theory can be traced to Emile Durkheim's book *Suicide.* Durkheim opined that crime is not so much a violation of a penal code as it is an act that outrages society. He was the first to suggest that deviant labeling satisfies that function and satisfies society's need to control the behavior.
- Labeling theory is based on the assumption that no act is intrinsically criminal. Definitions of criminality are established by those in power through the formulation of laws and the interpretation of those laws by police, courts, and correctional institutions.
- Deviance is therefore not a set of characteristics of individuals or groups, but rather, it is a process of interaction between deviants and nondeviants and the context in which criminality is being interpreted.
- According to the label theorists, most of the rules that define deviance and the contexts in which deviant behavior is labeled as deviant are framed by the wealthy for the poor, by men for women, by older people for younger people, and by ethnic majorities for minority groups.
- Once the individual is labeled as deviant, it is extremely difficult to remove that label. He or she becomes stigmatized as a criminal or deviant and is likely to be considered, and treated, as untrustworthy by others.
- Charles Cooley developed the social psychological concept of looking-glass self. He stated that a person's self grows out of society's interpersonal interactions and the perceptions of others. The term

refers to people shaping their self-concepts based on their understanding of how others perceive them. Because people conform to how they think others think them to be, it's difficult, or arguably impossible, to act differently from how a person thinks he or she is perpetually perceived.

- Frank Tannenbaum is considered the father of labeling theory. In his book *Crime and the Community*, Tannenbaum described the social interactions involved in crime. He contended that the criminal differs little or none at all from others in the original impulse to first commit deviant behavior. He blamed societal reactions for continued deviant acts that develop patterns of interest to sociologists.
- Tannenbaum labeled his theoretical model as the dramatization of evil or labeling theory. The labeling theory developed in the mid to late 1930s. During this time the nation was suffering under the Great Depression. The social climate was one of disillusionment with the government. The class structure was one of cultural isolationism.
- Sociologist Edwin Lemert introduced the concept of secondary deviance. The primary deviance is the first experience connected to deviant behavior or the first offense by an individual. Secondary deviation is the role created to deal with society's condemnation of and reaction to the behavior.
- Becker in *Outsider* noted that "social groups create deviance by making rules whose infraction creates deviance, and by applying those roles to particular people and labeling them as outsiders. From this point of view, deviance is not a quality of the act the person commits, but rather a consequence of the application by others of rules and sanctions to an offender."
- Conflict and critical theories are theories that examine the social, political, or material inequality of social groups. The theories focus on the power differentials, such as class conflict, and generally contrast historically dominant ideologies with a macro level analysis of society. Karl Marx is generally considered the founder of the social conflict theories.
- As early as the 16th century, theorists examining crime causation have linked deviant behavior with economic status. Karl Marx and Friedrich Engels are credited with originating the concept that crime or deviant behavior is a potential of capitalism.
- Critical criminology may be considered a mixture of the labeling and radical theories. These theories evolved from the social turbulence of the 1960s caused by the reaction to the American involvement in the Vietnam War, the development of the drug counterculture, and the war on drugs.

- The new criminology approach to explaining crime, which became popular in the 1960s, rejected the established paradigms and considered the paradigms incompatible with acceptable social and humanistic views of crime and deviance control. The theory asserts that crime is a political phenomenon. New criminology apparently offered a distinctive conceptual framework within which to conduct its work.

Questions in Review

1. What are the basic assumptions of the conflict theories?
2. Explain the labeling theories.
3. How does conflict or labeling theories explain the first involvement in deviant behavior by an individual that is subsequently labeled as a deviant?
4. If you were a follower of the labelist theories, how would you establish a crime prevention program?

Endnotes

1. Howard Becker. (1963). *Outsiders: Studies in the sociology of deviance* (p. 9). New York: Free Press.
2. Frank Tannenbaum. (1938). *Crime and the community*. Boston: Ginn.
3. Charles Horton Cooley. (1902). *Human nature and the social order* (p. 152). New York: Scribner's.
4. Cooley, 1902.
5. King-To Yeung & John Martin. (2003). The looking glass self: An empirical test and elaboration. *Social Forces*, *81*(3), 843–879.
6. B. David & J. C. Turner. (1992). Studies in self-categorization and minority conversion: Is being a member of the outgroup an advantage? *British Journal of Social Psychology*, *35*, 179–200.
7. Tannenbaum, 1938.
8. E. M. Lemert. (1951). *Social pathology* (pp. 75–76). New York: McGraw-Hill.
9. Herbert Becker. (1973). *Outsiders* (rev. ed., p. 9). New York: Free Press.
10. Erving Goffman. (1959). *The presentation of self in everyday life*. New York: Anchor Books.
11. Erving Goffman. (1963). *Stigma: Notes on the management of spoiled identity* (pp. 143–144). Englewood Cliffs, NJ: Prentice-Hall.
12. David Matza. (1969). *On becoming deviant*. Englewood Cliffs, NJ: Prentice Hall.
13. Thomas J. Scheff. (1984). *Being mentally ill* (2nd ed.). Piscataway, NJ: Aldine Transaction.
14. Tannenbaum, 1938, pp. 18–20.
15. Frank P. Williams III & Marilyn D. McShane. (1994). *Criminological theory* (2nd ed., p. 141). Englewood Cliffs, NJ: Prentice-Hall.
16. Bruce G. Link, Francis T. Cullen, Elmer Struening, Patrick E. Shrout, & Bruce P. Dohrenwend. (1989). A modified labeling theory approach to mental disorders: An empirical assessment. *American Sociological Review*, *54*(3), 400–423.

17. Ronald Akers. (1979, February). Theory and ideology in Marxist criminology: Comments on Turk, Quinney, Toby, and Klockers. *Criminology*, 442–444.
18. Ruth Masters & Cliff Roberson. (1990). *Inside criminology*. Englewood Cliffs, NJ: Prentice-Hall.
19. Akers, 1979.
20. C. Wright Mills. (1951). *White collar: American middle classes*. New York: Oxford University Press.
21. C. Wright Mills. (1959). *The sociological imagination*. New York: Oxford University Press.
22. C. Wright Mills. (1956). *The power elite*. New York: Oxford University.
23. Allan Sears. (2008). *A good book, in theory: A guide to theoretical thinking* (pp. 34–36). Toronto: Higher Education University of Toronto Press.
24. William J. Chambliss. (1988). *Exploring criminology*. New York: Macmillan.
25. George B. Vold. (1958). *Theoretical criminology*. New York: Oxford University Press.
26. Robert F. Meier. (1976, December). The new criminology: Continuity in criminological theory. *Journal of Criminal Law and Criminology*, *67*(4), 461–469.
27. Thomas J. Benard, Jeffery B. Snipes, & Alexander L. Gerould. (2010). *Vold's theoretical criminology* (6th ed.). New York: Oxford University Press.
28. Jason Ditton. (1979). *Controlology: Beyond the new criminology*. London: Macmillan.
29. Michael Foucault. (1967). *Madness and civilization: A history of insanity in the age of reason*. New York: Mentor.
30. Erich Goode. (2010). *Deviant behavior* (9th ed.). Upper Saddle River, NJ: Prentice-Hall.

chapter four

Interpersonal Violence

Chapter Objectives

What you should know and understand after studying this chapter:

- What constitutes interpersonal violence
- The different types of homicide
- The differences between manslaughter and murder
- Issues involved with sex crimes
- What constitutes rape and sexual assault
- What constitutes stalking
- The issues involved with hate crimes

Introduction

> Almost universally, historians agree that the United States has always been an extremely violent nation and that violence usually redounds to the ultimate advantage of those who control the levers of power.[1]
>
> We still kill each other at roughly three times the rate of most western nations.[2]

Worldwide, violence causes more than 1.6 million deaths every year. More than 90% of these occur in low- and middle-income countries. Violence is one of the leading causes of death in all parts of the world for persons ages 15 to 44.[3] As noted by the World Health Organization (WHO), precise estimates of the cost of violence are difficult to obtain. According to WHO, the cost of violence translates into billions of U.S. dollars in annual health care expenditures worldwide, and billions more for national economies in terms of days lost from work, law enforcement, and lost investments. The human cost in grief and pain cannot be calculated. Much of the grief and pain is almost invisible. WHO contends that much more violence occurs in the homes, the workplaces, and even medical and social institutions than in terroristic activities. Many of the victims are too young, weak, or ill to protect themselves.

Violence

Violence can be divided into three broad categories according to characteristics of those committing the violent act:

- **Self-directed violence:** Self-directed violence is subdivided into suicidal behavior and self-abuse. The former includes suicidal thoughts, attempted suicides—also called parasuicide or deliberate self-injury in some countries—and completed suicides. Self-abuse, in contrast, includes acts such as self-mutilation.
- **Interpersonal violence:** Interpersonal violence is divided into two subcategories: family and intimate partner violence, which is violence largely between family members and intimate partners, usually taking place in the home; and community violence, which is violence between individuals who are unrelated, and who may or may not know each other, generally taking place outside the home.
- **Collective violence:** Collective violence is subdivided into social, political, and economic violence. Unlike the other two broad categories, the subcategories of collective violence suggest possible motives for violence committed by larger groups of individuals or by states. Collective violence that is committed to advance a particular social agenda includes, for example, crimes of hate committed by organized groups, terrorist acts, and mob violence.

Interpersonal Violence

In this chapter, we will examine interpersonal violence. Interpersonal violence is defined by WHO as any behavior within an intimate relationship that causes physical, psychological, or sexual harm to those in the relationship. Violence is considered the intentional use of physical force or power, threatened or actually, against another person that results in a high likelihood of resulting in injury or psychological harm or death. According to WHO, interpersonal violence can be perpetrated by a partner or ex-partner, an acquaintance, or a stranger, though the latter occurs the least frequently. Though the majority of cases involve men perpetrating violence against women, interpersonal violence occurs in same-sex relationships, and women can perpetrate violence against men in different-sex relationships.[4] Domestic abuse or interpersonal partner violence is discussed in detail in Chapter 6. Figure 4.1 is a diagram of interpersonal violence by methods used to inflict the violence.

According to Scott Mire and Cliff Roberson, the more we study interpersonal violence, the more questions are generated. They contend

Methods used to inflict interpersonal violence	Examples
Physical	Assault or battery, fist fights, stabbings, and shootings
Sexual	Rape, inappropriate sexual touching or fondling
Psychological	Psychological and emotional control/abuse
Deprivation or neglect	Failure to feed young children or otherwise provide for them

Figure 4.1 Diagram of interpersonal violence.

that the basic questions when doing research on interpersonal violence should include the following[5]:

- To what extent are we, as a society, willing to commit to preventing violence?
- Who is most capable of engaging in interventions most able to prevent violence?

One of the problems that occur when researching interpersonal violence is that there are a number of fallacies that are accepted as true. Mire and Roberson concluded that most common fallacies include[6]

- Is the world more violent today than ever before? No.
- Is the United States more violent today than ever before? No. In fact, there is evidence that suggests trends in violence have been declining since around the year 1200 in Europe and the early 1600s in the United States.
- Is the United States more violent today than most other countries? Yes, especially in relation to homicide.
- Who is most likely to perpetrate violence? Young, minority males.

Figure 4.2 contains a chart regarding the relationship between the victim and the abuser.

Human Capital Approach

The human capital approach tries to explain crime using an approach based on economics—that crimes of opportunity that require little expertise generally are associated with the young, and that crimes that require more expertise are more likely to increase as education and skill increase. To support this theory, the theorists look to the fact that violent crime is generally committed by the youth, and white-collar crime by the more educated adult.

Property and violent crime rates typically increase with age during adolescence, reach a peak during the late teenage years, and then decline

SOCIETY IN ACTION

ARE THERE SEASONAL PATTERNS IN CRIMINAL VICTIMIZATIONS?

According to a June 2014 special report sponsored by the Bureau of Justice Statistics, seasonal patterns for violent victimizations vary depending upon the type of crime. Rape and sexual assault rates and aggravated assault rates are higher in the summer than in most other seasons. In comparison, simple assault rates are the highest in the fall. Robbery victimizations do not show significant variations according to seasons. Intimate partner violence fluctuates, with the highest rates in the summer and the lowest rates in the winter. Rates of violence involving weapons and those that result in serious injuries are also higher in the summer than in the winter. Motor vehicle thefts do not appear to have seasonal variations.[7]

Coauthor Cliff Roberson wrote his PhD dissertation on criminal homicides in San Francisco. During the years covered by the research he concluded that unlike cities like Detroit and Philadelphia, there were no significant seasonal variations in criminal homicides. Both Detroit and Philadelphia had higher rates of criminal victimizations in the summer months and lesser rates in the winter months. He concluded that since both Detroit and Philadelphia have cold winters, people tend to stay indoors rather than socialize during the winter months. During the summer months in those cities, people tend to socialize more, and it is the socializing that results in an increase in interaction with others, and thus an increase in criminal homicides. San Francisco, however, has an average mean temperature of 54°F with a normal variation of only 4°. Accordingly, unlike Detroit and Philadelphia, people tend to be engaged in outdoor activities 12 months a year.

thereafter. Nearly two centuries ago, Adolphe Quetelet observed this general pattern. And this pattern holds true today for both official arrest rates and self-reported offending rates. According to Lance Lochner, the age crime profile is one of the most documented relationships in criminology.[8] Lochner suggests that studying crime within a human capital framework may be useful. According to him, this approach recognizes that education and training increase human capital levels and market wage rates, which raises the costs of planning and engaging in crime.

Human capital investments also increase the costs associated with incarceration, since they increase the value of any time foregone. The fact that training and learning occur throughout life implies that the opportunity

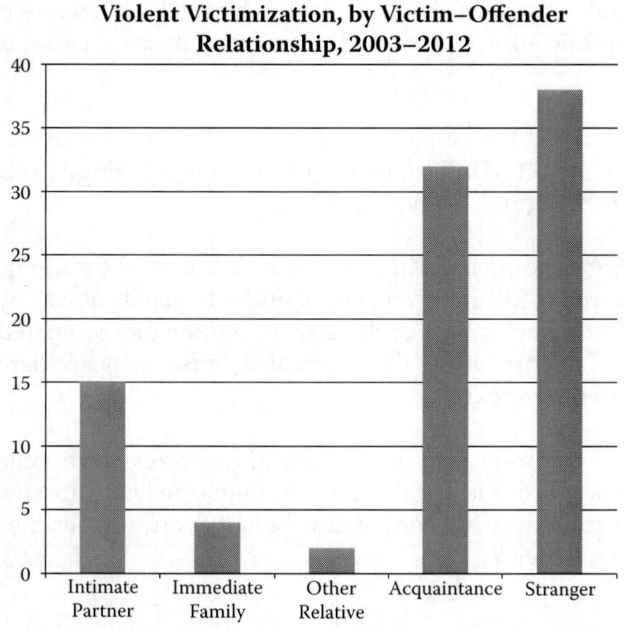

Figure 4.2 This figure illustrates the percentages of violent victimization by the victim–offender relationship. Note that in only 38 percent of the cases the offender was a stranger. (Authors' compilation based on Bureau of Justice Statistics, National Crime Victimization Survey, 2003–2012; Truman, J. L., and Morgan, R. E., Special Report: Nonfatal Domestic Violence, 2003–2012, NCJ 244697, U. S. Department of Justice, Bureau of Justice Statistics, 2014.)

costs of crime should generally rise with age, just as they rise with educational attainment. For crimes that require little market skill (e.g., larceny, assault, drug dealing), a human capital approach suggests that both age and education should be negatively correlated with crime among adults.

According to this approach, a policy that subsidizes schooling or job training is likely to reduce crime more in the long run than the short run by increasing skill levels. In contrast, a short-term wage subsidy targeted at younger workers may reduce crime among subsidized workers for the duration of the subsidy, but it may actually increase crime after the subsidy ends because it discourages investment in human capital. Human capital theory also offers insights useful for analyzing traditional law enforcement policies by recognizing that these policies can affect education and training decisions in addition to criminal behavior.

Lochner concludes that violent and property crimes are mostly a problem among young, uneducated men. The human capital approach argues that this can be explained by their low skill levels, which imply low opportunity and incarceration costs for committing crime. A human capital framework also suggests that the relationships between white-collar crime and both age and education should differ from those for less skilled crimes.

Homicide

Homicide is the act of killing another human being. English common law established three forms of homicide[9]:

- Justifiable homicide: Killing that is sanctioned by the government, for example, killing of an enemy under the rules of war by a military person during combat or the legal execution of a convicted murderer.
- Excusable homicide: Killing in self-defense or by accident.
- Criminal homicide.

At early common law, all criminal homicides were generally punished by death. Presently in the United States, the U.S. Supreme Court has approved capital punishment (death penalty) only for crimes involving aggravated murder.[10]

Criminal Homicide

In this section, we will discuss the third category, criminal homicide. This category of misconduct involves both the required mental intent and the required act. Criminal homicide may also be subdivided into murder, voluntary manslaughter, and involuntary manslaughter. In addition, some states have created other forms of criminal homicide, such as vehicle homicide and negligent manslaughter.

To constitute criminal homicide, the act and the required mental intent must be joined in time. For example, in the 1951 movie *A Place in the Sun,* George (Montgomery Cliff) planned to kill his wife. He rented a boat under a false name and took his wife out on it. While out in the lake, George begins to feel sorry for his wife and decides not to take her life. Alice, the wife, tries to stand up in the boat, causing it to capsize, and drowns. Since the actus reus and the mens rea were not joined in time, he was not guilty of murder. But in the movie he was convicted of murder based on the circumstantial evidence that he rented the boat under a false name, knew she could not swim, had a mistress, and the fact that he failed to immediately report her death.

To constitute criminal homicide, there must be a killing of another human being. The term *another human being* has different meanings under different state statutes. Generally, it refers to the fact that there must be a killing of a living person. While many people consider abortion murder, it is not because the fetus has not yet reached the status of a human being. Note: States vary on when a fetus is considered a living human being.

SOCIETY IN ACTION

THE QUEEN V. DUDLEY AND STEPHENS

14 Queen's Bench Digest 273

December 9, 1884

Facts: On July 5, 1884, Thomas Dudley and Edward Stephens, with one Brooks, all able-bodied English seamen, and the deceased also an English boy, between seventeen and eighteen years of age, the crew of an English yacht, a registered English vessel, were cast away in a storm on the high seas about 1600 miles from the Cape of Good Hope, and were compelled to put into an open boat belonging to the said yacht.

In this boat they had no supply of water and no supply of food, except two cans of turnips, and for three days they had nothing else to subsist upon. On the fourth day they caught a small turtle, upon which they subsisted for a few days, and this was the only food they had up to the twentieth day. On the twelfth day the remains of the turtle were entirely consumed, and for the next eight days they had nothing to eat. They had no fresh water, except such rain as they from time to time caught in their oilskin capes. The boat was drifting on the ocean, and was probably more than 1000 miles away from land. On the eighteenth day, when they had been seven days without food and five without water, the prisoners spoke to Brooks as to what should be done if no help came, and suggested that someone should be sacrificed to save the rest, but Brooks dissented, and the boy, to whom they were understood to refer, was not consulted. That on the 24th of July, Dudley proposed to Stephens and Brooks that lots should be cast who should be put to death to save the rest, but Brooks refused to consent, and it was not put to the boy, and in point of fact there was no drawing of lots. That on that day the prisoners spoke of their having families, and suggested it would be better to kill the boy that their lives should be saved, and Dudley proposed that if there was no vessel in sight by tomorrow morning the boy should be killed. That next day, the 25th of July, no vessel appearing, Dudley told Brooks that he had better go and have a sleep, and made signs to Stephens and Brooks that the boy had better be killed. Stephens agreed to the act, but Brooks dissented from it. The boy was then lying at the bottom of the boat quite helpless, and extremely weakened by famine and by drinking sea water, and unable to make any resistance, nor did he ever assent to his being killed. Dudley offered a prayer asking forgiveness for them all if either of them should be tempted to commit a rash act, and that their souls might be saved. Dudley, with the assent of Stephens, went to the boy, and telling him that his time was come, put a knife into his throat and killed him then and there; that the three men fed upon the body and blood of the boy for four days; that on the fourth day after the act had been committed the boat was picked up by a passing vessel, and the prisoners were rescued, still alive, but in the lowest state of prostration. They were carried to the port of Falmouth, England and committed for trial at Exeter. If the men had not fed upon the body of the boy they would probably not have survived to be so picked up and rescued, but would within the four days have died of famine. The boy, being in a much weaker condition, was likely to have died before them. At the time of the act in question there was no sail in sight, nor any reasonable prospect of relief. Under these circumstances there appeared to the prisoners every probability that unless they then fed or very soon fed upon the boy or one of themselves they would die of starvation. There was no appreciable chance of saving life except by killing someone for the others to eat. That assuming any necessity to kill anybody, there was no greater necessity for killing the boy than any of the other three men.

Was the killing justified?

Finding of the Jury: The jurors found the killing of Richard Parker by Dudley and Stephens to be a felony and murder. That killing an individual in order to save your life is not a justified defense to criminal homicide.

Sentence: The prisoners were sentenced to death, but the sentences were later commuted by the Crown to six months imprisonment.

The general rule is that it is considered a living human being if the fetus could survive outside the mother's body.

A common law school example of killing a living human being involves the scenario where Joe has been bitten by a poisonous snake and is dying a slow, painful death. His companion Sue, in order to relieve the pain, shoots Joe in the head, killing him instantly. Under this fact situation, did Sue commit criminal homicide? The answer of course is yes, because she killed a living human being. Does the fact that Joe was dying have any bearing on the act? No. While it may reduce the degree of criminal homicide, the killing of a person who is on his or her deathbed is still a criminal homicide.

Murder

Murder is defined as the purposeful, knowing, or reckless unlawful killing of another human being. Murder has two distinct elements:

- The defendant must have acted with the necessary—express or implied—specific intent to kill.
- The defendant's conduct must have caused the unlawful death of another human being. Note: If there are multiple potential causes of death, the defendant's conduct must be a substantial factor in the victim's death.

Murder with aggravating circumstances is generally considered murder in the first degree, and all others are considered murder in the second degree. While state laws may vary as to what constitutes aggravating circumstances, the most common aggravating circumstances include

- Murder that is premeditated (planned)
- Murder by poisoning
- Murder of a peace officer or public safety officer
- Murder of a crime witness
- Murder of a juror
- Murder committed for financial or other reward
- Murder committed in a brutal or cruel manner

At common law, to constitute murder, the death of a human being must occur within one year and a day after the act was inflicted. Most states have since abandoned this time requirement and require only proof that the death occurred as the result of the criminal act.

In those cases where the victim is considered brain dead, most states consider that this status is sufficient to establish the death of a living human being. For example, an individual is shot in the head. While she is brain dead, she is kept alive by devices until her organs may be used for transplants. At common law, the doctors who harvested her heart or other organs would be considered the individuals who caused her death.

Voluntary Manslaughter

The next most serious form of criminal homicide is voluntary manslaughter. The crime requires the same type of intent that is necessary to establish murder and an act or failure to act that resulted in the death of a living human being. The crime is downgraded from murder to voluntary manslaughter because of the presence of adequate provocation. While adequate provocation does not excuse the offender's action, it does reduce

SOCIETY IN ACTION

DEATH OF POLICE OFFICE WALTER BARCLAY

Philadelphia police officer Walter Barclay was shot by William Barnes on November 27, 1966. At the time, Barnes was attempting to burglarize a beauty shop. Barnes was convicted of attempted murder and served many years in prison for the crime.

On August 19, 2007, Officer Barclay died at a nursing home. The county coroner ruled that Barclay's death was a homicide because the gunshot wound resulted in paralysis, which eventually led to a urinary tract infection that killed him. The Commonwealth of Pennsylvania has no time limit requirement on when the death must occur. In 2010, Barnes (who was in prison for parole violations) was tried for the murder of Barclay.

Results

Barnes's attempts to prevent the trial 44 years after the shooting were unsuccessful in the appellate courts. The courts held that Barnes could be tried for the murder based on his 1966 shooting of Office Barclay. The Commonwealth's prosecutor, however, failed to prove to the satisfaction of the jury (beyond a reasonable doubt) that the urinary tract infection was directly caused by the gunshot wound, and Barnes was acquitted of the murder charge.

the crime from murder to voluntary manslaughter. To constitute adequate provocation, the provocation must be of such a nature as to cause a reasonable person to kill the victim. In addition, the killing must have occurred while the offender was in the heat of passion. For example, Joe catches his wife having sex with Jim. Joe, in a heat of passion, kills Jim. Under these circumstances, there may be adequate provocation. But if Joe waits until the next morning before shooting Jim, he is probably guilty of murder because there is a cooling-off period.

The test for sufficient provocation is an objective one, based on a reasonable person standard; the fact the defendant is intoxicated or suffers from a mental abnormality or has particular susceptibilities to events is irrelevant in determining whether the claimed provocation was sufficient. In addition, the claim of provocation cannot be based on events for which the killer was culpably reasonable. For example, an individual may not be the aggressor and then claim adequate provocation.

To constitute adequate provocation:

- The defendant must be so governed by passion that he or she is unable to reason to the extent necessary to form a deliberate purpose to take a life.
- The circumstances causing the state of passion must be such that a reasonable person would be similarly governed.

Involuntary Manslaughter

It is frequently stated that involuntary manslaughter is one of the most confusing forms of criminal homicide because it generally occurs under factual situations that do not establish a wicked or depraved mind. Frequently, the death results from activities that persons regularly engage in on a daily basis. Involuntary manslaughter may be defined as the unintentional killing of another human being during the commission of an unlawful but not inherently dangerous crime or as the result of criminal negligence. For example, you are late to work and are speeding in a school zone when you hit and kill an eight-year-old child. In most states this would be considered involuntary manslaughter.

An unintended killing during the commission of an inherently dangerous felony is not involuntary manslaughter, but murder under the felony murder rule. For example, while attempting to rob a bank, an employee of the bank is accidently shot and killed by one of the robbers. The crime would be murder and not involuntary manslaughter.

To constitute involuntary manslaughter:

- The killing of another human being must be unintentional.
- The death occurred either during the commission of an unlawful act that is not an inherently dangerous felony or as the result of criminal negligence.
- The defendant's unlawful act or negligence caused the death.

Some states have divided involuntary manslaughter into separate crimes, such as negligent manslaughter and vehicular manslaughter.

Euthanasia

Euthanasia is more commonly known as mercy killing. An example of euthanasia is the killing of a loved one to prevent further suffering. Under existing statutes, this killing would be classified as criminal homicide. Even though one who commits euthanasia bears no ill will toward the victim and believes his or her act is morally justified, he or she nevertheless acts with intent to kill if he or she is able to comprehend that society prohibits his or her act regardless of his or her personal belief.

Suicide

Since homicide is the killing of another human being, it is not homicide to kill yourself. Assisting another to commit suicide is a crime in most states. The modern trend is not to classify suicide as homicide, but to establish a separate crime for those persons who aid another to commit suicide.

Sexual Assault

The University of North Carolina at Chapel Hill's "Policy on Prohibited Harassment, Including Sexual Misconduct, and Discrimination" defines sexual misconduct as physical sexual acts perpetrated against a person without his or her consent or where a person is incapable of giving consent due to the person's use of drugs, alcohol, or other impairing substances. An individual also may be unable to give consent due to an intellectual or other disability. Sexual misconduct includes, but is not limited to, rape, sexual assault, sexual battery, and sexual coercion.[11]

Research has indicated that sexual violence does not discriminate, and it is rarely the victim's fault. The violence is often a method to hurt, humiliate, or gain control over the victim. The actions may be committed by spouses, boyfriends, girlfriends, friends, acquaintances, family, lovers, partners, and strangers. Sexual assault and rape affect people of all ages, races, genders, sexualities, and abilities. The fact that someone has been intimate with a partner in the past does not mean he or she must consent to any future sexual activity with that partner.

While sexual assault is frequently associated with women, men, women, and children of all ages frequently experience unwanted sexual contact. People are most at risk between 12 and 34 years of age, with risk peaking in the late teens.

We do not know how many sexual assaults occur because a large number of victims will suffer in silence and never report the crime to the police. The failure to report happens for many different reasons, including feelings of shame, guilt, or fear of reprisal from their attacker. Many people sexually assaulted as children do not tell anyone or get help until they are adults. Many offenders never go to jail.

Rape

Rape is the unlawful act of sexual intercourse with another person without the valid consent of the other person. The lack of valid consent may be in cases where the sexual act is committed by force on the victim, the victim, because of age or mental status, cannot give legal consent, or the victim consents to the sexual act because of fear or is tricked into consenting. In many jurisdictions, the crime of rape has been merged into the crime of unlawful sexual intercourse.

Consent

In this section, we will explore what constitutes a valid consent to sexual intercourse. In determining what constitutes legal consent, consider the fact situation in a 1950s case that occurred in Fort Worth, Texas. The victim's husband worked until midnight each night. The victim went to bed and was awaken late in the evening by an individual who wanted to have sex with her. Not fully awake and thinking it was her husband, she consented, and after the act was completed realized that she had sex with a stranger. In most states, unless the offender knew that the woman was mistaken, the courts would hold that the consent was legal.

In another case, the woman informed her boyfriend that she was not going to have sex with him until they were married. So the boyfriend arranged a phony marriage ceremony and had a friend act as the official who performed the ceremony. After a weekend at a hotel, the boyfriend then informed the woman that the ceremony was a sham. In this case, it is clear that the consent was not valid. And the man was guilty of rape.

Rape Shield Laws

Rape shield laws are designed to protect a victim when she (or he) is being cross-examined by the defense in court. In general terms, the law prevents the defense from requiring the witness to testify regarding her previous sexual experiences unless the defense can establish that her history is relevant to the case. Presently, all states in the United States, the District of Columbia, and the armed forces have some form of rape shield protections. The type of protection differs in each jurisdiction. Many states do not permit any evidence relating to the past sexual behavior of the victim. This exclusion of the evidence of the victim's prior or subsequent sexual conduct also includes opinion evidence or reputation evidence.

The Violence Against Women Act of 1994 created a federal rape shield law. The military rape shield law has been incorporated into Military Rules of Evidence, Rule 412.

A typical rape shield law is contained in the California Evidence Code. Section 782 concerns use of evidence, such as prior sexual history, to attack the credibility of the victim, and Section 1103 governs character evidence, such as sexual history, presented against the victim. Under California's rape shield law, a defendant is not allowed to introduce evidence about the alleged victim's past sexual conduct in order to prove that she (or he)

SOCIETY IN ACTION

BORO V. PEOPLE

163 Cal. App. 3rd 1224 (1985)

Dr. Stevens allegedly informed the victim that he had the results of her blood test and that she had contracted a dangerous, highly infectious, and perhaps fatal disease, that she could be sued as a result, that the disease came from using public toilets, and that she would have to tell him the identity of all her friends who would then have to be contacted in the interest of controlling the spread of the disease.

Dr. Stevens further explained that there were only two ways to treat the disease. The first was a painful surgical procedure—graphically described—costing $9,000, and requiring her uninsured hospitalization for six weeks. A second alternative, Dr. Stevens explained, was to have sexual intercourse with an anonymous donor who had been injected with a serum that would cure the disease. The latter, nonsurgical procedure would only cost $4,500. When the victim replied that she lacked sufficient funds, the doctor suggested that $1,000 would suffice as a down payment. The victim thereupon agreed to the nonsurgical alternative and consented to intercourse with the mysterious donor, believing "it was the only choice I had."

Is her consent to have sex with an anonymous donor valid consent?

Held: The victim's testimony was clear that she precisely understood the "nature of the act," but motivated by a fear of disease and death, she succumbed to the petitioner's fraudulent blandishments. (The court held that Boro (Dr. Stevens) was not guilty of rape, but that his conduct comprised crimes of a different order than a violation of the rape statutes.)

As the result of this case, California Penal Code 261 (which describes what constitutes rape) was amended to include situations where the victim was not "aware, knowing, perceiving, or cognizant of the essential characteristics of the act due to the perpetrator's fraudulent representation that the sexual penetration served a professional purpose when it served no professional purpose."

consented to the sexual act. However, a defendant can introduce evidence about the victim's past sexual conduct in order to show that her (or his) testimony is not trustworthy. Before the defense may present this evidence in open court before a jury, the defense must get prior permission from the judge in a closed hearing.

SOCIETY IN ACTION

PEOPLE V. JOVANOVIC

263 A.D. 2d 182, 700 N.Y.S. 2d 156

(N.Y. App. Div. 1st Dep't 1999)

In 1996, Oliver Jovanovic was accused of the sadomasochistic torture of a woman. He had met the victim shortly before on the Internet. He was convicted in 1998. His conviction was overturned on appeal. The appellate court ruled that the trial court had improperly ruled as inadmissible an e-mail in which the victim had expressed her consent to, and later approval of, the encounter. The trial court had ruled these e-mails were inadmissible on the basis of rape shield laws. The court of appeals ruled that the trial court had misapplied those laws.

Spousal Rape

Spousal rape is generally described as nonconsensual sex in which the perpetrator is the victim's spouse. It is a form of partner rape, domestic violence, and sexual abuse. Prior to the 1960s, most jurisdictions held that a husband could not be convicted of rape for having nonconsensual sex with his wife. Some jurisdictions would prosecute assault and battery charges against the husband. This concept changed during the 1960s and 1970s. Now in most jurisdictions the husband can be prosecuted for rape or sexual assault for forcing his wife to have sex. The original justifications for the legal noncriminalization of marital rape were simply the result of the way marriage was understood historically in most cultures, where the wife was required to obey the husband.

Stalking

According to the National Institute of Justice (NIJ) website, like domestic violence, stalking is a crime of power and control.[12] Stalking is defined by NIJ as "a course of conduct directed at a specific person that involves repeated (two or more occasions) visual or physical proximity, nonconsensual communication, or verbal, written, or implied threats, or a combination thereof, that would cause a reasonable person fear."

Stalking may include persistent patterns of leaving or sending the victim unwanted items or presents that may range from seemingly romantic to bizarre, following or lying in wait for the victim, damaging

SOCIETY IN ACTION

THE ATTORNEY GENERAL'S NATIONAL TASK FORCE ON CHILDREN EXPOSED TO VIOLENCE: EXCERPTS OF THE EXECUTIVE SUMMARY

Exposure to violence is a national crisis that affects approximately two out of every three of our children. Of the 76 million children currently residing in the United States, an estimated 46 million can expect to have their lives touched by violence, crime, abuse, and psychological trauma this year. In 1979, U.S. Surgeon General Julius B. Richmond declared violence a public health crisis of the highest priority, and yet 33 years later that crisis remains. Whether the violence occurs in children's homes, neighborhoods, schools, playgrounds or playing fields, locker rooms, places of worship, shelters, streets, or in juvenile detention centers, the exposure of children to violence is a uniquely traumatic experience that has the potential to profoundly derail the child's security, health, happiness, and ability to grow and learn—with effects lasting well into adulthood.

Exposure to violence in any form harms children, and different forms of violence have different negative impacts.

Sexual abuse places children at high risk for serious and chronic health problems, including posttraumatic stress disorder (PTSD), depression, suicidality, eating disorders, sleep disorders, substance abuse, and deviant sexual behavior. Sexually abused children often become hypervigilant about the possibility of future sexual violation, experience feelings of betrayal by the adults who failed to care for and protect them.

Physical abuse puts children at high risk for lifelong problems with medical illness, PTSD, suicidality, eating disorders, substance abuse, and deviant sexual behavior. Physically abused children are at heightened risk for cognitive and developmental impairments, which can lead to violent behavior as a form of self-protection and control.

These children often feel powerless when faced with physical intimidation, threats, or conflict and may compensate by becoming isolated (through truancy or hiding) or aggressive (by bullying or joining gangs for protection). Physically abused children are at risk for significant impairment in memory processing and problem solving and for developing defensive behaviors that lead to consistent avoidance of intimacy.

Intimate partner violence within families puts children at high risk for severe and potentially lifelong problems with physical health, mental health, and school and peer relationships as well as for disruptive behavior. Witnessing or living with domestic or intimate partner violence often burdens children with a sense of loss or profound guilt and shame because of their mistaken assumption that they should have intervened or prevented the violence or, tragically, that they caused the violence. They frequently castigate themselves for having failed in what they assume to be their duty to protect a parent or sibling(s) from being harmed, for not having taken the place of their horribly injured or killed family member, or for having caused the offender to be violent. Children exposed to intimate partner violence often experience a sense of terror and dread that they will lose an essential caregiver through permanent injury or death. They also fear losing their relationship with the offending parent, who may be removed from the home, incarcerated, or even executed. Children will mistakenly blame themselves for having caused the batterer to be violent. If no one identifies these children and helps them heal and recover, they may bring this uncertainty, fear, grief, anger, shame, and sense of betrayal into all of their important relationships for the rest of their lives….

The challenge of children's exposure to violence and ensuing psychological trauma is not one that government alone can solve. The problem requires a truly national response that draws on the strengths of all Americans. Our children's futures are at stake.

Every child we are able to help recover from the impact of violence is an investment in our nation's future. Therefore, this report calls for a collective investment nationwide in defending our children from exposure to violence and psychological trauma, in healing families and communities, and in enabling all of our children to imagine and claim their safe and creative development and their productive futures. The time for action is now. Together, we must take this next step and build a nation whose communities are dedicated to ending children's exposure to violence and psychological trauma….

Source: Office of Juvenile Justice and Delinquency Prevention, Office of Justice Programs, U.S. Department of Justice, Report of the Attorney General's National Task Force on Children Exposed to Violence, December 2012.

or threatening to damage the victim's property, defaming the victim's character, or cyberstalking.

Cyberstalking is the harassing of the victim via the Internet by posting personal information or spreading rumors about the victim. As part of the Violence Against Women Reauthorization Act of 2005, Congress extended the federal interstate stalking statute to include cyberstalking.[13]

SOCIETY IN ACTION

BAIRD V. BAIRD

322 P. 3d 728, Utah, 2014

Robert obtained an injunction or court order to prevent his mother from calling him every day. Is her action a form of stalking?

Facts: Robert Baird sought and obtained a stalking injunction against his mother, Gloria Baird. The district court entered the three-year injunction after determining that Gloria's nearly daily phone calls to Robert were causing him emotional distress. On appeal, we are asked to determine whether the district court erred in entering the injunction based solely on its finding that Gloria's conduct was causing Robert emotional distress, without considering whether her conduct would have caused emotional distress to a reasonable person in Robert's circumstances. We are also asked to interpret the definition of emotional distress contained in the 2008 amendment to Utah Code section 76-5-106.5(2) (Stalking Statute) to determine whether it departs from or encompasses the definition of emotional distress previously recognized. (Note: Apparently Robert's mother was concerned about his medical health.)

Appellate Court's Opinion: We hold that the district court erred by focusing solely on whether Gloria's conduct subjectively caused Robert emotional distress. The proper inquiry under the Stalking Statute is an objective inquiry into whether Gloria's conduct would have caused a reasonable person in Robert's circumstances emotional distress. We therefore remand the case to the district court for an objective determination of whether Gloria's conduct met the statutory requirement. Because we remand to the district court for this reason, we need not reach the claim that the district court misinterpreted the statutory definition of emotional distress.... However, because the district court will need to determine the elements of emotional distress on remand, we address that issue for the purpose of giving guidance to the district court.

Utah's civil stalking statute allows for the issuance of a temporary, ex parte injunction upon a petitioner's showing of a "reason to believe that an offense of stalking has occurred." Utah Code § 77-3a-101(5)(a). It also provides for entry of a permanent injunction after a hearing if the petitioner establishes "by a preponderance of the evidence that stalking of the petitioner by the respondent has occurred." Thus, the essential statutory element is proof of "stalking."

Utah's Stalking Statute defines the crime of stalking as follows:

> A person is guilty of stalking who intentionally or knowingly engages in a course of conduct directed at a specific person and knows or should know that the course of conduct would cause a reasonable person: (a) to fear for the person's own safety or the safety of a third person; or (b) to suffer other emotional distress. § 76-5-106.5(2)

The Stalking Statute defines "reasonable person" as "a reasonable person in the victim's circumstances." The Model Stalking Code, upon which Utah's Stalking Statute is based, explains that the offense of stalking does not focus on the particular emotional distress a particular victim suffers, but rather on how the defendant's conduct would affect a reasonable person....

Thus, to qualify for an injunction under the Model Stalking Code, a petitioner must meet an objective—not subjective—standard. Utah's Stalking Statute conforms to the Model Stalking Code's "solely objective" standard. In this regard, the Model Code and the Utah Stalking Statute differ from statutes of other states that explicitly require both an objective and a subjective analysis. The comments to the Model Code explain that the shift to a solely objective standard was motivated by the fact that a subjective standard "places an unnecessary burden on … victims … forcing the victim to have to justify his or her fear [or distress] in the presence of the perpetrator." Furthermore, a subjective standard inappropriately punishes only those stalkers who have successfully caused the victim fear or distress.

Under the Stalking Statute's solely objective standard, the subjective effect of the respondent's conduct on the petitioner is irrelevant. Rather, the petitioner must establish only that the respondent's conduct would cause emotional distress to a reasonable person in the petitioner's circumstances.

(**Note:** The appellate court did not make a decision as to whether calling Robert each day amounted to stalking, but sent the case back to the trial court to make the determination as to whether a reasonable person under the circumstances would feel fear or distress.)

SOCIETY IN ACTION

COMMON STALKING TACTICS

General Tactics	Specific Examples
Physical surveillance	Following
Telephone harassment	Continual calling or any unwanted calling
Other types of communications	U.S. mail, leaving notes at different places, etc.
Property invasion or damage	
Cyberstalking	Use of the Internet, e-mail, or other electronic communications devices, using GPS to track victims, and using cameras to take photos of the victim without consent

Three factors appear to have a direct impact on what charges a prosecutor is able to bring before a court:

- The decisions police officers make at the crime scene
- The information the officers record
- The demeanor of victims

According to an NIJ research report, police officers were more likely to charge suspects with misdemeanors than felony offenses. Suspects were routinely charged with harassment, intimidation, or violation of a restraining order—rarely with stalking.[14]

Some studies suggest police and other criminal justice system personnel are not always sensitive or helpful in partner stalking cases. It is common in these cases for the officers not to take a report, advise the victim to document his or her experiences, discuss safety planning, or refer him or her to victim services for more help. There is also an indication that in some jurisdictions, partner violence is a lower priority than other crimes.[15]

Hate Crimes

Hate crimes, also referred to as bias-motivated crimes, are usually violent, prejudice-motivated crimes that occur when offenders target victims because of their perceived membership in a certain social or ethnic group. Examples of such groups include ethnicity, gender identity, language,

SOCIETY IN ACTION

PREVALENCE OF STALKING BY ABUSIVE PARTNERS*

More than half of partner violence victims are stalked by their partners.

- Several studies have found that between 50% and 60% of partner violence victims report ever being stalked by that partner.
- The vast majority of partner violence victims who report ever being stalked by a violent partner report being stalked the year prior to obtaining a protective order (approximately 90%).
- Thirty percent of domestic violence offenders in offender treatment reported stalking behaviors toward their victim.

Danger of Violence From Stalking Versus Nonstalking Abusive Partners

- Research indicates that abusive partners who stalk are more violent than those who do not stalk.
- Stalking was highly prevalent in cases of actual or attempted femicides.
- Approximately 90% of actual or attempted lethality victims who experienced a physical assault in the preceding year were also stalked by the violent partner.
- Studies suggest that partner stalkers were more controlling and physically and sexually violent in the prior relationship compared to abusers who do not stalk their victims.
- A study of domestic violence police records concluded that domestic violence cases with elements or charges of stalking were more threatening and violent than domestic violence cases without stalking.
- Several studies indicate women stalked by a violent partner after obtaining a protective order are more likely to experience almost every other kind of abuse and violence than women not stalked after a protective order, even after controlling for a number of relevant factors.
- Women who were stalked by a violent partner after obtaining a protective order were 4 times more likely to experience physical assault, 9.3 times more likely to experience sexual assault, and 4.7 times more likely to be injured than women with protective orders who were not stalked.

* Adapted from the NIJ stalking website.

- Victims who were stalked after obtaining a protective order experienced more overall violations and more severe violence than victims who experienced ongoing violations but who were not stalked, even after controlling for past history of violence and other relevant factors.
- Prior history of stalking is associated with future stalking. For example, of those stalked after the protective order, 78% were stalked before the protective order was obtained; the other 22% indicated the stalking was initiated after the protective order was issued.
- Even though prior history of stalking is associated with future stalking behavior, several studies suggest that the majority of partner stalkers discontinue their stalking behavior after a civil protective order is obtained against them (61% to 65%). That means, however, that about 35% to 39% of stalkers continued to stalk their victims after a protective order was obtained.

Characteristics of Stalking Versus Nonstalking Abusive Partners

- Research on the characteristics of partner violence offenders who stalk compared with partner violence offenders who do not stalk is limited. A few studies suggest that abusive partners who stalk have higher rates of drug and alcohol use.

nationality, physical appearance, religion, and sexual orientation. Rebecca Stotzer states: "A hate crime or bias motivated crime occurs when the perpetrator of the crime intentionally selects the victim because of his or her membership in a certain group."[16]

The federal government has addressed hate crimes in three ways:

- By defining and prosecuting federal hate crimes
- By enhancing sentences for other federal offenses when motivated by bias against protected groups
- By requiring the FBI to track hate crimes from state and local agencies across the United States

The Federal Bureau of Investigation (FBI) has been investigating crimes of hatred and prejudice—from lynchings to cross burnings to vandalism of synagogues—since World War I when the Ku Klux Klan first attracted its attention. The term *hate crime* did not enter the nation's vocabulary until the 1980s, when emerging hate groups like the skinheads launched a wave of bias-related crime.[17]

A hate crime is not a distinct federal offense. However, the federal government (FBI) can and does investigate and prosecute crimes of bias as civil rights violations. The majority of hate crimes are handled by state and local authorities. The Violent Crime Control and Law Enforcement Act (1994) provided for the prosecution of hate crimes that constituted a violation of the Civil Rights Act of 1964. The 1994 Act also increased penalties for offenses proven to be hate crimes.

The Matthew Shepard and James Byrd Jr. Hate Crimes Prevention Act in 2009 included the first significant expansion of federal criminal civil

FOCUS ON PEOPLE

JAMES BYRD JR. (1949–1998)

James Byrd Jr. was an African American who was murdered by three white supremacists, in Jasper, Texas, on June 7, 1998. The three men dragged Byrd for three miles behind a pickup truck along an asphalt road. Byrd, who remained conscious throughout most of the ordeal, was killed when his body hit the edge of a culvert, severing his right arm and head. The men then drove on for another mile before dumping his torso in front of an African American cemetery in Jasper. Byrd's lynching-by-dragging gave impetus to passage of a Texas hate crimes law.

FOCUS ON PEOPLE

MATTHEW SHEPARD (1976–1998)

On October 12, 1998, near the outskirts of Laramie, Wyoming, 21-year-old gay college student Matthew Shepard was brutally beaten, tied to a fence, and left for dead. He was found 18 hours later and rushed to the hospital, where he lingered on the edge of death for nearly five days before dying due to his injuries. Two men were arrested shortly after the attack. During the trial of one, it was widely reported that Shepard was targeted because he was gay. A Laramie police officer testified at a pretrial hearing that the violence against Shepard was due to how the attacker felt about gays. The officer's opinion was based on an interview of the attacker's girlfriend.

The killings of Byrd and Shepard led to the federal Matthew Shepard and James Byrd Jr. Hate Crimes Prevention Act, commonly known as the Matthew Shepard Act, which passed on October 22, 2009, and which President Barack Obama signed into law on October 28, 2009.

SOCIETY IN ACTION

CALIFORNIA'S HATE CRIMES

There are two parts to California's hate crime law:

- Penal Code 422.6 PC makes it a stand-alone crime to interfere with someone else's civil rights, or damage or destroy his or her property, because that person has one of the characteristics in the list above.
- Penal Code 422.7 PC and Penal Code 422.75 PC provide that if (1) you commit a crime such as assault or vandalism and (2) you are motivated in part by the fact that the victim has one of the listed characteristics, the criminal offense is considered a hate crime and subject to an enhanced sentence.

List of characteristics: Disability, gender, nationality, race or ethnicity, religion, or sexual orientation.

rights law since 1994. The 2009 Act gave the federal government the authority to prosecute violent hate crimes, including violence and attempted violence directed at the gay, lesbian, bisexual, and transgender community, to the fullest extent of its jurisdiction. The act also provides funding and technical assistance to state, local, and tribal jurisdictions to help them to more effectively investigate, prosecute, and prevent hate crimes.

Practicum

Consider the following examples. Which would be murder and which are manslaughter?

- Jeff and Dan were standing next to each other at the top of a flight of stairs. They began to argue over who should be the next governor. The argument becomes increasingly animated and culminates when Jeff makes an obscene gesture toward Dan. At this time, Dan pushes Jeff backwards and causes Jeff to fall down the stairs. Jeff dies of his injuries.

  Answer: Dan would probably be guilty of involuntary manslaughter. It was criminally negligent of Dan to shove a person standing near the top of a stairway. The circumstances don't suggest that Dan's behavior was so reckless as to demonstrate extreme indifference to human life, which would have elevated the crime to murder.

- Joe comes home to find that his wife Diane has been beaten and sexually abused by Kenn. After taking his wife to the hospital, Joe drives to a gun shop and buys a gun. He hunts down Kenn and kills him.

  Answer: Joe probably committed murder, because his purchase of the gun suggests that the shooting was intentional and premeditated. There was probably enough time elapsed between the time Joe discovered the wife's condition and the time he found Kenn that the crime was not committed in a heat of passion and was not involuntary manslaughter.

- Susan and Jim have been married for about four years. Jim has frequently used violent force against Susan. Susan is afraid to leave Jim because she knows that if she does he will hunt her down and punish her. One night Jim comes home drunk and falls asleep. Susan sees this as her chance to be free. She pours gas on Jim and burns him to death. Does Susan commit murder or did she act in self-defense?

  Answer: Susan would be considered to have committed murder. The fact that she was abused by her husband may be used to mitigate the sentence.

Summary

- Interpersonal violence is defined as any behavior within an intimate relationship that causes physical, psychological, or sexual harm to those in the relationship.
- Violence is considered the intentional use of physical force or power, threatened or actually, against another person that results in a high likelihood of injury or psychological harm or death.
- Homicide is the act of killing another human being. English common law established three forms of homicide.
- To constitute criminal homicide, the act and the required mental intent must be joined in time.
- To constitute criminal homicide, there must be a killing of another human being.
- Murder is defined as the purposeful, knowing, or reckless unlawful killing of another human being.
- The next most serious form of criminal homicide is voluntary manslaughter. The crime requires the same type of intent that is necessary to establish murder and an act or failure to act that resulted in the death of a living human being. The crime is downgraded from murder to voluntary manslaughter because of the presence of adequate provocation.

- Involuntary manslaughter may be defined as the unintentional killing of another human being during the commission of an unlawful but not inherently dangerous crime or as the result of criminal negligence.
- Rape is the unlawful act of sexual intercourse with another person without the valid consent of the other person. The lack of valid consent may be in cases where the sexual act is committed by force on the victim; the victim, because of age or mental status, cannot give legal consent; or the victim consents to the sexual act because of fear or is tricked into consenting.
- Rape shield laws are designed to protect a victim when she is being cross-examined by the defense in court. In general terms the law prevents the defense from requiring the witness to testify regarding her previous sexual experiences unless the defense can establish that her history is relevant to the case.
- Stalking is defined by NIJ as "a course of conduct directed at a specific person that involves repeated (two or more occasions) visual or physical proximity, nonconsensual communication, or verbal, written, or implied threats, or a combination thereof, that would cause a reasonable person fear."
- Hate crimes, also referred to as bias-motivated crimes, are usually violent, prejudice-motivated crimes that occur when offenders target victims because of their perceived membership in a certain social or ethnic group.

Questions in Review

1. What constitutes interpersonal violence?
2. How does voluntary manslaughter differ from murder?
3. What are the issues involved when considering the crime of stalking?
4. How does the crime of assault differ from the crime of battery?
5. What constitutes a hate crime?
6. Explain the purposes of rape shield laws.
7. What constitutes the crime of robbery?
8. Can a female rape a male? Explain.
9. In sexual assault cases, what constitutes legal consent?

Key Terms

Adequate provocation: A killing in which the defendant is so governed by the heat of passion that he or she is unable to reason to the extent necessary to form a deliberate purpose to take a life. The circumstances causing the state of passion must be such that a reasonable person would be similarly governed.

Cyberstalking: The use of technology to stalk victims—shares some characteristics with real-life stalking. It involves the pursuit, harassment, or contact of others in an unsolicited fashion initially via the Internet and e-mail.

Euthanasia: More commonly known as mercy killing. An example of euthanasia is the killing of a loved one to prevent further suffering.

Excusable homicide: A killing in self-defense or by accident.

Homicide: The act of killing another human being.

Interpersonal violence: Any behavior within an intimate relationship that causes physical, psychological, or sexual harm to those in the relationship.

Involuntary manslaughter: The unintentional killing of another human being during the commission of an unlawful but not inherently dangerous crime or as the result of criminal negligence.

Justifiable homicide: A killing that is sanctioned by the government, for example, killing of an enemy under the rules of war by a military person during combat or the legal execution of a convicted murderer.

Murder: The purposeful, knowing, or reckless unlawful killing of another human being.

Rape: The unlawful act of sexual intercourse with another person without the valid consent of the other person.

Rape shield laws: Laws that are designed to protect a victim when she is being cross-examined by the defense in court.

Spousal rape: Nonconsensual sex in which the perpetrator is the victim's spouse. It is a form of partner rape, domestic violence, and sexual abuse.

Voluntary manslaughter: A killing that is downgraded from murder because of the presence of adequate provocation.

Endnotes

1. James Buenker. (1999). Overview of violence theories: History. In R. Gottesman (Ed.), *The encyclopedia of violence in America* (Vol. 3, pp. 314–315). New York: Scribner.
2. R. M. Brown. (1969). Historical patterns of American violence. In H. D. Graham & T. R. Gurr (Eds.), *The history of violence in America: Historical and comparative perspectives—A report to the National Commission on the Causes and Prevention of Violence* (pp. 45–84). New York: Bantam.
3. Etienne G. Krug, Linda L. Dahlberg, James A. Mercy, Anthony B. Zwi, & Rafael Lozano, Eds. (2002). *World report on violence and health*. Geneva: World Health Organization.
4. SAFE@UNC website. http://safe.unc.edu/get-info/interpersonal-violence. Retrieved May 12, 2014.

5. Scott Mire & Cliff Roberson. (2011). *The study of violent crime: Its correlates and concerns*. Boca Raton, FL: CRC Press.
6. Mire & Roberson, 2011, pp. 24–25.
7. Janet L. Lauritsen. (2014, June 14). *Special report: Seasonal patterns in criminal victimization trends*. NCJ 245959. Washington, DC: U.S. Department of Justice, Bureau of Justice Statistics.
8. Lance Lochner. (2004, August). Education, work, and crime: A human capital approach. *International Economic Review*, *45*(3), 811–843.
9. Harvey Wallace & Cliff Roberson. (2014). *Principles of criminal law*. Columbus, OH: Pearson.
10. *Coker v. Georgia*. 433 U.S. 584 (1977).
11. SAFE@UNC website.
12. National Institute of Justice website on stalking. http://www.nij.gov/topics/crime/stalking/Pages/welcome.aspx. Retrieved May 19, 2014.
13. 18 USC § 2261 A (2005).
14. Patricia Tjaden & Nancy Thoennes. (2002). *Stalking: Its role in serious domestic violence cases*. NCJ 187446, Grant 97-WT-VX-0002. Final report submitted to the National Institute of Justice. Washington, DC: U.S. Department of Justice, National Institute of Justice.
15. A. K. Klein, A. Salomon, N. Huntington, J. Dubois, & D. Lang. (2009). *A statewide study of stalking and its criminal justice response*. NCJ 228354. Final report to the National Institute of Justice. Washington, DC: U.S. Department of Justice, National Institute of Justice.
16. Rebecca Stotzer. (2007–2006). Comparison of hate crime rates across protected and unprotected groups. Williams Institute. Retrieved May 14, 2014, from http://williamsinstitute.law.ucla.edu/wp-content/uploads/Stotzer-Comparison-Hate-Crime-June-2007.pdf.
17. FBI website on hate crimes. http://www.fbi.gov/about-us/investigate/civilrights/hate_crimes/. Retrieved May 14, 2014.

chapter five

Self-Destructive Deviance

Chapter Objectives

What you should know and understand after studying this chapter:

- The nature of self-destructive behaviors
- What constitutes suicide
- Who commits suicide
- Why suicide is a national problem
- Some of the theoretical explanations for suicides
- Why the war on drugs is considered by most people to be a failure
- The issues involved in determining why people commit self-inflicted violence
- How poor personal health habits affect us
- The issues involved in diverse lifestyles

Introduction

For the most part, when we discuss deviant behavior, we focus on the harm caused to others. We tend to overlook the fact that deviant behavior can be very destructive to the actor. In this chapter we will explore some of the actions of individuals who commit self-destructive deviance. Self-destructive behavior includes destructive acts that harm the individual performing the harmful acts.

The phrase "self-destructive deviance" is derived from objective psychology, wherein all apparent self-inflicted harm or abuse toward oneself is treated as a collection of actions, and therefore as a pattern of behavior. Acts of self-destruction may be merely metaphorical, such as social suicide, or literal, such as suicide or cutting one's self. Self-destructive actions may be deliberate, born of impulse, or developed as a habit. The term is frequently applied when referring to acts of self-destructions that are potentially habit forming or addictive, and thus may eventually be fatal.

Humans, unlike most animals, tend to engage in a vast number of behaviors that are destructive to us. Numerous research studies have attempted to answer the question of why an intelligent species seems so nasty, spiteful, self-destructive, and hurtful to themselves. Humans are creatures of habit. Studies have found that even when the risks of a particular bad habit are well known, such as smoking, people find it hard to quit.

It is difficult to define what actions constitute self-destructive deviance. What behaviors sit within this definition? For example, in one recent court case, the court held that drunk driving is itself a self-destructive behavior.[1] Currently many researchers are using the term *self-directed violence* rather than *self-destructive deviance.* Self-directed violence (SDV) encompasses a range of violent behaviors, including acts of fatal and nonfatal suicidal behavior, and nonsuicidal intentional self-harm (i.e., behaviors where the intention is not to kill oneself, as in self-mutilation). In 2007, SDV was the third leading cause of death among persons aged 15 to 24 years, fourth among persons aged 25 to 44 years, and eighth among those aged 45 to 64 years.[2] The intent of the individual when inflicting self-directed violence may be either suicidal or nonsuicidal. Often the individual's intent remains unknown or unclear.

Suicide

Suicide has been described as the ultimate act of self-destruction. Suicide is the willful taking of one's own life. Steven Stack estimates that there are 22.5 suicide attempts for every completed suicide.[3] According to Stack, people are twice as likely to commit suicide as to be murdered by someone else. This supports the ancient saying "I have met the enemy and it is I."

History indicates that males are four times more likely than females to commit suicide. Elderly or retired individuals, especially males, have the highest suicide rates per 100,000. Whites tend to commit suicide at twice the rate as blacks.

Emile Durkheim

The first sociologist, Emile Durkheim, used his concept of anomie to explain suicides. He defined anomie as a state or condition that exists within people when a society evolves from a mechanical to an organic entity. To him, anomie was a condition of normlessness, not a lack of norms, but the condition whereby norms have lost their meaning and become inoperative for a large number of people. Anomie, a Greek term defined as lawlessness, may also be described as the fragmentation or disassociation of one's center; the feeling of being a number, not a person; social isolation; or social loneliness. According to Durkheim, the degree of integration of a society was inversely related to its rate of suicide. He also noted that there were low suicide rates in predominantly Catholic countries where religion provided a unifying theme. He stated that during wartime and in prolonged economic depressions the suicide rates were lower presumably because there was greater unification and social solidarity within a society.[5]

SOCIETY IN ACTION

BULLYING AND SUICIDE

According to the Centers for Disease Control and Prevention (CDC) there is a close relationship between bullying and youth suicides.[4]

- Youths who report any involvement with bullying behavior are more likely to report high levels of suicide-related behaviors than youths who do not report any involvement with bullying behavior.
- Researchers know enough about the relationship between bullying and suicide-related behavior to make evidence-based recommendations to improve prevention efforts.
- Youth who report frequently bullying others are at high, long-term risk for suicide-related behavior.
- Youth who report both being bullied and bullying others (sometimes referred to as bully victims) have the highest rates of negative mental health outcomes, including depression, anxiety, and thinking about suicide.
- Youth who act out through bullying others may be trying to fit in or reacting to stress, abuse, or other issues at home or school. Bullying behavior may be an important signal that they need mental health services and additional support.

What We Know or Don't Know About Bullying and Suicide

- We don't know if bullying directly causes suicide-related behavior.
- We know that most youth who are involved in bullying do *not* engage in suicide-related behavior.
- It is correct to say that involvement in bullying, along with other risk factors, increases the chance that a young person will engage in suicide-related behaviors.

Sociological Risk Factors

According to Durkheim, suicide was not the result of psychiatric morbidity, but a result of factors external to the individual, basically inadequate ties to social groups. Some of the sociological risk factors that influence suicide rates include the following[7]:

- **Marital ties:** He saw marital ties as a key source of integration into a society—that marriage increases meaning in life and should reduce deviant behavior.

SOCIETY IN ACTION

SUICIDE EPIDEMIC

Robin McLaurin Williams, an American actor and comedian, committed suicide on August 11, 2014. He started as a stand-up comedian in San Francisco and Los Angeles and rose to fame as Mork in the TV series *Mork & Mindy* (1978–1982). Williams went on to establish a career in stand-up comedy and feature film acting. It appears that at the time of his death he was suffering from depression and had recently been diagnosed with early stage Parkinson's disease.

Common Causes of Death in 2010

Suicide: 38,364
Automobile accidents: 35,332
Prostate cancer: 32,050
Leukemia: 21,840

Annual Growth in Number of Suicides

2002: 31,665
2005: 32,559
2008: 36,035
2011: 39,518

Source: Centers for Disease Control and Prevention's National Vital Statistics Report, 2013.

SOCIETY IN ACTION

SUICIDE DATA

- Suicide occurs almost twice as often as murder.
- Each year, about 36,000 people in the United States die by suicide.
- In the United States, suicide is the 10th leading cause of death.
- Suicide is the third leading cause of death for people ages 15 to 24, and the second leading cause for people ages 25 to 34.
- Suicide rates have increased for middle-aged and older adults.
- Women try suicide more often, but men are four times more likely to die from a suicide attempt.
- Using a gun is the most common method of suicide.

Source: WebMD website, http://www.webmd.com/mental-health/tc/suicidal-thoughts-or-threats-topic-overview, retrieved May 26, 2014.

SOCIETY IN ACTION

SUICIDE AND THE RECESSION

According to a study by Aaron Reeves, a researcher at Oxford University in England, during the world recession of 2007–2010 at least 10,000 more people took their lives during that period. Reeves concluded that there are large mental health implications of the economic crisis that are still being felt by many people. The suicide rate among countries did not rise evenly. He noted that two countries, Sweden and Austria, had little increase in suicide rates, and that these two countries provided strong support for their citizens who lost their jobs or were struggling financially.

Reeves also noted that the suicide rate was higher for men facing financial difficulties than women during this period. This may be based on the fact that men are more likely to be the breadwinners or less likely than women to seek help.

Before the recession, the suicide rates were falling in most European countries and rising in the United States. Reeves also noted that antidepressant prescriptions rose by nearly 20% in the United States and United Kingdom during the recession.[6]

- **Divorce:** Stark notes that divorce is the most widely researched sociological risk factor for suicide.
- **Cohabitation:** Couples living together without being married is an increasing trend in today's societies. Early research indicates that the suicide rate for these couples is higher than for married couples, but lower than for single persons living alone.
- **Living alone:** Generally persons living alone are about 1½ times more likely to commit suicide than persons not living alone.
- **Parents:** Because being a parent tends to increase one's sense of responsibility to others and provides the parent with a purpose to life, the rate of suicide of parents is lower than for nonparents. Married parents tend to have the lowest suicide rates.
- **Unemployed:** As noted by Stack, unemployment affects not only your income, but also your feelings of self-worthiness. Unemployed individuals commit suicide about 1.3 times more than persons who are employed.
- **Income level:** There are conflicting studies on the relationship between low incomes and suicide. Some researchers indicate that suicide rates are lower for people in the lower income brackets. Recent research tends to indicate that the rates are significantly higher. For example, the largest recent research study was a Danish

study that indicated that persons in the lowest quartile of the income brackets were almost six times more likely to die of suicide.

According to the Centers for Disease Control and Prevention, several factors can put a person at risk for suicide. However, having these risk factors does not always mean that suicide will occur. Some of the risk factors researchers identified include the following[8]:

- History of previous suicide attempts
- Family history of suicide
- History of depression or other mental illness
- History of alcohol or drug abuse
- Stressful life event or loss
- Easy access to lethal methods
- Exposure to the suicidal behavior of others

Threatening to Commit Suicide

Is threatening to commit suicide a form of abuse? Or is it a sign that the person needs help?

Consider the situation where a woman makes a decision to break up with her boyfriend. He has been abusive and the woman decides that she can no longer remain in this relationship. The boyfriend then threatens that if she breaks up with him, he will kill himself. Some researchers would consider that the threat of suicide is another abusive behavior by the male because he is trying to force her to remain in the abusive relationship. Others would indicate that the threat indicates that the boyfriend needs help. To some extent, probably both views are correct.

An online search by the authors of the "advice columns" found seven situations were a reader had sought advice in somewhat similar situations. The common response from the "advice gurus" was basically that the young woman was not responsible and should not consider his threat to commit suicide to be credible or a reason to stay in the abusive relationship. A couple of the gurus noted that the woman should advise someone close to the boyfriend of his threat. It appears that such threats rarely are carried out. The authors could find no research on this scenario. It would appear that no matter what the situation, a threat to commit suicide is at least a sign that the individual needs help.

Suicide Attempts

As noted earlier in this chapter, there is only about 1 suicide for every 22.5 attempts. It would improve our murder rates if only 1 of every 22.5 murder attempts were successful. Why the large number of unsuccessful

SOCIETY IN ACTION

UNITED STATES, APPELLEE V. EDWARD A. ST. JEAN, FIRST LIEUTENANT, U.S. AIR FORCE, APPELLANT

No. 95-0756

Crim. App. No. 29942

United States Court of Appeals for the Armed Forces

In the above-cited case, Dr. William H. Grant, a forensic psychologist, testified as an expert witness on suicide. Lieutenant St. Jean was convicted of murdering his wife. The defense contended that she committed suicide. Excerpts of Dr. Grant's testimony at the trial are presented to point out what types of individuals committed suicide.

When called as a witness by the prosecution, Dr. Grant explained that within the obvious limitations, he was trying to assess retrospectively the state of mind of the deceased. He explained his methodology and the general nature of the materials he drew from. He discussed the volumes of studies conducted to try to understand the causes of suicide and the means to prevent it.

Asked by trial counsel about "generally accepted indicators, characteristics, warning signals for individuals with a high risk of committing suicide," Dr. Grant described "two ways to look at it." According to Dr. Grant:

> If you look at it strictly statistically and strictly actuarial, the individual at high risk for suicide is male, over 45, living alone, no job, physically ill, and probably alcoholic….
>
> Really two types of people kill themselves, the depressed person and the highly impulsive person. The highly impulsive person who isn't really depressed, but who is angry, is at risk for suicide. But in the impulsive person, what one sees is a history of impulsivity. They see—you see someone whose reactions to stress and reactions to situations and reactions to other people have been impulsive and not always in their best interests over an extended period of time and recognizable from situation to situation. You know, if you were impulsive a year or two years ago and there's a pattern, you're

likely to be impulsive now and you're probably going to be impulsive in the future. And impulsive people like this are at times prone to suicide. They tend to alienate people so that they can have the support system—to give them an option other than suicide. And, yes, sometimes they get angry and do something destructive to themselves. But there has to be a pattern.

(The decision of the U.S. Air Force Court of Criminal Appeals, which upheld the murder conviction, was affirmed.)

suicide attempts? Some researchers contend that unlike people who threaten suicide, people to attempt to commit suicide are ambiguous in their intent to die, whereas those who threaten suicide actually do not want to die. Since the attempters are not certain that they want to die, frequently they change their mind after starting the process. In addition, frequently suicide attempts are made in a setting or manner that makes rescue possible, probable, or inevitable. In choosing this type of setting or manner, the individual may be indicating his or her lack of commitment to dying. In a *Psychology Today* article, the author indicates that most suicide attempts are not a road to death but a road to life.

Assisting a Person to Commit Suicide

In many states, it is not considered a crime for a person to attempt to commit suicide. But in almost all jurisdictions, it is considered a crime to assist another person to commit suicide. As noted in the excerpts from the U.S. Supreme Court case of *Washington v. Glucksberg*, states are moving away from punishing individuals' unsuccessful suicide attempts, but have continued to consider it criminal to assist someone else to commit suicide. Too many, this approach may not seem logical, but it is the law of the land.

What conduct is necessary to constitute helping someone to commit suicide? For example, is a pharmacist who sells the necessary drugs to a potential suicide victim committing the crime of assisting a suicide? Would it make a difference if the pharmacist knew or did not know that the buyer intended to use the drugs to commit suicide? This is a confusing issue, and not all jurisdictions agree on what constitutes the crime of assisting another to commit suicide. If the suicide is unsuccessful, would the aider and abettor (person who assists) still be guilty of attempting to assist another to commit suicide? He or she probably would be in most jurisdictions.

SOCIETY IN ACTION

EXCERPTS FROM THE U.S. SUPREME COURT DECISION *WASHINGTON V. GLUCKSBERG*

521 U.S. 702 (1997)

Facts: Three terminally ill patients, four physicians, and nonprofit organization brought action against State of Washington for declaratory judgment that statute banning assisted suicide violated due process clause. The Supreme Court, Chief Justice Rehnquist, held that: (1) asserted right to assistance in committing suicide was not a fundamental liberty interest protected by due process clause, and (2) Washington's ban on assisted suicide was rationally related to a legitimate government interest.

Court's opinion: It has always been a crime to assist a suicide in the State of Washington. In 1854, Washington's first Territorial Legislature outlawed "assisting another in the commission of self-murder." Today, Washington law provides: "A person is guilty of promoting a suicide attempt when he knowingly causes or aids another person to attempt suicide." Promoting a suicide attempt is a felony, punishable by up to five years' imprisonment and up to a $10,000 fine. At the same time, Washington's Natural Death Act, enacted in 1979, states that the withholding or withdrawal of life-sustaining treatment at a patient's direction shall not, for any purpose, constitute a suicide.

The plaintiffs asserted the existence of a liberty interest protected by the Fourteenth Amendment which extends to a personal choice by a mentally competent, terminally ill adult to commit physician-assisted suicide. Relying primarily on *Planned Parenthood of Southeastern Pa. v. Casey*, 505 U.S. 833 (1992), the District Court agreed and concluded that Washington's assisted-suicide ban is unconstitutional because it places an undue burden on the exercise of that constitutionally protected liberty interest. The District Court also decided that the Washington statute violated the Equal Protection Clause's requirement that all persons similarly situated…. The court of appeals upheld the district court's decision.

We now reverse that decision.

We begin, as we do in all due process cases, by examining our Nation's history, legal traditions, and practices. In almost every State—indeed, in almost every western democracy—it is a crime to assist a suicide. The States' assisted-suicide bans are not innovations. Rather, they are longstanding expressions of the States' commitment to the protection and preservation of all human life. The States—indeed, all civilized nations—demonstrate their commitment to life by treating homicide as a serious crime. Moreover, the majority of States in this country have laws imposing criminal penalties on one who assists another to commit suicide….

In total, forty-four states, the District of Columbia and two territories prohibit or condemn assisted suicide. A blanket prohibition on assisted suicide … is the norm among western democracies…. More specifically, for over 700 years, the Anglo-American common-law tradition has punished or otherwise disapproved of both suicide and assisting suicide. In the 13th century, Henry de Bracton, one of the first legal-treatise writers, observed that "just as a man may commit felony by slaying another so may he do so by slaying himself." The real and personal property of one who killed himself to avoid conviction and punishment for a crime were forfeit to the King; however, thought Bracton, "if a man slays himself in weariness of life or because he is unwilling to endure further bodily pain … only his movable goods were confiscated." Thus, the principle that suicide of a sane person, for whatever reason, was a punishable felony was … introduced into English common law.

For the most part, the early American Colonies adopted the common-law approach. For example, the legislators of the Providence Plantations, which would later become Rhode Island, declared, in 1647, that "self-murder is by all agreed to be the most unnatural, and it is by this present Assembly declared, to be that, wherein he that doth it, kills himself out of a premeditated hatred against his own life or other humor: … his goods and chattels are the king's custom, but not his debts nor lands; but in case he be an infant, a lunatic, mad or distracted man, he forfeits nothing." Virginia also required ignominious burial for suicides, and their estates were forfeit to the Crown.

Over time, however, the American Colonies abolished these harsh common-law penalties. William Penn abandoned the criminal-forfeiture sanction in Pennsylvania in 1701, and the other Colonies (and later, the other States) eventually followed this example. Zephaniah Swift, who would later become Chief Justice of Connecticut, wrote in 1796:

> There can be no act more contemptible, than to attempt to punish an offender for a crime, by exercising a mean act of revenge upon lifeless clay that is insensible of the punishment. There

> can be no greater cruelty, than the inflicting of a punishment, as the forfeiture of goods, which must fall solely on the innocent offspring of the offender…. Suicide is so abhorrent to the feelings of mankind, and that strong love of life which is implanted in the human heart, that it cannot be so frequently committed, as to become dangerous to society. There can of course be no necessity of any punishment.

This statement makes it clear, however, that the movement away from the common law's harsh sanctions did not represent an acceptance of suicide; rather, as Chief Justice Swift observed, this change reflected the growing consensus that it was unfair to punish the suicide's family for his wrongdoing.

That suicide remained a grievous, though non-felonious, wrong is confirmed by the fact that colonial and early state legislatures and courts did not retreat from prohibiting assisting suicide. Swift, in his early 19th-century treatise on the laws of Connecticut, stated that "if one counsels another to commit suicide, and the other by reason of the advice kills himself, the advisor is guilty of murder as principal." This was the well-established common-law view.

Attitudes toward suicide itself have changed since Bracton, but our laws have consistently condemned, and continue to prohibit, assisting suicide. Despite changes in medical technology and notwithstanding an increased emphasis on the importance of end-of-life decision making, we have not retreated from this prohibition. Against this backdrop of history, tradition, and practice, we now turn to respondents' constitutional claim.

The court identified and discussed six state interests: (1) preserving life; (2) preventing suicide; (3) avoiding the involvement of third parties and use of arbitrary, unfair, or undue influence; (4) protecting family members and loved ones; (5) protecting the integrity of the medical profession; and (6) avoiding future movement toward euthanasia and other abuses.

Washington has an "unqualified interest in the preservation of human life." The State's prohibition on assisted suicide, like all homicide laws, both reflects and advances its commitment to this interest. The interests in the sanctity of life that are represented by the criminal homicide laws are threatened by one who expresses a willingness to participate in taking the life of this interest is symbolic and aspirational as well as practical.

Nearly all states expressly disapprove of suicide and assisted suicide either in statutes dealing with durable powers of attorney in health-care situations, or in "living will" statutes. In addition, all states provide for the involuntary commitment of persons who may harm themselves as the result of mental illness, and a number of states allow the use of non-deadly force to thwart suicide attempts.

While suicide is no longer prohibited or penalized, the ban against assisted suicide and euthanasia shores up the notion of limits in human relationships. It reflects the gravity with which we view the decision to take one's own life or the life of another, and our reluctance to encourage or promote these decisions.

Throughout the Nation, Americans are engaged in an earnest and profound debate about the morality, legality, and practicality of physician-assisted suicide. Our holding permits this debate to continue, as it should in a democratic society. The decision of the Court of Appeals is reversed, and the case is remanded for further proceedings consistent with this opinion.

It is so ordered.

Preventing Suicide

If a person is unhappy and does not wish to continue living, do we have a right to prevent that individual from committing suicide? The answer to this question may depend upon your religious and moral beliefs. It may also depend on your assessment of the mental condition of the individual who wants to terminate his or her life.

According to the Centers for Disease Control and Prevention website, protective factors buffer individuals from suicidal thoughts and behavior. Some of the protective factors researchers have identified include[9]

- Skills in problem solving, conflict resolution, and nonviolent ways of handling disputes
- Effective clinical care for mental, physical, and substance abuse disorders
- Easy access to various clinical interventions and support for help seeking
- Family and community support (connectedness)
- Support from ongoing medical and mental health care relationships
- Cultural beliefs that discourage suicide and support instincts for self-preservation, including seeking help

SOCIETY IN ACTION

NATIONAL ACTION ALLIANCE FOR SUICIDE PREVENTION

The National Action Alliance for Suicide Prevention is the public-private partnership created for the purposes of advancing a National Strategy for Suicide Prevention.[10] The alliance consists of more than 200 public and private organizations. Its goal is to save 20,000 lives in the next five years. Its website is http://actionallianceforsuicideprevention.org/nssp.

In 2013, the alliance released the revised National Strategy for Suicide Prevention (NSSP). The revised strategy emphasizes the role every American can play in protecting their friends, family members, and colleagues from suicide. It also provides guidance for schools, businesses, health systems, clinicians, and many other sectors that takes into account nearly a decade of research and other advancements in the field since the last strategy was published.

The NSSP features 13 goals and 60 objectives with the themes that suicide prevention should:

- Foster positive public dialogue; counter shame, prejudice, and silence; and build public support for suicide prevention
- Address the needs of vulnerable groups, be tailored to the cultural and situational contexts in which it is offered, and seek to eliminate disparities
- Be coordinated and integrated with existing efforts addressing health and behavioral health and ensure continuity of care
- Promote changes in systems, policies, and environments that will support and facilitate the prevention of suicide and related problems
- Bring together public health and behavioral health
- Promote efforts to reduce access to lethal means among individuals with identified suicide risks
- Apply the most up-to-date knowledge base for suicide prevention

The Action Alliance has four priorities that are taken from the revised National Strategy for Suicide Prevention. The priorities were chosen because of their potential to produce the systems-level change necessary to substantially lower the burden of suicide in our nation, and because the Action Alliance has the public-private collaboration and national leverage required to do so. The four priorities are

- Integrate suicide prevention into health care reform and encourage the adoption of similar measures in the private sector.

- Transform health care systems to significantly reduce suicide.
- Change the public conversation around suicide and suicide prevention. This initiative is designed to transform attitudes and behaviors relating to suicide and suicide prevention. Messages that promote hope, connectedness, social support, resilience, treatment, and recovery can fundamentally change the course for those who are struggling with thoughts of suicide. This priority will promote stories of those who have struggled, yet were resilient, found help or treatment, and established a stronger will to go on living. It will also promote the cultural norm of providing social support and connectedness for vulnerable individuals to fundamentally change the course for those who are struggling with thoughts of suicide.
- Increase the quality, timeliness, and usefulness of surveillance data regarding suicidal behaviors.

SOCIETY IN ACTION

MILITARY SUICIDES

The Army Study to Assess Risk and Resilience in Servicemembers (Army STARRS) is a research study dealing with suicide prevention. It is also one of the largest, most complex studies ever administered by the National Institute of Mental Health (NIMH).

Army STARRS was launched in July 2009 to address the Army's concern about the rising suicide rate among soldiers. In the past, the suicide rate for Army personnel was lower than that for the civilian population. Since 2002, however, the suicide rate among soldiers has risen, reaching record levels in 2007, and again in 2008 and 2009, before falling slightly in 2010. These numbers prompted the Army to partner with NIMH to address the issue. The collaboration also includes investigators from the Uniformed Services University of the Health Sciences, Harvard Medical School, University of Michigan, and University of California, San Diego.

In an effort to find risk and protective factors that affect soldiers' well-being, the Army STARRS team has created a secure database with more than 1 billion Army data records and 3,000 types of information. The team is analyzing the data while using surveys to gather new information. Researchers are collecting data from soldiers in the United States, Afghanistan, and installations around the globe.

A research study by lead researcher Michael Schoenbaum of NIMH examined the suicide and accident death rates in relation to basic sociodemographic and Army experience factors in the 975,057 regular Army soldiers who served between January 1, 2004 and December 31, 2009. This study found that the suicide rates increased during this time period, even among those who had never deployed, and also found that being deployed increased suicide risk for women more than it did for men. However, suicide risk still remained higher for deployed women than for deployed men.

Additionally, the study identified a correlation between demotion and suicide risk. The study found that soldiers who had been demoted in the past two years experienced increased suicide risk compared to those without such demotions. There was also increased risk in soldiers without at least a high school diploma compared to soldiers with similar or higher degrees. The data suggest that being male, white, or a junior enlisted rank put individuals at the highest risk of suicide.

For recent updates on the STARRS program, check out its website at http://www.nimh.nih.gov/health/topics/suicide-prevention/suicide-prevention-studies/the-making-of-army-starrs-an-overview.shtml.

Theoretical Explanations of Suicide

Attempts to explain why people commit suicide generally focus on two broad categories: psychiatric and sociological. Psychiatry theories assume that there is something wrong with the individual who commits suicide. Sociological theories assumed that there is nothing wrong with the person who commits suicide. To the psychiatrist, the individual who commits suicide generally has some form of mental illness. And thus mental illness is considered the causation factor in suicides. Some psychiatrists use the classical Freudian concept of the death instinct to explain suicide and attribute suicides to a breakdown of the ego defenses. It is this breakdown that drives individuals to commit suicide.

Durkheim

Any discussion on the sociological theories of suicide begins with Emile Durkheim. Durkheim saw two major causes of suicide: social integration and social regulation. Durkheim's theory, although developed in the 1800s, is still the most influential theory on the sociological causation of suicide.

Social integration as used by Durkheim involves individuals voluntarily attaching themselves to a societal group of which they become members. Social regulation, on the other hand, involves individuals being restrained, constrained, or controlled by a group or to the societal group to which they belong. Durkheim opined that people who experience either too little social integration or too much social integration are more likely to commit suicide than those who experience modern integration. Likewise, those who are subject to too little social regulation or too much regulation are more likely to commit suicide.

Durkheim classified suicides in four different types: egoistic suicide, altruistic suicide, anomic suicide, and fatalistic suicide. Egoistic suicide is caused by too little social integration. Altruistic suicide is brought about by overintegration. Anomic suicide is caused by too little social regulation, whereas fatalistic suicide is caused by too much regulation.

According to Durkheim, an unmarried individual is more likely to commit egoistic suicide because he or she is less socially integrated. Members of a close-knit terrorist group are more likely to commit altruistic suicide by committing acts such as suicide bombing because they are more integrated into the group. More developed countries tend to have higher rates of anomic suicides than undeveloped countries because the individuals in the higher developed countries expect more from life, and are thus more likely to feel frustrated, and they are less socially regulated. According to Durkheim, in ancient times slaves were more likely to commit fatalistic suicide because they were more regulated and controlled.[11]

Andrew Henry and James Short

Andrew Henry and James Short updated Durkheim's theory on suicide. Henry and Short defined suicide as an act of aggression directed against oneself. They then listed three different factors for the self-directed aggression: sociological, psychological, and economic. Henry and Short considered that the sociological factor consisted of two parts: a weak relational system and weak external restraints. A weak relational system refers to a lack of involvement with other people, which is very similar to Durkheim's inadequate social integration. The weak external restraint condition is similar to Durkheim's inadequate social regulation. Henry and Short, like Durkheim, opined that individuals with higher socioeconomic status are more likely to commit suicide than those with lower economic status.

Henry and Short saw the superego as the psychological factor in suicides. They suggested that a strong superego produces a higher propensity to commit suicide. According to the researchers, individuals with a strong superego are more likely to blame themselves for their problems and frustrations. Accordingly, they are more likely to kill themselves than to kill others.

The researchers noted that suicide rates are higher during periods of a depressed economy and lower during periods of prosperity. Henry and Short noted that people, regardless of their economic status, tended to be depressed during an economic depression, and therefore individuals, regardless of their economic status, tended to commit suicide at a higher rate.[12]

Interpersonal–Psychological Theory of Suicidal Behavior

Thomas Joiner developed the interpersonal–psychological theory of suicidal behavior.[13] Joiner contends that in order to die by suicide, an individual must develop high levels of three specific variables:

- A sense of thwarted belongingness
- A perception of functioning as a burden on others
- The acquired capability for suicide

The first two variables, thwarted belongingness and perceived burdensomeness, comprise the desire for suicide. According to Joiner, evidence indicates that when individuals die by suicide, they often feel disconnected from others. This feeling can reflect a sense on the part of the individuals that nobody truly cares about them, or nobody can relate to them and understand their situation. The individuals have the feeling that they are intolerably isolated. The sense on the part of some individuals is that while others may care, they cannot relate to the individual's experience. Therefore, individuals may feel estranged from others who did not experience the same overwhelming events.

Perceived burdensomeness is generally driven by distorted automatic thoughts. Individuals experiencing elevations in this variable have the sense that they are not making any worthwhile contributions to their families or societies. They generally feel that they are liabilities, and that the family or others' lives would improve if they were dead.

Interpersonal Theory of Suicide

In 2010 several researchers developed the interpersonal theory of suicide to explain about suicide and to increase understandings of the etiology of suicide.[14] This theory is very similar to Joiner's interpersonal–psychological theory of suicidal behavior. The researchers wanted to more precisely delineate the interpersonal theory explained by Joiner.

The researchers noted that suicidal behavior is very difficult to understand because the base rates of suicide attempts and deaths are low in relationship to the general population. In addition, individuals with suicidal behaviors are often excluded from clinical trials due to safety concerns on the part of the researchers. They noted that few theoretical models have been offered to help understand self-injury in the manner that other manifestations of cycle pathology have been examined. In particular, they

SOCIETY IN ACTION

PEOPLE V. HOGG

2013 WL 6230844

Cal. App. 1 Dist., 2013

November 26, 2013

Below are excerpts from the testimony of the defendant in a case involving the crime of annoying or molesting a child under 18 years of age (California Penal Code 647.6).

Testimony of Defendant: The self-hatred led to years of self-destructive behavior that further fueled my emotional issues. By the time I reached the age of 23, I had been hospitalized eight times for intending to end my life. I didn't want to live anymore. I did not want to live anymore because I believed that I was a worthless person who did not deserve life. There's still many days that I go to sleep and hope that I won't wake up the following morning because I don't want to spend another day hating myself, but everyday gets a little bit easier as I continue to participate in therapy and support groups to work through the trauma.

I have spent thousands of dollars on therapy, medications, and hospitalizations. My sister and mother have entered therapy as well as a result of my downward spiral and attempts to end my life. I have been unable to maintain a full-time job or finish my undergraduate degree at the University of California, Santa Barbara. I have relied completely on the members of my family to provide for me financially during the past two years. My parents have also both had to take leave from their jobs at points in order to monitor me and provide transportation during the points when I was severely depressed.

noted that few studies have considered integrative models that address interplay between dynamic systems within the individual and between individuals and their environment. The researchers also concluded that the relatively low number of empirical advances in understanding the causes and correlates of suicide, as well as the methods for suicide prevention, may be caused by the absence of a theory that can comprehensively explain known facts about suicide. Reliable and precise identification of risk factors for future occurrences of suicidal behavior is also needed.

According to their theory, the most dangerous form of suicidal desire is caused by the simultaneous presence of two interpersonal constructs:

thwarted belongingness and perceived burdensomeness. The researchers also concluded that the third construct was the capability to engage in suicidal behavior. To them, the capability is separate from the desire to engage in suicidal behavior.

In referring to the thwarted belongingness, the researchers contend that social isolation is one of the strongest and most reliable predictors of suicidal ideation, attempts, and lethal suicidal behavior during the life span. Social isolation can be conceptualized as measuring one facet of the higher-order construct of social connectedness or social integration.

According to their theory, when the need to belong is unmet (thwarted belongingness), a desire for death develops. Perceived burdensomeness may occur because of family conflict, unemployment, and physical illness. They contended that an elevated likelihood of developing perceptions of their burdensomeness on others is a common thread that may be caused by family conflict, unemployment, and physical illness. In other words, the individual has the perception that the family would be better off without him or her. The perceived burdensomeness has two dimensions of interpersonal functioning: a belief that the self is so flawed as to be a liability on others, and affectionately laden cognitions of self-hatred, often expressed by the statement "I am useless" or "My family would be better off if I were dead."

According to the researchers, the feeling of not belonging and perception of burdensomeness are presumed to be distinct, but related constructs. They note that the construct of belongingness is not synonymous with a lack of human connections, and conversely, the need to belong is not fulfilled by the mere presence of connections to others.

Drugs and Alcohol Abuse

Alcohol Abuse

As most researchers will agree, alcoholism is a contributor to a wide range of illnesses and behaviors. According to the National Institute on Alcohol Abuse, about 7% of the American population has a drinking problem.[15] The institute states that alcoholism or alcohol dependence consists of four symptoms: craving, an inability to stop drinking once drinking has begun, withdrawal dependence, and tolerance.

Historically the consumption of alcoholic beverages has played a significant role in the patterns of everyday life in most societies. Alcohol fulfills a number of personal and social functions and includes numerous benefits to our social life. Its consumption, however, can be quite dysfunctional at both the personal and societal levels. In addition, it creates numerous social problems, including drunken driving, domestic violence, and extensive health problems.

Alcohol consumption was probably greater in the colonial era than it is today. It appears that during the colonial era, alcoholism was for the most part tolerated. By the late 18th century, many researchers concluded that alcoholism was not an evil, but a pathological, problem. By the end of the 19th century, the temperance movement had become quite active and viewed the consumption of alcohol as evil. This movement eventually resulted in the passage of the 18th Amendment to the U.S. Constitution.

Alcoholics Anonymous (AA) was founded in 1935. According to AA, the alcoholic must come to the realization that his or her life is unmanageable and turn it over to a higher power. AA uses a 12-step program as its long-term process of rehabilitation.

In recent years it appears that there has been a downward trend in heavy drinking. Heavy drinking is generally described as consuming five or more drinks a day. However, college binge drinking has remained steady despite prevention efforts by colleges and universities. There has been a slight decrease in binge drinking at the high school level.

War on Drugs

Any discussion on drug abuse probably should start with the war on drugs. This war was declared by President Richard Nixon on June 18, 1971 (Figure 5.1). President Nixon declared that drug abuse was public enemy number one. Over four decades later and many billions of dollars expended, the general consensus is that the war on drugs was a complete failure. The end result of the war on drugs is that the United States has become the world's largest market for illegal drugs.

The war on drugs treated drug abuse as a crime despite the fact that drug addiction is a disease that needs to be treated as a disease. Currently, individual states are modifying their drug abuse laws. Several states have legalized the medical use of marijuana even though it remains a federal crime.

The first federal law that restricted the distribution and use of certain drugs was the Harrison Narcotics Act of 1914. Prior to that, some states had passed state statutes that restricted the use and distribution of specified drugs as early as 1860. In 1919 the 18th Amendment to the U.S. Constitution was certified, and that amendment prohibited the sale or manufacture and transportation of alcohol for consumption. The 18th Amendment was repealed in 1933.

In 1930, the U.S. government established the Federal Bureau of Narcotics as a part of the Treasury Department. In 1935 President Franklin Roosevelt pushed for the adoption of a narcotics drug act. Later in 1973, the Drug Enforcement Administration was created and replaced the Federal Bureau of Narcotics. In 2008, it was reported that approximately 1.5 million Americans were arrested each year for drug offenses, and approximately one-third of them were incarcerated.[16]

Figure 5.1 President Richard M. Nixon, who declared the war on drugs in 1971. (Photo from Library of Congress Prints and Photographs Division, Washington, DC.)

In 2011, the Global Commission on Drug Policy noted that the global war on drugs had failed, with vast devastating consequences for individuals and societies around the world. The commission also stated that the emphasis on drug policy that focused on harsh law enforcement had not accomplished its goal and had in fact caused dramatic eruptions of violence.[17]

Some of the social-economic effects of the war on drugs include the creation of a permanent underclass of Americans and a cost to the taxpayers of billions of dollars. There is no easy solution to the drug abuse problem. One of the proposed alternatives includes legalizing drugs and treating drug abuse as a medical problem. There is no easy answer or solution to the dilemma. While the authors of this text are not proposing the decriminalization of drug abuse, they are concerned with the current approaches used by the governmental agencies.

Eating Disorders

Eating disorders are related to food consumption or nonconsumption. Eating disorders do not occur randomly in the population. Like other deviance issues, eating disorders tend to occur among certain groups. They are the most prevalent in females, especially those who are young and white.

According to the National Institute of Mental Health (NIMH), an eating disorder is an illness that causes serious disturbances to your everyday diet, such as eating extremely small amounts of food or severely overeating. A person with an eating disorder may have started out just eating smaller or larger amounts of food, but at some point, the urge to eat less or more spiraled out of control. Severe distress or concern about body weight or shape may also signal an eating disorder. Common eating disorders include anorexia nervosa, bulimia nervosa, and binge eating disorder.[19] Eating disorders frequently appear during the teen years or young adulthood, but may also develop during childhood or later in life.

Researchers have concluded that eating disorders are caused by a complex interaction of genetic, biological, behavioral, psychological, and social factors. Researchers are studying various combinations of genes to determine if any DNA variations are linked to the risk of developing eating disorders. According to the NIMH, neuroimaging studies are also providing a better understanding of eating disorders and possible treatments. One study showed different patterns of brain activity between women with bulimia nervosa and healthy women. Using functional magnetic resonance imaging (fMRI), researchers were able to see the differences in brain activity while the women performed a task that involved self-regulation (a task that requires overcoming an automatic or impulsive response).

Psychotherapy interventions are also being studied. One such study of adolescents found that more adolescents with bulimia nervosa recovered after receiving Maudsley model family-based treatment than those

SOCIETY IN ACTION

ARE OBESE WOMEN DISCRIMINATED AGAINST?

According to researchers Susan Averett and Sanders Korenman, there is a growing awareness of the social stigma attached to being overweight. There is evidence of labor market discrimination against obese women. Obese women have lower family incomes than women whose weight-for-height is in the recommended range. Results for men are weaker and mixed.[18] An unanswered question: Why are obese men discriminated against also?

receiving supportive psychotherapy that did not specifically address the eating disorder.

Researchers are studying questions about behavior, genetics, and brain function to better understand risk factors, identify biological markers, and develop specific psychotherapies and medications that can target areas in the brain that control eating behavior. Neuroimaging and genetic studies may provide clues for how each person may respond to specific treatments for these medical illnesses.

Anorexia Nervosa

Anorexia nervosa is an eating disorder characterized by severe food restriction, inappropriate eating habits or rituals, obsession with having a thin figure, and a fear of weight gain, as well as a distorted body self-perception. The disorder typically involves excessive weight loss and is diagnosed approximately nine times more often in females than in males.

Anorexia nervosa displays the following symptoms[20]:

- Extreme thinness (emaciation)
- A relentless pursuit of thinness and unwillingness to maintain a normal or healthy weight
- Intense fear of gaining weight
- Distorted body image, a self-esteem that is heavily influenced by perceptions of body weight and shape, or a denial of the seriousness of low body weight
- Lack of menstruation among girls and women
- Extremely restricted eating

According to the NIMH, treating anorexia nervosa involves three components:

- Restoring the person to a healthy weight
- Treating the psychological issues related to the eating disorder
- Reducing or eliminating behaviors or thoughts that lead to insufficient eating and preventing relapse

Bulimia Nervosa

Bulimia nervosa is an eating disorder resulting in binge eating and purging, or consuming a large amount of food in a short amount of time. Individuals with this disorder often have an extensive concern regarding their body weight. They generally have a feeling of a lack of control over these episodes. The binge eating is followed by behavior that compensates for the overeating, such as forced vomiting, excessive use of laxatives or diuretics, fasting, excessive exercise, or a combination of these behaviors.

Unlike anorexia nervosa, people with bulimia nervosa usually maintain what is considered a healthy or normal weight, while some are slightly overweight. But like people with anorexia nervosa, they often fear gaining weight, want desperately to lose weight, and are intensely unhappy with their body size and shape. Usually, bulimic behavior is done secretly because it is often accompanied by feelings of disgust or shame. The binge eating and purging cycle happens anywhere from several times a week to many times a day.[21]

Treatment options for binge eating disorder are similar to those used to treat bulimia nervosa. Psychotherapy especially has been shown to be effective. This type of therapy can be offered in an individual or group environment.

Eating Disorder Myths

- You can't tell if someone has a eating disorder by looking at him or her.
- Eating disorders do not discriminate; they affect males and females, young and old.
- You can't tell by someone's size whether they have an eating disorder.
- Families do not cause eating disorders—they can be patients' best allies in treatment.
- Both genetic and environmental factors influence eating disorders.
- Eating disorders are serious, biologically influenced mental illnesses, not passing fads.
- Complete recovery is possible.[22]

Self-Inflicted Violence

Why does a person cut, pierce, or mutilate his or her body? This question has been the subject of numerous medical and psychiatric studies. Some studies indicate that self-injury is a form of suicidal tendencies that require medical treatment or intervention. Other studies seem to indicate that the suicidal tendency theory should be discounted. A common criticism of the numerous studies on self-inflicted violence is that these studies are too judgmental and too closely tied to widely held notions of extreme violence or even evil. In addition, some studies have concluded that cutting is an aspect of renewal and restoration, while suicide is a compartmentalized event designed expressively for total destruction.[23]

Individuals who cut themselves do not appear to be a part of a unified group. The reasons frequently cited for engaging in self-injury practices are varied and highly complex. The studies do suggest substantial variations among the cutters in terms of function and form of cutting practices.

Self-injures are far more dynamic and diverse in their activities and reasons for engaging in their chosen form of deviance. Additional research in this area is vastly needed. In summary, there is no single accepted reason for self-inflicted injuries.

Poor Personal Health Habits

In discussing poor personal health habits, an interesting question arises: Are poor personal health habits deviant behavior? Since a good portion of Americans smoke, many are overweight, many are couch potatoes, and we tend to daily perform activities that are self-destructive to our health, it would appear that the behavior, while destructive, is not considered deviant because everyone is doing it, that is, if we define deviant as a deviation from the norm. For example, if the authors spend a significant portion of their day watching TV news, is that deviant behavior? It is certainly behavior that in the long run is self-destructive or, putting it a little milder, not healthful, but is it deviant?

Smoking

In the 1990s, the Texas prison system went tobacco-free. The system forbade smoking in any prison facility. By the end of 1998 in the prison underground market, the price of a cigarette on the illegal market was higher than the price of a marijuana reefer. The high demand for tobacco products indicates their addictive nature.

The history of smoking dates back to as early as 5000 BC. The ancient civilizations, such as the Babylonians, Indians, and Chinese, burnt incense as a part of religious rituals, as did the Israelites and the later Catholic and Orthodox Christian churches.

Cannabis smoking was common in the Middle East before the arrival of tobacco, and was a common social activity that centered on a water pipe called a hookah. Smoking, especially after the introduction of tobacco, was an essential component of Muslim society and culture and became integrated with important functions such as weddings and funerals, and was expressed in architecture, clothing, literature, and poetry. Smoking in the Americas probably had its origins in the incense burning ceremonies of shamans but was later adopted for pleasure, or as a social tool.[24]

Jean Nicot, from whose name the word *nicotine* was derived, introduced tobacco to France in 1560. From France tobacco spread to England. The first report of a smoking Englishman is of a sailor in Bristol in 1556, seen "emitting smoke from his nostrils." Tobacco, like tea, coffee, and opium, was originally used as a form of medicine.[25]

James Rolfe is considered the first colonial to raise tobacco as a cash crop. He started tobacco farming in 1612, six years after the settlement of

Jamestown. The demand quickly grew as tobacco, referred to as golden weed, revived the Virginia joint stock company from its failed gold expeditions. In order to meet demands from Europe, tobacco was grown in succession, quickly depleting the land. The depleted land motivated the settlers to move west on the new continent.

Smoking has been accepted in culture, in various art forms, and has developed many distinct, and often conflicting or mutually exclusive, meanings depending on time, place, and the practitioners of smoking. Cigarette smoking, which did not begin to become widespread until the late 19th century, has more associations of modernity and the faster pace of the industrialized world.

According to the World Health Organization, smoking is one of the leading causes of preventable death globally. In the United States about 500,000 deaths per year are attributed to smoking-related diseases, and a recent study estimated that as much as one-third of China's male population will have significantly shortened life spans due to smoking. Male and female smokers lose an average of 13.2 and 14.5 years of life, respectively. At least half of all lifelong smokers die earlier as a result of smoking.[26]

Is Sitting the New Smoking?

According to recent studies there are significant health risks of sitting at your desk for too long. Heart disease, diabetes, and certain types of cancers have all been shown in those individuals that lead a sedentary lifestyle. Studies are comparing sitting to smoking in terms of harm to overall health. In addition, many individuals spend hours at home sitting and watching television when they get home from work. Many researchers have concluded that we have become a culture of sedentary individuals.[27]

Killing Ourselves

A study by scientists at the U.S. Centers for Disease Control and Prevention (CDC) determined that avoidable behaviors like cigarette use, poor diet, and lack of exercise were the underlying cause of half of the deaths in the United States in the year 2000[28]:

- Tobacco: 435,000
- Inactivity and bad eating: 400,000
- Alcohol consumption: 85,000

Some of the reasons that the medical profession has assigned as the rationale for the self-destructive behaviors include the following:

- Innate human defiance
- Need for social acceptance

- Inability to truly understand the nature of risk
- Individualistic view of the world and the ability to rationalize unhealthy habits
- Genetic predisposition to addiction

You would think people were on a one-track mission to self-destruct rather than desiring immortality.

Diverse Lifestyles

In looking at the concept of diverse lifestyles, the first question we need to answer is: What is a diverse lifestyle? In today's present society, people tend to live a more varied lifestyle than in past decades. Does that make them deviant? Probably not. At one time homosexuality was considered by the vast majority of society as a diverse lifestyle. In recent years, however, societal views have either changed or are changing, and more and more people are accepting the concept that individuals involved with a homosexual lifestyle are no longer living in sin.

A dictionary definition of diverse lifestyles indicates that they are lifestyles that are different from the currently accepted mainstream lifestyles. Once a lifestyle is designated as diverse, the next question that needs to be asked is: Is it deviant? Do we as a society punish groups merely because they are different? It would appear that an additional element, that of harm to society or violation of moral codes, is necessary before a lifestyle can be labeled as deviant. As noted in Chapter 1, deviance generally describes actions that are behaviors that violate social norms, including formally enacted rules, as well as formal violations of social norms. We also learned that deviance can be relative to time and place because what is considered deviant in one social context may not be deviant in another.

During the 1960s, many individuals joined communes. Are communes where individuals share families, sex, and income deviant? To most of us, the answer would be yes. But that is based on our perceived "correct" norms of behavior. In a somewhat similar situation, being a part of a motorcycle gang would be considered by many groups as a deviant lifestyle.

Practicum

Some psychiatrists believe that for kids with emotional problems, self-injury has an effect similar to cocaine and other drugs that release endorphins to create a feel-good feeling. Assume that you are employed as a school nurse. A student you have treated has indicated that she has been thinking of cutting herself for the fun of it. What actions would you take?

Summary

- Self-destructive behavior includes destructive acts that harm the individual performing the harmful acts.
- The phrase "self-destructive deviance" is derived from objective psychology, wherein all apparent self-inflicted harm or abuse toward oneself is treated as a collection of actions, and therefore as a pattern of behavior.
- It is difficult to define what actions constitute self-destructive deviance. What behaviors sit within this definition?
- Suicide has been described as the ultimate act of self-destruction. Suicide is the willful taking of one's own life. Steven Stack estimates that there are 22.5 suicide attempts for every completed suicide.
- History indicates that males are four times more likely than females to commit suicide. Elderly or retired individuals, especially males, have the highest suicide rates per 100,000. Whites tend to commit suicide at twice the rate as blacks.
- The first sociologist, Emile Durkheim used his concept of anomie to explain suicides. He defined anomie as a state or condition that exists within people when a society evolves from a mechanical to an organic entity.
- According to Durkheim, suicide was not the result of psychiatric morbidity, but a result of factors external to the individual, basically inadequate ties to social groups.
- Why the large number of unsuccessful suicide attempts? Some researchers contend that unlike people who threaten suicide, people who attempt to commit suicide are ambiguous in their intent to die, whereas those who threaten suicide actually do not want to die.
- Really two types of people kill themselves, the depressed person and the highly impulsive person. The highly impulsive person who isn't really depressed, but is angry, is at risk for suicide. But in the impulsive person, what one sees is a history of impulsivity.
- In many states, it is not considered a crime for a person to attempt to commit suicide. But in almost all jurisdictions, it is considered a crime to assist another person to commit suicide.
- Attempts to explain why people commit suicide generally focus on two broad categories: psychiatric and sociological.
- Psychiatry theories assume that there is something wrong with the individual who commits suicide.
- Sociological theories assumed that there is nothing wrong with the person who commits suicide.
- Henry and Short saw the superego as the psychological factor in suicides. They suggested that a strong superego produces a higher propensity to commit suicide.

- According to the researchers, individuals with a strong superego are more likely to blame themselves for their problems and frustrations.
- As most researchers will agree, alcoholism is a contributor to a wide range of illnesses and behaviors. According to the National Institute on Alcohol Abuse, about 7% of the American population has a drinking problem.
- Any discussion on drug abuse probably should start with the war on drugs. This war was declared by President Richard Nixon on June 18, 1971. President Nixon declared that drug abuse was public enemy number one.
- Over four decades later and many billions of dollars expended, the general consensus is that the war on drugs was a complete failure.
- Eating disorders are related to food consumption or nonconsumption. Eating disorders do not occur randomly in the population.
- Like other deviance issues, eating disorders tend to occur among certain groups. They are the most prevalent in females, especially those who are young and white.
- Why does a person cut, pierce, or mutilate his or her body? This question has been the subject of numerous medical and psychiatric studies.
- In summary, there is no single accepted reason for self-inflicted injuries.
- In discussing poor personal health habits, an interesting question arises: Are poor personal health habits deviant behavior?
- Since a good portion of Americans smoke, many are overweight, many are couch potatoes, and we tend to daily perform activities that are self-destructive to our health, it would appear that the behavior, while destructive, is not considered deviant because everyone is doing it.
- In looking at the concept of diverse lifestyles, the first question we need to answer is: What is a diverse lifestyle? In today's present society, people tend to live a more varied lifestyle than in past decades. Does that make them deviant? Probably not.

Questions in Review

1. Should it be a crime to assist someone who is terminally ill to commit suicide? Justify your answer.
2. Should unsuccessful suicide attempts be considered a crime?
3. Explain the interpersonal theory of suicide.
4. How did Durkheim explain suicide?
5. Is smoking a form of deviant behavior? Explain your answer.
6. What are the two major eating disorders?
7. Why do people engage in personal habits that are self-destructive?
8. Why do some individuals cut themselves?
9. Why do people smoke?

Key Terms

Anorexia nervosa: The eating disorder that is characterized by severe food restriction, inappropriate eating habits or rituals, obsession with having a thin figure, and a fear of weight gain, as well as a distorted body self-perception.

Bulimia nervosa: An eating disorder resulting in binge eating and purging, or consuming a large amount of food in a short amount of time.

Interpersonal theory of suicide: The theory that suicide is the outcome of the convergence of an intense desire to die due to a sense of not belonging and not wanting to be a burden on others, and the capacity for lethal self-injury.

Nonsuicidal self-directed violence: Behavior that is self-directed and deliberately results in injury or the potential for injury to oneself. There is no evidence, whether implicit or explicit, of suicidal intent.

Self-directed violence: This term encompasses a range of violent behaviors, including acts of fatal and nonfatal suicidal behavior, and nonsuicidal intentional self-harm (i.e., behaviors where the intention is not to kill oneself, as in self-mutilation).

Suicidal self-directed violence: Behavior that is self-directed and deliberately results in injury or the potential for injury to oneself. There is evidence, whether implicit or explicit, of suicidal intent.

Suicide: The willful taking of one's own life.

Suicide attempt: A nonfatal self-directed potentially injurious behavior with any intent to die as a result of the behavior. A suicide attempt may or may not result in injury.

Unacceptable Terms and Definitions

The CDC and the World Health Organization have recommended against using the following terms[29]:

Failed attempt: This terminology gives a negative impression of the person's action, implying an unsuccessful effort aimed at achieving death. Alternate terms: *suicide attempt* or *suicidal self-directed violence.*

Nonfatal suicide: This terminology portrays a contradiction. *Suicide* indicates a death, while *nonfatal* indicates that no death occurred. Alternate term: *suicide attempt.*

Parasuicide: Formally used to refer to a person's self-directed violence, whether or not the individual had intent to die. However, the World Health Organization is now favoring the term *suicide attempt*. Alternate terms: *nonsuicidal self-directed violence* or *suicidal self-directed violence.*

Successful suicide: This term also implies achieving a desired outcome, whereas those involved in the mission of "reducing disease, premature death, and discomfort and disability" would view this event as undesirable. Alternate term: *suicide*.

Suicidality: This terminology is often used to refer simultaneously to suicidal thoughts and suicidal behavior. These phenomena are vastly different in occurrence, associated factors, consequences, and interventions, and so should be addressed separately. Alternate terms: *suicidal thoughts* and *suicidal behavior*.

Suicide gesture, manipulative act, and suicide threat: Each of these terms gives a value judgment with a pejorative or negative impression of the person's intent. They are usually used to describe an episode of nonfatal, self-directed violence. A more objective description of the event is preferable, such as *nonsuicidal self-directed violence* or *suicidal self-directed violence*.

Endnotes

1. *People v. Heidgen*. 22 N.Y. 3d 259, 3 N.E. 3d 657 (N.Y., 2013).
2. Alex E. Crosby, LaVonne Ortega, & Cindi Melanson. (2011). *Self-directed violence surveillance: Uniform definitions and recommended data elements* (Version 1.0). Atlanta, GA: Centers for Disease Control and Prevention, National Center for Injury Prevention and Control.
3. Steven Stack. (2011). Suicide as deviant behavior. In Clifton Bryant (Ed.), *The Routledge handbook of deviant behavior* (pp. 313–320). London: Routledge.
4. Centers for Disease Control and Prevention web page. http://www.cdc.gov/violenceprevention/pdf/bullying-suicide-translation-final-a.pdf. Retrieved June 1, 2014.
5. Cliff Roberson & Harvey Wallace. (1998). *Introduction to criminology*. Incline Village, NV: Copperhouse.
6. Karen Weintraub. (2014, June 12). Recession tied to suicide rise. *USA Today*, p. 4A, column 2-4.
7. Stack, 2011.
8. Centers for Disease Control and Prevention website. http://www.cdc.gov/Features/PreventingSuicide. Retrieved May 30, 2014.
9. Centers for Disease Control and Prevention website. http://www.cdc.gov/Features/PreventingSuicide. Retrieved May 30, 2014.
10. National Strategy for Suicide Prevention website. http://actionalliance forsuicideprevention.org/nssp. Retrieved June 1, 2014.
11. Emil Durkheim. (1897). *Suicide*. New York: Free Press.
12. Andrew Henry & James Short. (1954). *Suicide and homicide*. New York: Free Press.
13. Michael Anestis. (2009). Joiner's interpersonal-psychological theory of suicidal behavior. Posted on Psychotherapy Brownbag website. http://www.psychotherapybrownbag.com/psychotherapy_brown_bag_a/2009/03/joiners-interpersonalpsychological-theory-of-suicidal-behavior.html. Retrieved June 1, 2014.
14. Kimberly A. VanOrden, Tracy K. White, Kelly C. Cukrowicz, Scott Braithwaite, Edward A. Selby, & Thomas E. Joiner Jr. 2010. The interpersonal theory of suicide. *Psychological Review*, *117*(2), 575–600.

15. National Institute on Alcohol Abuse and Alcohol Dependence. (2000). *Alcohol and health: Tenth special report to the U.S. Congress*. Rockville, MD: NIAAA.
16. George F. Will. (2009, October 29). A reality check on drug use. *Washington Post*, p. A19.
17. George P. Shultz & Paul A. Volcker. (2011, June 11). A real debate about drug policy. *Wall Street Journal*.
18. Susan Averett & Sanders Korenman. (1993). *The economic reality of the beauty myth*. Working Paper 4521. Cambridge, MA: National Bureau of Economic Research.
19. National Institute of Mental Health web page. http://www.nimh.nih.gov/health/topics/eating-disorders/index.shtml. Retrieved May 30, 2014.
20. National Institute of Mental Health web page.
21. Ibid.
22. Cynthia M. Bulik. (2014, February 7). Eating disorders essentials: Replacing myths with realities. Presented at the NIMH Alliance for Research Progress Winter Meeting, Rockville, MD.
23. Jimmy D. Taylor. (2013). Cutting, piercing, and self-mutilation. In Clifton D. Bryant (Ed.), *The Routledge handbook of deviant behavior* (pp. 305–320). London: Routledge.
24. Iain Gately. (2003). *Tobacco: A cultural history of how an exotic plant seduced civilization*. New York: Grove Press.
25. John Mitchinson & John Lloyd. (2006). *The book of general ignorance*. London: Faber and Faber.
26. World Health Organization. (2008). *WHO report on the global tobacco epidemic 2008: The MPOWER package*. Geneva: World Health Organization.
27. Henry More. Is sitting the new smoking? http://www.philly.com/philly/blogs/sportsdoc/Is-sitting-the-new-smoking.html#xxf8MVpbjPa6sORr.99. Retrieved May 30, 2014.
28. Ali H. Mokdad, James S. Marks, Donna F. Stroup, & Julie L. Gerberding. (2004, March 10). Actual causes of death in the United States, 2000. *Journal of the American Medical Association*, *291*(10), 1238–1245.
29. Alex E. Crosby et al., 2011.

chapter six

Family Violence and Deviance

Chapter Objectives

What you should know and understand after studying this chapter:

- What constitutes family violence
- The leading theories on the causes of family violence
- Who does the battering
- Issues involving dating violence
- Law enforcement response to family violence

Introduction

Domestic violence is one of the most chronically underreported crimes.

In this chapter, we will explore family violence and deviance. Another name for family violence is domestic violence. As noted by Wallace and Roberson, family violence is a relatively new discipline in the United States.[1]

According to Sue Schuerman, incidents of domestic violence occur against women in the United States at epidemic rates, and up to 60% of all married women suffer physical abuse at the hands of their spouses at some time during marriage. The fact that police officers spend more time responding to domestic disturbances than to murders, rapes, and aggravated assaults reflects the pervasiveness of this problem (Figure 6.1).[2]

Some of the concepts and issues that the reader should be acquainted with regarding family violence include the following:

- It is difficult to define and agree on what constitutes family violence.
- There are mandatory reporting laws in all jurisdictions on child abuse. Should there be similar such laws on family violence issues?
- Proposed intervention strategies for dealing with family violence vary widely, and many are contradictory.
- The Violence Against Women Act, as reauthorized, has been a fundamental tool in the fight against family violence. It no longer protects just women; as currently reauthorized, the act is gender-neutral.

Figure 6.1 A 1909 photo of an 11-year-old boy who had been selling newspapers since he was 7 years old. He sold until 10:00 p.m. each day. His paper boss reported that the boy had shown him the marks on his arm where his father had bitten him for not selling more papers. (Photo from Library of Congress Prints and Photographs Division, Washington, DC.)

Family violence includes intimate partner violence, domestic abuse, and intimate partner abuse. Domestic violence is any form of maltreatment that takes place in a heterosexual or homosexual romantic relationship between adults or adolescents. Domestic abuse occurs with couples of all races, religions, social economic status, and sexual orientations. The risk factors that contribute to the likelihood of men or women becoming domestic violence victims or abusers include poverty, lack of a high school education, witnessing family violence as a child, attitudes of male domination, and substance abuse, especially alcohol abuse.

Relationship Violence

Relationship violence is a term used to include physical, sexual, and psychological abuse and stalking committed by one partner against the other in an intimate relationship. While relationship violence may involve both genders, since women are victimized more often and sustain more severe injuries than men, relationship violence is generally considered as violence against women. Relationship violence includes, but is not limited

SOCIETY IN ACTION

DATA FROM THE NATIONAL CRIME VICTIMIZATION SURVEY (NCVS), 2003–2012

- Domestic violence accounted for 21% of all violent crime.
- Intimate partner violence (15%) accounted for a greater percentage of all violent victimizations than violence committed by immediate family members (4%) or other relatives (2%).
- Current or former boyfriends or girlfriends committed most domestic violence.
- The majority of domestic violence was committed against females (76%) compared to males (24%).
- A similar percentage of violence by intimate partners and immediate family members was reported to police (56% each). An estimated 49% of violence by other relatives was reported to police.
- Most domestic violence (77%) occurred at or near the victim's home. Intimate partner violence resulted in injuries more often than violence perpetrated by immediate family members and other relatives.
- A weapon was involved in a larger percentage of violence committed by other relatives (26%) than intimate partners (19%) and immediate family members (19%).

Source: Jennifer L. Truman & Rachel E. Morgan, Special Report: Nonfatal Domestic Violence, 2003–2012, NCJ 244697, U.S. Department of Justice, Bureau of Justice Statistics, Washington, DC, April 2014.

to, acts committed by family members against other family members, so it may also fall within the topics examined in the field of family violence. Specifically excluded from relationship violence are acts committed by parents or other adult family members against children or elderly persons (i.e., child maltreatment and elder abuse, respectively) (Figure 6.2).

Myths About Family Violence

There are many myths and misconceptions about the discipline. A few are as follows:

- *Only males in the lower socioeconomic class are involved in domestic violence.* Anyone can be victimized by domestic violence. Victims can be of any age, sex, race, culture, religion, sexual orientation, education, employment, or marital status. Although both men and

Figure 6.2 An 1891 photo shows a child huddled on a door stoop in New York City wearing ragged clothing. (Photo from Library of Congress Prints and Photographs Division, Washington, DC.)

women can be abused, most domestic violence is committed against women by their male partners or ex-partners.

- *Contrary to popular belief, domestic violence is not caused by stress, mental illness, alcohol, or drugs.* The causes of domestic violence are the abusers' choices to act violently and control their intimate partners.
- *Domestic violence only happens to poor women and women of color.* Domestic violence happens in all kinds of families and relationships.

SOCIETY IN ACTION

DOMESTIC VIOLENCE ACCOUNTED FOR ABOUT A FIFTH OF ALL VIOLENT VICTIMIZATIONS BETWEEN 2003 AND 2012

Between 2003 and 2012:

- The majority of domestic violence was simple assault (64%), compared to serious violence (36%).
- Most domestic violence (77%) occurred at or near the victim's home.
- Intimate partner violence (48%) resulted in injuries more often than violence perpetrated by immediate family members (37%) and other relatives (26%).
- A weapon was involved in a larger percentage of violence committed by other relatives (26%) than intimate partners (19%) and immediate family members (19%).
- Rates of domestic violence were highest for persons ages 18 to 24 (11.6 victimizations per 1,000 persons) and lowest for persons age 65 or older (0.6 per 1,000).
- Non-Hispanic persons of two or more races (16.5 victimizations per 1,000 persons age 12 or older) and non-Hispanic blacks (4.7 per 1,000) had the highest rates of intimate partner violence, compared to non-Hispanic whites (3.9 per 1,000), Hispanics (2.8 per 1,000), and non-Hispanic persons of other races (2.3 per 1,000).

Source: Office of Justice Programs website, http://www.bjs.gov/index.cfm?ty=pbdetail&iid=4984, retrieved June 8, 2014.

Persons of any class, culture, religion, sexual orientation, marital status, age, and sex can be victims or perpetrators of domestic violence.

- *Domestic violence is a personal problem between a husband and a wife.* Domestic violence affects everyone. About one in three American women have been physically or sexually abused by a husband or boyfriend at some point in their lives.
- *If it were that bad, she would just leave.* There are many reasons why women may not leave. Not leaving does not mean that the situation is okay or that the victim wants to be abused. Leaving can be dangerous. The most dangerous time for a woman who is being abused is when she tries to leave.

Intimate Partner Violence

Intimate partner violence (IPV) is defined to include physical violence, sexual violence, stalking, and psychological aggression, including coercive tactics, committed by a current or former intimate partner. The violence may occur among cohabitating or noncohabitating romantic or sexual partners and among opposite or same-sex couples. IPV is considered a major public health problem with serious long-term physical and mental health consequences, as well as significant social and public health costs.

A number of studies have established that beyond injury and death, victims of IPV are more likely to report a range of negative mental and physical health conditions that are both acute and chronic in nature. Victims of IPV are more likely to smoke, engage in heavy/binge drinking, engage in behaviors that increase the risk of HIV, and endorse other unhealthy behaviors.

The recent studies have increased our understanding of the biologic response to acute and chronic stress that links IPV with negative health conditions. In addition, elevated health risks have been observed in relation to multiple body systems, including the nervous, cardiovascular, gastrointestinal, genitourinary, reproductive, musculoskeletal, immune, and endocrine systems.[3]

In a 2014 publication, the National Center for Injury Prevention and Control, Centers for Disease Control and Prevention reported the following findings[4]:

- Nearly 1 in 10 women in the United States (9.4%) has been raped by an intimate partner in her lifetime, including completed forced penetration, attempted forced penetration, or alcohol/drug-facilitated completed penetration.
- An estimated 16.9% of women and 8.0% of men have experienced sexual violence other than rape (being made to penetrate an intimate partner, sexual coercion, unwanted sexual contact, and noncontact unwanted sexual experiences) by an intimate partner in their lifetime.
- Women and men experienced many types of physical violence, ranging from being slapped to having a knife or gun used against them.
- Women had a significantly higher lifetime prevalence of stalking by an intimate partner (10.7%) than men (2.1%).
- Approximately one in four women and nearly one in seven men in the United States have experienced severe physical violence by an intimate partner at some point in their lifetime.
- More than 4 in 10 lesbian women, 6 in 10 bisexual women, and 1 in 3 heterosexual women have experienced rape, physical violence, or stalking by an intimate partner during their lifetime.

SOCIETY IN ACTION

THE VIOLENCE AGAINST WOMEN REAUTHORIZATION ACT OF 2013

The Violence Against Women Act (VAWA) is the foundation of the nation's response to domestic and sexual violence. The bill was first enacted in 1994. The latest reauthorization was signed into law on March 7, 2013.[5]

The 2013 version of VAWA reauthorized and improved upon lifesaving services for all victims of domestic violence, sexual assault, dating violence, and stalking, including Native women, immigrants, LGBT victims, college students and youth, and public housing residents. VAWA authorized appropriate funding to provide for VAWA's important programs and protections.

Key aspects of the act include

- Prior to the revision, Native American victims of domestic violence often could not seek justice because the tribal courts were not allowed to prosecute non-Native offenders—even for crimes committed on tribal land. VAWA 2013 included a provision that gives tribal courts the authority they need to hold offenders in their communities accountable.
- VAWA expanded protections against unjust evictions to individuals in all federally subsidized housing programs, explicitly protects victims of sexual assault, and created emergency housing transfer options.
- VAWA revisions added additional protections for students by requiring schools to implement a recording process for incidences of dating violence, as well as report the findings. In addition, schools are required to create plans to prevent this violence and educate victims on their rights and resources.
- Lesbian, gay, transgender, and bisexual survivors of violence experience the same rates of violence as straight individuals; however, they sometimes faced discrimination when seeking help and protection. VAWA prohibited such discrimination to ensure that all victims of violence have access to the same services and protection to overcome trauma and find safety.
- The revised VAWA provides important protections for immigrant survivors who are abused, while making key improvements to existing provisions, including strengthening the International Marriage Broker Regulation Act and the provisions around self-petitions and visas.

SOCIETY IN ACTION

UNITED STATES V. MORRISON

529 U.S. 598 (2000)

The original Violence Against Women Act, passed in 1994, provided a federal civil remedy for the victims of gender-motivated violence. Under the Act, a woman could sue her violator in federal civil court.

Former university student at Virginia Polytechnic Institute filed a federal civil claim under Violence Against Women Act (VAWA) against students who allegedly raped her. The United States District Court for the Western District of Virginia dismissed her claims. The student appealed. The Fourth Circuit Court of Appeals affirmed the dismissal. The Supreme Court upheld the dismissal and held that

(1) Commerce Clause did not provide Congress with authority to enact civil remedy provision of VAWA, inasmuch as provision was not regulation of activity that substantially affected interstate commerce, and
(2) enforcement clause of Fourteenth Amendment did not provide Congress with authority to enact provision.

The Court noted that every law enacted by Congress must be based on one or more of its powers enumerated in the U.S. Constitution. The powers of the legislature are defined and limited; and that those limits may not be mistaken or forgotten, the Constitution is written. Due respect for the decisions of a coordinate branch of government demands that the Supreme Court invalidate a congressional enactment only upon a plain showing that Congress has regulatory authority under the Commerce Clause is not without effective bounds.

The scope of the interstate commerce power must be considered in the light of our dual system of government and may not be extended so as to embrace effects upon interstate commerce so indirect and remote that to embrace them, in view of our complex society, would effectually obliterate the distinction between what is national and what is local and create a completely centralized government.

There are three broad categories of activity that Congress may regulate under its commerce power: first, Congress may regulate the use of the channels of interstate commerce; second, Congress is empowered to regulate and protect the instrumentalities of interstate commerce, or persons or things in interstate commerce, even though the threat may come only from intrastate activities; and, finally, Congress' commerce authority includes the power to regulate those activities having a substantial relation to interstate commerce, i.e., those activities that substantially affect interstate commerce.

Commerce Clause did not provide Congress with authority to enact civil remedy provision of Violence Against Women Act (VAWA), inasmuch as provision was not regulation of activity that substantially affected interstate commerce; gender-motivated crimes of violence were not economic activity, provision contained no jurisdictional element establishing that federal cause of action was in pursuance of Congress' power to regulate interstate commerce, and, although Congress made findings regarding impact of gender-motivated violence on victims and their families, such findings were based on unworkable "but-for" reasoning.

Congress may not regulate noneconomic, violent criminal conduct based solely on that conduct's aggregate effect on interstate commerce; the Constitution requires a distinction between what is truly national and what is truly local.

Petitioner filed suit, alleging that she was raped by respondents who were students at Virginia Polytechnic Institute, and that this attack violated 42 U.S.C. § 13981, which provides a federal civil remedy for the victims of gender-motivated violence. Respondents moved to dismiss on the grounds that the complaint failed to state a claim and that § 13981's civil remedy is unconstitutional. The United States intervened to defend the section's constitutionality. In dismissing the complaint, the District Court held that it stated a claim against respondents, but that Congress lacked authority to enact § 13981 under either the Commerce Clause or § 5 of the Fourteenth Amendment, which Congress had explicitly identified as the sources of federal authority for § 13981. The Fourth Circuit affirmed.

The Court upheld the decision by the United States Court of Appeals for the Fourth Circuit. The Court of Appeals had held that § 13981 was unconstitutional because Congress lacked the authority to enact the section's civil remedy noted. Section 42 U.S.C. § 13981 provided a federal civil remedy for the victims of gender-motivated violence.

Notes: Associate Supreme Court Justices David Souter, John Paul Stevens, Ruth Bader Ginsburg, and Stephen Breyer dissented in this 5-4 decision by the court.

The case holding that the civil remedy section was unconstitutional did not affect the remaining provisions of the VAWA.

- Men and women with a lifetime history of rape, physical violence, or stalking by an intimate partner were more likely to report frequent headaches, chronic pain, difficulty sleeping, activity limitations, and poor physical health in general than those without a history of these forms of IPV. Women who have experienced these forms of violence were also more likely to report asthma, irritable bowel syndrome, diabetes, and poor mental health than women who did not experience these forms of violence.

Why Is Family Violence So Common?

The National Council on Child Abuse and Family Violence (NCCAFV) attempts to answer the question as to why family violence is so common. According to the NCCAFV, the roots of family violence are embedded in attitudes toward women that have existed for hundreds of years. Even today there are numerous societies where a woman is treated as the property of her husband, and he is seen as having the right to use physical force in relating to her, if necessary. Although not spoken aloud, there are segments in our American society where this attitude still exists.[6]

As noted by the NCCAFV, the causes of family violence, as with most social problems, are many and sometimes complex. Factors that keep acts of family violence from being recognized as a crime include the following:

- A lack of understanding that verbal and physical violence are learned behaviors, often learned from role models such as parents, relatives, or friends
- A lack of understanding that violence in relationships is often used as a way to reduce emotional stress, as a defense mechanism, or as a way to maintain control in the relationship
- A lack of recognition that there is a high correlation between alcohol and substance abuse and domestic violence
- Continual exposure to violent behavior in entertainment, sports, and the media
- Reinforcement of sexual roles condoning aggressive and violent behavior by males
- A lack of public awareness regarding the severity of the problem, with many still believing it is a private matter within the family instead of a criminal issue, and therefore best left alone

Who Are the Victims of Family Violence?

There is no single profile of a family violence or domestic abuse victim. Men, women, and children are victims. The victims range in age from the very young to the very old. For the most part, however, the battered victim

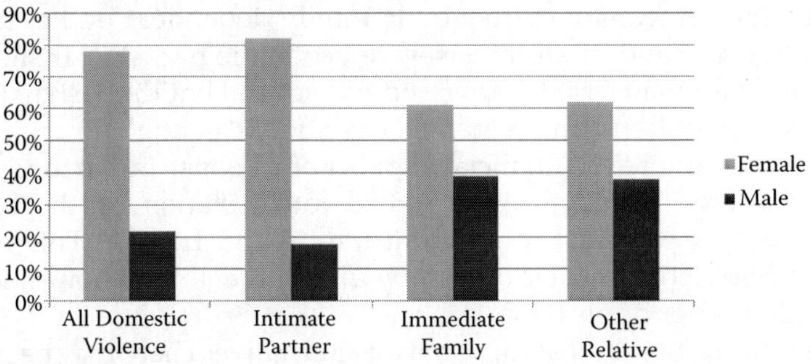

Figure 6.3 Victim–offender relationships in domestic violence victimizations, by victim's sex, 2003–2012. (Authors' compilation based on Bureau of Justice Statistics, National Crime Victimization Survey, 2003–2012; Truman, J. L., and Morgan, R. E., Special Report: Nonfatal Domestic Violence, 2003–2012, NCJ 244697, U. S. Department of Justice, Bureau of Justice Statistics, 2014.)

is a woman. The NCCAFV has identified, on its web page, some common characteristics that victims of spouse/partner abuse share. Men are rarely thought of as being victims of spouse/partner abuse and are less willing to report if they are being abused. Therefore, it is more difficult to determine the extent of male victimization in spouse/partner abuse.

Spouse/partner abuse may be considered a gender-neutral issue in rare instances when men suffer abuse at the hands of a spouse. However, the number of such cases, although no less important, is extremely small when compared to the number of women who suffer this type of abuse at the hands of a male. Figure 6.3 depicts the breakdown of domestic violence cases by gender.

The common characteristics include the following:

- Battered victims come from all sectors of society, from every social, economic, religious, and racial group.
- Victims come from all walks of life and from all lifestyles.
- Battered victims often feel degraded and worthless.
- A battered victim's lack of positive self-esteem may keep her or him from telling anyone about the abuse. She or he may fear being seen as a failure as a wife and mother or husband and father. Worse yet, the victim may believe he or she deserves the mistreatment.
- A battered victim may have been brought up to believe that there is a duty to keep the family together, no matter what the cost. The victim will therefore endure the abuse for the sake of the children or the family, often leaving only when the violence is directed at them.
- A battered victim may not reveal the abuse because of the belief that society generally ignores domestic violence, or that the victim will be blamed for provoking or accepting the violence.

- A battered woman is frequently totally dependent on her husband financially and often faces severe economic hardship if she leaves. If the victim married young and has several children, she may have few job skills to make her feel confident enough to support her family without the financial support of a spouse or partner.
- A battered victim is often forced into isolation by the battering spouse or partner, cut off from family and friends. This isolation further victimizes her or him by giving the abuser power and control over her or his life.
- For many victims leaving is not an alternative. There may be nowhere to go if few or no resources exist within the community to offer help.
- Battered persons frequently face the most physical danger when attempting to leave a domestic violence situation. The victim may be threatened with death or attacked if there are attempts to flee. Fearing for the person's safety and that of the children and those who may try to help the victim may cause the victim to endure the abuse in silence.
- It is important to remember that most victims want only the violence to end, not the relationship. When a victim of spouse/partner abuse leaves the home, it is often as a last resort, having previously tried many ways to stop the abuse.

What About the Batterer?

According to the NCCAFV, batterers, like victims of domestic violence, are found among all social, economic, racial, religious, and age groups. There is no typical batterer. Frequently, the batterer may exhibit one or more of the following characteristics:

- The batterer often denies the existence of violence and its effect on the victim and other members of the family.
- He or she often exhibits extreme possessiveness and jealousy, thus isolating the victim from family and friends.
- Batterers often refuse to accept responsibility for the abuse, blaming the behavior on stress, alcohol, drugs, or the victim.
- Frequently the batterer has grown up in a home where male dominance over women was modeled physically or verbally (or the reverse).
- He or she may believe in a traditional dominant sex role, or have developed a strong negative attitude toward women or men.

Why Batter?

This is no correct or simple answer to why one person batters his or her partner. We tend to think that the batterer is suffering some type of mental illness. While this is a natural response, most researchers in the area will disagree.

The following are some of the reasons given for the battering:

- It appears that in the vast majority of situations, battering is a learned behavior, not a mental disorder. There appears to be only isolated cases where mental illness is a part of the process.
- Many batterers were raised in a violent home where they witnessed the abuse of their mother, siblings, or perhaps were themselves a victim of childhood abuse. Wallace and Roberson discuss the "intergenerational transmission of violence and aggression." According to them, children who have been physically abused are more aggressive than children who have not been physically abused. In addition, they note that children raised in a violent home are more likely to become abusers than children raised in a nonviolent home.[7]
- Witnessing domestic violence in the childhood home is the most common risk factor for becoming a batterer in adulthood.
- The batterer has learned to use physical force as a way to maintain power and control in the relationship with his or her partner. Battering is the ultimate expression of a belief in the batterer's dominance over the battered.
- The batterer has learned to use physical violence as a means to handle anger, frustration, or guilt, and lacks the communication skills necessary to handle these emotions in nonviolent ways.
- The batterer generally has low self-esteem and low self-control, often displacing anger at a boss or self onto the spouse/partner and children.
- Frequently the batterer will experience some remorse after the battering and even seek forgiveness from the victim, promising it will never happen again. Such promises are rarely kept.
- Until recently there have been no consequences for the battering behavior.
- For the most part, acts of violence committed within the family, which would be considered assaults with penalties if perpetrated on a stranger, have gone unpunished.

Dating Violence

Dating violence is described as abusive and violent behavior that occurs in dating relationships. It happens in both heterosexual and same-sex relationships. It covers a wide range of behaviors that include verbal and emotional abuse, sexual abuse, and physical violence.

Researchers indicate that about one in four female college students will be raped at least once during their college career. Less than 5% of the completed rapes and 8% of the attempted rapes involved a stranger to the victim. The largest numbers of offenders, about one-third of the total number, were classified as classmates; friends accounted for almost another one-third, and boyfriends or ex-boyfriends accounted for about 24% of the rapes of the college women. Approximately 9% of high school students report being hit, slapped, or physically hurt on purpose by a boyfriend or girlfriend in the 12 months before surveyed.[8]

According to Centers for Disease Control and Prevention, the nature of dating violence can be physical, emotional, or sexual.[9] The violence includes

- Physical: This occurs when a partner is pinched, hit, shoved, slapped, punched, or kicked.
- Psychological/emotional: This means threatening a partner or harming his or her sense of self-worth. Examples include name calling, shaming, bullying, embarrassing on purpose, or keeping him or her away from friends and family.
- Sexual: This is forcing a partner to engage in a sex act when he or she does not or cannot consent. This can be physical or nonphysical, like threatening to spread rumors if a partner refuses to have sex.
- Stalking: This refers to a pattern of harassing or threatening tactics that are unwanted and cause fear in the victim.

Dating violence can take place in person or electronically, such as repeated texting or posting sexual pictures of a partner online. Unhealthy relationships can start early and last a lifetime. Teens often think some behaviors, like teasing and name calling, are a normal part of a relationship. However, these behaviors can become abusive and develop into more serious forms of violence.

Factors that increase risk for harming a dating partner include

- Belief that dating violence is acceptable
- Depression, anxiety, and other trauma symptoms
- Aggression toward peers and other aggressive behavior
- Substance use
- Early sexual activity and having multiple sexual partners
- Having a friend involved in dating violence
- Conflict with partner
- Witnessing or experiencing violence in the home

The Centers for Disease Control and Prevention (CDC) uses a four-step approach to address problems like dating violence[10]:

Step 1: Define the problem. Before we can prevent dating violence, we need to know how big the problem is, where it is, and who it affects. The CDC learns about a problem by gathering and studying data.

Step 2: Identify risk and protective factors. It is not enough to know that dating violence is affecting a certain group of people in a certain area. We also need to know why. The CDC conducts and supports research to answer this question.

Step 3: Develop and test prevention strategies. Using information gathered in research, the CDC develops and evaluates strategies to prevent violence.

Step 4: Ensure widespread adoption. In this final step, the CDC shares the best prevention strategies and may provide funding or technical help so communities can adopt these strategies.

What Causes Family Violence?

English common law during the 18th century recognized the right of husbands to physically discipline their wives. American common law in the early 19th century permitted a man to chastise his wife without subjecting himself to vexatious prosecutions for assault and battery, resulting in the discredit and shame of all parties concerned. At one time a husband was permitted to beat his wife so long as he didn't use a switch any bigger around than his thumb. In 1874 the Supreme Court of North Carolina nullified the husband's right to chastise his wife "under any circumstances." But the court's ruling became ambiguous when it added, "If no permanent injury has been inflicted, nor malice, cruelty, nor dangerous violence shown by the husband, it is better to draw the curtain, shut out the public gaze, and leave the parties to forgive and forget."[11]

In this section, we will examine some of the reported causes of family violence.

Intergenerational Transmission of Violence

The intergenerational transmission of violence theory was originally called the cycle of violence theory. It is a popular, yet controversial, explanation for explaining family violence. The theory asserts that violent behavior is learned within the family and passed from one generation to the next. There are several recent studies that indicate that the majority of abused children do not grow up to be abusers. While these studies question this theory of violence causation, they still note that a higher percentage of abusive parents were abused as children compared to the number of abusive parents who deny that they were abused as children.

According to the theory, children who are victims of child abuse or who witness violent aggression by one spouse against the other spouse will grow up and react to their children or spouses in the same manner. Thus, the childhood survivor of a violent family develops a predisposition toward violence in his or her own family. Accordingly, there is a never-ending chain of violence that is passed from one generation to the next.[12]

Social Stress

The stress theory states that though most people experience some level of stress, those individuals that lack resources and stable supports are more likely to turn to violence. The family system as it currently exists today is a set of contradictions. We retreat from the city streets and install locks and bars on our windows to keep out the violence. In so doing we secure one of the most violent settings a person is likely to encounter: the setting within the home. Family life has a different set of behaviors from all other social settings; how the family dresses and acts in a home is different from how they act when they attend social auctions and other public events. There is a significant amount of social stress within the dysfunctional family setting. Many researchers conclude that it is this social stress that causes family violence.

Strain Theories

The strain theories focus on negative interpersonal relations as a primary source of stress. According to the strain theorist, people are basically moral and desire to conform to society's laws. When an individual fails to conform to societal norms and commits acts such as those that occur in family violence situations, it is because there is excessive pressure or strain on the individual that causes him or her to commit those acts.[13]

Power

Power is generally defined as the ability to impose one's will on another and to make life decisions that affect others. When couples share power or are equals in the decision making, generally the decision making involves little or no violence or conflict. However, when there is an unequal balance of power in the relationship, there is a higher probability of family violence. In addition, most battered partners have reported a feeling of powerlessness.

Marital Dependency

The meaning of marital dependency has been subject to debate; generally it is used to mean economic dependency by one partner on the other partner. In many situations the female partner often has little or no earning power and is therefore dependent upon her male partner for the necessities of life. Marital dependency is a multifaceted concept that involves economic, emotional, and societal forces that result in one partner being dependent upon the other partner for support. This dependency often creates in the dependent partner a feeling of hopelessness and increases the partner's tolerance for physical abuse.

Alcohol

The relationship between alcohol use and family violence has been studied extensively, and there are several theories advanced regarding the relationship between alcohol and violence. The *disinhibition theory* is based on the principle that alcohol releases inhibitions and alters judgment. The *social learning and deviance disavowal theory* is based on the premise that individuals learn violence by observing others who drink can become violent, and that the violent behavior is excused, pardoned, or justified because the individual was drunk, and therefore not accountable for his or her actions. *Integrated theoretical models* are premised on the numerous factors that interact in alcohol and violence. These factors may include the inherent conflict present in marriage and societies that drinking is an acceptable and expected form of male behavior.

Generally the theories and studies on the relationship between alcohol and family violence have attempted to determine whether alcohol causes family violence. As many studies note, many people drink and yet do not commit family violence. Based on this aspect, many studies conclude that alcohol by itself cannot be defined as a cause of family violence.

Marriage

Straus and Gelles concluded that married couples suffer assaults at a much greater rate than strangers. The researchers stated that in many cases the marriage license is really a hitting license. They also noted that recent studies, however, indicate that unmarried cohabitating couples are involved in violence at a greater rate than married couples, and the violence tends to be more severe. Age could be a factor in this situation because dating and cohabitating couples tend to be younger than married couples.[14]

Straus and Gelles listed certain factors as having a direct impact on the degree of risk a woman faces in a cohabiting relationship. Those factors are

- **Isolation.** Couples who are living together may be more isolated than married couples. This may be because of the stigma that certain parts of society attach to cohabitation before marriage. It would appear that the stigma has disappeared or greatly reduced in today's society.
- **Anonymous and control.** Frequently people prefer cohabitation over marriage with the idea that they can retain their independence. However, the living arrangement brings with it duties, obligations, tensions, and resulting disagreements. Many researchers conclude that when the issue of control arises, violence occurs. In addition, it appears that as the relationship becomes more serious, the issue of control becomes more important, and thus violence is more likely to occur.

- **Investment in the relationship.** Frequently cohabitating couples share similar characteristics that trigger violence while lacking others shared by married couples. The absence of some triggers may stop the conflicts from escalating into physical violence.

Self-Control

According to Michael Gottfredson and Travis Hirschi, there is a lack of self-control in all forms of criminal activity. Persons who lack self-control tend to be impulsive, insensitive, physical, risk taking, shortsighted, and nonverbal. They also tend to engage in criminality and risk-taking behavior. According to the writers, often husbands and wives assault one another to simply end an explosive encounter. Therefore, an argument that neither side is willing to negotiate or to assert control over the person or the present situation ends in family violence. When self-control is weak, conflict between partners may erupt into acts of aggression or violence.[15]

Social Learning Theory

The social learning theorists consider factors that generate or cause deviant behavior. The theorists suggest deviant behavior involves four semirelated processes: differential association, definitions, differential reinforcement, and intimidation. Differential association refers to the interaction with persons who favor the violation of the law more so than with persons who advocate conformist behavior. According to this theory, the more an individual associates with individuals who use violence to solve problems, the more likely that individual will use violence in situations involving conflicts within the family. Accordingly, the abusive husband may use or condone the use of violence to keep the wife and children under control. The concept of definitions refers to meanings assigned to certain behaviors. In other words, what defines an act as acceptable or deviant determines whether the act will be routinely carried out in the home. Accordingly, if chastising the wife or partner is defined as acceptable behavior, then this action will be carried out in the home.[16]

Differential reinforcement is based on the concept of rewards and punishments. If an individual uses family violence to control his or her partner and there are no negative consequences, then the individual's use of violence has been reinforced. In addition, the use of family violence may be positively rewarded when the victim submits to the wishes of the abuser. If a wife submits to the wishes of her battering husband, she is reinforcing his behavior, and the acts of violence result in a favorable outcome for the batterer.

Feminist Theory

The feminist theorist focuses on the patriarchal structure of society to explain the violence of men toward their female partners. Male dominance is the key to understanding the victimization of wives and female cohabitants. The theorists argue that men have set expectations for the behavior of their partners. When the women fail to live up to those expectations, the men resort to violence to establish their position of dominance in the relationship. Frequently men learn to use physical force largely by participating in a violent male subculture. In other words, men resort to violence in order to exert coercive control over women. Not only does the violence result in male dominance, but it also establishes gender differences in the social relationship.[17]

Subculture of Violence

Marvin Wolfgang and Franco Ferracuti are credited with developing the subculture of violence theories. According to the researchers, families and neighborhoods that are characterized by norms and values that support the use of violence to settle interpersonal disputes are more likely to resort to violence to resolve family conflicts. Violent behavior is a learned response and an appropriate way to get what you want immediately or to control the behavior of other people.[18]

Psychopathological Theory

The psychopathological theory is based on the concept that certain individuals suffer from mental illness, personality disorders, and other dysfunctions that cause them to engage in aggressive acts within the family. According to this theory, the cause of family violence is that one or more members of the family suffer from some type of mental illness or other dysfunction. This theory is not widely accepted mainly because the large number of family violence cases would indicate that mental illness or other mental dysfunctions are very prevalent in today's society.

Sociocultural Model of Family Violence

The sociocultural model of family violence focuses on the roles of men and women in our society as well as the cultural attitudes toward women and the acceptance of violence as a cause of family violence. Under this theory family violence is an outgrowth of the cultural climate in our society and the roles that men and women play within the family. The theory also holds that our culture is responsible for many women accepting violence within the family.

Exchange Theory

The exchange theory notes that the potential punishment for engaging in family violence does not supersede the rewards of such actions, such as control over the victim. This theory states that people enter into relationships that are of direct benefit to the individual, and when that benefit is no longer viable, the relationship ends. The exchange theory can be applied to many forms of family issues, like how a partner is chosen, sexual bargaining, the quality of a marriage and who holds the power in the marriage, and the level of family violence.

Violence and abuse are used when the rewards (power, control, and domination) outweigh the cost (arrest, confinement, or the complete loss of the family) to that person, and if the behavior is an accepted part of cultures or ethnic groups that are poor and uneducated. Violence in society is related to many aspects of life: family background, social class, age, race, economic stress, and education levels.

Parent Abuse

When we think about abuse within the family, generally we tend to think about intimate partner, elder, or child abuse. There is a fourth type of family violence that is rarely discussed and has seldom been researched—parent abuse. Children, especially teenagers, can abuse their parents. The most obvious way is by physical abuse. Children can also abuse their parents emotionally by actions such as yelling, name calling, and throwing tantrums. The third way that children can abuse their parents is financially. They can steal money or other property, damage property, or conduct other actions that have a financial impact on the family.

Until recently, adolescent-to-parent violence was not officially defined as domestic violence if the adolescent was under the age of 18. The definition referred to any incidence of threatening behavior, violence, or abuse between adults aged 18 or over who are, or who have been, intimate partners or family members.[19] The first significant study on parental abuse was in 1979 by Harbin and Madden.[20] In their study, they coined the term *parent battery*. Studies indicate that the abuse generally starts with verbal abuse and then can escalate to physical violence and other forms.

Often, parents who are subject to parent abuse have a feeling of shame and humiliation, and therefore they rarely seek help or report the behavior. Generally young people who abuse their parents are between the ages of 12 and 24. There are reported cases of children younger than 10 years old abusing their parents. While children of both genders are involved, males are more often involved in physical abuse. In the reported cases, more frequently it is the female parent who is victimized. A 2013 English study of 1,896 cases reported in London indicated that 87% of adolescent perpetrators were male, 77% of victims were female, and 66% of cases involved a son-to-mother relationship. The English researchers concluded that adolescent-to-parent violence is clearly a gendered phenomenon.[21]

Generally when young people abuse their parents, we assume that it is caused by bad parenting, neglect, or from a child who has been abused. But in many cases, it appears that the abusing child had a normal upbringing and was not subject to abuse. Some of the causation factors attributed to parent abuse include the following:

- Out-of-control arguments
- Aggressive behavioral tenancies
- Breakdown of the family unit
- Poor or nonexistent relationship with an absent parent
- Lack of respect for parents
- Drugs
- Gangs or peer pressure
- Mental issues

Law Enforcement Response to Family Violence

Legal recourse against spousal abuse or family violence did not begin to take form until the late 19th century. In 1871, the Alabama Supreme Court delivered one of the first rulings that prohibited husbands from physically abusing their wives.[22] A Massachusetts court followed suit the same year, and in 1883, Maryland enacted the first law criminalizing spousal abuse.[23] Public sentiment toward domestic violence began to shift as well, due in part to the increasingly "companionate" conception of marriage as an institution.

Civil Protective Orders

Civil protection orders (CPOs) are civil remedies that provide protection to a victim of domestic violence by requiring the respondent to stay away from the petitioner. This protection is offered by statute in all 50 states, with most states having the option of issuing temporary or emergency protection orders, as well as permanent protection orders. To obtain an order, the victim petitions the court for a formal order that will prohibit the abuser from contacting the victim for a certain period of time. This provides the woman or man with the independence to decide whether she or he needs protection, as well as providing protection "whether or not the abuser will face criminal charges." Each state has its own procedure and requirements for obtaining a protection order, as well as variations in the relief, duration, and sanctions available.[24]

Most states require that the victim have a specific relationship with her abuser to qualify for the order. This relationship includes current and former spouses, family members related by blood, current or former household members, persons in or previously in intimate relationships, and individuals who have a child in common.

Civil protection orders are a leading tool in preventing the maltreatment of women in abusive relationships, offering an effective and low-cost solution to the hardship of domestic violence. These orders are designed to protect the victim of an abusive relationship, while also penalizing the perpetrator for his criminal actions.

Who Can Get a CPO?

Anyone who has been physically, emotionally, or sexually abused or threatened by someone they have been married to, lived with, have a child with, or dated can obtain a CPO. Some examples may include a current or former spouse, family member, partner, other parent of your child, current or former roommate, or current or former person you have dated.

Anyone who has been stalked can also obtain a CPO. Stalking is repeated harassment that makes you feel scared or upset. A stalker can be someone you know or a stranger. They often bother people by giving them attention they do not want. This can be unwanted phone calls or gifts, or following people by going to where they work or live. It can also be threats to you or your family.

Problem With CPOs

The problem with the current approach in using protective orders is that not all abusive relationships are one-sided, and while one partner may be considered the victim, there is often a more complex story, sometimes involving mutual abuse. A civil protection order is effective in the traditional model of abuse where there is one abuser and one victim; however, some abusive relationships involve mutual abuse and manipulation, which cannot be remedied in the same manner.[25]

Mandatory Arrests

Following the *Thurman* case, discussed later in this section, and the publication of an empirical study of the effects of mandatory arrest in domestic violence incidents, police departments began to look at mandatory arrests as a method to prevent or reduce domestic violence. The Minneapolis Domestic Violence Experiment in 1984 is considered one of the most rigorous studies of its kind and was the first controlled, randomized experiment in history on the use of arrest for any offense.

The experiment was funded by the National Institute for Justice and conducted by the Police Foundation. The study involved 314 incidents of domestic violence, each randomly assigned to one of three experimental conditions: mandatory arrest of batterers upon reasonable suspicion, counseling by officers, or temporary separation of the parties with the threat of arrest for future incidents. The results of the experiment were striking: "Arrest worked best." Arrest and a night in jail cut in half the risk of recidivism against the same victim over a six-month follow-up period.[26]

After the study was reported in *The New York Times,* the New York police commissioner issued orders that required mandatory arrest in domestic violence cases. The U.S. Attorney General also issued a report recommending that arrest be the standard law enforcement response to domestic violence cases. By the early 1990s, however, only seven states had passed mandatory arrest statutes for domestic violence.[27]

It was not until the infamous murder of Nicole Brown Simpson and the media firestorm it ignited that a majority of states enacted mandatory arrest laws. On June 12, 1994, Nicole Brown Simpson and Ron Goldman were found murdered on the walkway leading to Nicole's residence located at 875 South Bundy Drive in Los Angeles. Nicole had been stabbed multiple times and had a slash wound on her neck that went all the way to the spine. These brutal murders led many states to adopt the policy of mandatory arrest in domestic violence cases.

Mandatory arrest laws remove a police officer's discretion when called to an incident of intimate partner violence. The laws require that an officer arrest suspected abusers when there is probable cause to believe that abuse has occurred. Before mandatory arrest statutes were passed, many police officers felt that intimate partner violence was a private family problem that did not require the assistance of law enforcement.

Officers are not required to have seen the violence firsthand. Currently, 29 states mandate arrest when there is probable cause to believe that the batterer has violated a protective order. Twenty-one states and the District of Columbia mandate arrest in cases of domestic violence, regardless of whether a protective order has been violated. There is widespread public awareness of domestic violence. Intimate partner violence is no longer quarantined within the private sphere; it is considered a serious crime. Yet, despite these advances, domestic violence continues to be a pervasive and profound problem.[28]

As noted by Zelcer, mandatory arrest statutes are now widespread, but they are not universally beloved. Supporters of the statutes argue that such laws send a crucial societal message that intimate partner violence is unacceptable. Although the symbolic significance of these laws is certainly powerful, in operation, mandatory arrest statutes are both ineffective and injurious. Zelcer provides six arguments against mandatory arrest statutes[29]:

- The ineffectiveness of mandatory arrest on recidivism.
- The disempowerment of women.
- Increased arrests of women. It is noted that in the states with mandatory arrest laws, the rate of female arrests has risen from a range of 4% to 12%.
- Adverse effects on women with children.
- Discriminatory consequences for poor, minority, and immigrant women.
- Procedural challenges posed by mandatory arrest.

Zelcer argues that the *Castle Rock* decision (discussed later in this section) presents an opportunity to attack domestic violence from a different angle, rather than an occasion to further enshrine mandatory arrest statutes. She suggests a three-pronged strategy for effectively battling domestic violence: preferential arrest statutes, improved education of law enforcement officers regarding the seriousness of domestic violence, and mandatory treatment programs for batterers.

Zelcer contends that preferential arrest policies must be part of a more comprehensive effort to effectively tackle domestic and family violence. Another important component of the response to domestic violence is both the quantity and quality of training and education for police officers as well as dispatchers. Police officers serve as the gatekeepers to the criminal justice system. They are the most visible actors, and thus it is crucial that officers are prepared to respond effectively to calls of domestic violence and to enforce restraining orders.

According to Zelcer, the quality of law enforcement response to domestic violence has improved considerably over the last several decades. State legislatures have "done a service to the field" by including definitions of domestic violence in state statutes, providing consistency across departments. Additionally, the majority of police departments have written policies and procedures in place for how to respond to reports of domestic violence.

Zelcer notes that despite the drastic increase in the number of domestic violence arrests that have accompanied mandatory and preferential arrest statutes, arrest alone rarely deters further violence. She advocates that batterer treatment programs are also critical to effectively prevent recurring abuse. The goals of these treatment programs are victim safety as well as offender accountability and rehabilitation. To meet these goals, the programs use a variety of techniques and treatment plans to curb abusive behavior.

There are three major models of court-ordered batterer treatment programs: psychoeducational intervention programs known under the umbrella of the Duluth model, integrated treatment models that combine psychoeducational curriculum with mental health treatment, and individualized therapy programs.

The most common form of batterer intervention program is the Duluth model, which originated in Duluth, Minnesota. Parts of the well-respected Duluth model are incorporated in most treatment programs around the world. This program has also been adopted by most states. It is a psychoeducational intervention program that does not deal with men's individual psychological problems. Rather, it concentrates on sociocultural underpinnings of men's attitudes toward women, positing that patriarchal ideology, which encourages men to control their partners, causes domestic violence.

Numerous evaluations have been conducted to assess the efficacy of the Duluth model of batterer treatment. One such study found the Duluth model as implemented in the state of Florida to be generally successful at curbing recurrent violence among court-ordered participants. Individuals who completed the program were less likely to be arrested for domestic violence and scored higher on postassessments testing their knowledge of domestic violence. The partners of these individuals reported less physically abusive behavior. The study noted that power and control issues were still reported. And the self-awareness of violent behaviors did improve. Also, despite the reduction in violence for many participants, at least half of those who completed the program continued to engage in abusive behaviors.

Probably the biggest criticism of the Duluth model is that it tends to oversimplify the issue of family violence and offers a one-size-fits-all solution to the very complex issue of preventing family violence. Many critics are now calling for an integrated response that combines elements from the criminal justice system with educational and therapeutic methods.

The Duty of Law Enforcement to Come to the Rescue

In this section we will explore the duties of law enforcement officers and officials when a family violence situation occurs. To determine whether or not the officers have a duty to protect or rescue a victim, we need to look at leading cases: *Thurman v. City of Torrington* and *Castle Rock v. Gonzales*. Excerpts of both of these cases are presented in this section.

As you will note when you read the holding in the *Thurman* case, the court held that the police had a duty to intervene and prevent the family violence. However, in the *Castle Rock* case the court ruled that the officers had a degree of discretion as to whether or not to arrest the husband. In attempting to reconcile the two cases, in *Castle Rock* there appears to be

SOCIETY IN ACTION

THE DULUTH MODEL

In 1980 in Duluth, Minnesota, after a particularly brutal domestic homicide, the Duluth Domestic Abuse Intervention Project (DAIP) found that the community was willing to experiment with new practices to confront the problem of men's violence toward their partners. Organizers from DAIP negotiated with law enforcement agencies, the justice system, and human service providers to go beyond a superficial examination of the flaws in the system and committing to a comprehensive overhaul of the police, court, and human service system's response to these cases. The project argued for practices that would hold offenders accountable and place the onus of intervention on the community, not on the individual woman being beaten. Ensuring women's safety was the community's responsibility. Within a year policies and procedures were developed and a community experiment began.

The program attempts to coordinate the response of the many agencies and practitioners who respond to domestic violence cases in the community. The project involves community organizing and advocacy that examines training programs, policies, procedures and texts, intake forms, report formats, assessments, evaluations, checklists, and other materials.

When a woman being beaten by her husband calls 911, she dials into a complex community system, which often resolves cases based on institutional imperatives rather than making victim safety central. This reflects a historical tolerance for domestic violence, rather than the attitudes of individual practitioners. Negotiating common understandings among agencies lessens the negative impact of fragmented philosophies and responses on the victims of domestic violence. These understandings make central the victim's experience of violence and coercion and the ongoing threats to her safety.

The shared framework for community intervention is guided by practical questions: Who is doing harm to whom? How dangerous is this situation? Who needs protection? Community agencies include the communications center (911), police department, jail, prosecutor's office, sheriff's department, probation department, women's shelter, public health department, district bench, and several mental health agencies. With each agency, the goal is to make links between what individual practitioners do in a case and the overall effect of intervention. For more on the Duluth model, log on to http://www.duluth-model.org/.

SOCIETY IN ACTION

THURMAN V. CITY OF TORRINGTON

595 F. Suppl. 1521 (Conn. 1984)

Between early October 1982 and June 10, 1983, Tracey Thurman, a woman living in the City of Torrington, notified the police officers of the City of repeated threats upon her life and the life of her child made by her estranged husband, Charles Thurman. Her attempts to file complaints against her estranged husband were ignored or rejected by the police.

On May 6, 1983, Tracey filed an application for a restraining order against Charles Thurman in the Superior Court. The court issued a restraining order forbidding Charles Thurman from assaulting, threatening, and harassing Tracey Thurman. The police was informed of this order.

On May 27, 1983, Tracey Thurman requested police protection in order to get to the Torrington Police Department, and she requested a warrant for her husband's arrest upon her arrival at headquarters after being taken there by one of the unnamed defendant police officers. She was told that she would have to wait until after the Memorial Day holiday weekend and was advised to call on Tuesday, May 31, to pursue the warrant request.

On May 31, 1983, Tracey Thurman appeared once again at the Torrington Police Department to pursue the warrant request. She was then advised by one of the unnamed defendant police officers that Officer Schapp was the only policeman who could help her and that he was on vacation. She was told that she would have to wait until he returned. That same day, Tracey's brother-in-law called the Torrington Police Department to protest the lack of action taken on Tracey's complaint. Although the brother-in-law was advised that Charles Thurman would be arrested on June 8, 1983, no such arrest took place.

On June 10, 1983, Charles Thurman appeared at her residence in the early afternoon and demanded to speak to Tracey. Tracey, remaining indoors, called the police department asking that Charles be picked up for violation of his probation. After about 15 minutes, Tracey went outside to speak to her husband in an effort to persuade him not to take or hurt Charles Jr. Soon thereafter, Charles began to stab Tracey repeatedly in the chest, neck and throat.

Approximately 25 minutes after Tracey's call to the Torrington Police Department and after her stabbing, a single police officer arrived on the scene. Upon the arrival of the officer at the scene of the stabbing, Charles Thurman was holding a bloody knife. Charles then dropped the knife and, in the presence of the officer, kicked Tracey Thurman in the head and ran into the residence.

Charles returned from within the residence holding the child and dropped the child on his wounded mother. Charles then kicked Tracey in the head a second time. Soon thereafter, other officers arrived on the scene but still permitted Charles Thurman to wander about the crowd and to continue to threaten Tracey. Finally, upon approaching Tracey once again, this time while she was lying on a stretcher, Charles Thurman was arrested and taken into custody.

District Court's Decision

City officials and police officers are under an affirmative duty to preserve law and order, and to protect the personal safety of persons in the community. This duty applies equally to women whose personal safety is threatened by individuals with whom they have or have had a domestic relationship as well as to all other persons whose personal safety is threatened, including women not involved in domestic relationships. If officials have notice of the possibility of attacks on women in domestic relationships or other persons, they are under an affirmative duty to take reasonable measures to protect the personal safety of such persons in the community.

A police officer may not knowingly refrain from interference in such violence, and may not automatically decline to make an arrest simply because the assailant and his victim are married to each other. Such inaction on the part of the officer is a denial of the equal protection of the laws.

The court determined that such inaction on the part of the officers was a denial of the equal protection of the laws. And that the police could not claim that they were promoting domestic harmony by refraining from interference in a marital dispute. The court noted that research had conclusively demonstrated that police inaction supports the continuance of violence. There could be no question, the court concluded, that the city of Torrington, through its police department, had "condoned a pattern or practice of affording inadequate protection or no protection at all, to women who complained of having been abused by their husbands or others with whom they have had close relations." The police had, therefore, failed in their duty to protect Tracey Thurman and deserved to be sued.

Note: The court awarded Tracey Thurman $2.3 million in compensatory damages. Shortly after this court decision, the Connecticut legislature adopted a more comprehensive domestic violence law. In the 12 months after the new law took effect, the number of domestic violence assaults reported increased by 92%.

SOCIETY IN ACTION

CASTLE ROCK V. GONZALES

125 U.S. 417 (2005) (Excerpts)

Associate Justice Anthony Scalia delivered the opinion of the Court.

We decide in this case whether an individual who has obtained a state-law restraining order has a constitutionally protected property interest in having the police enforce the restraining order when they have probable cause to believe it has been violated.

The horrible facts of this case are contained in the complaint that respondent Jessica Gonzales filed in Federal District Court. (Because the case comes to us on appeal from a dismissal of the complaint, we assume its allegations are true.) Respondent Rebecca Gonzales alleges that the town of Castle Rock, Colorado, violated the Due Process Clause of the Fourteenth Amendment to the United States Constitution when its police officers, acting pursuant to official policy or custom, failed to respond properly to her repeated reports that her estranged husband was violating the terms of a restraining order.

Petitioner claims that respondent's complaint did not allege that she ever notified the police of her contention that her husband was actually in violation of the restraining order. The complaint does allege, however, that respondent showed the police a copy of the temporary restraining order (TRO) and requested that it be enforced. We may assume that this reasonably implied the order was being violated.

The restraining order had been issued by a state trial court several weeks earlier in conjunction with respondent's divorce proceedings. The order commanded him not to molest or disturb the peace of her or of any child, and to remain at least 100 yards from the family home at all times. On June 4, 1999, the state trial court modified the terms of the restraining order and made it permanent. The modified order gave husband the right to spend time with his three daughters (ages 10, 9, and 7) on alternate weekends, for two weeks during the summer, and, upon reasonable notice, for a midweek dinner visit arranged by the parties; the modified order also allowed him to visit the home to collect the children for such parenting time.

According to the complaint, at about 5 or 5:30 p.m. on Tuesday, June 22, 1999, respondent's husband took the three daughters while they were playing outside the family home. No advance arrangements had been made for him to see the daughters that evening. When respondent noticed the children were missing, she suspected her husband had taken them. At about 7:30 p.m., she called the Castle Rock Police Department, which dispatched two officers. The complaint continues: "When [the officers] arrived …, she showed them a copy of the TRO and requested that it be enforced and the three children be returned to her immediately." The officers stated that there was nothing they could do about the TRO and suggested that respondent call the Police Department again if the three children did not return home by 10:00 p.m.

At approximately 8:30 p.m., respondent talked to her husband on his cellular telephone. He told her "he had the three children [at an] amusement park in Denver." She called the police again and asked them to "have someone check for" her husband or his vehicle at the amusement park and "put out an all-points bulletin" for her husband, but the officer with whom she spoke "refused to do so," again telling her to "wait until 10:00 p.m. and see if" her husband returned the girls.

At approximately 10:10 p.m., respondent called the police and said her children were still missing, but she was now told to wait until midnight. She called at midnight and told the dispatcher her children were still missing. She went to her husband's apartment and, finding nobody there, called the police at 12:10 a.m.; she was told to wait for an officer to arrive. When none came, she went to the police station at 12:50 a.m. and submitted an incident report. The officer who took the report "made no reasonable effort to enforce the TRO or locate the three children. Instead, he went to dinner."

At approximately 3:20 a.m., respondent's husband arrived at the police station and opened fire with a semiautomatic handgun he had purchased earlier that evening. Police shot back, killing him. Inside the cab of his pickup truck, they found the bodies of all three daughters, whom he had already murdered.

On the basis of the foregoing factual allegations, respondent brought an action under Rev. Stat. § 1979, 42 U.S.C. § 1983, claiming that the town violated the Due Process Clause because its police department had "an official policy or custom of failing to respond properly to complaints of restraining order violations" and "tolerated the non-enforcement of restraining orders by its police officers." The complaint also alleged that the town's actions "were taken either willfully, recklessly or with such gross negligence as to indicate wanton disregard and deliberate indifference to" respondent's civil rights.

The Fourteenth Amendment to the United States Constitution provides that a State shall not "deprive any person of life, liberty, or property, without due process of law." In 42 U.S.C. § 1983,

Congress has created a federal cause of action for "the deprivation of any rights, privileges, or immunities secured by the Constitution and laws." Respondent claims the benefit of this provision on the ground that she had a property interest in police enforcement of the restraining order against her husband; and that the town deprived her of this property without due process by having a policy that tolerated non-enforcement of restraining orders.

The procedural component of the Due Process Clause does not protect everything that might be described as a "benefit": To have a property interest in a benefit, a person clearly must have more than an abstract need or desire and more than a unilateral expectation of it.

Our cases recognize that a benefit is not a protected entitlement if government officials may grant or deny it in their discretion. The Court of Appeals in this case determined that Colorado law created an entitlement to enforcement of the restraining order because the "court-issued restraining order … specifically dictated that its terms must be enforced" and a "state statute commanded" enforcement of the order when certain objective conditions were met (probable cause to believe that the order had been violated and that the object of the order had received notice of its existence).

The critical language in the restraining order came not from any part of the order itself (which was signed by the state-court trial judge and directed to the restrained party, respondent's husband), but from the preprinted notice to law-enforcement personnel that appeared on the order. That notice effectively restated the statutory provision describing "peace officers' duties" related to the crime of violation of a restraining order. At the time of the conduct at issue in this case, that provision read as follows:

(a) Whenever a restraining order is issued, the protected person shall be provided with a copy of such order. A peace officer shall use every reasonable means to enforce a restraining order.

(b) A peace officer shall arrest, or, if an arrest would be impractical under the circumstances, seek a warrant for the arrest of a restrained person when the peace officer has information amounting to probable cause that:

  (I) The restrained person has violated or attempted to violate any provision of a restraining order; and

  (II) The restrained person has been properly served with a copy of the restraining order or the restrained person has received actual notice of the existence and substance of such order.

(c) In making the probable cause determination, a peace officer shall assume that the information received from the registry is accurate. A peace officer shall enforce a valid restraining order whether or not there is a record of the restraining order in the registry.

The entire criminal justice system must act in a consistent manner, which does not now occur. The police must make probable cause arrests. The prosecutors must prosecute every case. Judges must apply appropriate sentences, and probation officers must monitor their probationers closely. And the offender needs to be sentenced to offender-specific therapy. The entire system must send the same message that violence is criminal.

We do not believe that these provisions of Colorado law truly made enforcement of restraining orders mandatory. A well-established tradition of police discretion has long coexisted with apparently mandatory arrest statutes.

In each and every state there are long-standing statutes that, by their terms, seem to preclude non-enforcement by the police.... However, for a number of reasons, including their legislative history, insufficient resources, and sheer physical impossibility, it has been recognized that such statutes cannot be interpreted literally.... They clearly do not mean that a police officer may not lawfully decline to ... make an arrest. As to third parties in these states, the full-enforcement statutes simply have no effect, and their significance is diminished.

The deep-rooted nature of law-enforcement discretion, even in the presence of seemingly mandatory legislative commands, is illustrated by *Chicago v. Morales*, 527 U.S. 41 (1999), which involved an ordinance that said a police officer "shall order" persons to disperse in certain circumstances. This Court rejected out of hand the possibility that the mandatory language of the ordinance ... afforded the police no discretion. It is, the Court proclaimed, simply "common sense that all police officers must use some discretion in deciding when and where to enforce city ordinances." The U.S. Supreme Court dismissed her suit.

Questions: Didn't she have a right to expect the police to aid her in protecting her children? Do you agree with the decision?

no immediate danger of injury, whereas in the *Thurman* case, the officers witnessed actual physical violence. This is a confused area. Some lawyers have argued that the *Castle Rock* case has overruled the *Thurman* case, while others have argued that *Thurman* is still valid case law.

An interesting fact noted in the *Thurman* case is that research had conclusively demonstrated that police inaction supports the continuance of violence.

Practicum

MARSHALL V. STATE

2014 WL 1744103

Ala. Crim. App., 2014.

May 2, 2014

Marshall was convicted of two counts of murder for the killing of his stepdaughter, Alicia Nicole Bentley—one count of murder made capital because it occurred during a burglary, see § 13A-5-40(a)(4), Ala. Code 1975, and one count of murder made capital because it occurred while Marshall, who was over the age of 19 years, sexually abused or attempted to sexually abuse Alicia, who was between the ages of 12 and 16 years, see § 13A-5-40(a)(8), Ala. Code 1975. This Court, on direct appeal, summarized the facts underlying Marshall's convictions as follows:

> Marshall did not deny that he killed 15-year-old Alicia. Indeed, while in police custody he confessed to the killing and eventually led police to Alicia's body. His attorneys, however, presented a defense in which Marshall attempted to call into question the allegation that he had had any kind of sexual contact with Alicia.

Marshall was found guilty of murder. During the sentencing portion of the trial, the prosecution calls a clinical psychologist who testified in substance as follows:

> Based on all the information available and defendant's current presentation, it is my

> opinion that he has never suffered from a serious mental illness. There also is no indication of a serious mental defect on his part and he opined functioning within the low average to average range of intelligence. In my opinion his history is remarkable for antisocial behaviors, substance abuse and narcissistic personality traits. Most critically, Marshall also has a significant history of violence against women, including sexual aggression. Such aggression coupled with his narcissism has clearly resulted in impaired personal relationships. In my opinion Marshall has harbored animosity and disdain towards women in part due to his less than ideal relationship with his own mother. Within relationships he has been domineering, aggressive, and has essentially denigrated the rights and welfare of his previous female partners.
>
> In my opinion, Marshall's animosity towards women coupled with his narcissism provides the best explanation for his actions related to the alleged offense. He was not mentally ill at the time in question or suffering from cognitive deficits which could have precluded his ability to understand right from wrong and appreciate the nature and potential consequences of his actions. Marshall, in my opinion, was angry with the victim, struck out aggressively and in doing so caused her death. He then made attempts to conceal his actions and for nearly twenty-four hours lied to officials when searchers were looking for the child.

Assume that you are the trial judge in this case. What sentence would you pronounce in this case? Explain why you selected that sentence.

Summary

- Incidents of domestic violence occur against women in the United States at epidemic rates, and up to 60% of all married women suffer physical abuse at the hands of their spouses at some time during marriage.

- The fact that police officers spend more time responding to domestic disturbances than to murders, rapes, and aggravated assaults reflects the pervasiveness of this problem.
- It is difficult to define and agree on what constitutes family violence.
- The Violence Against Women Act, as reauthorized, has been a fundamental tool in the fight against family violence. It no longer protects just women; as currently reauthorized, the act is gender-neutral.
- Family violence includes intimate partner violence, domestic abuse, and intimate partner abuse.
- Domestic violence is any form of maltreatment that takes place in a heterosexual or homosexual romantic relationship between adults or adolescents.
- Domestic abuse occurs with couples of all races, religions, social economic status, and sexual orientations.
- Relationship violence is a term used to include physical, sexual, and psychological abuse and stalking committed by one partner against the other in an intimate relationship.
- Intimate partner violence (IPV) is defined to include physical violence, sexual violence, stalking, and psychological aggression, including coercive tactics, committed by a current or former intimate partner.
- According to the NCCAFV, the roots of family violence are embedded in attitudes toward women that have existed for hundreds of years. Even today there are numerous societies where a woman is treated as the property of her husband and he is seen as having the right to use physical force in relating to her, if necessary.
- There is no single profile of a family violence or domestic abuse victim. Men, women, and children are victims.
- The victims range in age from the very young to the very old. For the most part, however, the battered victim is a woman.
- Batterers, like victims of domestic violence, are found among all social, economic, racial, religious, and age groups. There is no typical batterer.
- This is no correct or simple answer to why one person batters his or her partner.
- Dating violence is described as abusive and violent behavior that occurs in dating relationships. It happens in both heterosexual and same-sex relationships. It covers a wide range of behaviors that include verbal and emotional abuse, sexual abuse, and physical violence.
- Civil protection orders (CPOs) are civil remedies that provide protection to a victim of domestic violence by requiring the respondent to stay away from the petitioner. This protection is offered by statute in all 50 states, with most states having the option of issuing temporary or emergency protection orders, as well as permanent protection orders.

- Mandatory arrest laws remove a police officer's discretion when called to an incident of intimate partner violence.
- Numerous evaluations have been conducted to assess the efficacy of the Duluth model of batterer treatment. One such study found the Duluth model as implemented in the state of Florida to be generally successful at curbing recurrent violence among court-ordered participants. Individuals who completed the program were less likely to be arrested for domestic violence and scored higher on postassessments testing their knowledge of domestic violence. The partners of these individuals reported less physically abusive behavior.

Questions in Review

1. What types of conduct are considered intimate partner abuse?
2. What are the issues involved when studying family violence?
3. Why do abused individuals involved in dating violence continue in the relationship with the abuser?
4. What duties do police officers have to protect a person from being abused?
5. Why do batterers batter?
6. Should a state require mandatory arrest in family violence cases?

Key Terms

Domestic violence: Any form of maltreatment that takes place in a heterosexual or homosexual romantic relationship between adults or adolescents.

Intimate partner abuse (IPA) or violence: When one person in a relationship purposely hurts another person physically or emotionally. Intimate partner violence includes physical violence, sexual violence, stalking, and psychological aggression, including coercive tactics, committed by a current or former intimate partner.

Physical violence: Includes a range of behaviors, from slapping, pushing, or shoving to severe acts such as being beaten, burned, or choked.

Psychological aggression: Includes expressive aggression (such as name calling, insulting, or humiliating an intimate partner) and coercive control, which includes behaviors that are intended to monitor and control or threaten an intimate partner.

Sexual violence: Includes rape, being made to penetrate someone else, sexual coercion, unwanted sexual contact, and noncontact unwanted sexual experiences.

Endnotes

1. Harvey Wallace & Cliff Roberson. (2014). *Family violence: Legal, medical, and social perspectives* (7th ed.). Columbus, OH: Pearson.
2. Sue Schuerman. (1992). Establishing a tort duty for police failure to respond to domestic violence. *Arizona Law Review, 35*, 355–383.
3. Matthew J. Breiding, J. Chen, & Michelle C. Black. (2014). *Intimate partner violence in the United States—2010*. Atlanta, GA: National Center for Injury Prevention and Control, Centers for Disease Control and Prevention.
4. Breiding et al., 2014.
5. U.S. Public Law 113-4 (2013, March 7).
6. National Council on Child Abuse and Family Violence website. http://www.nccafv.org/spouse.htm. Retrieved June 3, 2014.
7. Wallace & Roberson, 2014.
8. B. S. Fisher, F. T. Cullen, & M. G. Turner. (2000). *The sexual victimization of college women*. NCJ 182369. Washington, DC: U.S. Department of Justice, Office of Justice Programs. www.ojp.usdoj.gov/nij.
9. Centers for Disease Control and Prevention website. http://www.cdc.gov/ViolencePrevention/intimatepartnerviolence/teen_dating_violence.html. Retrieved June 4, 2014.
10. Centers for Disease Control and Prevention website.
11. Barbara K. Finesmith. (1983). Police response to battered women: Critique and proposals for reform. *Seton Hall Law Review, 14*, 74, 79.
12. Wallace & Roberson, 2014.
13. Cliff Roberson & Harvey Wallace. (1998). *Introduction to criminology*. Incline Village, NV: Copperhouse.
14. Murray A. Straus & Richard J. Gelles. (1990). *Physical violence in American families*. New Brunswick, NJ: Transaction.
15. Michael Gottfredson & Travis Hirschi. (1990). *A general theory of crime*. Palo Alto, CA: Stanford University Press.
16. Ronald Akers. (1985). *Deviant behavior: A social learning theory* (3rd ed.). Belmont, CA: Wadsworth.
17. Russell Dobash & R. Emerson Dobash. (1988). Research as social action: The struggle for battered women. In Kersti Yllo & Michelle Bograd (Eds.), *Feminist perspectives on wife abuse*. Newberry Park, CA: Sage.
18. Marvin Wolfgang & Franco Ferracuti. (1967). *The subculture of violence*. London: Travistock.
19. Rachel Condry & Caroline Miles. (2014). Adolescent to parent violence: Framing and mapping a hidden problem. *Criminology and Criminal Justice, 14*(3), 257–275.
20. Henry T. Harbin & David J. Madden. (1979). Battered parents: A new syndrome. *American Journal of Psychiatry, 139*(10), 1288–1291.
21. Condry & Miles, 2014.
22. *Fulgham v. State*. 46 Ala. 143, 146–147 (1871).
23. Thomas L. Hafemeister. (2011). If all you have is a hammer: Society's ineffective response to intimate partner violence. *Catholic University Law Review, 60*, 919, 926.
24. Olivia M. Fritsche. (2014, Spring). The role of enforcement in a violation of a protection order. *Washington and Lee Law Review*, 71, 1473–1513.

25. Fritsche, 2014.
26. Amy M. Zelcer. (2014). Battling domestic violence: Replacing mandatory arrest Laws with a trifecta of preferential arrest, officer education, and batterer treatment programs. *American Criminal Law Review*, 51, 541–566.
27. Philip M. Boffey. (1983, April 5). Domestic violence: Study favors arrest. *New York Times*. http://www.nytimes.com/1983/04/05/science/domestic-violence-study-favors-arrest.html. Retrieved June 4, 2014.
28. Alexandra Pavlidakis. (2009). Mandatory arrest: Past its prime. *Santa Clara Law Review*, *49*, 1201–1233.
29. Zelcer, 2014, p. 542.

chapter seven

Social Inequality and Deviance Issues

Chapter Objectives

What you should know and understand after studying this chapter:

- The issues involved with economic inequality
- How inequality affects crime rates
- How inequality and incarceration in prison are associated
- The issues involved in law enforcement and inequality

Introduction

> An imbalance between rich and poor is the oldest and most fatal ailment of all republics.
>
> **—Plutarch (c. 46–127 A.D.)**[1]

According to David Troutt, Americans have good reasons to worry about the way to a middle-class future.[2] The Great Recession, which started in 2008, revealed fault lines in banking and on Wall Street. It diminished home ownership as a family's central asset, weakened college prospects, and altered for millions the likelihood of a stable job or even retirement. The recession wiped out all the wealth gained by the middle class during the 1990s. According to Troutt, these changes have shaken our personal belief in mobility, deestablishing our local faith in environments that were designed to support the American middle-class dream. Troutt states that we are challenged by two indisputable forces:

- The growing instability of the middle class
- The rising proportion of previously excluded groups

According to Troutt, of the many reasons that we should address the inequities, the foremost is that we need each other's success.

Troutt contends that nearly every choice we make affecting opportunity—attending private instead of public schools, stealing a car, or demanding a reappraisal of our property tax bill—influences the context in which other people's choices are made. He contends that this holds true for murder, obesity, and sprawl. He notes that the city of Oakland estimates that homicides cost city taxpayers an average of $1 million per homicide. However, when it comes to opportunity and social mobility, our insecurities about class differences and racial meanings make it harder to acknowledge connections to one another's welfare. According to him, equity is always the last voice to be heard.

Troutt contends that we need to think about specific approaches along three straightforward principles of integration: mixing income, increasing equitable arrangements, and decreasing local inequities. We need to alter structures that have separated people by race, class, and place.

According to Phillip J. Cook, if you look at the crime map of any large city, you will note that it lights up in those neighborhoods characterized by a high concentration of disadvantaged minorities, joblessness, single-parent households, drug abuse, substandard housing, inadequate public services, and high population turnover. According to Cook, it is reasonable to assume that such a confluence of conditions holds the key to understanding the social and economic conditions that foster crime.[3]

In this chapter, we will examine how social inequality affects and influences the issues involved in understanding deviant behavior. Social inequality refers to relational processes in society that have the effect of limiting or harming a group's social status, social class, and social circle.[4]

Generally when we use the term *inner city* we have images, almost all of them negative: broken windows, graffiti, abandoned buildings, and littered alleys, symbols of endemic disinvestment and marginalization. Edwin Sutherland argued as early as 1947 that crime rates are low in egalitarian, consensual societies and high in inequitable societies characterized by conflicting beliefs.[6] Ross L. Matsueda and Maria S. Grigoryeva opined that it was likely that crime rates are high in inequitable societies because members of disadvantaged groups or classes have particularly high rates of offending.[7] They noted that high rates of crime and violence have traditionally been associated with the disadvantaged inner-city urban areas when the areas were compared to affluent urban neighborhoods and rural areas.

If inequality and disadvantage are associated with crime, then we must question why, and what is the association between inequality, disadvantage, and crime? Another question is: What roles do crime and incarceration play in the reproduction of social inequality?

One standard economic prediction is that material inequality increases crime. The economic theory of crime views the decision to offend as a rational response to the costs and benefits of various alternative actions.[8]

SOCIETY IN ACTION

IS IT DEVIANT BEHAVIOR TO SEND YOUR CHILDREN TO A BETTER SCHOOL THAN THE SCHOOL THEY SHOULD ATTEND?

A report on the *Huffington Post* website concluded that schools that enroll 90% or more nonwhite students spend $733 less per pupil per year than schools that enroll 90% or more white students. The "racially isolated" schools make up one-third of the country's schools. Nationwide, schools spend an average of $334 more on every white student than on every nonwhite student.[5]

Most researchers and educators will agree that public schools in the United States are not all equal. As any realtor will advise you, check out the school district before your select an area in which to live.

Kelley Williams-Bolar stated, like most mothers, that she would do anything to help her two daughters. Because of this commitment, she spent nine days in jail and now has a felony conviction. At press time, there was a movement requesting the governor of Ohio to pardon her.

Ms. Williams-Bolar, whose children attended schools in one district and lived in another, was sentenced to 10 days in jail and community service for falsifying records so that her children could attend a high-achieving suburban district school rather than Akron public schools.

Ms. Williams-Bolar, who said she was trying to keep her daughters safe, is also facing the risk of being disqualified as a schoolteacher. As of June 2014, she was an aide for special education classes and was near completion of a college degree that would allow her to become a teacher. Felons in Ohio can be disqualified from working as teachers. She was charged with using her father's address to enroll her children in a neighboring school district.

Prosecutors defended the felony charges, saying Williams-Bolar willingly broke the law by using her father's address and misrepresenting other information on school documents. Her case drew national attention as a high-profile example of schools getting tougher on parents who improperly send their children to other districts, usually with better-funded and higher-performing schools.

This case leads to the question: Why are some schools better funded and higher performing than other schools, and why is it that schools with a high percentage of minority enrollment tend to get less money?

The decision to steal, for example, involves a choice between two different ways of generating income: One can invest time in lawful production or in appropriating the property of others. The model predicts that an individual will steal when his expected returns from illegal work exceed those of legal work.

Equality for Women

In 1618, an anonymous author wrote a thorough and documented article entitled "Are Women Human Beings?"[9] Probably no serious journal or magazine would print such an article today. While the rights of women have advanced considerably since that era, research still indicates that they lag behind men in income and in leadership and management positions. As late as 1970, the rights of women to have equal pay and employment benefits were denied by the British Hong Kong government. Women in Japan got the right to vote in 1945, and in Kuwait only in 2005.

In the United States, in the 19th century women were denied the right to their property once they were married.

The International Council of Women was the first major women's organization to work across national boundaries to advocate women's rights. In the United States the National Organization for Women (NOW) was created in 1966 with the goal of bringing about equality for all women. NOW tried unsuccessfully to pass an equal rights amendment that would provide that equality of rights under the law shall not be denied or abridged by the United States or any state on the account of sex. The amendment died in 1982 because not enough states had ratified it (Figure 7.1).

In 1948, the United Nations General Assembly adopted the Universal Declaration of Human Rights that advocated for the equal rights of men and women. And in 1979, the General Assembly adopted the Convention of the Elimination of All Forms of Discrimination Against Women. The convention states:

> Any distinction, exclusion or restriction made on the basis of sex which has the effect or purpose of impairing or nullifying the recognition, enjoyment or exercise by women, irrespective of their marital status, on a basis of equality of men and women, of human rights and fundamental freedoms in the political, economic, social, cultural, civil or any other field.[10]

The issues that need to be addressed in our society today include women's rights to bodily integrity and autonomy, hold more public offices,

Figure 7.1 A commemorative print marking the enactment of the 15th Amendment on March 30, 1870, giving women the right to vote. The artist was James Carter Beard. (Print from the Library of Congress Prints and Photographs Division, Washington, DC.)

fairer wages, and more equal treatment in general. In a September 26, 2011, issue of *Newsweek*, a study was published evaluating the rights and quality of life of women in countries around the world. The worst were Pakistan, Ethiopia, and the Sudan. The United States was listed as eighth best, behind Iceland, Sweden, Canada, Denmark, Finland, Switzerland, and Norway.[11]

Women's rights have experienced numerous opponents and roadblocks. As noted in Figure 7.2, there have been congressional investigations attempted over the issues of women's rights.

Racial Equality

The biggest problem when considering racial equality is in determining where to start. History is replete with instances where people have been discriminated against merely because of their race or color. The authors grew up in the 1950s and 1960s, when black Americans were fighting for

Figure 7.2 A 1939 picture of Senator Allen J. Ellender, Democrat of Louisiana, chairman of the Special Senate Committee, investigating charges of favoritism in the promotion of feminine workers in government service. Principal charges were that the beauties were being promoted, regardless of their ability, over the heads of their homelier co-workers. (Photo courtesy of Library of Congress Prints and Photographs Division, Washington, DC.)

the right to vote in many southern states. Minorities, as have women, have suffered discrimination over our long history. As noted in later sections in this chapter, minorities have continued to suffer economic disadvantages (Figure 7.3).

Racial equality often has different meaning in different contexts. To the authors, it means equal rights to all races, genders, and cultures. This includes social equality, employment equality, and political equality. Human identity is unique, and we are the only mammals that have the ability to think and plan. We must use this ability to show respect for the rights of all humans and move away from our stereotyped boundaries.

Economic Inequality

According to Richard Freeman, neighborhoods with little stable adult and youth employment are vulnerable to predatory crime, partly because of

Figure 7.3 A 1946 photo of African Americans marching near the Capitol building in Washington, DC, to protest the lynching of four African Americans in Georgia. (Photo from Library of Congress Prints and Photographs Division, Washington, DC.)

the effect of persistent unemployment on household stability.[12] Freeman opines that the unstable and economic deprived households account for a disproportionate amount of total unemployment and poverty in the United States.

The authors are not aware of any country that has not had economic inequality issues. It appears that all countries have had a wide gap between the wealthy and the economically depressed groups in the country. According to most researchers, it appears that income inequality in the United States has grown significantly in the past 40 years. A 2011 study by the U.S. Congressional Budget Office (CBO) concluded that the top earning 1% of households in the United States increased their income by about 275% after federal taxes and income transfers over a period between 1979 and 2007, compared to a gain of less than 40% for the 60% in the middle of America's income distribution.[13] See Figure 7.4 for a graphic display of the differences.

The CBO concluded that as a result of that uneven income growth, the distribution of after-tax household income in the United States was

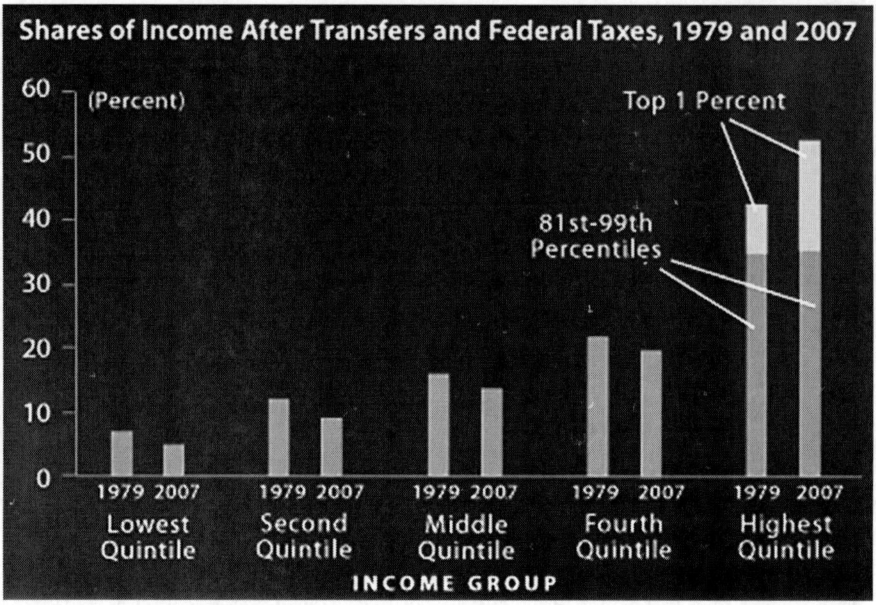

Figure 7.4 The growing inequality in the United States from 1970 to 2007. It appears that this inequality continues to increase. (From U.S. Congressional Budget Office, October 2011.)

substantially more unequal in 2007 than in 1979: The share of income accruing to higher-income households increased, whereas the share accruing to other households declined. In fact, between 2005 and 2007, the after-tax income received by 20% of the population with the highest income exceeded the after-tax income of the remaining 80%. In other words, the rich are getting richer and the poor are getting poorer.

This concept is the main theme of a book by Jeffery H. Reiman: *The Rich Get Richer and the Poor Get Prison: Ideology, Class, and Criminal Justice.* The first edition of his book was published in 1979.[14] Reiman examined the premise that the criminal justice system is biased against the poor from start to finish, from the definition of what constitutes a crime through the process of arrest, trial, and sentencing. Also, he discussed how this bias is accompanied with a general refusal to remedy the causes of crime—poverty, lack of education, and discrimination. Figure 7.4 illustrates the point that inequity is growing in the United States.

According to the Federal Reserve, the inequality is not uniform among the states, with Texas having the highest rate of inequality and Maine the lowest.[15] According to the Organization for Economic Cooperation and Development (OECD), only two nations who are members of the organization, Mexico and Russia, display greater income inequality than the United States.[16]

The 2010 U.S. Census data determined that the top-earning 20% of Americans—those making more than $100,000 each year—received 49.4% of all income generated in the United States, compared with the 3.4% made by the bottom 20% of earners, those who fell below the poverty line. The ratio of income received by the highest compared to that of the lowest indicated that the ratio of 14.5:1 was an increase from 13.6 in 2008, and nearly double the 7.69 in 1968. According to the census data, three states—New York, Connecticut, and Texas—and the District of Columbia had the largest gaps between rich and poor. Big gaps were also evident in large cities such as New York, Miami, Los Angeles, Boston, and Atlanta, home to both highly paid financial and high-tech jobs and clusters of poorer immigrant and minority residents. The states with the lowest income gaps were Alaska, Utah, Wyoming, Idaho, and Hawaii.[17]

The 2010 census data also indicated that 11.7 million Americans were receiving food stamps, or 1 in 10 families. This number is the highest on record. Twenty-eight states had increases in the percentage of citizens whose average annual income was less than $10,977. The one bright spot in the census data trends is that while women's average pay was still below that of men's average pay, the gap between the two is narrowing. Women with full-time jobs are currently making about 78.2% of men's pay. This is up from 77.7% in 2008 and 64% in 2000. The income gap between the richest and poorest Americans grew last year to its largest margin ever.

The 2010 data indicate that marriages fell to a record low, with just 52% of adults 18 and over saying they were joined in wedlock, compared to 57% in 2000. This drop in percentages of people being married probably indicates a larger percentage of couples living together without the benefit of marriage. How will this affect the number of intimate partner abuse cases? We may expect an increase because past statistics indicate that law enforcement agencies are called more frequently in cases where the partners are living together without the benefit of marriage than in cases involving married partners.

The foreign-born population edged higher to 38.5 million, or 12.5%, following a dip in the previous year, due mostly to increases in naturalized citizens. The share of U.S. residents speaking a language other than English at home also rose, from 19.7% to 20%, mostly in California, New Mexico, and Texas.

Economics of Unauthorized Migration

In 2014 the United States and Mexico had an influx of young unaccompanied migrants from Central America. It appeared that poor families were sending their children north in hopes they would have a better life. Neither the United States nor Mexico was prepared to handle this large number of migrants, especially because of their age. There is no easy solution to the problem. Neither country could handle the vast numbers, yet the children were not to blame. Situations similar to this may become the wave of the future. Strong government leadership will be needed to solve the issues involved.

Stanford researcher Emily Ryo attempted to answer the question of why there are so many unauthorized migrants in the United States.[18] According to a recent estimate, more than 11 million unauthorized migrants currently live in the United States. This means that unauthorized migrants make up a large proportion—about 30%—of the nation's foreign-born population. Using data collected in Mexico through the Mexican Migration Project, she developed and tested a new decision-making model of unauthorized labor migration. The model considered the economic motivations of prospective migrants, as well as their beliefs, attitudes, and social norms regarding U.S. immigration law and legal authorities. She concluded that perceptions of certainty of apprehension and severity of punishment are not significant determinants of the intent to migrate illegally; however, perceptions of availability of Mexican jobs and the dangers of border crossing are significant determinants of these intentions. In addition, individuals' general legal attitudes, morality about violating U.S. immigration law, views about the legitimacy of U.S. authority, and norms about border crossing are significant determinants of the intent to migrate illegally. Perceptions of procedural justice are significantly related to beliefs in the legitimacy of U.S. authority, suggesting that, all else being equal, procedural fairness may produce greater deference to U.S. immigration law. Together, the results show that the decision to migrate illegally cannot be fully understood without considering an individual's underlying values and norms.

Ryo notes that personal morality as a determinant of legal noncompliance has been conceptualized in a variety of ways, including moral beliefs, moral commitment, ethical beliefs, and conscience. The basic idea underlying this line of research is that people generally see themselves as moral beings who want to do the right thing as they perceive it.

Ryo also notes that among too many would-be migrants, as well as many U.S. citizens, there is a lack of moral credibility to a law perceived as preventing individuals from working to support their families. For many, there is also no moral credibility to a law that seems to punish individuals for satisfying the demands of U.S. households and corporations for cheap foreign labor. Ryo concludes that immigration law is fraught with these and other moral tensions, which is significant to understanding the widespread noncompliance with U.S. immigration law.

Inequality and Law Enforcement

According to researcher Richard McAdams, inequality adversely affects the level of policing. We can assume that more policing raises the probability of detecting crime and therefore decreasing crime. But the provision of a public good like policing requires collective political action that is most likely when the actors are homogeneous in their demand for the good. When citizens are instead heterogeneous, differing in the type and quantity of public goods they value, the cost of their political organization is higher, and the government will provide less of such goods.

McAdams sees it easier to organize political support for paying taxes to fund police if everyone agrees on the priorities the police should have. The rich will probably want a legal system focused on protecting property interests, while the poor might be more concerned with preventing interpersonal violence in disadvantaged areas. Because these groups disagree on the desired focus of the police, there is less willingness to invest in a common legal system than there would be if the population shared a common set of legal needs.[19]

Inequality and Crime

Researchers Lauren J. Krivo and Ruth D. Peterson conducted a research project using two hypotheses concerning the relationship between neighborhood disadvantage and crime. The two hypotheses were

1. Extremely disadvantaged neighborhoods have unusually high rates of crime.
2. Local structural disadvantage is equally important in influencing crime in black and white neighborhoods.

They examined if the racial differences in structural disadvantage account for black-white differences in crime across communities. To test their hypotheses, they examined the 1990 census and crime data for local areas in the city of Columbus, Ohio. The researchers concluded that both hypotheses were supported by the data.[20]

The evidence generally supports the claim that inequality increases crime. Ehrlich examined crime levels among the states in 1940, 1950, and 1960 and concluded that crimes against property (robbery, burglary, larceny, and auto theft) vary positively with the percentage of families below one-half of the median income.[21] Hsieh and Pugh conducted a meta-analysis of the literature in 1993 and found a significant link between income inequality and violent crime.[22] Many studies found a positive relationship between inequality and crime, many found no significant relationship, and virtually no study found a negative relationship.[23]

Recently the issue of inequality and crime has attracted increased attention. The new studies tend to confirm that inequality causes crime. Soares noted that prior studies relied overwhelmingly on reported crime, even though there is significant underreporting of crime. While there appears to be a significant relationship between inequality and crime, there are many who dispute this relationship. It does appear that there is real and substantial evidence of a strong relationship between the two, especially when considering street crime.

Soares found that underreporting systematically distorted the analysis of the link between inequality and crime, and therefore examined the connection in two new ways: using victimization surveys and using a statistical adjustment to reported crime. In the two cross section analyses of international data, he found a significant and positive relationship: Economic inequality increases thefts, burglaries, and contact crimes such as robbery and assault.[24] Matz Dahlberg and Magnus Gustavsson separated the effects of transitory changes in income from permanent changes. Using Swedish panel data from 1974 to 2000, they found that while an increase in inequality of transitory income had no effect on crime, an increase in the inequality of permanent income significantly increased total crime.[25]

In a famous study, Shaw and McKay mapped rates of juvenile delinquency by neighborhood and over time in the city of Chicago.[26] They concluded that delinquency rates were highest in the center of the city in which residential areas were being overtaken by industry. They found that delinquency rates dropped monotonically as one moved from the center of the city to the periphery, and that the patterns remained stable over decades despite ethnic turnovers of the zone in transition. Shaw and McKay argued that city growth, especially business and industry that invaded residential neighborhoods, produced community social disorganization and the breakdown of social controls.

Following the research of Shaw and McKay, later researchers have specified the causal mechanisms—particularly informal social control—by which disorganization produces high rates of crime.[27] Shaw and McKay also found evidence of interlocking networks of delinquent groups over time, and case study evidence that young delinquents learned delinquent traditions from older groups of offenders. They used the term *cultural transmission* to describe this intergenerational transmission of a delinquent tradition. The cultural transmission concept is considered the early development of the learning theories.

There are some researchers and politicians who have suggested that welfare assistance actually contributes to the development of deviant subcultures and related behavioral problems by undermining individual responsibility and desire to legitimately pursue the American dream.[28] According to their viewpoint, the poor interpret welfare as society's admission of guilt and as evidence that an unjust social system exists.

They then realize it is the unjust system and not their personal failing that is to blame for their economic problems. Thus, welfare teaches the poor that they are entitled to both a certain amount of theft and occasional outbursts of angry frustration.

In general, proponents of this view believe that welfare has become a way of life that corrupts traditional family values and sustains a rebellious subculture of poverty or a black subculture of violence.[29] Hannon and Defronzo conducted a research project to test this assumption. The researchers concluded that the findings presented suggested that the convergence of such factors as the prevalence of female-headed families, percent black, and family poverty rate (a combination that is often seen as indicating an underclass) is more related to crime in areas with relatively high levels of welfare support. According to their conclusions, welfare assistance may help prevent crime. They noted that welfare's overall impact may be limited by the condition that the mean level of welfare support in the United States is far below the average for most Western industrialized nations. Moreover, the welfare spending gap between the United States and other industrialized nations is likely to widen.

According to Steven E. Barkan and Steven F. Cohn, not all whites who perceive African Americans as more violent want more money spent on crime.[30] According to the researchers, this relationship is limited to one segment of the whites: the most racially prejudiced. The researchers noted that the United States adopted a get-tough approach that has guided the criminal justice policy since the 1970s. This approach emphasized the goals of deterrence, incapacitation, and retribution over the goal of rehabilitation.

Barkan and Cohn noted that although scholars dispute the reasons for the rise and popularity of the get-tough approach, many agree that public opinion has played an important role. They noted that some scholars have tried to explain why the get-tough approach arose and flourished in the first place. And some see it as a legitimate response to growing public concern over the rising crime rates of the 1960s. The researchers looked at the question of whether racial prejudice also leads white Americans to support greater spending to reduce crime.

The researchers concluded that the more racially prejudiced whites perceive that African Americans are prone to violence, the more likely they are to want more money spent to reduce crime. This finding extends prior studies of the influence of racial prejudice on punitiveness into another important dimension of public opinion on crime. They note that there may be many good reasons to favor greater spending to reduce crime, but racial prejudice is an unacceptable reason in a democracy that espouses equal opportunity and egalitarian treatment. Because racial prejudice does prompt whites to support such spending, and also, as previous studies have shown, the more punitive treatment of criminals, policy makers must be careful not to be unduly swayed by public opinion on crime, as such opinion rests in part upon the racial prejudices of white Americans.

Crime and Incarceration in the United States

As noted by the Hamilton Project, the U.S. incarceration rate in 2012 was significantly higher than those of its neighbors: Canada's and Mexico's incarceration rates were 118 and 210, respectively, per 100,000 citizens.[31] The U.S. incarceration rate is more than six times higher than the typical rate of 115 for a nation in the Organization for Economic Cooperation and Development (OECD).

As noted by the Brookings Institute, crime rates in the United States have been on a steady decline since the 1990s; however, in 2010, the United States spent more than $80 billion on corrections expenditures at the federal, state, and local levels. Crime-related expenditures generate a significant strain on state and federal budgets, leading some to question whether public funds are best spent incarcerating nonviolent criminals.[32]

The Brookings Institute notes that preliminary evidence from the recent policy experience in California—in which a substantial number of nonviolent criminals were released from state and federal prisons—suggests that alternatives to incarceration for nonviolent offenders (e.g., electronic monitoring and house arrest) can lead to slightly higher rates of property crime, but have no statistically significant impact on violent crime. These conclusions have led some experts to suggest that public safety priorities could better be achieved by incarcerating fewer nonviolent criminals, combined with spending more on education and policing.

Income and Crime

The Hamilton Project noted that youths from low-income families at or below the federal poverty level are equally likely to commit drug-related offenses as their counterpoints in higher-income groups. The project noted that low-income youths are more likely to engage in violent and property crimes than youths from middle- and high-income families. In particular, low-income youths are significantly more likely to attack someone or get into a fight, join a gang, or steal something worth more than $50. Youths from low-income families are more likely to engage in crimes that involve or affect other people than youths from higher-income families.[33]

The Hamilton Project researchers concluded that if employment opportunities are limited for teens living in poor neighborhoods, then property crime becomes relatively more attractive. The heightened likelihood of violent crime among poor youths raises the issue of automatic behaviors—in other words, youths intuitively responding to perceived threats—which is the focus of recent research in this field. However, the similar rates of

SOCIETY IN ACTION

TEN ECONOMIC FACTS ABOUT CRIME AND INCARCERATION IN THE UNITED STATES

1. Crime rates have steadily declined over the past twenty-five years.
2. Low-income individuals are more likely than higher income individuals to be victims of crime.
3. The majority of criminal offenders are younger than age thirty.
4. Disadvantaged youths engage in riskier criminal behavior.
5. Federal and state policies have driven up the incarceration rate over the past thirty years.
6. The U.S. incarceration rate is more than six times that of the typical OECD nation.
7. There is nearly a 70 percent chance that an African American man without a high school diploma will be imprisoned by his mid-thirties.
8. Per capita expenditures on corrections more than tripled over the past thirty years.
9. By their fourteenth birthday, African American children whose fathers do not have a high school diploma are more likely than not to see their fathers incarcerated.
10. Juvenile incarceration can have lasting impacts on a young person's future.

Source: This section was reprinted with permission from the Brooking Institute's Hamilton Project, Ten Economic Facts About Crime and Incarceration in the United States.

drug use across teens from different income groups is consistent with a more general model of risky teenage activity associated with the so-called impaired decision-making capabilities of the adolescent brain.

Low-income individuals are more likely than higher-income individuals to be victims of crime. The victimization rate for all personal crimes among individuals with family incomes of less than $15,000 was over three times the rate of those with family incomes of $75,000 or more. The most prevalent crime for low-income victims was assault, followed closely by acts of attempted violence, at 33 victims and 28 victims per 1,000 residents, respectively. For those in the higher-income bracket, these rates were significantly lower at only 11 victims and 9 victims per 1,000 residents.[34] The Hamilton Project noted that since crime tends to concentrate in disadvantaged areas, the lower-income individuals living in those communities are even more likely to be victims. Research tends

SOCIETY IN ACTION

VIOLENT VICTIMIZATION IN NEW AND ESTABLISHED HISPANIC AREAS, 2007–2010

This report describes violent victimization rates by victims' race and ethnicity within four types of Hispanic areas using National Crime Victimization Survey data from 2007 to 2010. Hispanic areas are classified based on their historical Hispanic population and the growth in their Hispanic population between 1980 and 2010:

(1) established slow-growth areas,
(2) established fast-growth areas,
(3) new Hispanic areas, and
(4) small Hispanic areas.

- From 1980 to 2010, the Hispanic population increased 246%, compared to 44% for non-Hispanic blacks and 9% for non-Hispanic whites.
- From 2007 to 2010, new Hispanic areas had a lower overall rate of violent victimization compared to small Hispanic areas that had relatively little growth in Hispanic populations.
- Unlike blacks and whites, Hispanics experienced higher rates of violent victimization in new Hispanic metropolitan areas (26 per 1,000) than in other areas (16 to 20 per 1,000).
- Hispanics ages 18 to 34 exhibited the largest variation in victimization rates by type of area. Those in new Hispanic areas experienced violence at higher rates than those in established and small Hispanic areas.
- Among all age groups, new Hispanic areas did not show statistically significant higher rates of violent victimization for non-Hispanic white and black residents.
- Blacks experienced higher rates of violent victimization in small Hispanic metropolitan areas (50 per 1,000) than in new Hispanic areas (27 per 1,000).
- For whites, the overall rate of violent victimization was lower in established slow-growth areas, while the other areas showed no significant differences in the overall rate of violent victimization.

Source: Min Xie & Michael Planty, Violent Victimization in New and Established Hispanic Areas, 2007–2010, Special Report NCJ 246311, U.S. Department of Justice, Office of Justice Programs, Bureau of Justice Statistics Washington, DC, August 2014.

to imply that moving families with low incomes from disadvantaged areas to areas where the neighborhoods are economically better off will reduce the likelihood of being victimized.

The majority of criminal offenders are younger than 30 years old (about 60%). Juveniles make up a significant portion (about 27%) of the known offenders.

Structured Inequality

Research has indicated that individuals who are high in one dimension of inequality, for example, economics, power, or status, tend to be high in other dimensions. Structured inequality refers to the fact that inequality is not arbitrary. Inequality tends to be systematic, and generally the same people and groups who are high in one dimension are high in the other dimensions.[35] Accordingly, the rich are generally more powerful, and the powerful have more social status than one who is less powerful.

Keister and Southgate note that there are two common approaches to use when thinking about the structure of inequality: the categorical approach and the continuous approach.[36] The categorical approach refers to the fact that when individuals study inequality, they assume that society is grouped into distinct groups. Thus, those included in the higher social class are considered elite or upper class and will be assumed as a member of any higher social dimension. Those who have wealth are also considered powerful and in an elite class.

The continuous approach refers to those who argue that social class should be considered a continuum along which people are arrayed from lower class to upper class. This approach assumes that there is a linear progression from the very poor in society to the very rich.

Behavior of Law

In an influential 1976 book, *The Behavior of Law*, Donald Black argued that much of what occurs in the legal system can be explained by the relative social status of the participants. According to Black, one of the universal truths is that the law moves more easily down social hierarchies than up. For example, it is far easier for a rich man to get a policeman to arrest a poor man in the street, for example, than the other way around.[37]

Donald Black uses the concept of stratification to explain how law differs according to social rank. By stratification he is referring to the vertical aspect of social class. He states that stratification has several variable aspects. One aspect is the magnitude of the difference in wealth. Another is the degree to which wealth is distributed into layers, each separate from the next, rather than a continuum.

Black sees the law as a governmental social control agent. The amount of law that a person will experience varies according to that person's social status and where in the stratification the person fits. A homeless person is subject to more control by the law than a rich person. In addition, a law that appears to be equal to everyone may affect the poor more than the rich. For example, in Los Angeles it is illegal to live in your car. It is highly unlikely that Warren Buffett would ever consider living in his car, whereas a homeless person may have no better accommodations.

In reading Black's comments, the authors considered the famous quote by Anatole France, who won the 1921 Nobel Prize for Literature: "In its majestic equality, the law forbids rich and poor alike to sleep under bridges, beg in the streets, and steal loaves of bread."[38] Anatole France begs the question of what rich man would sleep under a bridge and beg in the streets.

Black contends that certain types of people attract law to themselves. The poor, the culturally marginal, and social deviants of all types are more likely to attract bad legal outcomes—to be arrested, to be convicted, to lose civil lawsuits—when they do the same things as more socially favored people. Researchers in the early 1970s sent two groups into a store to shoplift, some dressed as hippies, with long hair and dirty blue jeans, and others who looked more conventional. Not surprisingly, customers in the store turned the hippies in far more often than the "straights," and with much more enthusiasm.

Black suggested that the uneven distribution of material resources among different groups (inequality of wealth) was a key factor that determines the quantity of law. According to Black, people in the lower social strata have less access to the law, and different racial groups will vary in their willingness to report to the police when crime occurs.

Historically, because blacks have had less wealth than whites, black victims are expected to be less likely than white victims to report crimes to the police. He also noted that wealth was an advantage for the offenders. Black theorized that victims are expected to be more likely to report to the police when victimized by black offenders than by white offenders, holding the victims' race constant. Both offender and victim racial groups act as proxies for social status. Accordingly, the racial groups in which the victim and the offender belong will determine the likelihood that an incident will be reported to the police. According to him, the likelihood of reporting a crime is ranked from high to low[39]:

1. Black offender with white victim
2. White offender with white victim
3. Black offender with black victim
4. White offender with black victim

This racial hierarchy in Black's theory is formed and maintained by the location of blacks and whites in the stratification system in American society. This racial stratification hypothesis is based on the assumption that there is economic inequality among the two racial groups. This assumption may be questioned in various situations within the United States. If Black's hypothesis is modified to substitute social status or economic status in lieu of racial groups in determining the likelihood of reporting crime, it would appear to be more relevant in today's society.

Summary

- It appears that we are challenged by two indisputable forces: the growing instability of the middle class and the rising proportion of previously excluded groups.
- If you look at the crime map of any large city, you will note that it lights up in those neighborhoods characterized by a high concentration of disadvantaged minorities, joblessness, single-parent households, drug abuse, substandard housing, inadequate public services, and high population turnover.
- A report on the *Huffington Post* website concluded that schools that enroll 90% or more nonwhite students spend $733 less per pupil per year than schools that enroll 90% or more white students.
- Generally when we use the term *inner city* we have images, almost all of them negative: broken windows, graffiti, abandoned buildings, and littered alleys, symbols of endemic disinvestment and marginalization.
- Edwin Sutherland argued as early as 1947 that crime rates are low in egalitarian, consensual societies and high in inequitable societies characterized by conflicting beliefs.
- According to Richard Freeman, neighborhoods with little stable adult and youth employment are vulnerable to predatory crime, partly because of the effect of persistent unemployment on household stability.
- According to most researchers, it appears that income inequality in the United States has grown significantly in the past 40 years.
- According to researcher Richard McAdams, inequality adversely affects the level of policing.
- Evidence generally supports the claim that inequality increases crime.
- While there appears to be a significant relationship between inequality and crime, there are many who dispute this relationship. It does appear that there is real and substantial evidence of a strong relationship between the two, especially when considering street crime.

- As noted by the Hamilton Project, the U.S. incarceration rate in 2012 was significantly higher than those of its neighbors: Canada's and Mexico's incarceration rates were 118 and 210, respectively, per 100,000 citizens.
- The Hamilton Project noted that youths from low-income families at or below the federal poverty level are equally likely to commit drug-related offenses as their counterpoints in higher-income groups. The project noted that low-income youths are more likely to engage in violent and property crimes than are youths from middle- and high-income families.
- Donald Black uses the concept of stratification to explain how law differs according to social rank. By stratification he is referring to the vertical aspect of social class. He states that stratification has several variable aspects.

Questions in Review

1. Why are more poor people incarcerated in prisons?
2. How does law enforcement differ based on inequities?
3. Why is the middle class in the United States not progressing as much as the upper class?
4. Why are racial minorities more likely to be victimized?
5. Explain Donald Black's comments on inequity.
6. What suggestions do you have to combat the inequity issues?

Key Terms

Crimes against persons: Crimes whose victims are always individuals (e.g., assault, murder, and rape).

Crimes against property: Those crimes with the goal of obtaining money, property, or some other benefit (e.g., bribery, burglary, and robbery).

Crimes against society: Those crimes that represent society's prohibition against engaging in certain types of activity (e.g., drug violations, gambling, and prostitution).

Social inequality: Refers to relational processes in society that have the effect of limiting or harming a group's social status, social class, and social circle.

U.S. crime rate: The sum of the violent crime rates (i.e., aggravated assault, forcible rape, murder and nonnegligent manslaughter, and robbery) and property crime rates (i.e., burglary, larceny-theft, and motor vehicle theft) from the FBI's Uniform Crime Reporting Program.

Endnotes

1. Jon D. Wisman. (2011). Inequality, social respectability, political power, and environmental devastation. *Journal of Economic Issues, XLV*(4), 877.
2. David Dante Troutt. (2013). *The price of paradise: The costs of inequality and a vision for a more equitable America*. New York: New York University Press.
3. Phillip J. Cook. (2009). Crime control in the city: A research-based briefing on public and private measures. *Cityscape, 11*(1), 53–79.
4. Lawrence E. Cohen, James R. Kluegel, & Kenneth C. Land. (1981). Social inequality and predatory criminal victimization: An exposition and test of a formal theory. *American Sociological Review, 46*(5), 505–525.
5. *Huffington Post* web page. http://www.huffingtonpost.com/2012/09/20/state-and-local-school-fi_n_1898225.html. Retrieved June 10, 2014.
6. Edwin H. Sutherland. (1949). *White collar crime*. New York: Dryden Press.
7. Ross L. Matsueda & Maria S. Grigoryeva. (No date). Social inequality, crime, and deviance. http://faculty.washington.edu/matsueda/Papers/Inequality.pdf. Retrieved June 7, 2014.
8. Gary S. Becker. (1968). Crime and punishment: An economic approach. *Journal of Political Economy, 76*, 169–184. Richard H. McAdams. (2010). Economic costs of inequality. In *2010 University of Chicago Legal Forum*, pp. 23–37.
9. As reported by Elisabeth Gossman & Iudicium Verlag. (1996). Berlangend die frag ob die weiber menschen seyn oder nicht? *Archiv fur Philosophie-Geschichtliche, IV*, 101–104.
10. United Nations General Assembly. (1979). Convention on the elimination of all forms of discrimination against women. Article 2e. Geneva: United Nations.
11. Lauren Streib. (2011, September 26). The best and worst places to be a woman. *Newsweek*, 30–33.
12. Richard B. Freeman. (1981). *Troubled workers in the labor market*. Working Paper 816. Cambridge, MA: National Bureau of Economic Research.
13. U.S. Congressional Budget Office. (2011, October). *Trends in the distribution of household income between 1970 and 2007*. Washington, DC: Government Printing Office.
14. Jeffery H. Reiman. (2006). *The rich get richer and the poor get prison: Ideology, class, and criminal justice* (8th ed.). Boston: Allyn and Bacon.
15. Daniel H. Cooper, Byron F. Lutz, & Michael G. Palumbo. (2011, September 22). *Quantifying the role of federal and state taxes in mitigating income inequality*. Boston: Federal Reserve.
16. Timothy M. Smeeding. (2005). Public policy, economic inequality, and poverty: The United States in comparative perspective. *Social Science Quarterly, 86*(Suppl.), 955–983.
17. U.S. Census Bureau website. http://www.census.gov/. Retrieved June 2014.
18. Emily Ryo. (2013). Deciding to cross: Norms and economics of unauthorized migration. *American Sociological Review, 78*, 574–585.
19. McAdams, 2010, pp. 23–37.
20. Lauren J. Krivo & Ruth D. Peterson. (1996). Extremely disadvantaged neighborhoods and urban crime. *Social Forces, 75*(2), pp. 619–664.
21. Isaac Ehrlich. (1974). Participation in illegitimate activities: An economic analysis. In Gary S. Becker & William M. Landes (Eds.), *Essays in the economics of crime and punishment* (pp. 68–87). New York: National Bureau of Economic Research.

22. Ching-Chi Hsieh & M. D. Pugh. (1993). Poverty, income inequality, and violent crime: A meta-analysis of recent aggregate data studies. *Criminal Justice Review, 18*, 182–198.
23. Rodrigo Reis Soares. (2004). Development, crime, and punishment: Accounting for the international differences in crime rates. *Journal of Developmental Economy, 73*, 155–165.
24. Soares, 2004.
25. Matz Dahlberg & Magnus Gustavsson. (2008). Inequality and crime: Separating the effects of permanent and transitory income. *Oxford Bulletin of Economy and Statistics, 70*, 141–148.
26. Clifford R. Shaw & Henry D. McKay. (1969). *Juvenile delinquency and urban areas* (rev. ed.). Chicago: University of Chicago.
27. Robert J. Sampson & W. Bryon Groves. (1989). Community structure and crime: Testing social-disorganization theory. *American Journal of Sociology, 94*(4), 774–802.
28. James Q. Wilson. (1995). Crime and public policy. In James Q. Wilson & Joan Petersilia (Eds.), *Crime* (pp. 489–507). San Francisco: ICS Press.
29. Lance Hannon & James Defronzo. (1998). The truly disadvantaged, public assistance, and crime. *Social Problems, 45*(3), 383–392.
30. Steven E. Barkan & Steven F. Cohn. (2005). Why whites favor spending more money to fight crime: The role of racial prejudice. *Social Problems, 52*(2), 300–314.
31. Melissa S. Kearney, Benjamin H. Harris, Elisa Jacome, & Lucie Parker. (2014, May). *The Hamilton Project: Ten economic facts about crime and incarceration in the United States*. New York: Brookings Institute.
32. Brooking Institute website. http://www.brookings.edu/research/reports/2014/05/10-crime-facts. Retrieved June 7, 2014.
33. Kearney et al., 2014.
34. Kearney et al., 2014.
35. Lisa A. Keister & Darby E. Southgate. (2012). *Inequality: A contemporary approach to race, class, and gender*. Cambridge, England: Cambridge University Press.
36. Keister & Southgate, 2012.
37. Donald Black. (1976). *The behavior of law*. New York: Academic Press.
38. Anatole France. (1894). *The red lily* (chap. 7). http://www.online-literature.com/anatole-france/red-lily/8/. Retrieved July 29, 2014.
39. Black, 1976, p. 28.

chapter eight

Physical and Mental Differences as Deviance

Chapter Objectives

What you should know and understand after studying this chapter:

- The importance that society places on physical appearance
- The role of stigma in deviance issues
- Stereotype threat
- How some people perceive the presence of tattoos
- The different types of mental illnesses
- Why some people consider mental illness a form of deviance
- The history of the concept of insanity
- The legal issues involved with the insanity defense

Introduction

In this chapter, the forms of deviance caused not by misconduct but by the physical and mental characteristics of the individual will be explored. The individuals are deviant simply because they are different from others and not because of their actions, beliefs, or conduct. These individuals are considered deviant merely because they are different from the majority in their society. In this chapter, we will focus on four conditions: deviant physical appearance, deviant physical functionality, the developmentally handicapped, and mental illness.

Stigma

The Greeks originated the term *stigma* to refer to bodily signs designed to expose something unusual and bad about the moral status of the signifier. The signs were cut or burnt into the body and advertised that the bearer was a slave, a criminal, or a traitor—a blemished person, ritually polluted, to be avoided, especially in public places. Presently, the term is applied more to the disgrace itself than to the bodily evidence of it.

In 1963, Erving Goffman published his fascinating text on stigma and what it is like to be a stigmatized person. He described the world of persons who society does not consider normal. According to him, stigmatized people are those that do not have full social acceptance and are constantly striving to change their social identities. He was referring to physically deformed people, mental patients, drug addicts, prostitutes, and so forth.[1] Stigma, as defined by Goffman, pertains to the shame that a person may feel when he or she fails to meet other people's standards, and to the fear of being discredited—which causes the individual not to reveal his or her shortcomings. Accordingly, a person with a criminal record may simply withhold that information for fear of being judged by whomever that person happens to encounter.

Goffman divided an individual's relation to a stigma into three groups:

1. The stigmatized are those who bear the stigma.
2. The normals are those who do not bear the stigma.
3. The wise are those among the normals who are accepted by the stigmatized as "wise" to their condition.

In 1984, a group of psychologists and one sociologist added six dimensions to Goffman's concepts of stigma[2]:

1. Concealable: Extent to which others can see the stigma.
2. Course of the mark: Whether the stigma's prominence increases, decreases, or remains consistent over time.
3. Disruptiveness: The degree to which the stigma or others' reaction to it impedes social interactions.
4. Aesthetics: The subset of others' reactions to the stigma comprising reactions that are positive/approving or negative/disapproving, but representing estimations of qualities other than the stigmatized person's inherent worth or dignity.
5. Origin: Whether others think the stigma is present at birth, accidental, or deliberate.
6. Peril: The danger that others perceive (whether accurately or inaccurately) the stigma to pose to them.

Stereotype Threat

"You throw like a girl." This statement has been heard on baseball fields for years. It establishes a stereotype that girls cannot throw a baseball. Anyone who has watched the NCAA's women's softball tournaments each year knows that women softball players are very adept at throwing the ball. A stereotype is a thought that can be adopted about specific types of individuals or certain ways of doing things. These thoughts or beliefs may or may not accurately reflect reality.

Researchers have demonstrated that people can underperform at tasks when thinking about the negative performance expectations for their group. This concept is referred to as a stereotype threat. Under this concept, a woman's performance on a difficult math test may suffer if she is told that women tend to underperform in math or on that particular test. Thoughts about the negative gender stereotype may cause the woman to worry that her performance, if poor, would verify the negative stereotype of her group. Consequently, she may become particularly motivated to disprove the stereotype. Unfortunately, this excessive concern about performance may sometimes impair actual performance outcomes.[3]

Physical Appearance

As noted by Druann Heckert, physical appearance, like behavior, is subject to social evaluation and differential social reaction.[4] According to Heckert, appearance norms are consequential and thus not benign. She also indicates that persons with unattractive culturally constructed appearance will encounter diminished experiences. Both men and women are subject to appearance norms. Heckert points out that women are especially challenged in this area and are judged more harshly on the basis of appearance. In a study by Heckert and Joel Best, she also notes that redheaded men are more harshly judged than women.

Research indicates that the appearance norms are not only gendered but also raced. Frequently individuals with physical disabilities may also need to use a device such as a wheelchair or a cane, which also compromises experience expectations. As noted by the researchers, an important source of any quality in appearance idealization is age. Our preferred image of beauty is youth. Gray hair is, once again, especially problematic for women.

As noted by several researchers, the labeling theory is perhaps the most descriptive theory on the impact or stigma of physical appearance on individuals. There appears to be a cultural variation in which appearances are defined as deviant. For example, one culture may stress thinness, whereas another culture may stress overweight as a sign of abundance. In some cultures redheaded women are viewed as hot-tempered and with a fiery personality. Several studies have shown that females who are of size are considered by many in one culture as lazy and out of control, whereas in another culture they may be considered wives of successful businessmen. Coauthor Cliff Roberson once attended a legal seminar on jury selection. The presenter indicated that overweight people should not be selected for the jury panel because they lacked self-control.

In our current society blondes have benefited from social attributions of beauty. However, there are jokes about their mental abilities. The descriptive term *dumb blonde* is frequently used in our society. The color of a woman's hair should not be used as a measure of her mental abilities. Clearly appearance is a potential classifier of how other people will define them. For example, a tattooed professional basketball player may be classified by many based merely on his appearance and many tattoos. The authors were surprised to find out that one professional basketball player with numerous tattoos was not from New York City or Chicago but a small town in East Texas.

Fritz Heider developed a seminal theory in social psychology termed attribution theory.[5] Essentially, Heider suggested that humans observe other people's actions, draw inferences concerning those actions, and attribute meaning to those actions based on the inferences drawn. Researchers have used attribution theory to analyze the effects of a person's physical appearance.[6] Researchers have concluded that humans observe a person's physical appearance, draw inferences concerning that appearance, and attribute meaning to that appearance based on the inferences drawn. This attribution suggests that humans tend to judge a person's disposition and personality based on that person's physical appearance.[7]

Numerous studies indicate that we tend to associate physical attractiveness with positive personal characteristics and physical unattractiveness with socially deviant behavior, despite the indication that the process of attribution is often inaccurate. Social psychology teaches that humans make false substantive assumptions about other people's dispositions based on image alone.[8]

David Wiley concluded that physical appearance discrimination plays a substantive and all-too-frequent role in American criminal trials. He states that research suggests that people viewed as facially unattractive are more likely to be perceived as criminal than are facially attractive persons. Similarly, physically unattractive people are more likely to be reported for committing a crime than are their physically attractive counterparts. Wiley opined that it was not surprising, therefore, that jurors tend to base their decisions on the physical appearance of the defendant and the victim in simulated jury trials. Simulated juries tend to recommend lighter sentences for physically attractive defendants and harsher sentences for physically unattractive defendants, regardless of the severity of the crime.[9]

In a National Office Management Association study, about 28% of the 2,000 companies surveyed indicated that sex appeal is a qualification of some office jobs and is given serious consideration in the employment of receptionists, switchboard operators, secretaries, and stenographers.[10]

Sex appeal can also operate to the detriment of attractive female workers. In one case decided by the Iowa Human Rights Commission, the commission agreed with a lady who claimed she was fired from her job with a company that manufactures tractors because her striking physical appearance prompted male coworkers to hang around her workstation instead of working.[11]

SOCIETY IN ACTION

Is it legal for a university to fire a security guard because he has a beard?

SIMPSON V. CHARLES DREW UNIVERSITY OF MEDICINE AND SCIENCE

2013 WL 4407677 (Cal. App. 2 Dist., 2013)

Plaintiff argued defendant discriminated against him based on physical appearance because he wore a beard. He contends he has a constitutional right to wear a beard. The court disagreed.

The court noted that in one case, a high school teacher was transferred from the classroom to home teaching because he insisted on wearing a beard in violation of the school's administrative policy. (*Finot v. Pasadena City Bd. of Education* (1967) 250 Cal. App. 2d 189, 197–199). The appellate court in Finot held plaintiff possessed a constitutional right to wear a beard while teaching in a high school classroom. The Finot court found plaintiff's wearing of his beard was protected by the due process clauses of the federal and state Constitutions. The federal and state due process clauses prohibited the state and its agents, including the education board, from depriving plaintiff of his liberty to wear his beard without due process of law. The appellate court explained: "A beard, for a man, is an expression of his personality. On the one hand it has been interpreted as a symbol of masculinity, of authority and of wisdom. On the other hand it has been interpreted as a symbol of nonconformity and rebellion. But symbols, under appropriate circumstances merit constitutional protection." In Finot, the appellate court considered whether the state or governmental agency may restrict a public employee's constitutional right of personal liberty as a condition of employment. Here, there is no evidence in the record to suggest defendant is a governmental agency. Thus, Finot is inapplicable.

Finot involved the constitutional rights of a bearded public employee (a high school teacher), as distinguished from one employed in the private sector, but we perceive no essential distinction. The state is constitutionally inhibited from denying unemployment compensation benefits to an applicant who has been discharged from employment because of personal action which is constitutionally protected.

Plaintiff contends he is entitled to constitutional protection for wearing a beard regardless of whether he is a public or private

> employee. Plaintiff's argument is unavailing. The court explicitly limited its holding to the state and its agencies and refused to impose a constitutional obligation on private employers such as defendant: "We neither hold nor suggest that a bearded person has a constitutional right to a job and we do not reach or affect a private employer's right to manage its own business." We decline to impose a constitutional obligation on defendant. As a private employer, defendant is entitled to enforce its no-beard policy which contains religious and medical condition exceptions.

Tattoos

Tom Leppard of Scotland was considered the most tattooed man in the world because 99% of his body was covered in tattooed leopard spots. Leppard lived as something of a hermit in a shack with no electricity or furniture on the Scottish island of Skye. It is reported that he spent 5,500 pounds to complete the tattoos.

Tattoos have been around for more than 5,000 years. The Egyptians used tattoos to differentiate peasants from slaves. In the last three decades, the number of persons getting tattoos has mushroomed. In the 1940s and 1950s in the United States, getting a tattoo was considered by many as a form of deviant behavior. In today's world a large percentage of young and old have at least one tattoo, and no one considers them as deviant. This is a reflection of how social norms change.

Many people get tattooed to mark a significant aspect of themselves or their life. The U.S. Food and Drug Administration estimates that at least 45 million Americans are now tatted up. Another study estimated that 38% of Americans have some type of long-term body art. Some individuals consider tattooing as no longer just tattooing, but a culturally sanctioned form of delicate cutting. So what was once considered self-multilatory behavior and a psychiatric issue is now normative behavior.[12]

During the Second World War, the Germans tattooed persons who were designated for shipment to concentration camps. Assigned serial numbers were tattooed on the arms of those individuals prior to being shipped to a concentration camp as a method of identifying prisoners. This was done despite the fact that Judaism forbids tattoos.

Prison Tattoos

Frequently, especially with tattoos obtained while the individual is in prison, tattoos carry certain messages. For example, the tattoo of the number 1488 is a tattoo used by white supremacists. The 14 refers to a quote by

SOCIETY IN ACTION

As recently as 1970, a federal court in Florida determined that women were better suited for duties as flight attendants than men for airlines. Note: The decision is no longer valid law.

DIAZ V. PAN AM. WORLD AIRWAYS, INC.

311 F. Supp. 559, S.D. Fla. 1970

Excerpts from the opinion

The Court was impressed with this expert testimony and analysis, particularly since it was confirmed by the actual experience of Pan Am and Eastern that the male stewards whom they did hire, until recent years, and who therefore survived a selection process which did not exclude males, did not perform as well as the females selected in the same process. The Court further notes that Pan Am and United airlines have tried and abandoned available psychological tests as inadequate for testing the suitability of personality characteristics of applicants for the cabin attendant position, and that the industry is nevertheless continuing its efforts to find or develop suitable tests.

On the basis of this and other evidence, the Court finds that at the time of the plaintiff's application for employment and at the time of trial, there were few men who possessed the aggregate of personality characteristics which Pan Am was entitled to seek in its flight attendants; that it was not practically possible to identify in the hiring process those few men who did; that given the present requirements of the job, the admission of men to the hiring process, in the present state of the art of employment selection, would have increased the number of unsatisfactory employees hired, and reduced the average level of performance of Pan Am's flight attendants; and that the requirement that one be of the female sex was reasonably designed to improve the average performance of Pan Am's complement of flight attendants and was accordingly a bona fide occupational qualification reasonably necessary to the normal operation of Pan Am's business.

supremacist David Lane that contained 14 words. The 88 is shorthand for the eighth letter of the alphabet twice (H or HH—Heil Hitler). Reportedly, the Nuestra Familia gang uses the number 14 in their tattoos.

Prison tattoos can also symbolize toughness or refusal to accept authority, gang membership, or racist feelings. Since prison tattoos are frequently made with homemade needles and ink from pens, they are generally of one color.

The authors have worked extensively on prison research projects. When they notice an individual who has tattoos that are of one dark color, generally dark blue, they consider the individual an ex-con.

Physical Disability

Are physical disabilities deviant? The authors do not feel that physical disabilities are a form of deviance, but there are many in society who do. A physical disability is really a condition rather than a behavior. A physical disability is a limitation on a person's physical functioning, mobility, dexterity, or stamina.

According to Diane Taub, Elaine Blinde, and Kimberly Greer, individuals with physical disabilities are often stigmatized because their bodies are assumed to vary from norms of physical competence and bodily appearance. Possession of a discrediting attribute may impair social interactions and result in the devaluation of an individual.[13] According to the researchers, physical disability constitutes one of several socially defined categories of stigma, an attribute that is deeply discrediting. Individuals with a physical disability fall outside the range of what is considered normative or ordinary, thus spoiling their social identity and complicating interactions with able-bodied individuals. They conclude that when a physical disability becomes the defining feature of an individual, others often focus on the disability to the exclusion of relevant personal characteristics. They note that even with increased mainstreaming and political lobbying, individuals with physical disabilities frequently experience various forms of devaluation and discrimination. Harlan Hahn noted that those individuals who depart from normative images of human physique and "fail to meet prescribed standards of physical attractiveness" are devalued and stigmatized.[14]

Americans With Disabilities Act of 1990

The Americans with Disabilities Act (ADA) was signed into law on July 26, 1990. The ADA is one of America's most comprehensive pieces of civil rights legislation that prohibits discrimination and guarantees that people with disabilities have the same opportunities as everyone else to participate in the mainstream of American life—to enjoy employment opportunities, to purchase goods and services, and to participate in state and local government programs and services. Modeled after the Civil Rights Act of 1964, which prohibits discrimination on the basis of race, color, religion, sex, or national origin—and Section 504 of the Rehabilitation Act of 1973—the ADA is an equal opportunity law for people with disabilities.

To be protected by the ADA, one must have a disability, which is defined by the ADA as a physical or mental impairment that substantially limits one or more major life activities, have a history or record of such impairment, or be perceived by others as having such impairment. The ADA does not specifically name all of the impairments that are covered. The implementing regulations of the Americans with Disabilities Act of 1990, 42 USC §§ 12101 et seq. (U.S. Code), follow:

29 CFR Parts 1602, 1630 (Title I, EEOC) (Code of Federal Regulations)
28 CFR Part 35 (Title II, Department of Justice)
49 CFR Parts 27, 37, 38 (Titles II, III, Department of Transportation)
28 CFR Part 36 (Title III, Department of Justice)
47 CFR §§ 64.601 et seq. (Title IV, FCC)

Individuals With Disabilities Education Act

The Individuals with Disabilities Education Act (IDEA) (formerly called Public Law 94-142 or the Education for All Handicapped Children Act of 1975) requires public schools to make available to all eligible children with disabilities a free appropriate public education in the least restrictive environment appropriate to their individual needs.

IDEA requires public school systems to develop appropriate Individualized Education Programs (IEPs) for each child. The specific special education and related services outlined in each IEP reflect the individualized needs of each student.

IDEA also mandates that particular procedures be followed in the development of the IEP. Each student's IEP must be developed by a team of knowledgeable persons and must be reviewed at least annually. The team includes the child's teacher; the parents, subject to certain limited exceptions; the child, if determined appropriate; an agency representative who is qualified to provide or supervise the provision of special education; and other individuals at the parents' or agency's discretion.

If parents disagree with the proposed IEP, they can request a due process hearing and a review from the state educational agency if applicable in that state. They also can appeal the state agency's decision to state or federal court.

The implementing regulation of the Individuals with Disabilities Education Act, 20 USC §§ 1400 et seq., is 34 CFR Part 300.

Fair Housing Act

The Fair Housing Act, as amended in 1988, prohibits housing discrimination on the basis of race, color, religion, sex, disability, familial status, and national origin. Its coverage includes private housing, housing that receives federal financial assistance, and state and local government housing. It is unlawful to discriminate in any aspect of selling or renting housing or to deny a dwelling to a buyer or renter because of the disability of that individual, an individual associated with the buyer or renter, or an individual who intends to live in the residence. Other covered activities include, for example, financing, zoning practices, new construction design, and advertising.

The Fair Housing Act requires owners of housing facilities to make reasonable exceptions in their policies and operations to afford people with disabilities equal housing opportunities. For example, a landlord with a "no pets" policy may be required to grant an exception to this rule and allow an individual who is blind to keep a guide dog in the residence. The Fair Housing Act also requires landlords to allow tenants with disabilities to make reasonable access-related modifications to their private living space, as well as to common use spaces. (The landlord is not required to pay for the changes.) The act further requires that new multifamily housing with four or more units be designed and built to allow access for persons with disabilities. This includes accessible common use areas, doors that are wide enough for wheelchairs, kitchens and bathrooms that allow a person using a wheelchair to maneuver, and other adaptable features within the units.

The implementing regulation of the Fair Housing Amendments Act of 1988, 42 USC §§ 3601 et seq., is: 24 CFR Parts 100 et seq.

Air Carrier Access Act

The Air Carrier Access Act prohibits discrimination in air transportation by domestic and foreign air carriers against qualified individuals with physical or mental impairments. It applies only to air carriers that provide regularly scheduled services for hire to the public. Requirements address a wide range of issues, including boarding assistance and certain accessibility features in newly built aircraft and new or altered airport facilities. People may enforce rights under the Air Carrier Access Act by filing a complaint with the U.S. Department of Transportation, or by bringing a lawsuit in federal court.

The implementing regulation of the Air Carrier Access Act of 1986, 49 USC § 41705, is 14 CFR Part 382.

The Pregnancy Discrimination Act of 1978

The Pregnancy Discrimination Act of 1978 amended Title VII of the Civil Rights Act of 1964 to prohibit sex discrimination on the basis of pregnancy. Pregnancy discrimination involves treating a woman (an applicant or employee) unfavorably because of pregnancy, childbirth, or a medical condition related to pregnancy or childbirth.

If a woman is temporarily unable to perform her job due to a medical condition related to pregnancy or childbirth, the employer or other covered entity must treat her in the same way as it treats any other temporarily disabled employee. For example, the employer may have to provide light duty, alternative assignments, disability leave, or unpaid leave to pregnant employees if it does so for other temporarily disabled employees.

Additionally, impairments resulting from pregnancy (for example, gestational diabetes or preeclampsia, a condition characterized by pregnancy-induced hypertension and protein in the urine) may be disabilities under the Americans with Disabilities Act (ADA). An employer may have to provide a reasonable accommodation (such as leave or modifications that enable an employee to perform her job) for a disability related to pregnancy, absent undue hardship (significant difficulty or expense). The ADA Amendments Act of 2008 makes it much easier to show that a medical condition is a covered disability.

It is unlawful to harass a woman because of pregnancy, childbirth, or a medical condition related to pregnancy or childbirth. Harassment is illegal when it is so frequent or severe that it creates a hostile or offensive work environment or when it results in an adverse employment decision (such as the victim being fired or demoted). The harasser can be the victim's supervisor, a supervisor in another area, a coworker, or someone who is not an employee of the employer, such as a client or customer.

Mental Illness

Mental illness is generally considered any disease or condition that influences the way a person thinks, feels, behaves, or relates to others and to his or her surroundings. The symptoms of mental illness can range from mild to severe and are different depending on the type of mental illness; a person with an untreated mental illness often is unable to cope with life's daily routines and demands.

The exact causes of most mental illnesses are not known. Researchers have concluded that many of these conditions are caused by a combination of genetic, biological, psychological, and environmental factors—not personal weakness or a character defect. Most researchers have concluded that recovery from a mental illness is not simply a matter of will and self-discipline.

Ashley Crossman states that deviance and mental illness often go hand in hand. She notes that while not all deviants are considered mentally ill, almost all mentally ill persons are considered deviant (since mental illness is not considered normal).[15] Unfortunately, too many individuals equate mental illness with deviance.

According to Crossman, sociologists have two possible explanations for the link between social status and mental illness:

- It is the stresses of being in a low-income group, being a racial minority, or being a woman in a sexist society that contribute to higher rates of mental illness because this harsher social environment is a threat to mental health.
- Others argue that the same behavior that is labeled mentally ill for some groups may be tolerated in other groups and so therefore not labeled as such. If a homeless woman were to exhibit crazy, "deranged" behavior, she would be considered mentally ill, whereas if a rich woman exhibited the same behavior, she might be seen as merely eccentric or charming.

Functionalists believe that by recognizing mental illness, society upholds values about conforming behavior, whereas symbolic interactionists see mentally ill persons not as sick, but as victims of societal reactions to their behavior.

Conflict and labeling theorists contend that the people in a society with the fewest resources are the most likely to be labeled mentally ill. They point out that women, racial minorities, and the poor all suffer higher rates of mental illness than groups of higher social and economic status. The conflict and labeling theorists note that research has consistently shown that middle- and upper-class persons are more likely to receive some form of psychotherapy for their mental illness. Minorities and poorer individuals are more likely to only receive medication and physical rehabilitation, and not psychotherapy.

Research also indicates that women have higher rates of mental illness than men. Some sociologists believe that this stems from the roles that women are forced to play in society. Poverty, unhappy marriages, physical and sexual abuse, the stresses of rearing children, and spending a lot of time doing housework all contribute to higher rates of mental illness for women.

Genetics

Many mental illnesses run in families. This fact suggests that the illnesses are passed on from parents to children through genes. Genes contain instructions for the function of each cell in the body and are responsible for how we look, act, think, and so on. If your mother or father has some sort of mental illness, this does not mean you will have one. Hereditary just means that you are more likely to get the condition than if you didn't have an affected family member. Experts believe that many mental conditions are linked to problems in multiple genes—not just one, as with many diseases. This explains why a person who inherits a susceptibility to a mental disorder doesn't always develop the condition. The disorder itself occurs from the interaction of these genes and other factors—such as psychological trauma and environmental stressors—which can influence, or trigger, the illness in a person who has inherited a susceptibility to it.[16]

Biology

Certain types of mental illnesses have been linked to an abnormal functioning of brain circuits that connect different brain regions that control thinking, mood, and behavior. Nerve cells within those brain circuits pass information along from one cell to the next through brain chemicals called neurotransmitters. Scientists have concluded that if treatment procedures alter the activity of certain neurotransmitters (through medicines, psychotherapy, brain stimulation, or other treatments), those faulty brain circuits may work more efficiently, thereby controlling symptoms.

Other Conditions

Defects or injuries to certain areas of the brain also have been linked to some mental conditions. Some studies have indicated that inflammation may cause the development of mental illness. Even psychological trauma may have caused the mental illness. For example, mental illnesses may be triggered by psychological trauma suffered as a child or teenager, such as severe emotional, physical, or sexual abuse. Even a significant early loss, such as the loss of a parent, or neglect has apparently caused some mental illness. Certain stressor, such as a death or divorce, a dysfunctional family life, changing jobs or schools, and substance abuse, can trigger a disorder in a person who may be at risk for developing a mental illness.

Narcissistic Personality Disorder (NPD)

Narcissistic personality disorder (NPD) is a personality disorder that describes a person who is excessively preoccupied with personal adequacy, power, prestige, and vanity, and is mentally unable to see the destructive damage he or she is causing to himself or herself and others in the process. NPD was first formatted in 1968 and was originally labeled "megalomania." It is a form of severe egocentrism.[17]

Megalomania is defined as an unrealistic belief in one's superiority, grandiose abilities, and even omnipotence. It is characterized by a need for total power and control over others, and is marked by a lack of empathy for anything that is perceived as not feeding the self. It is estimated that about 1% of the population is afflicted by NPD. An example of megalomania in modern history is Adolf Hitler. Hitler wasn't content rising through the ranks to become the military leader of Germany; his megalomania drove him to aspire to conquer the entire world.

Megalomania is sometimes associated with bipolar disorder, a depressive illness that is characterized by mood swings from extreme lows to extreme highs. The NPD characteristics can be expressed in lesser degrees or in a different fashion by persons in society who may be considered to appear normal or near normal.

Narcissism

Narcissism is defined as excessive self-love. While it may be healthy to care about your own well-being and have a healthy self-esteem, when someone loves himself to the exclusion of all else and others become objectified to be used only to serve the self, this is no longer considered healthy or normal and is a form of mental illness.

Schizophrenia

Schizophrenia is a mental disorder generally characterized by abnormal social behavior and the failure to recognize what is real and what is not real. Common symptoms include false beliefs, auditory hallucinations, confused or unclear thinking, inactivity, and reduced social engagement and emotional expression. Generally a schizophrenia diagnosis is based on observed behavior and a person's reported experiences.

Schizophrenia symptoms generally begin in early adulthood. The disorder is thought to mainly affect the ability to think, but it also usually contributes to chronic problems with behavior and emotion. People with schizophrenia frequently have additional conditions, including major depression and anxiety disorders; the lifetime occurrence of substance use disorder is almost 50%. Social problems, such as long-term unemployment, poverty, and homelessness are common. The symptoms in the patients are vastly different. Virtually none present with the same group of symptoms. Moreover, even in the same patient, symptoms can show dramatic change over time, and there is significant interplay between different sets of symptoms.[18]

Posttraumatic Stress Disorder (PTSD)

Posttraumatic stress disorder may develop after a person is exposed to one or more traumatic events, such as sexual assault, fighting in a war, sustaining a serious injury, or the threat of death, in which he or she experiences intense fear, horror, or powerlessness. PTSD is used to indicate a person is experiencing one or more symptoms, such as disturbing recurring flashbacks, avoidance or numbing of memories of the event, and hyperarousal, which continue for more than a month after the traumatic event.

The majority of people who experience a traumatizing event will not develop PTSD. Women are more likely to experience higher impact events, and are also more likely to develop PTSD than men. Children are less likely to experience PTSD after trauma than adults, especially if they are less than 10 years of age. War veterans are at risk for PTSD.

The *Diagnostic and Statistical Manual of Mental Disorders,* Fifth Edition (DSM-V), published by the American Psychiatric Association, classifies PTSD as an anxiety disorder. With PTSD, the characteristic symptoms are not present before exposure to the violently traumatic event. In the typical case, the individual with PTSD persistently avoids all thoughts and emotions and discussion of the stressor event, and may experience amnesia for it. However, the event is commonly relived by the individual through intrusive, recurrent recollections, flashbacks, and nightmares. The symptoms are considered acute if they last less than 3 months and chronic if they persist for 3 months or longer. Often with delayed onset, the symptoms first occur after 6 months or some years later.

The term *posttraumatic stress disorder* was first recognized in the mid-1970s, based on the efforts of anti-Vietnam War activists and the antiwar group Vietnam Veterans Against the War. In 1978, the term was used in a working group finding presented to the Committee of Reactive Disorders. The diagnosis PTSD was formally recognized in 1980.[19]

Acute Stress Disorder (ASD)

Acute stress disorder is acute stress that is experienced in the immediate aftermath of a traumatic event. This is a newly categorized disorder that was first listed in the *Diagnostic and Statistical Manual of Mental Disorders,* 4th Edition (DSM-IV) in 1994. The characteristics of ASD are the development of anxiety, dissociative symptoms, and other manifestations that occur within one month of exposure to the traumatic event. To be diagnosed with ASD, the victim must first have experienced, witnessed, or been confronted with an event that involved actual or threatened death, serious injury, or a threat to the physical safety of the victim or others. In addition, the victim's response to such a condition must involve intense fear, helplessness, or horror. The diagnosis requires that the victim experience three of five posttraumatic stress disorder dissociative symptoms during or immediately after the traumatic incident. These symptoms must persist for at least 2 days but last no more than 30 days. The dissociative symptoms are de-realization, depersonalization, dissociative amnesia, subjective sense of numbing, and reduction in awareness of surroundings. If these symptoms last longer than 30 days, the victim may be suffering from PTSD.[20]

Long-Term Crisis Reaction

The National Organization for Victim Assistance (NOVA) termed the phrase "long-term crisis reaction." Professionals from NOVA working with crisis victims have observed this reaction on a number of occasions. Long-term crisis reaction is a condition that occurs when victims do not suffer from PTSD, but may reexperience feelings of the crisis reaction when certain events trigger the recollection of the trauma in their lives. The trigger event may be a number of situations, including the anniversaries of the crisis, birthdays, or holidays of loved ones lost during the trauma; significant life events such as marriages, divorces, births, and graduations; media events that broadcast similar types of incidents; and involvement in the criminal justice system.

The intensity and frequency of long-term crisis reactions usually diminish with the passage of time. As the victim develops coping mechanisms to deal with the trauma, resources or mechanisms of the victim may lessen the victim's reaction to triggering events. In most cases, the victim learns to continue to function despite these reactions.

Developmental Disability

Developmental disability is a term used to describe a diverse group of severe chronic conditions that are due to mental or physical impairments. These disabilities generally cause individuals who are living with the impairments difficulties in certain areas of life, especially in language, mobility, learning, self-help, and independent living.

The terms used to describe this condition are generally subject to a process called the euphemism treadmill. The euphemism treadmill refers to the fact that whatever term is used to describe this condition, eventually the term becomes perceived as an insult. For example, *mental retardation* and *mentally retarded* were developed to replace the previous set of terms, which were deemed to have become offensive. By the end of the 20th century, these terms themselves had come to be widely seen as disparaging, politically incorrect, and in need of replacement.[21]

Developmental disabilities generally are detected early in the individual's life, and persist throughout his or her life span. They can begin anytime during the developmental period and usually last throughout a person's lifetime. Most developmental disabilities begin before a baby is born, but some can happen after birth because of injury, infection, or other factors. The Centers for Disease Control and Prevention estimates that about one in six children in the United States have one or more developmental disabilities or other developmental delays.[22]

Children and adults with developmental disabilities are frequently treated poorly by society, just because they are different. Having a disability does not mean a person is a deviant or not healthy.

Common developmental disabilities include the following:

- **Attention-deficit hyperactivity disorder (ADHD).** People with ADHD may have trouble paying attention, controlling impulsive behaviors, and frequently act without thinking about what the result will be. Generally they are overly active. Although ADHD can't be cured, it can be successfully managed, and some symptoms may improve as the child ages.
- **Autism spectrum disorder (ASD).** This disorder refers to a group of developmental disabilities that can cause significant social, communication, and behavioral challenges. Frequently there is nothing about how people with ASD look that sets them apart from others. But individuals with this disorder may communicate, interact, behave, and learn in ways that are different from most other people. The learning, thinking, and problem-solving abilities of people with ASD can range from gifted to severely challenged. Frequently, people with ASD need a lot of help in their daily lives; others need less. A diagnosis of ASD now includes several conditions that used to be diagnosed separately: autistic disorder, pervasive developmental disorder not otherwise specified (PDD-NOS), and Asperger syndrome. These conditions are now all called autism spectrum disorder.[23]
- **Cerebral palsy (CP).** CP is a group of disorders that affect a person's ability to move and maintain balance and posture. CP is the most common motor disability in childhood. The symptoms of CP may vary from person to person. A person with severe CP probably needs to use special equipment to be able to walk, or might not be able to walk at all. A person with mild CP may be able walk awkwardly, but may not need any special help.

  CP is caused by abnormal development of the brain or damage to the developing brain that affects a child's ability to control his or her muscles. There are several possible causes of the abnormal development or damage. People used to think that CP was mainly caused by lack of oxygen during the birth process. Presently, scientists think that this causes only a small number of CP cases.

  Doctors classify CP according to the main type of movement disorder involved. Depending on which areas of the brain are affected, one or more of the following movement disorders can occur: stiff muscles, uncontrollable movements, and poor balance and coordination.

  The most common type of CP is spastic CP. Spastic CP affects about 80% of people with CP.

  People with dyskinetic CP have problems controlling the movement of their hands, arms, feet, and legs, making it difficult to sit and walk. Their movements are uncontrollable and can be slow and writhing or rapid and jerky.

People with ataxic CP have problems with balance and coordination. They might be unsteady when they walk. They often have a hard time with quick movements or movements that need a lot of control, like writing. They may have a hard time controlling their hands or arms when they reach for something.

Mixed cerebral palsy is where the individual has symptoms of more than one type of CP.

- **Down syndrome.** Down syndrome is a condition in which people are born with an extra chromosome. Normally a person is born with 46 chromosomes. However, if one is born with Down syndrome, there is an extra copy of one of the chromosomes. The extra copy changes the body and brain's normal development. It also causes mental and physical struggles for the individual.
- **Fetal alcohol spectrum disorders (FASDs).** FASDs are a group of conditions that can occur in a person whose mother drank alcohol during pregnancy. FASDs are preventable if the mother does not drink alcohol during pregnancy.
- **Fragile X syndrome (FXS).** FXS causes autism and intellectual disability, usually in people with XY chromosomes.
- **Intellectual disability.** Refers to an individual whose IQ is below 70, along with limitations in adaptive functioning and onset before the age of 18 years.
- **Pervasive developmental disorders (PDDs).** PDDs are a group of developmental disabilities that can cause significant social, communication, and behavioral challenges.

Insanity

Insanity is a legal term and no longer a medical term.

The term *insanity* refers to a legal defense and not a medical condition. It is used to describe a condition of unsoundness of mind that constitutes a defense and absolves one from legal responsibility for committing a crime. In civil law issues it refers to one's lack of legal capacity, as for entering into a contractual agreement or making a valid will.

Although it is no longer used in the medical profession, it was originally used to describe a person with certain abnormal mental or behavioral patterns. Frequently it is used by nonmedical persons to describe persons who commit violations of societal norms. Sometimes it is used to refer to a person who is a danger to himself or herself or others. The term *insanity* is used as an informal unscientific term denoting mental instability.

FOCUS ON PEOPLE

ISAAC RAY (1807–1881)

Isaac Ray, an American psychiatrist, was one of the founders of the discipline of forensic psychiatry. In 1838, he published *A Treatise on the Medical Jurisprudence of Insanity*. This treatise was the authoritative text on insanity for many years.[24]

Ray was a native of Beverly, Massachusetts, and a graduate of Phillips Academy and received his medical degree from the Medical College of Maine (Bowdoin College). While living in the coastal village of Eastport, he wrote his *Treatise on the Medical Jurisprudence of Insanity*. After several years in Eastport, he was appointed superintendent of the state hospital for the insane in Augusta in 1841. In 1845, he moved to Providence, Rhode Island, to supervise the building of the private Butler Hospital and became its first superintendent.

The *Treatise on the Medical Jurisprudence of Insanity* was very influential and was used by defense lawyer Sir Alexander Cockburn in the famous English trial of Daniel M'Naghten in 1843. At the trial, Cockburn used the treatise to argue that the insanity defense should be based on the defendant's ability to distinguish right from wrong.

Ray was a founding member of the Association of Medical Superintendents of American Institutions for the Insane and served as its president from 1855 to 1859. Between 1828 and 1880, he published numerous articles dealing with insanity and its legal implications.

The Trial of Daniel M'Naghten: The Trial of the Century

Daniel M'Naghten was tried for the murder of Edward Drummond, secretary to Sir Robert Peel. The trial started on Friday, March 3, 1843, at the Old Bailey Criminal Court in London. The presiding judge was Sir Nicholas Tindal, the Lord Chief Justice of Common Pleas. Public attendance at the trial included Albert, Prince Consort of Queen.

The Solicitor General, Sir William Webb Follett, opened the prosecution with a description of the facts of the crime and then discussed in detail the laws on criminal insanity as they had been formulated in the English courts.

The defense counsel, Alexander Cockburn, in his speech to the jury the following day, stated: "I hold in my hand perhaps the most scientific treatise that the age has produced upon the subject of insanity in relation to jurisprudence—it is the work of Dr. Ray, an American writer on medical jurisprudence, and a professor in one of the great national establishments of that country."

Cockburn based his insanity defense argument on the works of Isaac Ray. The jury was instructed by the chief judge to enter a finding of not guilty. After the finding of not guilty, M'Naghten was confined to a mental hospital where he remained until his death in 1856.

According to Bernard Diamond, who has researched extensively on the M'Naghten trial, "It is safe to say that never since, in English or an American courtroom, has a scientific work by a psychiatrist been treated with such respect as was *The Medical Jurisprudence of Insanity*."[25] In spite of the public and parliamentary indignation over M'Naghten's acquittal, the M'Naghten rule was developed. The M'Naghten test for insanity is currently used in most of the states in the United States.

The medical profession avoids the use of the term and uses terms associated with diagnoses of specific mental disorders. For example, the presence of delusions or hallucinations is referred to as psychosis. The medical professional generally uses the term *psychopathology* when referring to mental illness in general terms.

In English, the word *sane* derives from the Latin adjective *sanus*, meaning "healthy." The phrase *mens sana in corpore sano* is often translated to mean a "healthy mind in a healthy body." From this perspective, insanity can be considered poor health of the mind, not necessarily of the brain as an organ (although that can affect mental health), referring to defective function of mental processes such as reasoning. Another Latin phrase related to our current concept of sanity is *compos mentis* (literally "sound of mind"), and a euphemistic term for insanity is *non compos mentis*. In law, *mens rea* means having had criminal intent, or a guilty mind, when the act (*actus reus*) was committed.

A more informal use of the term *insanity* is to denote something considered highly unique, passionate, or extreme, including in a positive sense. The term may also be used as an attempt to discredit or criticize particular ideas, beliefs, principles, desires, personal feelings, attitudes, or their proponents, such as in politics and religion.

Legal Tests for Insanity

As noted by Harvey Wallace and Cliff Roberson, insanity is a controversial defense. It is the subject of numerous articles and news stories each year. One study, however, indicated that the public should not be too concerned about the frequency with which the defense is used. That study concluded that the insanity defense was used in fewer than 2% of all trials involving serious crimes. Because of the complexity of this form of

SOCIETY IN ACTION

FAKING INSANITY

There are numerous cases in which a defendant has been accused of faking insanity to avoid a criminal conviction. Probably the most famous was Vincent Gigante (1928–2005).

Gigante was a New York Italian American and reportedly the boss of the Genovese crime family. Gigante, as a young adult, was a professional boxer who fought 25 bouts between 1944 and 1947. Reportedly after his boxing career, he became an enforcer for the mob. After serving a term in prison where he met with Vito Genovese, he became an overseer of his own crew of Genovese associates and operated out of Greenwich Village.

By 1981, Gigante became the family's boss. For about 30 years, Gigante feigned insanity in an effort to throw law enforcement off his trail. He was called The Oddfather and The Enigma in the Bathrobe by the press. Gigante often wandered the streets in his bathrobe and slippers, mumbling incoherently to himself. He later admitted that this was an act to avoid prosecution. He was indicted on federal racketeering charges in 1990, but was determined to be mentally unfit to stand trial. In 1997, however, he was tried and convicted of racketeering and was given a 12-year sentence. Facing new charges in 2003, he pleaded guilty and admitted that his supposed insanity was an elaborate effort to avoid prosecution. He died while in prison custody in 2005 at the U.S. Medical Center for Federal Prisoners.[26]

defense, it is normally raised only in the most serious cases, such as murder or attempted murder. The question of insanity may arise at the time of the criminal conduct, at the time of trial (referred to as incompetency), during incarceration, or just prior to execution.[27]

If insanity exists at the time the criminal act was committed, the defense acts to negate the required mental state of the actor, and therefore the individual has not committed the crime. Insanity at trial time is referred to as incompetency to stand trial. The accused must have a sufficient mental state in order to assist her attorney in the defense of the case. If the accused is not sufficiently competent, the trial must be delayed. Unlike the question of mental state at the time of the act, which negates the guilt, incompetency to stand trial refers only to the ability of the accused to assist his or her counsel and does not negate the commission of the offense. If the accused is determined to be incompetent to stand trial, the state is required to delay the trial until the individual is competent. The practical effect of this requirement is that in most cases, the trial can never be held, because the accused's mental state either does not change or gets worse.

Five basic tests for insanity have been used in the American court system:

- M'Naghten test
- Irresistible impulse test
- Durham rule
- Federal test
- American Law Institute (ALI) test

Under the M'Naghten rule, also referred to as the right and wrong test, individuals are presumed to be sane and to possess a sufficient degree of reason to be responsible for their crimes, until the contrary is proven. For individuals not to be legally responsible for their acts, they must be laboring under such a defect of reason, from diseases of the mind, as not to know the nature and quality of the acts that they were doing, or if they did know it, that they did not know that it was wrong.

The irresistible impulse test holds that a person will be considered insane if, as a result of a disease of the mind, he or she was unable to control his or her behavior. Just as the name of this test implies, if the defendant could prove that he or she was suffering from a disease of the mind so that he or she could not control an impulse to commit criminal acts, then he or she would be considered insane.

The Durham test does away with the right or wrong requirement of the M'Naghten rule and states that a person is insane if he or she committed a criminal act that was a product of a mental disease or defect.

The federal test, also known as the severe mental disease test, requires that the defendant, as a result of severe mental disease or defect, be unable to appreciate the nature and quality of the wrongfulness of his or her act or acts.

Under the ALI test, a person is not responsible for criminal conduct if at the time of such conduct, as a result of mental disease or defect, he or she lacks substantial capacity either to appreciate the criminality (wrongfulness) of his or her conduct or to conform his or her conduct to the requirements of the law.

Diminished Responsibility

This is when a defendant suffers from a mental disease or stress that, while it does not completely impair the reasoning ability, affects the person's reasoning. The concept of diminished responsibility is similar to the insanity defense, except that it is a partial defense. It tends to diminish the responsibility of the defendant, for example, to reduce first-degree murder to a lesser offense. Many states reject this personal defense, and those that allow it limit its use to specific intent crimes, permitting evidence to prove that the defendant lacked the mental state to commit an element of the offense.

Intoxication

Generally voluntary intoxication is not a defense. In many cases, it is considered an aggravating element and may increase the maximum allowable punishment.

Involuntary intoxication may provide a complete excuse for criminal liability under some circumstances. The problem involves exactly what is considered involuntary. The case law recognizes several situations in which involuntary intoxication is a complete defense. The first and most obvious case is that in which the defendant was tricked into drinking or ingesting alcohol or drugs that rendered him or her incapable of forming the necessary intent for the crime that was committed.

The second instance of involuntary intoxication as a defense occurs when the defendant claims he was forced to consume the substance. The courts have been very restrictive in allowing this intoxication by duress defense.

Practicum

You are a small business owner. You need to hire a secretary. One woman who applies is definitely pregnant. Can you exclude her as an applicant because of her condition? Can you base the exclusion on the fact that you need a secretary who will be available every workday and cannot afford to allow her to take medical leave?

Summary

- The Greeks originated the term *stigma* to refer to bodily signs designed to expose something unusual and bad about the moral status of the signifier.
- According to Goffman, stigmatized people are those that do not have full social acceptance and are constantly striving to change their social identities.
- A stereotype is a thought that can be adopted about specific types of individuals or certain ways of doing things. These thoughts or beliefs may or may not accurately reflect reality.
- Physical appearance, like behavior, is subject to social evaluation and differential social reaction.
- Both men and women are subject to appearance norms. Heckert points out that women are especially challenged in this area and are judged more harshly on the basis of appearance.

- Heider suggested that humans observe other people's actions, draw inferences concerning those actions, and attribute meaning to those actions based on the inferences drawn.
- Numerous studies indicate that we tend to associate physical attractiveness with positive personal characteristics and physical unattractiveness with socially deviant behavior, despite the indication that the process of attribution is often inaccurate.
- Tattoos have been around for more than 5,000 years. The Egyptians used tattoos to differentiate peasants from slaves. In the last three decades, the number of persons getting tattoos has mushroomed.
- A physical disability is really a condition rather than a behavior. A physical disability is a limitation on a person's physical functioning, mobility, dexterity, or stamina.
- The Americans with Disabilities Act (ADA) was signed into law on July 26, 1990. The ADA is one of America's most comprehensive pieces of civil rights legislation that prohibits discrimination and guarantees that people with disabilities have the same opportunities as everyone else to participate in the mainstream of American life.
- Mental illness is generally considered as any disease or condition that influences the way a person thinks, feels, behaves, or relates to others and his or her surroundings.
- The symptoms of mental illness can range from mild to severe and are different depending on the type of mental illness; a person with an untreated mental illness often is unable to cope with life's daily routines and demands.
- Developmental disability is a term used to describe a diverse group of severe chronic conditions that are due to mental or physical impairments. These disabilities generally cause individuals who are living with the impairments difficulties in certain areas of life, especially in language, mobility, learning, self-help, and independent living.
- The term *insanity* refers to a legal defense and not a medical condition. It is used to describe a condition of unsoundness of mind that constitutes a defense and absolves one from legal responsibility for committing a crime.

Questions in Review

1. When is involuntary intoxication a defense in a criminal case?
2. Why is insanity presently considered a legal term and not a medical one?
3. What is the difference between a person's condition and a person's illness?

4. When is diminished responsibility considered a defense in a criminal case?
5. What law protects handicapped workers?
6. Define *physical disability*.

Key Terms

Euphemism treadmill: The process that refers to the fact that whatever term is used to describe this condition, eventually the term becomes perceived as an insult.

Megalomania: A mental condition that is defined as an unrealistic belief in one's superiority, grandiose abilities, and even omnipotence.

Physical disability: A limitation on a person's physical functioning, mobility, dexterity, or stamina.

Stereotype: A thought that can be adopted about specific types of individuals or certain ways of doing things.

Stereotype threat: A concept that holds that people can underperform at tasks when thinking about the negative performance expectations for their group.

Stigma: Pertains to the shame that a person may feel when he or she fails to meet other people's standards, and to the fear of being discredited.

Endnotes

1. Erving Goffman. (1963). *Stigma: Notes on the management of spoiled identity*. London: Penguin
2. Edward Jones, Amerigo Farina Albert Hastorf, Hazel Markus, Dale T. Miller, & Robert A. Scott. (1984). *Social stigma: The psychology of marked relationships*. New York: Freeman.
3. Laurie T. O'Brien & Christian S. Crandall. (2003). Stereotype threat and arousal: Effects on women's math performance. *Personality and Social Psychology Bulletin*, *29*, 782–789.
4. Druann Maria Heckert. (2013). The stigma of deviant physical appearance. In Clifton D. Bryant (Ed.), *The Routledge handbook of deviant behavior* (pp. 553–558). London: Routledge.
5. Fritz Heider. (1958). *The psychology of interpersonal relations*. New York: Wiley.
6. Linda A. Jackson. (1992). *Physical appearance and gender: Sociobiological and sociocultural perspectives*. New York: SUNY Press.
7. David L. Wiley. (1995). Beauty and the beast: Physical appearance discrimination in American criminal trials. *St. Mary's Law Journal*, *27*, 193–239.
8. Wiley, 1995.
9. Wiley, 1995.
10. V. K. Oppenheimer. (1968, May). The sex-labeling of jobs. *Industrial Relations: A Journal of Economy and Society*, *7*, 219–234.

11. Martha Chamallas. (1984). Exploring the 'entire spectrum' of disparate treatment under Title VII: Rules governing predominantly female jobs. *University of Illinois Law Review*, 1–62.
12. U.S. Food and Drug Administration web page. http://www.fda.gov/Cosmetics/ProductsIngredients/Products/ucm108530.htm. Retrieved June 28, 2014.
13. Diane E. Taub, Elaine M. Blinde, & Kimberly R. Greer. (1999). Stigma management through participation in sport and physical activity: Experiences of male college students with physical disabilities. *Human Relations*, 52(11), 1469–1484.
14. Harlan Hahn. (1988). The politics of physical differences: Disability and discrimination. *Journal of Social Issues*, *44*(1), 39–47.
15. Ashley Crossman. (No date). Deviance and mental illness. http://sociology.about.com/od/Deviance/a/Deviance-And-Mental-Illness.htm. Retrieved June 29, 2014.
16. Mental illness basics. Human Relations, 52(11). http://www.medicinenet.com/mental_illness/article.htm. Retrieved June 25, 2014.
17. R. Kayne & L. S. Wynn (Eds.). (2013, March 4). What is megalomania? https://web.archive.org/web/20130311080518/http://www.wisegeek.org/what-is-megalomania.htm. Retrieved June 25, 2014.
18. Peter F. Buckley, Brian J. Miller, Douglas S. Lehrer, & David J. Castle. (2009). Psychiatric comorbidities and schizophrenia. *Schizophrenia Bulletin*, 35(2), 383–402.
19. World Health Organization. (2007). *International statistical classification of diseases and related health problems* (10th rev.). Geneva: World Health Organization (UN).
20. Harvey Wallace & Cliff Roberson. (2014). *Victimology: Legal, psychological, and social perspectives* (4th ed.). Columbus, OH: Pearson.
21. Nicholas A. Cummings & Rogers H. Wright. (2005). Psychology's surrender to political correctness. In Rogers H. Wright & Nicholas A. Cummings (Eds.), *Destructive trends in mental health: The well-intentioned path to harm* (chap. 1). New York: Routledge.
22. Centers for Disease Control and Prevention website. http://www.cdc.gov/ncbddd/developmentaldisabilities/index.html. Retrieved June 26, 2014.
23. Centers for Disease Control and Prevention website.
24. 19th century psychiatrists of note: Diseases of the mind: Highlights of American psychiatry through 1900. U.S. National Library of Medicine. http://www.nlm.nih.gov/hmd/diseases/note.html. Retrieved June 26, 2014.
25. Bernard L. Diamond. (1956). Isaac Ray and the trial of Daniel M'Naghten. *American Journal of Pyschiatry*, *112*(8), 651–656.
26. Selwyn Raab. (2005, December 19). Vincent Gigante, mob boss who feigned incompetence to avoid jail, dies at 77. *New York Times*, p. A-1. William K. Rashbaum. (2005, December 24). Gigante, mafia boss, is mourned and buried with little fanfare. *New York Times*, p. C-1.
27. Harvey Wallace & Cliff Roberson. (2013). *Principles of criminal law* (5th ed.). Columbus, OH: Pearson.

chapter nine

Business and Organized Crime

Chapter Objectives

What you should know and understand after studying this chapter:

- How white-collar crime is different from street crime
- What crimes are considered as white-collar crimes
- The issues involved in determining the appropriate punishment for white-collar criminals
- Why individuals commit white-collar crimes
- What constitutes money laundering
- Why money laundering offenses are used to target certain criminal activities
- The RICO statutes

Introduction

In this chapter, white-collar crime and organized crime are explored. By joining the two subjects in one chapter, we do not intend to imply that they are closely related. The joiner was because of space limitations. A separate text could be written on each of the issues. Accordingly, we will explore only the highlights of those criminal activities. This does not mean they are insignificant. Quite the opposite, they are very significant and affect each of us.

White-Collar Crimes

As noted by Frank DiMarino and Cliff Roberson, the introduction of the concept of white-collar crime into the study of criminal behavior revolutionized the thinking of the field by making it no longer possible to employ class-specific explanations to interpret such behavior.[1] Defining what constitutes white-collar crime is no easy chore. The content of the phrase "white-collar crime" is difficult to pin down. The term *white-collar crime* was first used by Edwin Sutherland in 1939, and the first reported U.S. court case in which the term was used was *United States v. Standard Ultramarine & Color Co.*, 137 F. Supp. 167, 168–173 (D.N.Y. 1955).

Generally, when we refer to white-collar crime, we are referring to offenses where there is a family resemblance to some type of concept of untruthfulness, such as perjury, fraud, false statements, obstruction of justice, bribery, extortion and blackmail, insider trading, tax evasion, and certain regulatory offenses. As noted by DiMarino and Roberson, what distinguishes white-collar crime from traditional crime is that white-collar crimes are the product in many ways of an advanced economy with high-speed communications, a large administrative apparatus, and a pervasive legal system that makes enforcement of the law a priority.

White-collar crimes are those crimes that are committed by individuals in their profession, and they do not involve the use of weapons or force. Frequently, they are also called business crimes. White-collar crimes are committed by individuals at all economic levels, but most are committed by the persons in the higher economic income levels. The term was originally intended as a classification of offenders but has since expanded to include a broad range of nonviolent offenses where cheating and dishonesty in normally legal business transactions are the central element. The name *white collar* comes from the fact that originally the offenders worked in positions that required the wearing of a white shirt and a tie.

The Department of Justice defines white-collar crime as offenses classified as nonviolent illegal activities that principally involve traditional notions of deceit, deception, concealment, and manipulation, breach of trust, subterfuge, or illegal circumvention.[2]

How serious is white-collar crime? According to the Federal Bureau of Investigation (FBI), white-collar crime cost the citizens of the nation more than $300 billion each year.

Edwin H. Sutherland

Edwin H. Sutherland, a professor at Indiana University, was the first to use the phrase "white-collar crime," in his address to the American Sociological Association in Philadelphia, Pennsylvania, in December 1939. His speech was reprinted in the *America Sociological Review* in February 1940.[3]

Sutherland stated:

> The "robber barons" of the last half of the nineteenth century were white-collar criminals, as practically everyone now agrees. Their attitudes are illustrated by the statements: Col. Vanderbilt asked, "You don't suppose you can run a railroad in accordance with the statutes, do you?" A. B. Stickney, a railroad president, said to 16 other railroad presidents in the home of J. P. Morgan in 1890, "I have the

> utmost respect for you gentlemen, individually, but as railroad presidents I wouldn't trust you with my watch out of sight." …
>
> The present day white-collar criminals, who are more swallowed and deceptive than the robber barons, are represented by Krueger, Stavisky, … and many other merchant princes and captains of finance and industry, and by a host of lesser followers. Their criminality has been demonstrated again and again in the investigation of land offices, railways, insurance, munitions, banking, public utilities, stock exchanges, the oil industry, real estate, reorganization committees, receiverships, bankruptcies, and politics…. White-collar criminals are found in every occupation, as can be discovered readily in casual conversation with a representative of an occupation by asking him, "What crooked practices are found in your occupation?"[4]

Frequently, you hear the statement that there are no individual victims in white-collar crime. The statement implies that only big businesses and banks are involved as victims. This is an incorrect statement since many investors have lost their retirement funds in investment schemes.

SOCIETY IN ACTION

SALE OF THE EIFFEL TOWER

While the term *white-color criminal* was not used in 1925, Victor Lustig (1890–1947) was clearly an early white-collar criminal. He became famous as the man who sold the Eiffel Tower. Lustig could speak five different languages and is known to have used 45 aliases. In the spring of 1925, Lustig noted an article in a Paris newspaper stating that the French government was having problems maintaining the Eiffel Tower and was considering having it dismantled. Using fake French government stationery, he invited six of France's leading scrap metal dealers to a meeting at the Hotel de Crillon in Paris. At the meeting, he introduced himself as a deputy minister in France's Ministry of Posts and Telegraphs. He invited the six dealers to bid on buying the tower for scrap metal. Not only did he get paid from one of the dealers, but he also accepted a bribe from the buyer for giving the buyer an inside track on the bids.[5]

Theories on Causation

Sutherland noted that with a small number of expectations, the generalization that criminality is closely associated with poverty does not apply to white-collar criminals. He concluded that white-collar criminality, like other criminality, is learned.

DiMarino and Roberson explored the questions: Is white-collar crime caused by societal or organizational pressures? Is the crime caused by organizational-specific pressures? They noted that executives are prone to overstate the earnings and understate the liabilities of their companies because they are judged by the profit margin during their stewardship. They asked: Are certain personality characteristics more associated with white-collar criminals? For example, is an individual with a competitive personality more likely to commit white-collar crime than an individual who does not have that type of personality?

Strain theories assume that excessive pressures or strain on the individual often result in criminal conduct. According to strain theorists, people are basically good. Excessive pressures placed on us by society cause some people to commit criminal acts.

Robert Merton contended that there are institutionalized paths to success in society, and that crime is caused by the difficulty that individuals have in achieving socially valued goals by legitimate means. Those who do not have the opportunity to achieve success, for example, an individual who cannot afford to attend college, have difficulty achieving wealth and status by securing well-paid employment. Accordingly, they are more likely to use criminal means to obtain these goals. Does this apply to white-collar criminals, most of whom are college graduates and in the higher economic income level? For example, consider Kenneth Lay of Enron fame, a college classmate of coauthor Cliff Roberson at the University of Missouri, was certainly not from the lower class, and he was CEO of one of the largest corporations in the United States. Lay's goals were not to achieve socially valued goals, but to exceed all others in obtaining wealth.

Social control theorists, unlike strain theorists, contend that individuals are by nature amoral and will commit deviant acts if they have the chance. The control theorists contend that people are by nature inclined to break the law, but if societal controls are present, the controls will restrain their unlawful behavior. One could argue that a white-collar criminal both has the opportunity to commit criminal behavior and is less likely to be detected, apprehended, and convicted than the individual who robs a liquor store.

Early in his teaching career, Cliff Roberson agreed to teach a course in criminology in a federal prison for a local community college. At the time he accepted the assignment, he thought that he was agreeing to teach a continuing education course to the correctional staff. It was only later that he learned that his students were all federal prisoners. As the class of prisoners discussed each of the theories on the causes of crime, he would ask the prisoners which criminological theory they considered the most relevant. After receiving their answers and rationale, he would then ask the prisoners if it applied to their case. In each case, the prisoner would answer that it did not apply to them because …, and then the prisoner would rationalize why his case was different. Applying this concept to Kenneth Lay's actions, which resulted in the loss of retirement savings for many Americans, he would probably answer that he committed the crimes to save the corporation, that is, for the good of the corporation.

Cultural deviance theories assume that individuals are not capable of committing criminal acts, and what are considered deviant acts are deviant only by mainstream standards, not by the offender's standards. This concept may apply to white-collar criminals. In most conventional crime prosecutions the issue is: Was the defendant the one who committed the crime? Attorneys frequently call this the SODDIT defense (some other dude did it). The white-collar criminal frequently admits committing the acts, but argues that they were not criminal.

Social disorganization theories hold that there is a relationship between increasing crime and the increasing complexity of our society. They also contend that social disorganization is a causal factor in crime. Social disorganization is defined as a breakdown in the bonds of society, especially those involving relationships, teamwork, and morale. In addition, they hold that in communities where the traditional clubs, groups, and so on, are no longer in existence, the community is disrupted and there is a lack of consensus of values and norms. Subsequently, this lack of consensus causes higher incidences of criminal behavior. A rational argument can be made that the white-collar criminal has the opportunity and is encouraged to commit the crime because of our complex society.

The two leading symbolic interactionist (SI) theories of crime causation are differential association and labeling. The SI theories examine the process of becoming a criminal.

Both SI theories hold that criminal behavior is a learned activity. Both theories also place the causes of our behavior in our interpretation of reality. As noted earlier, Sutherland considered that white-collar crime was caused by learned behavior.

Sutherland originated the differential association theory, which is based on the concept that criminal behavior is learned behavior. His theory focuses on how individuals learn how to become criminals, but does not concern itself with why they become criminals. They learn how to commit criminal acts; they learn motives, drives, rationalizations, and attitudes. A person learns to commit criminal acts the same way we learn to play basketball, baseball, and other childhood games.

SOCIETY IN ACTION

DOES AN INDIVIDUAL'S ECONOMIC LEVEL DETERMINE NOT WHETHER HE OR SHE WILL BE A CRIMINAL, BUT INSTEAD THE TYPE OF CRIME THE INDIVIDUAL WILL COMMIT?

The above question has been the subject of many interesting discussions. Many researchers contend that some individuals will commit crime regardless of their economic status. According to this line of thought, the choice to rob a convenience store or embezzle from a bank depends not on whether or not you will commit a crime, but on the opportunities that you have to commit the crime. The individual who is unemployed and living on the wrong side of the tracks has little opportunity to embezzle money. Accordingly, he robs the store. The bank officer who embezzles is probably an individual who is not comfortable with using a gun or confronting a possible violent situation, so he or she embezzles. Accordingly, under this line of reasoning, a criminal is a criminal, but his or her crime of choice depends on his or her opportunities.

SOCIETY IN ACTION

Dan Ariely, professor of behavioral economics at Duke University, in his book *Predictably Irrational* contends that people are more ethical when dealing with paper money than when dealing with other items that have the same dollar value. In an experiment, Ariely placed six packs of soda in refrigerators located in a common area of a college dormitory. He also placed in other refrigerators at similar locations six $1 bills. After 72 hours, all the sodas were gone, but not the bills. He opined that this revealed hidden biases that we all have to some degree. He also opined that office workers were more likely to steal office pens and pencils than they were to steal from the petty cash drawer. Another conclusion of Ariely was that people were more dishonest when the reward was something other than money. According to Ariely, the white-collar criminal rarely steals actual currency; more often, it is stocks, bonds, and so forth.[6] Ariely contends that we would cheat by a factor bigger than we could ever imagine if the rewards were something other than cash.

Organizational Needs

According to Sally Simpson, corporate crime results when managers take organizational needs and pressures into account when solving business problems or when managers act in accordance with the dominant culture of the firm, subunit, or team in which they work.[7] Under this concept, Kenneth Lay's crimes were committed in an unsuccessful attempt to save Enron. Enron Corporation was an American energy, commodities, and services company based in Houston, Texas. Before its bankruptcy on December 2, 2001, Enron employed approximately 20,000 staff and was one of the world's major electricity, natural gas, communications, and pulp and paper companies, with claimed revenues of nearly $101 billion during 2000. *Fortune* magazine named Enron America's Most Innovative Company for six consecutive years.

Theorists uniformly hold that structures, processes, and tasks are opportunity structures for misconduct because they provide the following:

- Normative support for misconduct
- The means for carrying out violations
- Concealment that minimizes detection and sanctioning

While some degree of self-interest may underlie offending decisions, corporate crime is not reducible to individuals and their characteristics because the individual and the organization are symbiotic. Managers are affected by and in turn contribute to the culture and structure of the organization. In short, corporate criminologists expect organizational characteristics as manifested in the behavior of individuals, not low self-control, to explain corporate illegality.

Routine Activity Theory

> Criminal opportunities are now recognized as an important cause of all crime. Without an opportunity, there cannot be a crime.[8]

The routine activity theory was developed by Lawrence E. Cohen and Marcus Felson in 1979, when they were trying to find a reason for high urban crime rates. The basic theory stated that criminal events originate in the routines of everyday life. The researchers stated that there must be three elements involved in order for a crime to be committed:

- A motivated offender
- A suitable target
- The lack of guardianship

If these three elements are present, a crime will occur in the absence of an effective controller.

The routine activity theory is controversial among sociologists who believe in the social causes of crime. The theory is based on the classical school of criminology, in that criminals decide that to commit the crime or not commit it is based on whether it will be beneficial to them.

What do the routine activity theorists mean when they use the phrase "lack of a capable guardianship?" While it includes the presence of a big strong person to guard you, the term is used in a broader sense by these theorists. It means anything or any person that can keep the offender from getting to a target. For example, automobile locks may or may not be a capable guardian depending on the type of lock and the skill of the offender.

The phrase "capable guardian" refers to anything that may discourage or prevent an offender from accomplishing his or her mission. It may also be a passing police officer. In addition to blocking the offender, a capable guardianship may make the target too risky in the eyes of the offender. If the offender believes that the piece of property may easily be traced, the offender may decide that it is too risky to steal the item.

When a medical doctor considers defrauding the government on a Medicare claim, the fact that the doctor can easily perform this action within the safety of his or her office probably increases the likelihood that the doctor may attempt to commit the fraud. If, however, the doctor had to break into the offices of the federal Medicare to commit the crime, he or she would likely decide that the risks involved are too great.

The primary technique used by almost all white-collar criminals is deception; rarely is there a need to resort to violence, as there may when committing a street crime such as robbing the convenience store. Does the routine activity theory provide an explanation that can be used when studying white-collar crime?

One of the most often repeated maxims in embezzlement prevention classes is: "No one can embezzle from you unless you trust them." This maxim is based on the premise that unless you trust someone with access to or information on your financial accounts, the person does not have the opportunity to embezzle from the accounts. If in a small retail business only one person opens the mail, that person is probably the only one who has an opportunity to steal from the incoming mail.

The crime pattern theory was developed by Canadian environmental criminologists Pat and Paul Brantingham.[9] The theory suggests that crime sites and opportunities are not random.

Using the principles of the routine activity theory, the crime pattern theory (also labeled the offender search theory) contends that offenders become aware of criminal opportunities as they engage in their normal legitimate activities. Under this theory, offenders tend to find their targets in familiar places. Therefore, criminal opportunities that are close to the areas that an offender moves through during their everyday activities are more likely to be taken advantage of by the offender than opportunities in areas less familiar to the offender. In cases of white-collar crime, almost always the offender takes advantage of his or her professional environment to commit the crime.

The crime pattern theory can be adapted to detect and explain the distribution of white-collar crimes across targets. In the case of white-collar offenders, they do not discover their opportunities by walking down familiar streets. Rather, their awareness of white-collar crime opportunities arises out of their employment or occupation. White-collar offenders take advantage of criminal opportunities that arise out of the patterns and activities associated with their occupational positions

Situational Crime Prevention Theory

The situational crime prevention theory contends that to prevent crime, we need to reduce the opportunities for criminals to commit crime, change the criminals' ideas about whether they can get away with the crime, and make it harder and more risky for them to commit crime. Situational crime prevention is focused on the settings for crime, rather than upon those committing criminal acts. It seeks to forestall the occurrence of crime, rather than to detect and sanction offenders. As noted by Clarke, it seeks not to eliminate criminal or delinquent tendencies through improvement of society or its institutions, but merely to make criminal action less attractive to offenders.

Central to this concept is not law enforcement, but a host of public and private organizations and agencies—schools, hospitals, transit systems, shops and malls, manufacturing businesses, and phone companies that should work to prevent crime.[10] For example, as mentioned earlier, no one can embezzle from you unless you trust him or her. In other words, to prevent an employee from embezzling from your business, trust no one.

Clarke contends that the problem of explaining crime has been confused with the problem of explaining the criminal. He correctly notes that most criminological theories have been concerned with explaining why certain individuals or groups, exposed to particular psychological or social influences, or with particular inherited traits, are more likely to become involved in delinquency or crime. However, according to Clarke, this is not the same as explaining why crime occurs. The commission of a crime requires not merely the existence of a motivated offender, but, as he points out that every detective story reader knows, also the opportunity for crime.[11]

Structural Dimensions of Opportunity

The structural dimensions of opportunity refer to the fact that in many white-collar crime situations, there is an excellent chance that the criminal conduct will not be detected. Unlike the street criminal who robs a local convenience store, the white-collar criminal's acts have a high probability of not being detected.

The opportunity to commit financial crimes is also available to the white-collar criminal. The average street criminal is never entrusted with other people's money, and therefore he or she cannot commit embezzlement or other financial crimes.

Money Laundering

In recent years, detecting and prosecuting money laundering offenses has been the government's primary weapon in its fight against organized crime. It is also an important tool in fighting terrorism. The accumulation of large sums of legal currency is a problem with white-collar criminals, drug cartels, and other organized crime groups. Currency is of no value unless it can be used, and before it can be used, it must be cleaned or "laundered." In addition, large sums of currency are bulky and often alert law enforcement to criminal activity. It is often stated that to investigate organized or white-collar crime, follow the money.

Money laundering is the practice of converting the illicit proceeds of criminal activity into funds that are "clean," or that cannot be demonstrated to have come from criminal activity, thus making them usable for spending or investment.

Money laundering has wide-ranging negative impacts on the economy and can take on a number of forms that are not easily identifiable. It is difficult to control. The extent of the crime is unknown. It is global in nature. Money laundering facilitates not only the proliferation of many types of crime, but also terrorism. As such, money laundering poses a significant problem worldwide.[12]

The laundering process generally involves several steps. These steps are designed to avoid detection by law enforcement and conceal the illicit proceeds of criminal activity in such a manner that they appear as the proceeds from some legitimate endeavor. Money launderers typically resort to a three-step process when converting illicit proceeds into apparently legal monies or goods:

- Placement: The criminally derived money is placed into a legitimate enterprise.
- Layering: The funds are layered through various transactions to obscure the original source.

- Integration: The newly laundered funds are integrated into the legitimate financial world in the form of bank notes, loans, letters of credit, or other recognizable financial instruments.

The U.S. Code (USC) criminalizes knowingly engaging in a broad array of financial transactions that involve money either derived from or meant to promote various illegal activities.

The current efforts of the government in its anti-money laundering efforts are designed to target a wide range of profitable criminal activities, including narcotics trafficking, terrorism activities, illegal sales of weapons, human trafficking, fraud, political corruption, and child pornography. Organized criminal groups need to be able to launder the proceeds of drug trafficking and commodity smuggling. Terrorist groups use money laundering channels to get cash to buy arms. The social consequences of allowing these groups to launder money can be disastrous.[13]

The U.S. Supreme Court held that it is not necessary for the government to prove that the defendant attempted to make illegal funds appear legitimate to satisfy the designed-to-conceal element; instead, the government must establish that the defendant did more than merely hide the funds during transport. To obtain a conviction, the government must prove that a defendant knew that a purpose of the transportation was to conceal or disguise the nature, location, source, ownership, or control of funds.[14]

In 1970, the United States enacted the Currency and Foreign Transaction Reporting Act, which is commonly referred to as the Bank Secrecy Act (BSA). The BSA was designed to address tax evasion and organized crime use of financial institutions to launder money. The act requires banks (financial institutions) to keep certain records and make certain reports. Under BSA, financial institutions are required to report currency transactions over $10,000. The BSA was amended by the USA Patriot Act in 2002. The amendment broadened the definition of financial institutions and expanded the requirements for financial and business transactions record keeping. The amendment also increased the civil and criminal penalties for certain BSA violations involving foreign financial institutions.[15]

Insider Trading

Insider trading is the buying or selling of a security by someone who has access to material, nonpublic information about the security. For example, the president of a company that is traded on the New York Stock Exchange realizes that his company is in serious financial trouble and will seek bankruptcy within the next few days. Before this information is known to the public, the president sells all of his stock in his company. In this situation, the president of the company has committed the crime of insider trading. In a reverse situation, if the company has discovered a new process that will increase the price of the company's stock, the president should not, based on this inside information, purchase large numbers of his or her company's stock.

Insider trading can be illegal or legal, depending on when the insider makes the trade: It is illegal when the material information is still nonpublic—trading while having special knowledge is unfair to other investors who do not have access to such knowledge. Illegal insider trading therefore includes tipping others when you have any sort of nonpublic information. Directors are not the only ones who have the potential to be convicted of insider trading.

People such as brokers and even family members can be guilty. Insider trading is legal once the material information has been made public, at which time the insider has no direct advantage over other investors.

Punishment for White-Collar or Business Crime Offenses

Punishment is generally defined as a government-authorized imposition of a deprivation of freedom, privacy, or goods to which the person would otherwise have a right, or the imposition of special burdens because the individual receiving the punishment has been found guilty of some crime. Generally, unlike street crime, the public is unconcerned about white-collar criminals unless the crime directly affects them. However, white-collar crime indirectly causes losses and hardship to many people. For example, in the Enron case, thousands of investors lost their life savings or retirement funds.

Unlike common criminals, the white-collar criminal tends to be mature, middle class or higher, white, and male. Sutherland, in his famous work on white-collar crime, observed the following:

> Those who become white-collar criminals generally start their careers in good neighborhoods and good homes, graduate from college with idealism, and, with little selection on their part, get into a particular business situation in which criminality is practically a folkway, becoming inducted into that system of behavior just as into any other folkway.[16]

Organized Crime

The federal government's primary statutory weapon in the fight against organized crime is the Racketeer Influenced Corrupt Organizations Act of 1970 (RICO). Where did the name RICO originate? The popular myth or folklore is that it was taken from the 1931 Hollywood film *Little Caesar*, in which Edward G. Robinson, playing the role of Caesar Enrico Bandello (aka Rico), dies at the hands of the police while uttering the famous last words: "Is this the end of Rico?"[17]

The RICO statute (18 USC §§ 1961–1968) prohibits any "person" from "investing in," "acquiring," or "conducting the affairs of" an "enterprise" engaged in or affecting interstate and foreign commerce by means of a "pattern" of "racketeering activity," including collection of an unlawful debt, and also prohibits conspiring to accomplish these goals.

18 USC § 1961 defines several key terms pertaining to RICO. *Racketeering activity* is defined as any act or threat involving certain generic state felonies—murder, kidnapping, gambling, arson, robbery, bribery, extortion, and narcotics trafficking (§ 1961(1)(A)(J))—and acts indictable or punishable under certain federal statutes, including, inter alia, bribery, counterfeiting, gambling, extortion, obstruction of justice, labor law violations, mail fraud, wire fraud, bankruptcy fraud, fraud in the sale of securities, violation of the Currency Transaction Reporting Act, and narcotics dealing.

Pattern of racketeering activity is defined as at least two acts of racketeering activity committed within 10 years of each other, one of which occurred since the enactment of the statute in 1970.

Enterprise is defined as "any individual, partnership, corporation, association or other legal entity" as well as "any union or group of individuals associated in fact although not a legal entity."

18 USC § 1962 list four activities that are controlled by RICO:

1. Using or establishing an enterprise involved in illegal activities.
2. Acquiring or maintaining an interest in, or control of, an enterprise through a pattern of racketeering activity.
3. Conducting or participating in the conduct of an enterprise's affairs through a pattern of racketeering activity.
4. Conspiring to violate 18 USC § 1962(a), (b), or (c), RICO may be prosecuted as a civil or criminal violation.

Section 1963 defines the criminal penalties, including forfeitures of property, and § 1964 provides for various civil remedies, including the following: allowing federal district courts to prevent violations by ordering divestiture of any interest in an enterprise and restricting future activities of the violator, civil actions by the attorney general in which injunctive relief is available, and a private right of action for treble damages, costs, and attorney's fees to any person injured in his business or property by reason of a violation of § 1962.

RICO contains severe criminal penalties for persons engaging in a "pattern of racketeering activity" or "collection of an unlawful debt" that has a specified relationship to an "enterprise" affecting interstate commerce.

Criminal Gangs and Drug Cartels

Criminal Gangs

The common definition of a gang is a group of recurrently associating individuals or close friends with identifiable leadership and internal organization, identifying with or claiming control over territory in a community, and engaging either individually or collectively in violent or other forms of illegal behavior. The word *gang* derives from the early English word *gan*, meaning "to go" on a journey.

Frequently criminal gang members are "jumped in" or have to prove their loyalty by committing acts such as theft or violence. Although there are international gangs, most gang research is based on gangs specifically located in the United States. A member of a gang is called a gangster.

Gangs are most prominent in larger cities and urban areas in many countries such as the United States, and in prisons and jails. However, many branches of them are also present in small towns and suburbs. American gangs originated in New York City and Chicago and the surrounding areas. Gangs became popular in the United States during the Prohibition Era. During that period gangs competed with one another for control of illegal alcoholic drinks, and would often beat or even murder an opposing gang member for attempting to sell or distribute illegal liquor on their "turf." This resulted in retaliation and frequently a "war" between the opposing gangs.

Today, the word *gang* is generally used to describe a criminal organization or else a criminal affiliation. The word *gang* often carries a negative connotation; however, within a gang that defines itself in opposition to mainstream norms, members may adopt the phrase as a statement of identity or defiance. A frequent justification for being a gang member is that membership provides a sense of belonging. To many individuals, the gang replaces their families as their primary social unit.

Drug Cartels

Drug cartels are criminal gangs developed with the primary purpose of promoting and controlling drug trafficking operations. They range from loosely managed agreements among various drug traffickers to formalized commercial enterprises. The term was applied when the largest trafficking organizations reached an agreement to coordinate the production and distribution of cocaine. Since that agreement was broken up, drug cartels are no longer actually cartels, but the term stuck, and it is now popularly used to refer to any criminal narcotics-related organization, such as those in Guatemala, Honduras, El Salvador, Jamaica, Trinidad and Tobago, South

Korea, Dominican Republic, Mexico, Japan, Italy, France, United States, Colombia, United Kingdom, Netherlands, Russia, Brazil, Argentina, Peru, Bolivia, Paraguay, Afghanistan, and Pakistan.

The Texas Department of Public Safety in 2013 singled out the Mexican cartels as the most significant organized crime threat to the state and its people. The report noted that six of eight cartels currently have command and control networks operating in the state, and that they move people, drugs, cash, weapons, and stolen merchandise back and forth across the border.

The report noted also that statewide prison gangs posed the second most significant organized crime threat in Texas—and that many of the prison gangs now work directly with the Mexican cartels, gaining substantial profits from drugs and human trafficking. Prison gangs operate within and outside the prison system, and are considered responsible for a disproportionate amount of violent crime.

The report noted that the impact of cartel crime is painfully obvious when we consider that our neighbors in Mexico have experienced some 60,000 deaths from 2006 to 2013. Director of Public Safety Steven McCraw stated that it was a top priority of the department to severely obstruct the range and power of Mexican drug organizations.[18]

Mafia

When we refer to the Mafia, we are generally referring to either the Sicilian Mafia or the American Mafia. Both are Italian criminal organizations. Both are secret criminal societies. Sometimes the American Mafia is referred to as the Cosa Nostra. Frequently, the press uses the phrase "National Crime Syndicate" to refer to the entire network of U.S. organized crime, including the Mafia.

Sicilian Mafia

The Sicilian Mafia became famous in the 1970s with the Hollywood film *The Godfather.* After the film became famous, Corleone became known as the Mafia capital of the world. *The Godfather* was not, however, filmed in Corleone. Apparently, the filmmakers thought that Corleone was too developed to adequately portray the Mafia.

Presently, Corleone is working hard to become known as the anti-Mafia capital. In Corleone there is an anti-Mafia museum. In a 2014 visit to Corleone, the authors observed a pleasant town to walk around in. The cobblestone streets with bars and trattorias gave the impression of a small peaceful village. Figure 9.1 provides a view of the peaceful village.

Figure 9.1 The village of Corleone seems peaceful, as noted in this picture, despite its history of violence. (Photo by Cliff Roberson.)

The Sicilian Mafia started in the mid-1800s. It started as a secret society designed to unify the Sicilian peasants against their enemies. In Sicily, the word *Mafia* tends to mean "manly." The Sicilian Mafia changed from a group of honorable Sicilian men to an organized criminal group in the 1920s.

In the 1950s, Sicily enjoyed a massive building boom. Taking advantage of the opportunity, the Sicilian Mafia gained control of the building contracts and made millions of dollars. Today, the Sicilian Mafia has evolved into an international organized crime group. Some experts estimate it is the second largest organization in Italy.

In the 1980s, Toto Riina took control of the Mafia. He was a Corleonese known for his brutality and considered responsible for the killing of two anti-Mafia judges, Falcone and Borsellino. Figure 9.2 is a picture of a statue located in the anti-Mafia museum honoring Judge Borsellino. After Riina was arrested and imprisoned, the anti-Mafia faction, known as the cooperative Libera Terra, managed to force a change in Italian law so that land confiscated from the Mafia could be turned over to local villagers.

The Sicilian Mafia specializes in heroin trafficking, political corruption, and military arms trafficking. It has also been known to engage in arson, frauds, counterfeiting, and other racketeering crimes. According to the FBI, with an estimated 2,500 Sicilian Mafia affiliates, it is the most

Figure 9.2 Bust of Judge Paolo Borsellino (January 19, 1940–July 19, 1992) in the anti-Mafia museum located in Corleone, Sicily. The judge was an Italian anti-Mafia magistrate. He was killed by a Mafia car bomb in July 1992.

powerful and most active Italian organized crime group in the United States. The FBI website states:

> The Sicilian Mafia is infamous for its aggressive assaults on Italian law enforcement officials. In Sicily the term "Excellent Cadaver" is used to distinguish the assassination of prominent government officials from the common criminals and ordinary citizens killed by the Mafia. High-ranking victims include police commissioners, mayors, judges, police colonels and generals, and Parliament members.
>
> On May 23, 1992, the Sicilian Mafia struck Italian law enforcement with a vengeance. At approximately 6 p.m., Italian Magistrate Giovanni Falcone, his wife, and three police body guards were killed by a massive bomb. Falcone was the director of Criminal Affairs in Rome. The bomb made a crater 30 feet in diameter in the road. The murders became known as the Capaci Massacre.[19]

As noted in Figure 9.2, Judge Paolo Borsellino, an Italian anti-Mafia magistrate, was killed by a Mafia car bomb on July 19, 1992.

American Mafia

Charles "Lucky" Luciano, a Mafioso from Sicily, came to the United States and is credited by many for making the American La Cosa Nostra what it is today. Luciano structured the La Cosa Nostra after the Sicilian Mafia. When Luciano was deported back to Italy in 1946 for operating a prostitution ring, he became a liaison between the Sicilian Mafia and La Cosa Nostra.

The American Mafia is considered to have started in the late 19th century in New York City's Lower East Side, following shortly thereafter in New Orleans and other cities on the East Coast. While it has its roots and origin in the Sicilian Mafia, it is a completely separate criminal organization. There is evidence that currently the American Mafia cooperates in many of its activities with the Sicilian Mafia.

The most important unit of the American Mafia is that of a "family," as the various criminal organizations that make up the Mafia are called, but unlike a traditional family, succession is not necessarily hereditary. Currently, the Mafia operates to some extent in all major U.S. cities.

The Federal Bureau of Investigation (FBI) currently identifies the five main New York City Mafia families, also known as the Five Families, as the Gambino, Lucchese, Genovese, Bonanno, and Colombo families. For many years, the Mafia dominated organized crime in the United States. That domination has been weakened by the intrusion of other criminal organizations, such as the drug cartels. Each Mafia crime family operates independently but appears to have nationwide coordination provided by a commission consisting of the bosses of each of the strongest families.

The FBI estimates that the Mafia families have approximately 25,000 members total, with 250,000 affiliates worldwide. And there are more than 3,000 members and affiliates in the United States, scattered mostly throughout the major cities in the Northeast, the Midwest, California, and the South. Their largest presence centers in New York, southern New Jersey, and Philadelphia.[20]

The FBI still considers the Mafia the largest organized crime group in the United States. It has maintained control over much of the organized crime activity in the United States and certain parts of Canada. Much of the Mafia's activities are directed to the northeastern United States and Chicago.

According to the FBI, the major threats to American society posed by these groups are drug trafficking and money laundering. They have been involved in heroin trafficking for decades. Two major investigations that targeted Italian organized crime drug trafficking in the 1980s were known as the French Connection and the Pizza Connection. There were popular Hollywood films made about these two operations.

The Mafia families do not limit themselves to drug running. They're also involved in illegal gambling, political corruption, extortion, kidnapping, fraud, counterfeiting, infiltration of legitimate businesses, murders, bombings, and weapons trafficking. Industry experts in Italy estimate that their worldwide criminal activity is worth more than $100 billion annually.

Practicum

Consider the Ford Pinto case as an indication of the problems involving the use of financial sanctions against large business. On August 10, 1978, a Ford Pinto was rear-ended. The Pinto burst into flames, killing three teenage girls. In September 1978, Ford Motor Company was indicted in Elkhart, Indiana, on three charges of reckless homicide. The company was charged with recklessly designing and manufacturing the automobile in such a manner as would be likely to cause the automobile to burn up on rear-end impact. If convicted, the maximum punishment would have been a fine of $30,000. Since the defendant was a corporation, it could not be incarcerated. At the time, the Ford Motor Company was the fourth largest corporation in the world.

The Pinto, a small car, was developed to sell for about $2,000 (late 1960 prices). The design was completed on a rushed schedule. For design reasons, the gas tank was placed behind, rather than over, the rear axle of the automobile. When the automobile was hit from behind, the gas tank could be crushed against the rear axle, and the car had a tendency to burst into flames.

Evidence was presented that the company was aware of the problem, and that the car could have been modified for a cost of $15.30 per car, but apparently the executives and the board decided to go ahead with the present design to save money.

The company contended that it was not sociopathic and did not randomly victimize its customers, but rather was a responsible citizen that obeyed federal regulations and carefully weighed all factors in manufacturing a product that the public wanted: a small affordable American car. The Ford Motor Company was found not guilty by the jury on March 13, 1980. The maximum penalty had the company been convicted was only $30,000, but why did the Ford Motor Company spend millions of dollars in legal fees and expenses in defending this case? Fining the Ford Motor Company $30,000 would have been the equivalent of fining an individual making $150,000 a year a quarter.

In 2014, there were accusations that General Motors knew about problems with several models of their automobiles, but failed to recall them—and that some deaths have occurred because of their failure to recall and correct the problems.

If General Motors were found guilty in a court case and you were the trial judge responsible for deciding the appropriate sanctions, how would you handle the punishment?

Summary

- The introduction of the concept of white-collar crime into the study of criminal behavior revolutionized the thinking of the field by making it no longer possible to employ class-specific explanations to interpret such behavior.
- The content of the phrase "white-collar crime" is difficult to pin down.
- The term *white-collar crime* was first used by Edwin Sutherland in 1939.
- White-collar crimes are those crimes that are committed by individuals in their profession, and they do not involve the use of weapons or force. Frequently, they are also called business crimes.
- Social disorganization theories hold that there is a relationship between increasing crime and the increasing complexity of our society. They also contend that social disorganization is a causal factor in crime.
- According to Sally Simpson, corporate crime results when managers take organizational needs and pressures into account when solving business problems or when managers act in accordance with the dominant culture of the firm, subunit, or team in which they work.
- The structural dimensions of opportunity refer to the fact that in many white-collar crime situations, there is an excellent chance that the criminal conduct will not be detected.
- Unlike the street criminal who robs a local convenient store, the white-collar criminal's acts have a high probability of not being detected.
- Money laundering is the practice of converting the illicit proceeds of criminal activity into funds that are clean or that cannot be demonstrated to have come from criminal activity, thus making them usable for spending or investment.
- Insider trading is the buying or selling of a security by someone who has access to material, nonpublic information about the security.
- The federal government's primary statutory weapon in the fight against organized crime is the Racketeer Influenced Corrupt Organizations Act of 1970.
- The common definition of a gang is a group of recurrently associating individuals or close friends with identifiable leadership and internal organization, identifying with or claiming control over territory in a community, and engaging either individually or collectively in violent or other forms of illegal behavior.

- Drug cartels are criminal gangs developed with the primary purpose of promoting and controlling drug trafficking operations. They range from loosely managed agreements among various drug traffickers to formalized commercial enterprises.

Questions in Review

1. What constitutes money laundering?
2. Explain the purposes of money laundering statutes.
3. How does Sutherland explain white-collar crime?
4. In your opinion, why do successful businesspersons commit white-collar crime?
5. Why are money laundering offenses used as weapons in the fight against organized crime?
6. What constitutes insider trading?
7. Explain how the RICO statutes function.

Key Terms

Drug cartel: Criminal gangs developed with the primary purpose of promoting and controlling drug trafficking operations.

Insider trading: The buying or selling of a security by someone who has access to material, nonpublic information about the security.

Money laundering: The practice of converting the illicit proceeds of criminal activity into funds that are clean or that cannot be demonstrated to have come from criminal activity, thus making them usable for spending or investment.

White-collar crimes: Those crimes that are committed by individuals in their profession, and they do not involve the use of weapons or force.

Endnotes

1. Frank J. DiMarino & Cliff Roberson. (2013). *An introduction to corporate and white-collar crime*. Boca Raton, FL: CRC Press.
2. White collar crime. (2010). www.hg.org/whitecollar-crime.html. Retrieved June 29, 2014.
3. Edwin H. Sutherland. (1940, February). White-collar criminality. *American Sociology Review*, *5*(1), 1–12.
4. Sutherland, 1940, p. 12.
5. Cliff Roberson. (2009). *Identify theft investigations*. New York: Kaplan Publishing.
6. Dan Ariely. (2009). *Predictably irrational: The hidden forces that shape our decisions*. New York: Harper-Collins.
7. Sally Simpson. (2002). Low self-control, organizational theory, and corporate crime. *Law and Society Review*, *36*, 509–511.

8. Michael L. Benson & Sally S. Simpson. (2009). *White-collar crime: An opportunity perspective* (p. 76). New York: Routledge.
9. P. J. Brantingham & P. L. Brantingham. (1984). *Patterns in crime*. New York: Macmillan.
10. Ronald Clarke. (1997). *Situational crime prevention successful case studies*. Guilderland, NY: Harrow and Hester.
11. Clarke, 1997, p. 6.
12. National White Collar Crime Center web page. http://nw3c.org/services/research/whitepapers/page/2. Retrieved July 1, 2014.
13. DiMarino & Roberson, 2013, p. 137.
14. *Cuellar v. United States*, 553 U.S. 550 (2008).
15. 12 USC 1829b and 31 USC § 5311.
16. Sutherland, 1940.
17. *Little Caesar* (film). (2014). http://www.filmsite.org/littc.html. Retrieved July 30, 2014.
18. Mexican drug cartels biggest threat to Texas and its residents. http://latino.foxnews.com/latino/news/2013/03/29/mexican-drug-cartels-biggest-threat-to-texas-and-its-residents/. Retrieved July 31, 2014.
19. FBI website. http://www.fbi.gov/about-us/investigate/organizedcrime/italian_mafia. Retrieved August 1, 2014.
20. FBI website.

chapter ten

Governmental Deviance

Chapter Objectives

What you should know and understand after studying this chapter:

- The elements of the federal crimes of bribery and illegal gratuity
- The differences between bribery and illegal gratuity
- The types of intent involved in bribery and illegal gratuity offenses
- The problems with establishing honest services fraud
- What constitutes criminal conflict of interest
- The theoretical causes of government deviance
- What constitutes environmental crime

Introduction

The problem with governmental deviance is that we are discussing individuals who have significant power over citizens within their jurisdiction. Unlike the individual who robs the convenience store, these individuals' actions have far more impact on the public in general. As the reader examines the various crimes discussed in this chapter, the reader should remember that these crimes are committed by people who are not economically or socially depressed.

Probably the most powerful person in the criminal justice system is the prosecutor. Under the American scheme of justice, it is the prosecutor who determines whether or not to prosecute or dismiss a case. To a great extent, the prosecutor controls the sentences by the use of plea bargains. That is why the following comments by Justice Jackson are so alarming.

Justice Robert H. Jackson, former associate justice, U.S. Supreme Court and U.S. Attorney General, once noted a "prosecutor has more control over life, liberty, and reputation than any other person in America." Justice Jackson also noted that if the prosecutor is obliged to choose his cases, it follows that he can choose his defendants. Jackson concluded that this was the most dangerous power of the prosecutor: that he will pick people that he thinks he should get, rather than cases that need to be prosecuted. With the law books filled with a great assortment of crimes, a prosecutor stands a fair chance of finding at least a technical violation of some act on the part of almost anyone.[1]

Samuel Clemens, aka Mark Twain, is reported to have stated: "It could probably be shown with facts and figures that there is no distinctly American criminal class except Congress."

While we admire and expect our leaders, often they perform actions that are not in our best interest but for personal gain. Probably the abuse of power is the most frequent deviant behavior of public officials. Abuse of power includes graft or bribery.

Most state and federal officials have some sort of power of the citizens in their district, county, state, or federal government. In this chapter we will discuss some of the steps that governments have or are taking to keep those officials from abusing their power. Clearly the abuse of power by a public official is a negative form of deviance. In addition, many of those acts are criminal.

Consider the following scenario: James Bell is a candidate for the U.S. House of Representatives. You want to support Bell for the office, but you are concerned that he may raise income taxes. Accordingly, you meet with Bell and inform him that if he promises not to vote for a tax raise, you will provide him financial support for his campaign. He promises not to support any tax increases. Have you bribed him?

Consider this scenario: June Singleton is running for governor. She promises you that if you work on her campaign and she wins, you will be appointed as a state appellate justice. Is this a crime?

In both scenarios, whether the conduct constitutes criminal deviance may depend upon state or federal statutes. Both scenarios are probably typical of election issues in the modern-day United States. When we vote for a candidate because he or she has promised to either restrict abortion or insure women's freedom of choice, we are acting on our beliefs. But is the candidate who is making the promise bribing us to vote for him or her?

Many congressional bills induced into Congress by all major parties are written or strongly supported by special interest groups. In addition, candidates must often agree to support certain actions in order to receive financial support of special interest groups.

There are a number of federal statutory crimes that were enacted to deter and punish public officials who are involved in acts of corruption. Those crimes include bribery and illegal gratuity, illegal outside income by government employees, kickbacks, and the honest services crimes. This chapter contains a brief summary of those statutes.

The chapter ends with a short discussion on environmental crime. While it may not be a form of governmental deviance, the failure of governments to protect our environment is certainly a form of deviance.

Bribery and Illegal Gratuity

Public officials are probably prosecuted more for taking bribery or illegal gratuities than for other types of offenses. The present federal bribery and illegal gratuity crimes are based on the federal conflict of interest law enacted in 1962. All states have similar statutes in order to prosecute deviant public officials.

The distinction between the crimes of bribery and illegal gratuity is that bribery requires the government to have a specific intent in giving or demanding something of value, whereas the crime of illegal gratuity does not require a specific intent to receive or give something of value. The crime of illegal gratuity requires only that an illegal gratuity be given for or because of an official act. Both bribery and illegal gratuity apply to present and future public officials. The crime of illegal gratuity, unlike bribery, applies to former officials. For example, to commit the crime of bribery, the offender must be either a present public official or a future official at the time of the criminal act. Note that the status of the defendant refers to the status at the time of the act, not the time of prosecution. Accordingly, a former executive may be prosecuted for bribery if he or she committed the act either during his or her service as a public officer or prior to accepting the position.

Another major difference between the two offenses is that bribery requires that the subject of misconduct be for or because of an officer act, whereas an illegal gratuity requires only that a gratuity be given. The conflict of interest crimes created or modified by the 1962 legislation include the following[2]:

- 18 U.S. Code (USC) § 201(b): Making the offering or receipt of a bribe to or by a public official or witness of a crime.
- 18 USC § 201(c): Making the offering or receipt of illegal gratuity to or by a public official or witness of a crime.
- 18 USC § 203 prohibits the unauthorized compensation of government officials for representing persons before the government.
- 18 USC § 205 prohibits government officials from representing persons prosecuting claims against the federal government or before the federal government.
- 18 USC § 207 restricts the postemployment activities of former federal government executive branch officials. (Note: This statute only applies to former officials of the executive branch and not to former congressional personnel.) The 1962 statute restricted the employment of former executives for one year. This restriction was extended to two years by the Honest Leadership and Open Government Act of 2007.
- 18 USC § 208 prohibits executive branch officials from participating in matters that affect their financial interest.

Elements of Bribery and Illegal Gratuities

To convict a defendant of bribery, the government must establish the following:

- A thing of value was either offered, given, or promised to a recipient, or
- A recipient demanded, sought, received, or accepted something of value, done by a present or future public official:
- For an official act
- With corrupt intent or intent to influence.[3]

To establish the offense of illegal gratuity, the government must prove the following:

- A thing of value was given, offered, or promised to (or, in the case of a recipient, demanded, sought, received, or accepted by)
- A present, past, or future public official
- For or because of any official act performed or to be performed by such public official.

Public Official or Witness

The requirement that the bribery or illegal gratuity be directed at a public official or a witness has provided some interesting cases. The Supreme Court and the federal appellate courts have interpreted the term *public official* broadly. In general, it is a person who occupies a position involving public trust with official responsibilities. In some cases, because state and local officials are involved in implementing federal programs, they may be considered public officials for the purposes of federal bribery and illegal gratuity crimes.

In the *Dixon* case,[4] the Supreme Court stated that Congress intended for such local officials to be covered by the statute, with the conclusion that employment by the United States or some other similarly formal contractual or agency bond is not a prerequisite to prosecution under the federal bribery statute.

Title 18 USC has defined a public official as a

- Member of Congress,
- Delegate, or
- Resident commissioner,
- Either before or after such official has qualified, or an officer or
- Employee or person acting for or on behalf of the United States or

- Any department, agency, or branch of government thereof, including the District of Columbia, in any official function, under or by authority of any such department, agency, or branch of government, or a juror.[5]

A person who has been selected to be a public official is defined as any person who has been nominated or appointed to be a public official or has been officially informed that such person will be so nominated or appointed.[6] A witness is defined as any person who testifies at a trial, hearing, or other proceeding. This includes any proceedings before any court; any committee of the Senate, House, or both; or any agency, commission, or officer authorized by the laws of the United States to hear evidence or take testimony.

The court in *United States v. Kenney*[7] concluded that a defense contractor employee who did not have the final word but whose recommendations were given sufficient weight to influence the outcome of the decisions at issue was a public official for the purposes of Section 201(c).

The U.S. Court of Appeals for the Second Circuit decision in *Dixon v. United States* stated that Congress never intended the open-ended definition of public official in Section 201(a) to be given a cramped reading.[8] The court noted that the interpretation of the meaning of *public official* was not intended to bring all employees of local organizations that administer federal funds within the definition of *public official,* and that the term *public official* applied only to those individuals who possess some degree of official responsibility for carrying out a federal program or policy. The court in that decision indicated that a person merely receiving federal assistance is not sufficient to be considered a public official.

The actual ability of a public official to complete the objective of the scheme is not important. Mere misrepresentation as to the scope of the official's authority has been sufficient. Even undercover agents acting as public officials qualify under the statutes as a public official.[9] An immigration inspector's promise to commit immigration fraud was sufficient to sustain a conviction for bribery even if the inspector did not have the authority to perform on his promise.[10]

Value

The term *thing of value* is broadly defined by the courts. It includes checks and negotiable instruments. The courts have found that it also includes the promise of future employment, overseas travel, sexual acts, shares of stock, and any item that the recipient subjectively believes to have value, even if it has little or no commercial value.[11] The court in *United States v. Williams* upheld a lower court's decision that worthless shares of stock were things of value to the defendant senator because he had a subjective belief that they were valuable.[12]

The item of value need not be conveyed to the official; it can be conveyed to a third party for the benefit of the official; for example, the awarding of a public contract to the senator's son is a thing of value to the senator. The fact that the receipt of the thing of value may be delayed until after the individual is no longer a public official is immaterial. The promise of a thing of value has been held to include the promise to testify in court proceedings.

Official Act Requirement

Under both the bribery and illegal gratuity offenses, an official act is required. An official act is defined by 18 USC § 201(a)(3) as any decision or action on any question, matter, cause, suit, proceeding, or controversy, which may be pending or brought before any public official in his or her official capacity, or in such official's place of trust or profit.

The U.S. Supreme Court has taken a narrow definition of the phrase "official capacity." The court stated in *United States v. Sun-Diamond Growers of California* that 18 USC § 201 requires a showing that a gift was motivated by the recipient's capacity to exercise governmental power or influence in the donor's favor without necessarily showing that it was connected to a particular official act.[13] The court, in that case, noted that a broad interpretation of Section 201 would criminalize the giving of token gifts during public ceremonies—a sports jersey for the president during a White House visit by the sports team, a school cap for the Secretary of Education during a high school visit, and a complimentary lunch from the farmers during a visit by the Secretary of Agriculture—all assuredly official acts in some sense.[14] Note: In a prosecution under Section 201, the government must allege and establish some particular act.

The required act may be a failure to act. For example, the court held that the failure to report a licensing violation by a massage parlor constituted an official act.[15]

Prosecution and Informant Agreements

A thing of value has been held to include a promise of leniency by a federal prosecutor, although there is a serious question as to whether leniency-induced testimony is included in the concept.[16] Note in the *Singleton* case that the court held that when a federal prosecutor enters into a plea agreement with a defendant, the plea agreement is between the U.S. government and the defendant; therefore, the prosecutor does not receive a thing of value.[17]

In *United States v. Dawson*, a U.S. Court of Appeals held that a government payment of 20% of the proceeds from the government sale of illegal narcotics was not a violation of the bribery or illegal gratuity statutes.[18]

In *United States v. Barnett*,[19] a federal appellate court concluded that a government payment of $7,500 to a witness for assistance and testimony in a murder-for-hire prosecution was not in violation of 18 USC § 201(c). The court noted that government payments for assistance and testimony in criminal cases were not prohibited by the U.S. Code.

The *United States v. Feng*[20] case concluded that the government's offer of letters recommending asylum on behalf of testifying witnesses was not a violation of the federal antigratuity statute because immigration benefits or leniency should not be differentiated from criminal leniency.

Intent

The major distinction between the crimes of bribery and illegal gratuity is that bribery requires the government to have a specific intent in giving or demanding something of value, whereas the crime of illegal gratuity does not require a specific intent to receive or give something of value. In *United States v. Jennings*,[21] an appellate court stated that a goodwill gift to an official to foster a favorable business climate, given simply with the generalized hope or expectation of ultimate benefit on the part of the donor, did not constitute a bribe.

Intent Required to Establish Bribery

To establish a bribery offense under Section 201(b), the government must prove a corrupt intent to influence, or be influenced in, the performance of an official act. The Supreme Court has stated that this element requires proof of a quid pro quo, that is, a specific intent to give or receive something of value in exchange for an official act. While the court has indicated a requirement of a quid pro quo, the court has stated that it need not be fully executed, and that bribery requires only the specific intent of performing an official act in return for something of value. Vague expectations of some future benefit do not satisfy the statutory intent requirement.

The specific intent requirement to establish bribery may be established by circumstantial evidence.[22] The promises need not be specifically correlated to a particular official act, as long as the offeror of the bribe intended for the payment to induce the official to adopt a specific course of action. In addition, a payment or promise need not alter a public official's actual course of conduct, as long as the parties to the transaction possessed corrupt intent.[23]

Question: Candidate Jamison is running for the U.S. Senate. She has promised that if elected, she will reduce the taxes on foreign stock profits. Based on this promise, Fred makes a large contribution to her campaign fund. Does this constitute bribery?

An appellate court in *United States v. Tomblin*[24] stated that intending to make a campaign contribution does not constitute bribery, even though many contributors hope that the official will act favorably because of their contributions. In *United States v. Allen*,[25] the court noted that accepting a campaign contribution does not equal taking a bribe unless the payment is made in exchange for an explicit promise to perform or not perform an official act.

A goodwill gift to an official to foster a favorable business climate, given simply with the generalized hope or expectation of ultimate benefit on the part of the donor, does not constitute a bribe.[26]

Intent in Illegal Gratuity Offenses

To establish an illegal gratuity offense under Section 201(c)(1), the government need only prove that the gratuity was given or accepted for or because of any official act. Corrupt intent or a quid pro quo agreement need not be established. The court, in *United States v. Bustamante*, held that it was sufficient for the government to show that the defendant was given the gratuity simply because he held public office.[27]

In *United States v. Schaffer*, the court stated that a gratuity can be given with the intent to induce a public official to propose, take, or shy away from some future official act.[28] Under the rule in this case, it would be an offense to give a gift if it was given in the hope that when the particular official's actions move to the forefront, the public official will listen hard to, and hopefully be swayed by, the giver's proposals, suggestions, or concerns. It would appear that maybe the authors committed the offense when they made donations to their favorite presidential candidate with the goal of getting him elected in order to have a president more favorable to their business or political beliefs.

Criminal Conflict of Interest

The use of a public office for private gain is prohibited by 18 USC § 203. The offense applies to the public official receiving the unauthorized compensation and also to the individual attempting to influence a public official. The elements of the criminal conflict of interest offense are as follows:

- The person was covered by the statute (generally a public official)
- In connection with a particular matter in which influence was sought, demanded, accepted, or agreed to receive compensation
- With corrupt intent
- To provide services before a particular governmental forum.

Section 203 applies to all individuals employed by the federal government. This includes members of Congress, federal judges, and employees of the executive, legislative, and judicial branches. It also covers those who knowingly give, promise, or offer compensation to public officials for representational services rendered or to be rendered in the future. The statute exempts retired military officers who are not otherwise government employees, individuals working under grants for the benefit of the national interest, those giving testimony under oath or statements under penalty of perjury, and those representing family members or other personal fiduciaries.

Section 203 prohibits public officials from accepting compensation for representational services in relation to a particular matter in which the United States is a party or has a direct and substantial interest. Section 203 is violated only when compensation is demanded, sought, received, accepted, or agreed upon by a public official or knowingly given, promised, or offered to a public official. The offense does not require specific intent or an intent to be corrupted or influenced. The acceptance of an unauthorized compensation is all that the government needs to establish in a trial under Section 203.

There are some exceptions under Section 203. Section 205 allows government employees to provide unpaid representation to a person who is the subject of disciplinary, loyalty, or other personnel administrative proceedings if it is not inconsistent with the employees' duties. The pro bono exception ensures that government employees with grievances against their employer agency will have representation in those proceedings without having to hire a private attorney.

This exception, however, has been interpreted as applying only to administrative proceedings, and not to representation before a court. Two Georgetown University law students who also worked for the government were prohibited from participating in an appellate litigation clinic representing indigent clients because of the potential for a conflict of interest between their duties to their employers and their duties to their clients.[29]

Another exception is that special government employees may represent parties who are grant recipients or who are under contract with the federal government, if the head of the federal agency involved certifies that such representation is necessary. Federal employees may also testify in court proceedings, even if the case is against the United States.

Acts Affecting Financial Interest

Title 18 USC § 208 generally prohibits an officer or employee of the executive branch from personally and substantially participating in any particular matter in which, to his or her knowledge, the officer, his or her spouse, general partner, or organization with which he or she is involved, has a financial interest. This section was enacted to ensure honesty in the government's business dealings by preventing federal agents who have interests adverse to those of the government from advancing their own interests at the expense of the public's welfare, and to preserve the integrity of the decision-making process. Courts have interpreted Section 208 broadly in order to achieve the objectives.

Illegal Outside Salaries for Federal Employees

Title 18 USC § 209 prohibits the receipt or payment of a salary as compensation, except from the government, for services rendered as an officer or employee of the executive branch, an executive agency, or the District of Columbia government. The statute has no intent or mens rea requirement.

When determining whether the payment was for government services, subjective intent is not a relevant inquiry. The purpose of the statute is to avoid improper quid pro quos. It was drafted with the intent to proscribe any gift giving or salary supplementation, regardless of the payment's purpose.

In *Crandon v. United States,* the Supreme Court held that severance payments made to future federal employees before they begin government service do not violate the statute.[30] The court determined that Congress intended to help the government attract personnel with special knowledge and skills, and that Section 209 accordingly applies only to those persons who are employed by the government at the time the outside payments are received.

Honest Services Fraud

Honest services fraud refers to a 28-word sentence of 18 USC § 1346: "For the purposes of this chapter, the term, scheme or artifice to defraud includes a scheme or artifice to deprive another of the intangible right of honest services."

The first federal mail fraud statute was enacted in 1872. Later in 1909, Congress added the language to 18 USC § 1346 that prohibited any scheme or artifice to defraud, or for obtaining money or property by means of false or fraudulent pretenses, representations, or promises. The statute, more commonly known as the Honest Services Doctrine, criminalized both schemes to defraud and schemes for obtaining money and property via fraudulent methods. The section protects the public from traditional fraudulent schemes that enrich the purveyor of the fraud at the expense of the victim, as well as fraudulent schemes that enrich the purveyor of the fraud as well as a complicit third party and deprive the victim of only honest services.

In *Skilling v. United States*,[31] the U.S. Supreme Court addressed the conviction of an officer of a corporation who was alleged to have denied the corporation's shareholders honest services by committing fraud regarding the corporation's finances. Skilling's attorneys argued that Section 1346 was a facially invalid violation of due process because (1) the statute was not definite enough to be understood by an ordinary person, and (2) the statute was so vague it encouraged arbitrary enforcement. The court acknowledged that a broad interpretation of the statute could run afoul of the Void for Vagueness Doctrine. The court interpreted the right to honest services to be violated only when the perpetrator of the fraud received a bribe or kickback from a third party. The court also found that a corporate officer convicted of fraudulently paying himself noncompetition fees and failing to disclose such fees had not violated Section 1346, because there was no bribe or kickback from a third party.

Election Deviance

Basic to our democracy is the concept that we choose our leaders fairly and without corruption. However, this is not always the case. Some of the election improprieties or election deviance includes denial of voting rights, political dirty tricks, and campaign finance abuses. An additional form of campaign deviance includes those cases where individuals use campaign funds for personal or private means.

Explanation of Governmental Deviance

In trying to determine why public officials commit deviant behavior or why candidates abuse or commit campaign deviance, we can look at the theoretical reasons provided earlier in the textbook for why people commit ordinary street crime. For example, the opportunity theorists Richard Cloward and Lloyd Ohlin would probably contend that these individuals are in a subculture or organization that provides the opportunities for the commission of these types of offenses. The conflict theorist would probably indicate that the higher the status and the more power the social political group has, the greater the likelihood that they will commit deviance.

Sutherland and his differential association theory would probably attribute the election deviance to the learning process. According to the differential association theorists, these individuals learned from their mentors how to beat the system, very similar to the manner in which street criminals learn to rob a convenience store.

Law Enforcement Deviance

A frequent question that is asked by individuals who are outspoken about the police is: "Who polices the police?" The United States probably has the best trained police officers in the world. But because of the large number of police officers in the States, a few are bad, and some make mistakes that are amplified. According to the CATO Institute, from January through December 2010 the National Police Misconduct Statistics and Reporting Project recorded 4,861 unique reports of police misconduct that involved 6,613 sworn law enforcement officers and 6,826 alleged victims.[32]

About 24% of the reports of misconduct involved the excessive use of force, and about 9% involved sexual misconduct, the two highest categories of alleged misconduct recorded. There were 127 fatalities associated with credible excessive force allegations within the 2010 report. The cities with the highest reported misconduct rates were New Orleans, Denver, and Atlanta. The cities with the lowest reported rates were Nashville, Milwaukee, and Miami.

The report noted that during the time period, the police misconduct rate was approximately 978 officers per 100,000 officers. This means that approximately 1 officer out of every 100 officers either committed misconduct or made a critical mistake during the time period in question. While employers would love to have only 1 employee out of every 100 involved in misconduct, this rate is too high for the guardians of our society.

In August 2014, in the city of Ferguson, Missouri, riots erupted over the shooting death of Michael Brown. Ferguson is a suburb of St. Louis. St. Louis was not one of the major cities involved in the riots in 1964. Reports indicated that there were two versions of what happened that August evening. Nobody knows for certain what happened, but studies of the incident and its aftermath indicate that black Americans are 20% to 30% less likely to trust the police. According to Professor Thomas Tyler of Yale Law School, this gap is not diminishing. And it's not going away.[33]

Observers indicated that the riots in Ferguson resembled a military action rather than a police response, and that the police officers were looking and acting more like soldiers than cops. As the result of the riots, the federal government was criticized for increasing the militarization of the police because of the federal policy of providing police forces with military equipment. As several outspoken opponents of this policy noted, soldiers and police are supposed to be different. The soldier is trained to meet the enemy and destroy, whereas the police are trained to protect the public.

Why do law enforcement officers commit misconduct? Some mistakes or misconduct may be attributed to lack of proper training. Some can be attributed to honest mistakes. And unfortunately, some of the misconduct can be traced to deliberate misconduct on the part of the law enforcement officer. Some researchers have attributed law enforcement misconduct to be related to personality and education. They also note that it can be significantly affected by the culture of the police agency. Education may help predict misconduct; research indicates that better-educated officers receive fewer complaints on average.[34]

Environmental Crime

> In 1984, the Union Carbide Corporation negligently released methyl isocyanate and hydrogen cyanide gas into the atmosphere from their plant in Bhopal, India. According to the Indian government's count, the incident killed 3,329 people and seriously injured some 20,000.[35]

According to Neal Shover and Aaron S. Routhe, the costs of environmental crime are numerous and varied, and no one seriously disputes that its aggregate financial toll is enormous. As with street crime, the tangible costs of environmental crime include victims' loss of money and property, and physical injuries or death.[36]

The designation *environmental crime* is applied to crimes that contravene statutory provisions designed to protect the ecological and physical environment.[37] The formal statutory and analytic designation is of recent origin, but efforts to prevent or mitigate harm to the environment were attempted in England in 1876 by Disraeli's Rivers Act, and in the United States by the Refuse Act of 1899 (Figure 10.1).

Shover and Routhe noted that there is no doubt that the financial and human costs of environmental crime are enormous, if indeterminable—and that both aggregate rates of environmental crime and crime commission by individuals and organizations vary substantially. They also noted that research points to a number of factors that influence aggregate rates or the likelihood of environmental crime. These risk and protective factors include the state of the economy, the degree of competition in an industry, the prevalence of socially acceptable rhetorical explanations for noncompliance, and the style of oversight. Oversight of environmental practices varies internationally, but controls are more intense where well-organized and sustained political movements press for state action. As noted by the researchers, the first line of oversight for environmental practices is regulatory agencies; criminal prosecution is rare, although there is some movement toward more severe sanctions.[38]

Like private citizens, governments can turn a blind eye toward harmful behaviors or choose to make them the focus of attention. It can take the lead in identifying and crafting controls, or it can wait until pressed to do so through action by citizens and organized groups.

Summary

- The distinction between the crimes of bribery and illegal gratuity is that bribery requires the government to have a specific intent in giving or demanding something of value, whereas the crime of illegal

Figure 10.1 Environmental Protection Agency photo showing a million-gallon reservoir, facing east-southeast. Nevada Test Site, Environmental Protection Agency Farm, Area 15, Yucca Flat, 10-2 Road near Circle Road, Mercury, Nye County, Nevada. The area was polluted because of Yucca Flats bomb testing. (Photo courtesy of Library of Congress Prints and Photographs Division, Washington, DC.)

gratuity does not require a specific intent to receive or give something of value.

- The crime of illegal gratuity requires only that an illegal gratuity be given for or because of an official act.
- Another major difference between the two offenses is that bribery requires that the subject of misconduct be for or because of an official act, whereas an illegal gratuity requires only that a gratuity be given.
- The Supreme Court and the federal appellate courts have interpreted the term *public official* broadly. In general, it is a person who occupies a position involving public trust with official federal responsibilities.
- The term *thing of value* is broadly defined by the courts. It includes checks and negotiable instruments.
- The courts have found that a thing of value also includes promise of future employment, overseas travel, sexual acts, shares of stock, and

any item that the recipient subjectively believes to have value, even if it has little or no commercial value.
- Under both the bribery and illegal gratuity offenses, an official act is required.
- To establish a bribery offense under Section 201(b), the government must prove a corrupt intent to influence, or be influenced in, the performance of an official act.
- To establish an illegal gratuity offense under Section 201(c)(1), the government need only prove that the gratuity was given or accepted for or because of any official act.
- The use of a public office for private gain is prohibited by 18 USC § 203.
- Honest services fraud refers to a 28-word sentence of 18 USC § 1346: "For the purposes of this chapter, the term, scheme or artifice to defraud includes a scheme or artifice to deprive another of the intangible right of honest services."
- The designation *environmental crime* is applied to crimes that contravene statutory provisions designed to protect the ecological and physical environment.

Questions in Review

1. How did the Supreme Court limit the scope of honest services fraud in the *Skilling* decision?
2. What are differences in required intent between bribery and illegal gratuities?
3. Explain the types of misconduct involved in the criminal conflict of interest crimes.
4. Why are there restrictions on the postemployment activities of former federal officials?
5. What are the elements of honest services fraud?

Key Terms

Bribery: The giving or demanding of something of value for or because of an official act.

Illegal gratuity: The giving up of something of value to a public official for or because of an official act.

Official act: Any decision or action on any question, matter, cause, suit, proceedings, or controversy, which may be pending or brought before any public official in his or her official capacity, or in such official's place of trust or profit.

Public official: An individual who occupies a position involving public trust with official responsibilities.

Thing of value: Broadly defined by the courts and includes checks negotiable instruments, promise of future employment, or anything that has value even if its commercial value is negligible.

Endnotes

1. Robert H. Jackson. (1940). The federal prosecutor. *Journal of American Judicature Society*, *18*, 18–22.
2. Frank DiMarino & Cliff Roberson. (2013). *An introduction to corporate and white-collar crime*. Boca Raton, FL: CRC Press.
3. Public Law 110-81, Sections 101 and 121 (2007).
4. *Dixon v. United States*, 465 U.S. 497–498.
5. 18 USC § 201(a)(1).
6. 18 USC § 201(a)(1) and 201(a)(2).
7. *United States v. Kenney*, 185 F. 3d 1217, 1221–1222 (11th Cir. 1999).
8. *United States v. Dixon*. 536 F. 2d 1388 (2d Cir. 1976).
9. *United States v. Romano*. 879 F. 2d 1056, 1060 (2d Cir. 1989).
10. *United States v. Vega*. 184 F. App'x 236, 242 (3d Cir. 2006).
11. *United States v. Ostrander*. 999 F. 2d 27, 31 (2d Cir. 1993). *United States v. Crozier*. 987 F. 2d 893, 901 (2d Cir. 1993).
12. *United States v. Williams*. 705 F. 2d 603 (2d Cir. 1983).
13. 526 U.S. 398, 406–407 (1999).
14. 526 U.S. 398, 407.
15. *United States v. Alan*, 231 F. 3d 26, 32 (D.D.C. 2000).
16. *United States v. Singleton*, 144 F. 3d 1343, 1348 (10th Cir. 1998).
17. *United States v. Singleton*, 165 F. 3d 1297, 1299–1301 (10th Cir. 1999).
18. *United States v. Dawson*, 425 F. 3d 389, 394–95 (7th Cir. 2005).
19. *United States v. Barnett*, 197 F. 3d 138, 145 (5th Cir. 1999).
20. 277 F. 3d 1151, 1153–54 (9th Cir. 2002).
21. 160 F. 3d 1006, 1013 (4th Cir. 1998).
22. *United States v. Jennings*, 160 F. 3d 1006 (4th Cir. 1998).
23. *United States v. Quinn*, 359 F. 3d 666 (4th Cir. 2004).
24. 46 F. 3d 1369, 1379 (5th Cir. 1995).
25. 10 F. 3d 405, 411 (7th Cir. 1993).
26. *United States v. Jennings*, 160 F. 3d 1006, 1013 (4th Cir. 1998).
27. 45 F. 3d 933 (5th Cir. 1995).
28. 183 F. 3d 833, 842 (D.C. Cir. 1999).
29. *United States v. Bailey*, 498 F. 2d 677 (D.C. Cir. 1974).
30. 359, 494 U.S. 152 (1990).
31. 130 S. Ct. 2963 (2010).
32. Police Misconduct website. http://www.policemisconduct.net/statistics/2010-annual-report/. Retrieved August 27, 2014.
33. David Von Drehle & Alex Altman. (2014, September 1). The tragedy of Ferguson. *Time*, 22–27.
34. Robert J. Kane. (2002, November). Social ecology of police misconduct. *Criminology*, 40(4), 867–877.

35. Frank Pearce & Steven Tombs. (1998*). Toxic capitalism: Corporate crime and the chemical industry*. Brookfield, CT: Dartmouth.
36. Neal Stover & Aaron S. Routhe. (2005). Environment crime. *Crime and Justice, 32*, 321–371
37. Stover & Ruothe, 2005.
38. Stover & Ruothe, 2005.

chapter eleven

Cybercrimes

Chapter Objectives

What you should know and understand after studying this chapter:

- What constitutes cybercrime
- The issues involved in controlling cybercrime
- How the Internet has changed society
- The types of cybercrime deviants
- Why some people commit cybercrime

Introduction

On November 8, 2008, a wave of thieves fanned out across the globe nearly simultaneously. With cloned or stolen debit cards in hand—and the PINs to go with them—they hit more than 2,100 money machines in at least 280 cities on three continents, in such countries as the United States, Canada, Italy, Hong Kong, Japan, Estonia, Russia, and the Ukraine. When it was all over—incredibly within 12 hours—the thieves walked off with a total of more than $9 million in cash. And that figure would've been more had the targeted ATMs not been drained of all their money.

Cybercrime is generally defined as criminal activity committed using computers and the Internet. The term includes anything from downloading illegal music or video files to stealing millions of dollars from online bank accounts. In addition, it includes nonmonetary criminal offenses such as cheating, introducing viruses, and posting trade secrets or confidential information on the Internet. Included in any discussion regarding online deviance is cyberbullying.

In today's modern world the most prominent form of cybercrime is probably identity theft. Identity theft includes login information such as usernames and passwords, phone numbers, addresses, credit card numbers, bank account numbers, and other information that may be used by criminals to steal and take advantage of another person's identity.

In this chapter, we will briefly discuss some of the various forms of cybercrime. However, each day it appears that new forms of cybercrime are committed.

FOCUS ON PEOPLE

KEVIN DAVID MITNICK

Kevin Mitnick is an American computer security consultant, author, and hacker. In 1999, he was convicted of various computer and communications-related crimes. At the time of his arrest, he was the most wanted computer criminal in the United States. Mitnick presently operates a security firm named Mitnick Security Consulting. The firm provides services that test a company's security strengths and weaknesses.[1]

In his 2002 book *The Art of Deception*, Mitnick states that he compromised computers solely by using passwords and codes that he gained by social engineering. He claims he did not use software programs or hacking tools for cracking passwords or otherwise exploit computer or phone security. He also stated that the reason he was involved in hacking was because of the intellectual challenge involved.[2]

Extent of the Problem

According to the Federal Bureau of Investigation (FBI), every day criminals are invading countless homes and offices across the nation. They are invading not by breaking down windows and doors, but by breaking into laptops, personal computers, and wireless devices via hacks and bits of malicious code. The FBI estimates that billions of dollars are lost each year repairing systems hit by such attacks. The attacks have taken down vital systems, disrupting and sometimes disabling the works of banks, hospitals, and 911 services around the country.[3]

According to the FBI, the individuals and organizations involved in cybercrime run the gamut from computer geeks looking for bragging rights to businesses trying to gain an upper hand in the marketplace, from rings of criminals wanting to steal your personal information and sell it on the black market to attempts by spies and terrorists to rob our nation of vital information or launch cyber strikes.

Common Cybercrime Fraud Schemes

The common cybercrime fraud schemes include Internet auction fraud, nondelivery of merchandise, credit card fraud, investment fraud, business fraud, and the ever-popular Nigerian letter. In addition, senior citizens have been targeted with healthcare fraud, counterfeit prescription drugs, funeral and cemetery insurance fraud, fraudulent antiaging products,

SOCIETY IN ACTION

Probably you have received an e-mail message very similar to this one:

Dear customer:

We regret to inform you that your bank account has been compromised. You need to take immediate action to prevent any fraudulent actions against your account. Please log in to the below Internet link and provide your username and password so that a complete assessment may be made of your account. We need you to provide the bank with your username and password in order to ensure that it is actually you, the authorized account holder, who is making the corrective action.

Link to click on: ————

Thank you for your prompt attention to this serious matter.

Sincerely,

Your Bank Manager

While this e-mail may seem legitimate, it is clearly an attempt to obtain your password and username. Generally a legitimate e-mail would advise you to either contact your bank or log in to your online account without providing a link. In other words, in a legitimate e-mail you would probably need to look up your bank's phone number and not use the number or link provided.

telemarketing fraud, investment schemes, and reverse mortgage scams. The common investor-related scams include letters of credit fraud, prime bank note fraud, Ponzi schemes, and pyramid schemes. In addition, it appears that a new scheme is invented each week.

Tips for Avoiding Internet Auction Fraud

The FBI has listed the following tips for avoiding Internet auction fraud:

- Understand as much as possible about how the auction works, what your obligations are as a buyer, and what the seller's obligations are before you bid.
- Find out what actions the website/company takes if a problem occurs, and consider insuring the transaction and shipment.
- Learn as much as possible about the seller, especially if the only information you have is an e-mail address. If it is a business, check the Better Business Bureau where the seller/business is located.

FOCUS ON PEOPLE

CARLOS ENRIQUE PEREZ-MELARA

In 2014, Carlos Enrique Perez-Melara was one of the FBI's most wanted cyber-deviants (Figure 11.1). The FBI is offering a reward of up to $50,000 for information leading to his arrest. He is wanted for alleged involvement in manufacturing spyware that was used to intercept the private communications of hundreds, if not thousands, of victims. As part of the scheme, he ran a website offering customers a way to catch cheating lovers by sending spyware masqueraded as an electronic greeting card. Victims who opened the greeting card unwittingly installed a program on their computers. The program collected keystrokes and other incoming and outgoing electronic communications on the victim's computers. The program would periodically send e-mail messages back to the purchasers of the service containing the acquired communications, including the victims' passwords, list of visited websites, and keystroke logs.

An arrest warrant was issued by the U.S. District Court, Southern District of California in July 2005. Perez-Melara was charged with the crimes of manufacturing an interception device, sending deceptive advertising, unlawfully intercepting electronic communications, and disclosing unlawfully intercepted electronic communications. He was in the United States on a travel visa and attended college in San Diego, California. His last known location was in San Salvador, El Salvador.

- Examine the feedback on the seller.
- Determine what method of payment the seller is asking from the buyer and where he or she is asking to send payment.
- If possible, purchase items online using your credit card, because you can often dispute the charges if something goes wrong.
- Be cautious when dealing with sellers outside the United States. If a problem occurs with the auction transaction, it could be much more difficult to rectify.
- Ask the seller about when delivery can be expected and whether the merchandise is covered by a warranty or can be exchanged if there is a problem.
- Make sure there are no unexpected costs, including whether shipping and handling is included in the auction price.
- There should be no reason to give out your social security number or driver's license number to the seller.

Figure 11.1 This picture of Carlos Enrique Perez-Melara was used on the wanted poster issued by the FBI. (Photo courtesy of U.S. Library of Congress.)

Tips for Avoiding Nondelivery of Merchandise

The FBI has listed the following tips for avoiding nondelivery of merchandise fraud:

- Make sure you are purchasing merchandise from a reputable source.
- Do your homework on the individual or company to ensure that they are legitimate.
- Obtain a physical address (rather than simply a post office box) and a telephone number, and call the seller to see if the telephone number is correct and working.
- Send an e-mail to the seller to make sure the e-mail address is active, and be wary of those that utilize free e-mail services where a credit card wasn't required to open the account.
- Consider not purchasing from sellers who won't provide you with this type of information.
- Check with the Better Business Bureau from the seller's area.
- Check out other websites regarding this person/company.
- Don't judge a person or company by their website. Flashy websites can be set up quickly.
- Be cautious when responding to special investment offers, especially through unsolicited e-mail.

- Be cautious when dealing with individuals/companies from outside your own country.
- Inquire about returns and warranties.
- If possible, purchase items online using your credit card, because you can often dispute the charges if something goes wrong.
- Make sure the transaction is secure when you electronically send your credit card numbers.
- Consider using an escrow or alternate payment service.

Tips for Avoiding Credit Card Fraud

The FBI's tips for avoiding credit card fraud include the following:

- Don't give out your credit card number online unless the site is secure and reputable. Sometimes a tiny icon of a padlock appears to symbolize a higher level of security to transmit data. This icon is not a guarantee of a secure site, but provides some assurance.
- Don't trust a site just because it claims to be secure.
- Before using the site, check out the security/encryption software it uses.
- Make sure you are purchasing merchandise from a reputable source.
- Do your homework on the individual or company to ensure that they are legitimate.
- Obtain a physical address (rather than simply a post office box) and a telephone number, and call the seller to see if the telephone number is correct and working.
- Send an e-mail to the seller to make sure the e-mail address is active, and be wary of those that utilize free e-mail services where a credit card wasn't required to open the account.
- Consider not purchasing from sellers who won't provide you with this type of information.
- Check with the Better Business Bureau from the seller's area.
- Check out other websites regarding this person/company.
- Don't judge a person or company by their website. Flashy websites can be set up quickly.
- Be cautious when responding to special investment offers, especially through unsolicited e-mail.
- Be cautious when dealing with individuals/companies from outside your own country.
- If possible, purchase items online using your credit card, because you can often dispute the charges if something goes wrong.
- Make sure the transaction is secure when you electronically send your credit card number.

- Keep a list of all your credit cards and account information along with the card issuer's contact information. If anything looks suspicious or you lose your credit card(s), contact the card issuer immediately.

Tips for Avoiding Investment Fraud

The FBI's tips for avoiding investment fraud include the following:

- Don't judge a person or company by their website. Flashy websites can be set up quickly.
- Don't invest in anything you are not absolutely sure about. Do your homework on the investment and the company to ensure that they are legitimate.
- Check out other websites regarding this person/company.
- Be cautious when responding to special investment offers, especially through unsolicited e-mail.
- Be cautious when dealing with individuals/companies from outside your own country.
- Inquire about all the terms and conditions.

Tips for Avoiding Business Fraud

The FBI's tips for avoiding business fraud include the following:

- Purchase merchandise from reputable dealers or establishments.
- Obtain a physical address (rather than simply a post office box) and a telephone number, and call the seller to see if the telephone number is correct and working.
- Send an e-mail to the seller to make sure the e-mail address is active, and be wary of those that utilize free e-mail services where a credit card wasn't required to open the account.
- Consider not purchasing from sellers who won't provide you with this type of information.
- Purchase merchandise directly from the individual/company that holds the trademark, copyright, or patent.

Extortion

According to a special report issued by FBI special agent Michelle Lee,[4] there has been a rise in virtual kidnapping extortion schemes. She notes that in the past several years, San Antonio FBI, along with many state and local enforcement partners, has received reports from the public regarding extortion schemes, often referred to as virtual kidnapping. Typically the scheme involves an individual or criminal organization contacting a victim by telephone and demanding payment for the return of a kidnapped family member or friend. While no actual kidnapping has taken place, the callers often use co-conspirators to convince their victims of the legitimacy of the threat. For example, a caller might attempt to convince a victim that his or her daughter was kidnapped by having a young female scream for help in the background during the call.

The callers, sometimes representing themselves as members of a drug cartel or a corrupt law enforcement agency, will provide the victim with specific instructions to ensure the safe return of the alleged kidnapped victim. The instructions normally demand the payment of a ransom and involve techniques designed to instill a sense of fear, panic, and urgency in an effort to rush the victim into making a hasty decision. Frequently, the callers will go to great lengths to engage the victim in ongoing conversations to prevent them from verifying the status and location of the allegedly kidnapped victim. Frequently, the callers will convince their victims that they are being watched and were personally targeted.[5]

The FBI advises that to avoid becoming a victim of this extortion scheme, look for the following possible indicators:

- Incoming calls made from an outside area code
- Multiple successive phone calls
- Calls that do not come from the kidnapped victim's phone
- Callers going to great lengths to keep you on the phone
- Callers preventing you from calling or locating the kidnapped victim
- Ransom money is only accepted via wire transfer service

The FBI recommends that if you receive a phone call from someone who demands payment of a ransom for a kidnapped victim, the following should be considered:

- Stay calm.
- Slow the situation down.
- Avoid sharing information about you or your family during the call.
- Listen carefully to the voice of the kidnapped victim.
- Attempt to call or determine the location of the kidnapped victim.
- Request to speak to the victim.
- Ask questions only the victim would know.
- Request the kidnapped victim call back from his or her cell phone.

Nigerian Letter or 419 Fraud

As noted by the FBI, the Nigerian letter frauds combine the threat of impersonation fraud with a variation of an advance fee scheme in which a letter mailed from Nigeria offers the recipient the opportunity to share in a percentage of millions of dollars that the author—a self-proclaimed government official—is trying to transfer illegally out of Nigeria. The recipient is encouraged to send information to the author, such as blank letterhead stationery, bank name and account numbers, and other identifying information using a fax number provided in the letter. Some of these letters have also been received via e-mail through the Internet. The scheme relies on convincing a willing victim, who has demonstrated a "propensity for larceny" by responding to the invitation, to send money to the author of the letter in Nigeria in several installments of increasing amounts for a variety of reasons.

Payment of taxes, bribes to government officials, and legal fees are often described in great detail with the promise that all expenses will be reimbursed as soon as the funds are spirited out of Nigeria. In actuality, the millions of dollars do not exist, and the victim eventually ends up with nothing but loss. Once the victim stops sending money, the perpetrators have been known to use the personal information and checks that they received to impersonate the victim, draining bank accounts and credit card balances. While such an invitation impresses most law abiding citizens as a laughable hoax, millions of dollars in losses are caused by these schemes annually. Some victims have been lured to Nigeria, where they have been imprisoned against their will, along with losing large sums of money. The Nigerian government is not sympathetic to victims of these schemes, since the victim actually conspires to remove funds from Nigeria in a manner that is contrary to Nigerian law. The schemes themselves violate Section 419 of the Nigerian criminal code, hence the label "419 fraud."[6]

Tips for Avoiding the Nigerian Letter or 419 Fraud

- If you receive a letter from Nigeria asking you to send personal or banking information, do not reply in any manner. Send the letter to the U.S. Secret Service, your local FBI office, or the U.S. Postal Inspection Service. You can also register a complaint with the Federal Trade Commission's complaint assistant.
- If you know someone who is corresponding in one of these schemes, encourage that person to contact the FBI or the U.S. Secret Service as soon as possible.
- Be skeptical of individuals representing themselves as Nigerian or foreign government officials asking for your help in placing large sums of money in overseas bank accounts.
- Do not believe the promise of large sums of money for your cooperation.
- Guard your account information carefully.

Causation

It is often difficult to determine why some people are engaged in cybercrime. A huge percentage is engaged for monetary gains, but others appear to engage in the deviant behavior only to harass or cause individuals problems.

Many researchers list computer crime and cybercrime as the most widespread criminal activity in the world. Cybercriminals are always searching for new and unprotected computer technologies to exploit and take advantage of. These criminals, unlike street criminals, operate in the electronic world. The deviants vary in age, gender, personality, and social and economic status. In other words, cybercriminals can be anyone, including your next-door neighbor. It is easy to hide your identity from others when committing cybercrime and the criminal has a strong sense of anonymity.

There are also cybercrime professionals. These are the criminals who have profited significantly from their cybercrime and are actively involved with various criminal organizations. If cybercrime opportunities were not available, these individuals undoubtedly would be engaged in similar criminal misconduct.

Another reason for the popularity of cybercrime is the fact that currently our legal statutes are inadequate and there are significant jurisdictional issues. For example, a credit card of one of the authors was stolen in Houston, Texas, and the card number was used the next day in Hong Kong.

As noted earlier, many cybercriminals are not in the game for monetary reasons. It is the excitement, fame, and challenge of exploiting a computer system that causes them to commit the acts. Frequently, the cybercriminals who invade computer systems with worms and viruses are looking to cause harm to an individual company or person. This grudge attitude may arise from losing a job, perceived unethical business conduct, jealousy, or envy. Such criminals intend to destroy or cripple their targets for the personal satisfaction of getting even. It does not matter to them that others will also be injured.

For many cybercriminals, it is the excitement and challenge of exploiting a computer system. This challenge is too great to resist. Computer gurus are notorious for obtaining information from computer systems and have many times an irresistible urge to put to the test the information they have obtained. Thus, the lure of cracking the code is a major factor in enticing certain gurus to commit cybercrime.

In a somewhat similar manner, cybercrime is an opportunistic crime for some individuals. The individuals who spend a significant amount of time on their computer and have many opportunities to commit crimes have suddenly gained a whole variety of opportunities to commit crime.

To these individuals, cybercrime is easy to commit and the chances of being detected are slim.

Donn Parker, in a study of 80 computer hackers, identified the following psychological and behavior traits that were commonly held by the 80 cyber-deviants.[7]

- Precociousness, curiosity, and persistence
- Habitual lying, cheating, stealing, and exaggerating
- Idealism
- Hyperactivity
- History of drug or alcohol abuse

Parker states that law enforcement in general has determined that there are two kinds of cybercriminals: the outside hackers who attack others' computers for pleasure, challenge, curiosity, educational experience, or to warn society of vulnerabilities, and the computer technologist insiders who are motivated by greed. Parker contends that these two classifications are too simplistic in today's time. He indicates that cybercriminals range from the juvenile delinquents playing pranks to malicious hackers, white-collar criminals, members of organized gangs, terrorists, and unethical businesspersons and bureaucrats. He contends that the criminals often migrate from one role to another or play multiple roles.

Parker brings out an important item in stating that unfortunately, the successful computer criminals generally do not look or act like stereotypic criminals. He also notes that most do not see themselves as greedy criminals, but as problem solvers. Parker opines that while computer criminals' motives vary, they often begin their criminal acts in an attempt to recover from errors, get even, beat competitors, eliminate debts, win sympathetic attention, get better jobs, or survive short-term business losses. He states that an experienced investigator in an insurance company told him that the trusted employees who are undergoing divorce are among the people most likely to commit computer crimes. Probably the reason that more criminals do not commit computer-related crimes is because of the lack of opportunity or lack of technical skill.

Under the rational choice theories of Derek Cornish and Ronald Clarke, the decision to commit a deviant act is influenced by the need to maximize pleasure and minimize pain. Computer crime tends to involve a deliberate process that could involve maximum pleasure and the low chance of being detected.[8] Under Sutherland's differential association, the individual commits computer crime when he or she has been sufficiently socialized into the computer underworld, or other acts of computer ingenuity are admired and copied. Greshman Sykes and David Matza's techniques of neutralization have been used by computer criminals to justify or neutralize guilt associated with their deviance.[9]

Preventing Cybercrime

The U.S. Department of Justice has established the Computer Crime and Intellectual Property Section (CCIPS), which is responsible for implementing the department's national strategies in combating computer and intellectual property crimes worldwide. CCIPS prevents, investigates, and prosecutes computer crimes by working with other government agencies, the private sector, academic institutions, and foreign counterparts. Section attorneys work to improve the domestic and international infrastructure—legal, technological, and operational—to pursue network criminals most effectively.[10]

The section's enforcement responsibilities against intellectual property crimes are similarly multifaceted. Intellectual property (IP) has become one of the principal U.S. economic engines, and the nation is a target of choice for thieves of material protected by copyright, trademark, or trade secret designation. In pursuing all these goals, CCIPS attorneys regularly run complex investigations, resolve unique legal and investigative issues raised by emerging computer and telecommunications technologies, litigate cases, provide litigation support to other prosecutors, train federal, state, and local law enforcement personnel, comment on and propose legislation, and initiate and participate in international efforts to combat computer and intellectual property crime.

Prosecution by CCIPS

An example of the work of CCIPS is noted in an August 2014 prosecution in which a California investment manager was found guilty in federal district court in Salt Lake City, Utah, for his role in a $33 million investment fraud scheme. The manager, Robert L. Holloway, was found guilty after a seven-day trial by a federal jury in the district of Utah of four counts of wire fraud and one count of making and subscribing a false income tax return.

Evidence presented at trial established that Holloway operated an investment entity called US Ventures LC, which was founded in 1999. Holloway served as the chief executive officer and managing partner of US Ventures. From October 2005 until at least April 2007, Holloway recruited investors for US Ventures by making false representations about the company, including that US Ventures used proprietary trading software that was consistently profitable, US Ventures generated returns of 0.8% per trading day, and US Ventures would retain a 30% share of investors' profits as a management fee.

Computer-Related Criminal Statutes

Generally the federal criminal statutes involving cybercrime and crime committed by use of computers are contained in Title 18 of the U.S. Code (USC). Laws concerning computer crimes have been enacted at the state and federal levels.

A general definition of *computer* in the statutes includes a device or group of devices that can automatically perform arithmetic, logical, storage, or retrieval operations with or on computer data. In addition, the definition also includes peripheral equipment, such as internal and external drives, faxes, modems, and printers, which are designed to store, retrieve, or communicate the results of computer operations, programs, or data.

In 1986, Congress passed the Computer Fraud and Abuse Act (CFAA). This act has been amended and expanded as Internet technology has advanced. It continues to be the basis for federal prosecutions of computer-related criminal activities. Other relevant federal statutes include the Electronic Communications Privacy Act (ECPA), the Identity Theft Enforcement and Restitution Act of 2008 (ITERA), and certain provisions of the USA Patriot Act.

For the most part, states have enacted similar state legation to cover state crimes in this area. For example, Article 156 of the New York Penal Code criminalizes a wide range of computer crimes. The article addresses five distinct offenses involving computers: unauthorized use of a computer, computer trespass, computer tampering, unlawful duplication of computer-related material, and criminal possession of computer-related material.[11]

A list of the most popular federal statutes is set forth below:

- 18 USC § 1028: Fraud and related activity in connection with identification documents, authentication features, and information.
- 18 USC § 1028A: Aggravated identity theft.
- 18 USC § 1029: Fraud and related activity in connection with access devices.
- 18 USC § 1030: Fraud and related activity in connection with computers.
- 18 USC § 1037: Fraud and related activity in connection with electronic mail.
- 18 USC § 1343: Fraud by wire, radio, or television.
- 18 USC § 1362: Malicious mischief related to communications lines, stations, or systems.
- 18 USC § 1462: Importation or transportation of obscene matters.
- 18 USC § 1466A: Obscene visual representation of the sexual abuse of children.
- 18 USC § 2251: Sexual exploitation of children.
- 18 USC § 2252B: Misleading domain names on the Internet.
- 18 USC § 2252C: Misleading words or digital images on the Internet.

Cyberbullying

Cyberbullying in recent years has grown because of the popularity of the Internet. When the authors were in school, kids could go home and be safe from neighborhood bullies. That is not the case nowadays. In addition to physical assaults, many bullies now harass people via e-mail, social media, instant message, and other online forums.

Cyberbullying may generally be defined as any message or image sent or shared on the Internet that is intended to hurt or embarrass another person. Because of the prevalence of social media in our present-day culture, it is difficult to control cyberbullying. Simply asking the child to cut off all electronics is not an acceptable answer. In so doing so, you isolate the child from potential friends and sources of support. In addition, the cutting off of all electronics would likely increase the child's feeling of being victimized and may result in depression and anxiety.

Several researchers have estimated that more than one-half of kids have been cyber bullied at one time or another online. In addition, about half of the kids who use the media have admitted to saying mean or hurtful things to someone at least on one occasion. Other researchers have indicated that more than one in three kids has experienced cyber threats. About 25% of teenagers are routinely bullied through their cell phones or over the Internet.

One of the problems in this regard is that most young people, approximately 60%, do not inform their parents when cyberbullying first takes place. Once a bullying comment or picture is posted on the Internet, it frequently goes viral. The effects of going viral are that more people see, comment, and pass on the posted image, message, or rumor. The speed at which a harmful message can spread on the Internet is unbelievable. The victim has little time to react to process the hurtful comments that can result.

Recovering from cyberbullying can be difficult for the victim because the words or images become a part of the permanent record of the Internet, and it is almost impossible to track down and erase all mentions of it online. This can make a person feel hopeless and like he or she can never escape the attack.

Why do cyberbullying incidents occur? While there is very little research in this area, it appears that the individual who commits cyberbullying is the same type of individual who would otherwise commit physical bullying if that avenue was more appropriate. Thus, it appears that some individuals get pleasure from causing pain or shame to victims. Each of the theoretical causation theories discussed in the earlier chapters of this text would appear to apply to cyberbullying. The one exception is that cyberbullying is not normally motivated by the desire for financial gain.

Cyberbullying Signs

There are certain signs that parents should be aware of which can indicate that their child is subject to cyberbullying. First, if the child suddenly spends either much more time or much less time texting, gaming, or using social network sites, this is an indicator of cyberbullying activity. Any rapid change in behavior in this regard should be accepted by the parents as a warning. If after being online or texting the child appears to be withdrawn or upset, this is another indication of the presence of cyberbullying. Frequently, a child who has been cyber bullied will suddenly avoid formerly enjoyable social situations. If a child starts blocking telephone numbers or e-mail addresses from his or her phone account, this may indicate bullying. If the child's behavior seems frustrated or if the child acts out more, this is another indication of cyberbullying. For many young people, the first reaction when they are attacked online is to seek revenge, avoid their friends and normal activities, or even launch cyberbullying tactics on their own.

Tips to Overcome Cyberbullying

First and foremost, any victim of cyberbullying should block any communications from the bully. Accordingly, it is important that the child understands how to block communications from certain individuals. Second, the child should be instructed never to open or read messages by cyber bullies. The child should be encouraged to report cyberbullying to a trusted adult. In addition, a report of the problem should be made to the Internet provider or website moderator. Parents should keep computers in a family or public area and not in a child's room. This location can help with monitoring for appropriate use of the computer and make it easier to detect when your child receives a message from a cyberbully.

Research indicates that cyber bullies are less inclined to send an attack on social media if an adult can see the impact. Accordingly, talk to children about being friends with their parents on Facebook, Twitter, and so on. If the child is resistant to "friending" a parent, consider asking the child to accept a grandparent, aunt, or uncle.

Summary

- Cybercrime is generally defined as criminal activity committed using computers and the Internet.
- The term includes anything from downloading illegal music or video files to stealing millions of dollars from online bank accounts.
- In addition, it includes nonmonetary criminal offenses such as cheating, introducing viruses, or posting trade secrets or confidential information on the Internet.

- Included in any discussion regarding online deviance is cyberbullying.
- The most prominent form of cybercrime is probably identity theft.
- The attacks have taken down vital systems, disrupting and sometimes disabling the works of banks, hospitals, and 911 services around the country.
- The common cybercrime fraud schemes include Internet auction fraud, nondelivery of merchandise, credit card fraud, investment fraud, business fraud, and the ever-popular Nigerian letter.
- Typically the virtual kidnapping extortion scheme involves an individual or criminal organization contacting a victim by telephone and demanding payment for the return of a kidnapped family member or friend.
- It is often difficult to determine why some people are engaged in cybercrime. A huge percentage is engaged for monetary gains, but others appear to engage in the deviant behavior only to harass or cause individuals problems.
- Cyberbullying in recent years has grown because of the popularity of the Internet. In addition to physical assaults, many bullies now harass people via e-mail, social media, instant message, and other online forums.

Questions in Review

1. Why do individuals engage in cybercrime?
2. Explain how virtual extortion works?
3. What should you do if you received an e-mail asking for your password and username?
4. How serious is cybercrime?
5. What steps can be taken to reduce your exposure to cybercrime?

Key Terms

Computer: A device or group of devices that can automatically perform arithmetic, logical, storage, or retrieval operations with or on computer data. In addition, the definition also includes peripheral equipment, such as internal and external drives, faxes, modems, and printers, which are designed to store, retrieve, or communicate the results of computer operations, programs, or data.

Cyberbullying: Generally defined as any message or image sent or shared on the Internet that is intended to hurt or embarrass another person.

Cybercrime professionals: Criminals who have profited significantly from their cybercrime and are actively involved with various criminal organizations.

Cyber-deviance: Conduct that ranges from relatively benign invasive acts directed at a particular computer to intentionally destructive attacks against computer systems or unknown Internet users.

Virtual extortion: A scheme involving an individual or criminal organization contacting a victim by telephone and demanding payment for the return of a kidnapped family member or friend.

Endnotes

1. Kevin Mitnick. (2011). *Ghost in the wires: My adventures as the world's most wanted hacker*. New York: Little, Brown and Company.
2. Kevin Mitnick & William L. Simon. (2003). *The art of deception: Controlling the human element of security*. New York: Wiley.
3. FBI website. http://www.fbi.gov/about-us/investigate/cyber/cyber. Retrieved August 8, 2014.
4. Michelle Lee. (2014). FBI warns of "digital kidnappings in South Texas." http://www.woai.com/articles/woai-local-news-sponsored-by-five-star-cleaners-119078/fbi-warns-of-virtual-kidnappings-in-south-texas-12645329. Retrieved April 30, 2014.
5. FBI website. http://www.fbi.gov/sanantonio/press-releases/2014/virtual-kidnapping-extortion-calls-on-the-rise. Retrieved August 7, 2014.
6. FBI website. http://www.fbi.gov/scams-safety/fraud/fraud#419. Retrieved August 9, 2014.
7. Donn B. Parker. (2010). *Fighting computer crime: A new framework for protecting information*. New York: Wiley.
8. Derek Cornish & Ronald Clarke. (1986). *The reasoning criminal*. New York: Springer.
9. Greshman Sykes & David Matza. (1957). Techniques of neutralization. *American Sociological Review*, 22, 664–670.
10. CCIPS website. http://www.justice.gov/criminal/cybercrime. Retrieved August 9, 2014.
11. Find Law website. http://statelaws.findlaw.com/new-york-law/new-york-computer-crimes-laws.html. Retrieved August 9, 2014.

chapter twelve

Human Trafficking and Commercial Sex

Chapter Objectives

What you should know and understand after studying this chapter:

- What constitutes human trafficking
- The gravity of the human trafficking problem
- The extent of slavery in the world
- The major forms of human trafficking
- What is considered commercial sex
- Why individuals become prostitutes
- Who the victims are of sex trafficking
- Who are the customers of prostitutes

Human Trafficking

> Nearly 30 million people around the world are living as slaves, according to a new index ranking 162 countries. The Global Slavery Index 2013 says India has the highest number of people living in conditions of slavery at 14 million....
>
> The U.S. may be land of the free and home of the brave, but not for everyone. The 2013 Global Slavery Index reports that 60,000 individuals within its borders live as slaves. Of those 60,000, two-thirds are U.S. citizens.[1]
>
> In April 2014, the terrorist group Boko Haram abducted more than 300 Nigerian school girls. Shortly afterward, a video of the group's leader revealed his plans: "I will sell them in the market.... There is a market for selling humans."[2]

The threat by Boko Haram to engage in selling humans is a concept that is hard to understand. According to a report by Susan Tiano and Moira Murphy-Aguilar, human trafficking is the third largest criminal enterprise in the world—surpassed only by the illegal drug and weapons trade.[3] The majority of human trafficking cases involve women to be used in the sex industry.

As noted on the FBI website, the term *human trafficking* is used in common parlance to describe many forms of exploitation of human beings. While these words often evoke images of undocumented migrants being smuggled across international borders, the term has a different and highly specific meaning under Title 18 of the U.S. Code (USC).

Human trafficking crimes, as defined in Title 18, focus on the act of compelling or coercing a person's labor, services, or commercial sex acts. The coercion can be subtle or overt, physical or psychological. Coercion is the essential element except in cases where minors are offered for commercial sex. It is the forcing of a victim into performing labor, services, or commercial sex acts. The federal government has jurisdiction over human trafficking crimes because the statutes are based on the prohibition against slavery and involuntary servitude set forth in the 13th Amendment to the U.S. Constitution.[4]

To constitute a violation of one of the human trafficking crimes, there is no requirement that there be any smuggling or movement of victims. Undocumented migrants are particularly vulnerable to coercion because of their fear of authorities. Human traffickers have demonstrated, however, their ability to exploit other vulnerable populations. In addition, the traffickers have also focused on documented guest workers and U.S. minors.

What Constitutes Slavery?

According to the Walk Free Foundation, modern slavery takes many forms and is known by many names: slavery, forced labor, or human trafficking. The definitions used by the foundation and the United Nations include the following:

- Slavery refers to the condition of treating another person as if he or she were property—something to be bought, sold, traded, or even destroyed.
- Forced labor is a related but not identical concept, referring to work taken without consent, by threats or coercion.
- Human trafficking is another related concept, referring to the process through which people are brought, through deception, threats, or coercion, into slavery, forced labor, or other forms of severe exploitation.

The Walk Free Foundation indicates that whatever term is used, the significant characteristic of all forms of modern slavery is that they involve one person depriving others of their freedom: their freedom to leave one job for another, their freedom to leave one workplace for another, their freedom to control their own body.

Where Does Trafficking Take Place?

According to the National White Collar Crime Center (NW3C), human trafficking takes place all over the world, including in the United States. The U.S. State Department estimates that of the more than 27 million people currently enslaved, 75% are sexually exploited, and most of the remaining people are subjected to other types of bondage, including forced labor, bonded labor, involuntary domestic servitude, and debt bondage. Enslaved people work on farms, in restaurants, hotels, nail salons, shops, factories, slaughterhouses, brothels, and in domestic situations in private homes. They live in large cities, small towns, suburban neighborhoods, and rural areas.[15]

Who Are the Victims?

Researcher Kim Williams states that the victims of human trafficking are often disadvantaged members of society. They may be poor, victims of wars or armed conflicts, undocumented immigrants, children, or the unschooled. The majority of those exploited are women and children; the U.S. Department of State's *Trafficking in Persons Report* estimates that 50% are under 18. Men are also victims of both sexual exploitation and forced labor. Trafficked victims also include members of the lesbian, gay, bisexual, and transgender (LGBT) community.[6]

Antislavery Legislation

In recent years, the U.S. Department of Justice has successfully prosecuted human trafficking crimes in agricultural fields, sweatshops, suburban mansions, brothels, escort services, bars, and strip clubs. Because of enhanced criminal statutes, victim protection provisions, and public awareness programs introduced by the Trafficking Victims Protection Act of 2000, as well as sustained dedication to combating human trafficking, the numbers of trafficking investigations and prosecutions have increased dramatically.

The Trafficking Victims Protection Act (TVPA)[7] was enacted by the United States in 2000. In addition, the United Nations has adopted the Protocol to Prevent, Suppress, and Punish Trafficking in Persons, Especially Women and Children, also known as the Palermo Protocol.[8]

As noted in the *Trafficking in Persons Report* for 2014,[9] the TVPA defines severe forms of trafficking as (1) sex trafficking in which a commercial sex act is induced by force, fraud, or coercion, or in which the person induced to perform such an act has not attained 18 years of age, or (2) the recruitment, harboring, transportation, provision, or obtaining of a person for labor or services through the use of force, fraud, or coercion for the purpose of subjection to involuntary servitude, peonage, debt bondage, or slavery.

The TVPA states that a person may be a trafficking victim regardless of whether he or she once consented, participated in a crime as a direct result of being trafficked, was transported into the exploitative situation, or was simply born into a state of servitude. At the heart of this phenomenon are the myriad forms of enslavement—not the activities involved in international transportation. The major forms of human trafficking include the following:

Forced labor
Sex trafficking
Bonded labor
Debt bondage among migrant laborers
Involuntary domestic servitude
Forced child labor
Child soldiers
Child sex trafficking

Indications of Trafficking

As noted by Kim Williams, citizens can play a key role in preventing and stopping human trafficking. In her report, she noted that the indications of trafficking include the following:

- There may be heavy security at a residence or work site, including barred windows, electronic surveillance, and guards.
- Victims often live where they work. If they leave the premises, an escort or guard accompanies them.
- At a doctor's office or any public place, victims are accompanied by an escort of some type. The escort often translates or speaks for them.
- Victims may appear to be malnourished, have poor personal hygiene, or have bruises or signs of physical mistreatment.
- Victims often appear frightened, anxious, or submissive, avoiding eye contact.
- Victims may be disoriented or seem confused. They may not know what city they are in or to where they are traveling.
- Victims have few, if any, personal belongings. Someone else is usually in control of their passports, identification, and money.

Williams advises that if you believe you have observed a situation that could be trafficking, report the incident immediately to your local law enforcement agency. You could save a life and help combat modern-day slavery as well.

FOCUS ON PEOPLE

POPE FRANCIS, 2013

I exhort the international community to adopt an even more unanimous and effective strategy against human trafficking, so that in every part of the world, men and women may no longer be used as a means to an end.[10]

SOCIETY IN ACTION

VICTIMS' RIGHTS

As mandated by the *Attorney General's Guidelines for Victim and Witness Assistance*,[11] all victims of federal crime are entitled to certain rights under the law. These rights include

- The right to be reasonably protected from the accused
- The right to reasonable, accurate, and timely notice of any public court proceeding, or any parole proceeding, involving the crime or of any release or escape of the accused
- The right not to be excluded from any such public court proceeding, unless the court, after receiving clear and convincing evidence, determines that testimony by the victim would be materially altered if the victim heard other testimony at that proceeding
- The right to be reasonably heard at any public proceeding in the district court involving release, plea, sentencing, or any parole proceeding
- The reasonable right to confer with the attorney for the government in the case
- The right to full and timely restitution as provided in law
- The right to proceedings free from unreasonable delay
- The right to be treated with fairness and with respect for the victim's dignity and privacy

SOCIETY IN ACTION

SLAVES

According to a 2014 webinar presented by the National Center for Victims of Crime:

- Globally, the average cost to buy a slave is $90.
- Approximately 80% of trafficking involves sexual exploitation, and about 19% involves labor exploitation.
- There are between 20 million and 30 million slaves in the world today.
- The average age a teen enters the sex trade in the United States is 12 to 14 years old. Many victims are runaway girls who were sexually abused as children.
- Los Angeles, San Francisco, and San Diego are three of the 13 highest child sex trafficking areas according to the FBI.
- The National Human Trafficking Hotline receives more calls from Texas than any other state in the United States—15% of those calls are from the Dallas–Fort Worth area.[12]

Sex Trafficking

> Every day in the United States, children and adolescents are victims of commercial sexual exploitation and sex trafficking. Despite the serious and long-term consequences for victims as well as their families, communities, and society, efforts to prevent, identify, and respond to these crimes are largely under supported, inefficient, uncoordinated, and unevaluated.[13]
>
> **Cambodia:** Kieu's family relied on their local pond for their livelihood. When her father became ill, the nets they used fell into disrepair. Mending them would cost the equivalent of approximately $200 they did not have. Her parents turned to a loan shark whose exorbitant interest rates quickly ballooned their debt to the equivalent of approximately $9,000. "Virgin selling" was a common practice in their community, and Kieu's mother, after acquiring a "certificate of virginity" from the hospital, sold her to a man at a hotel. Kieu was 12 years old. Upon hearing that she was to be sold again, Kieu fled, making her way to a safe house where she could recover. Kieu is now self-sufficient and hopes to start her own business.[14]

Sex trafficking is generally defined as a form of slavery in which a commercial sex act is induced by force, fraud, or coercion, or in which the person induced to perform such an act is under the age of 18 years. As defined by the TVPA, *commercial sex act* refers to any sex act on account of which anything of value is given to or received by any person.

The TVPA recognizes that traffickers use psychological as well as physical coercion and bondage, and it defines coercion to include threats of serious harm to or physical restraint against any person, any scheme, plan, or pattern intended to cause a person to believe that failure to perform an act would result in serious harm to or physical restraint against any person, or the abuse or threatened abuse of the legal process.

Victims of Sex Trafficking

The victims of sex trafficking are women or men, girls or boys, with the majority being women and girls. Some of the common patterns for luring victims into situations of sex trafficking include the following:

- The promise of a good job in another country.
- A false marriage proposal turned into a bondage situation.
- Being sold into the sex trade by parents, husbands, or boyfriends.
- Being kidnapped by traffickers.
- Sex traffickers frequently subject their victims to debt bondage. This the illegal practice in which the traffickers tell their victims that they owe money (often relating to the victims' living expenses and transport into the country) and that they must pledge their personal services to repay the debt.

Sex traffickers are known to use a variety of methods to condition their victims. The methods include starvation, confinement, beatings, physical abuse, rape, gang rape, threats of violence to the victims and the victims' families, forced drug use, and the threat of shaming their victims by revealing their activities to their family and their families' friends.

Types of Sex Trafficking

Victims of trafficking are forced into various forms of commercial sexual exploitation. The forms include prostitution, pornography, stripping, live sex shows, mail order brides, military prostitution, and sex tourism.

Most victims who are trafficked into prostitution and pornography are usually involved in the most exploitive forms of commercial sex operations. Sex trafficking operations can be found in highly visible venues, such as street prostitution, as well as more underground systems, such as closed brothels that operate out of residential homes. Sex trafficking also takes place in a variety of public and private locations, such as massage parlors, spas, strip clubs, and other fronts for prostitution. Frequently,

SOCIETY IN ACTION

U.S. V. MI SUN CHO

713 F. 3d 716, C.A. 2 (N.Y.), 2013 (Excerpts)

In October 2010, after losing money gambling at a casino, Mei Hua Jin telephoned Cho from Atlantic City to see whether Cho could find her employment as a prostitute. Cho was aware that Jin was calling from Atlantic City. Cho had extensive contacts in the sex-trafficking industry and worked to provide prostitutes to brothels, often determining prostitutes' placement based on their age and physical appearance. Cho and Jin had previously worked together at a Connecticut brothel and at a prostitution business that Cho operated in Manhattan. After receiving Jin's phone call, Cho arranged to have one of her contacts inform Jin that a position at a Manhattan brothel was available. This contact was a confidential informant (CI) for law enforcement who had a lengthy relationship with Cho in the sex-trafficking industry. On October 7, 2010, the CI spoke with Jin about traveling from Atlantic City to New York so that she could be placed at the Manhattan brothel designated by Cho. On October 8, after speaking to Cho and the CI, Jin bought a bus ticket with her own money and traveled from Atlantic City to Manhattan. She then took the subway to Flushing, where Cho and the CI awaited her arrival. The three then began driving to the Manhattan brothel, though Cho was dropped off at home before Jin and the CI reached their destination. The brothel rejected Jin because she was too old, and Jin then returned to Flushing.

On October 25, 2011, the government filed a three-count Superseding Indictment. As relevant to this appeal, Count Two charged Cho with transporting Jin from New Jersey to New York to work at a brothel, and willfully causing her to be so transported in violation of 18 U.S.C. §§ 2241 and 2. On November 7, 2011, after a five-day trial, the jury convicted Cho of all three counts.

After the verdict, Cho renewed her motion under Rule 29 of the Federal Rules of Criminal Procedure for a judgment of acquittal on Counts Two and Three. In the alternative, Cho requested a new trial on those counts pursuant to Rule 33. The district court denied Cho's motion, finding that there was ample evidence to support the jury's verdict. The district court sentenced Cho to an aggregate term of 70 months' imprisonment, to be followed by two years of supervised release, and a $300 special assessment.

Under 18 U.S.C. § 2421, it is a crime to "knowingly transport any individual in interstate or foreign commerce … with intent that such individual engage in prostitution, or in any sexual activity for which any person can be charged with a criminal offense." 18 U.S.C. § 2421. "A defendant will be deemed to have transported an individual under Section 2421 where evidence shows that the defendant personally or through an agent performed the proscribed act of transporting." *United States v. Holland,* 381 F. 3d 80, 86 (2d Cir. 2004). As the district court properly instructed the jury, without objection from defense counsel:

> The prosecution does not need to prove that the defendant personally transported the individual across a state line. This element is satisfied if you find that the defendant prearranged the transportation of a person across a state line and that the defendant personally or through an agent arranged intrastate transportation as a continuation of the interstate travel.

SOCIETY IN ACTION

COMMERCIAL SEXUAL EXPLOITATION AND SEX TRAFFICKING OF MINORS IN THE UNITED STATES: MYTHS AND FACTS

Myth: Sex trafficking only happens overseas to young girls.

Fact: Commercial sexual exploitation and sex trafficking occur every day in the United States. Its victims—both male and female—live in cities and small towns across America.

Myth: Minors who are commercially sexually exploited or trafficked for sex are recognized as victims of crime and abuse.

Fact: Sexual exploitation and sex trafficking are forms of child abuse, but the children and adolescents who are victims can still be arrested for prostitution, detained or incarcerated, and subject to permanent records as offenders in most states.

Myth: People who buy sex with minors or engage in the sale of sex with minors are caught and punished for these crimes.

Fact: Despite laws in every state that enable the prosecution of these individuals, and despite the hard work of prosecutors and law enforcement in many jurisdictions, those who sexually exploit children and adolescents have largely escaped accountability.

Myth: It is easy for professionals who interact with minors to recognize victims, survivors, and youth at risk of commercial sexual exploitation and sex trafficking.

Fact: Many teachers, doctors and nurses, child welfare workers, and other individuals who interact with youth are unaware that commercial sexual exploitation and sex trafficking of minors occurs in their communities or lack the knowledge or training to identify and respond to it.

Myth: Help is readily available for victims and survivors of commercial sexual exploitation and sex trafficking.

Fact: There are too few services to meet current needs. The services that do exist are unevenly distributed geographically, lack adequate resources, and vary in their ability to provide specialized care.

Source: Adapted from Ellen Wright Clayton, Richard D. Krugman, & Patti Simon (Eds.), *Confronting Commercial Sexual Exploitation and Sex Trafficking of Minors in the United States*, National Academies Press, Washington, DC, 2013.

the victims start off dancing or stripping in clubs and then are coerced into prostitution and involved in pornography.[15]

Prostitution

Prostitution is generally defined by criminal statutes as the business or practice of engaging in sexual relations in exchange for payment or some other benefit. Prostitution is sometimes described as commercial sex. Under our federalist government, prostitution is a state crime unless committed on federal property. Prostitution is frequently referred to as the world's oldest profession.

In all states except Nevada it is a state crime. In Nevada, whether or not prostitution is a crime depends on the county statutes. Nevada is the only jurisdiction in the United States where prostitution is permitted. Nevada allows regulated brothels to operate in isolated rural areas, away from the majority of Nevada's population. Prostitution is illegal in the following counties: Clark (Las Vegas), Washoe (Reno), Douglas, and Lincoln. Prostitution is also illegal in Carson City. The rest of Nevada's counties are permitted by state law to license brothels, but only eight counties have done so. As of August 2013, there are 19 brothels in Nevada.

Individuals who are engaged in prostitution are generally referred to as prostitutes. Prostitute is derived from the Latin *prostituta*. The literal translation of the Latin word is "to put up front for sale" or "to place forward."

Why Do People Engage in Prostitution?

The popular stereotype of a prostitute is a woman who is a streetwalker, drug addicted, controlled by her pimp, and willing to accept a few dollars for her services. In reality, there are several categories of prostitutes and many reasons why they are involved in the profession. In addition to the streetwalkers, who are generally considered the lowest form of prostitutes, there are the women who provide sexual favors in massage parlors, small hotels, and out of their apartments or homes. In addition, there are escorts who collect large sums of money for a "date."

Some women have claimed that they were attracted to the profession for financial reasons. Some have stated that it was the best method to pay for a college education. Frequently, those on the higher financial end of the profession claim that they are helping men save their marriages by supplying something they cannot get at home, or helping them chase away loneliness when they are on business trips. At the lower financial end of the profession are those women who see it as a way to obtain money to buy drugs. In addition, there are many who claim that they were forced into prostitution, and once involved, it is difficult to leave.

Probably many are in the profession because of sex trafficking, which is an international, multi-billion-dollar business involving criminals who kidnap and enslave girls. There are numerous reports of young girls, as young as 10 years of age, being kidnapped and moved from their countries and sold into prostitution far away from their homeland.

Customers of Prostitution

Martin Monto and Christine Milrod conducted a research study and surveyed almost 2,500 men regarding the issue of why men become clients of prostitutes. They concluded that only about 14% of the men admitted to having paid a prostitute.[16] They concluded that one-third of the men who regularly went to prostitutes expressed feelings of intimacy and connection to the women involved. Some of them even professed a desire to take things to the next level. To these men they weren't just paying for sex—many of them also enjoyed the intimacy and emotional connection that came with the experience as well.

It's important to note that the men surveyed in the study were not the typical "john," in the sense that they were not meeting prostitutes on the street or finding different women every night. Instead, these men used a sex escort website and regularly saw the same woman, as opposed to different women each time. It's easy to see how this arrangement could lead to more intimacy and familiarity. The men might feel comfortable experimenting with a prostitute in ways that they never would with a woman who wasn't in the sex trade, and they might also feel more comfortable opening up about their feelings or what is going on in their lives. Over time, they might even feel as though there is more to the relationship than just sex and money.

The researchers concluded that the average client doesn't look all that different from the average man who has never paid for sex—clients are more likely to have served in the military, only slightly less likely to be married and white, and only slightly more likely to have a full-time job and be more sexually liberal. To some men, the ease and availability of a sex escort website might make the temptation too much for some, especially those with sex addiction or those who have high-risk personalities. While the researchers argue that hiring prostitutes is not necessarily an ordinary behavior, they say there's also little evidence to show that it's inherently deviant or linked to psychological deficiencies.

A word of caution regarding their research is that it appears that the sample population used in their study did not deal with men who accepted the services of a streetwalker. Why men engage in prostitution with a streetwalker is an area that needs additional research, as well as what type of men are involved with this type of prostitution.

An individual who preferred not to be identified stated that he experienced childhood cruelty and neglect and linked this to his inability to form close relationships with anyone, particularly women. He admitted that sex with prostitutes made him feel empty, but he had no idea how to get to know women through the normal routes. When he engages with a prostitute, he wants the prostitute to pretend to be his girlfriend.

Summary

- Human trafficking is the third largest criminal enterprise in the world—surpassed only by the illegal drug and weapons trade.
- The majority of human trafficking cases involve women to be used in the sex industry.
- Human trafficking crimes as defined in Title 18 focus on the act of compelling or coercing a person's labor, services, or commercial sex acts.
- To constitute a violation of one of the human trafficking crimes, there is no requirement that there be any smuggling or movement of victims.
- Modern slavery takes many forms, and is known by many names: slavery, forced labor, or human trafficking.
- Slavery refers to the condition of treating another person as if he or she were property—something to be bought, sold, traded, or even destroyed.
- Forced labor is a related but not identical concept, referring to work taken without consent, by threats or coercion.

- Human trafficking is another related concept, referring to the process through which people are brought, through deception, threats, or coercion, into slavery, forced labor, or other forms of severe exploitation.
- The Trafficking Victims Protection Act (TVPA) was enacted by the United States in 2000. In addition, the United Nations has adopted the Protocol to Prevent, Suppress, and Punish Trafficking in Persons, Especially Women and Children, also known as the Palermo Protocol.
- Sex trafficking is generally defined as a form of slavery in which a commercial sex act is induced by force, fraud, or coercion, or in which the person induced to perform such an act is under the age of 18 years.
- As defined by the TVPA, *commercial sex act* refers to any sex act on account of which anything of value is given to or received by any person.
- The victims of sex trafficking are women or men, girls or boys, with the majority being women and girls.
- Prostitution is generally defined by criminal statutes as the business or practice of engaging in sexual relations in exchange for payment or some other benefit. Prostitution is sometimes described as commercial sex.
- Under our federalist government, prostitution is a state crime unless committed on federal property.
- Prostitution is frequently referred to as the world's oldest profession.

Questions in Review

1. Why do individuals become prostitutes?
2. Who are the customers of prostitutes?
3. What constitutes slavery?
4. How big of a problem is human trafficking?
5. How has the federal government attempted to prevent human trafficking?

Key Terms

Forced labor: Work taken without consent, by threats or coercion.

Human trafficking: Term used in common parlance to describe many forms of exploitation of human beings. It also refers to the process through which people are brought, through deception, threats, or coercion, into slavery, forced labor, or other forms of severe exploitation.

Prostitution: Generally defined by criminal statutes as the business or practice of engaging in sexual relations in exchange for payment or some other benefit. Prostitution is sometimes described as commercial sex.

Sex trafficking: A form of slavery where commercial sex acts are induced by force, fraud, or coercion, or in which the person induced to perform such an act is under the age of 18 years. Alternative definition: The recruitment, harboring, transportation, provision, or obtaining of a person for the purpose of a commercial sex act in which that act is induced by force, fraud, or coercion.

Slavery: The condition of treating another person as if he or she were property—something to be bought, sold, traded, or even destroyed.

Endnotes

1. The Global Slavery Index is produced by the Walk Free Foundation and its partners. It is the first index of its kind, providing an estimate, country by country, of the number of people living in modern slavery today. The index may be downloaded at http://www.globalslaveryindex.org/about/. Retrieved August 11, 2014.
2. Kim Williams. (2014, August). Human trafficking: The return of an ancient malaise and what law enforcement can do about it. http://www.nw3c.org/docs/briefing/d8_july_2014.pdf?sfvrsn=8. Retrieved August 15, 2014.
3. Susan Tiano & Moira Murphy-Aguilar. (2012). *Borderline slavery: Mexico, United States, and the human trade*. Burlington, VT: Ashgate.
4. U.S. Department of Justice website. http://www.justice.gov/crt/about/crm/htpu.php. Retrieved August 10, 2014.
5. Williams, 2014.
6. Williams, 2014.
7. The Victims of Trafficking and Violence Protection Act of 2000 (P.L. 106-386), the Trafficking Victims Protection Reauthorization Act of 2003 (H.R. 2620), the Trafficking Victims Protection Reauthorization Act of 2005 (H.R. 972), and the Trafficking Victims Protection Reauthorization Act of 2008 (H.R. 7311).
8. United Nations. (2000). Protocol to prevent, suppress and punish trafficking in persons, especially women and children. Supplementing the United Nations Convention Against Transnational Organized Crime. Geneva: United Nations. https://www.ncjrs.gov/spotlight/trafficking/Summary.html. Retrieved August 11, 2014.
9. The *Trafficking in Persons Report* is an annual report published by the U.S. Department of State. A copy of the current report may be obtained online at http://www.state.gov/documents/organization. Retrieved August 11, 2014.
10. U.S. State Department. (2014). *The trafficking in persons report* (p. 8). http://www.state.gov/documents/organization/226844.pdf. Retrieved August 11, 2014.
11. Office for Victims of Crime, U.S. Department of Justice. (2012, May). *Attorney general's guidelines for victim and witness assistance*. Washington, DC: DOJ.
12. Webinar: Fighting trafficking with the power of forensic science. Presented by National Center for Victims of Crime, June 26, 2014. www.victimsofcrime.org. Retrieved June 27, 2014.
13. National Academy of Sciences. (2014). *Confronting commercial sexual exploitation and sex trafficking of minors in the US* (video). Washington, DC: National Academy of Sciences.
14. U.S. State Department, 2014.

15. See Administration for Children and Families, U.S. Department of Health and Human Services. http://www.acf.hhs.gov/accessibility. Retrieved August 11, 2014.
16. Martin Monto & Christine Milrod. (2013). Ordinary or peculiar men? Comparing the customers of prostitutes with a nationally representative sample of men. *International Journal of Offender Therapy and Comparative Criminology*. http://www.sagepublications.com. Retrieved August 11, 2014.

chapter thirteen

Unconventional Beliefs and Behaviors

Chapter Objectives

What you should know and understand after studying this chapter:

- The problem with labeling behavior as unconventional
- What constitutes social belief systems
- Issues involved in deviant drinking behavior
- What constitutes workplace deviance
- What constitutes computer or Internet addiction
- Issues involved with paranormal claims
- Issues involved in defining abnormal religious practices

Introduction

In this concluding chapter we will explore unconventional beliefs that are considered by many as forms of deviance. In addition, we will explore selected behaviors that may be considered unconventional. Belief is a state of the mind, treated in various academic disciplines, especially philosophy and psychology, as well as traditional culture, in which a subject roughly regards a thing to be true.[1]

What is an unconventional belief? To a person who holds a questionable belief, it is probably unconventional to him or her. For the most part, each of us has certain beliefs that others may not agree with, but that does not make them unconventional. To beg the question or provide an easy answer, in this chapter we will define unconventional beliefs as beliefs that are not generally accepted by the society in which we belong or in which we are examining.

Social Belief Systems

A belief system is a set of mutually supportive beliefs. The beliefs of any such system can be classified as religious, philosophical, ideological, or a combination of these. Philosopher Jonathan Glover stated that beliefs are always part of a belief system, and that tenanted belief systems are difficult for the tenants to completely revise or reject.[2]

It is often difficult to define belief systems cross-culturally because different societies have different ways of expressing faith. Although all cultures have belief systems, the forms these beliefs take vary widely from society to society. In most societies, beliefs play the all-important role in social control by defining what is right and wrong behavior. If individuals do the right things in life, they may earn moral approval. If they do the wrong things, they may suffer retribution.

Belief systems play an important role in social change. In many cases, these changes are taking place through liberation theology (whereby believers are for social reform and justice for the poor) and religious nationalism (whereby religious beliefs are merged with government institutions). Belief systems fulfill social needs. They can be powerful, dynamic forces in society. Beliefs often provide a basis for common purpose and values that help maintain social solidarity. The beliefs, by reinforcing group norms, help bring about social homogeneity. A uniformity of beliefs also helps bind people together to reinforce group identity. Beliefs enhance the overall well-being of the society by serving as a mechanism of social control, and also reduce the stress and frustrations that often lead to social conflict, thereby helping intensify group solidarity.

In a community, city, or state in which there is not a uniformity of beliefs, there may be numerous social groups that are not accepted by the majority within that society. This can cause unrest, hostility, and the mistreatment of those who do not conform to the generally accepted belief system.

Deviant Drinking Behavior

What constitutes deviant drinking behavior? Generally, the label refers to behaviors that involve repetitive, usually heavy, and always consequential drinking. Is it pathological, learned behavior, or a sickness? The answer to that question is beyond the scope of this section. The idea that repetitive drinking could be the result of forces beyond the control of the drinker was explored many centuries ago. In 1784, Benjamin Rush studied the bodily effects of various forms of alcoholic drink and concluded that there was a connection between the drinker and the addiction to alcohol.[3] Rush called the connection a "disease of the will."

Rush, in his research study on alcohol and why people drink, noted that a known drunkard was once followed by his favorite goat to a tavern, into which he was invited by his master and drenched with some liquor. The poor animal staggered home with his master, a good deal intoxicated. The next day the goat followed his master to the accustomed tavern. When the goat came to the door, he paused: His master made signs to him to follow him into the house. The goat stood still. An attempt was made to thrust the goat into the tavern. He resisted, as he was struck with the recollection of what he suffered from being intoxicated the night before. His master was so much affected by a sense of shame, in observing the conduct of his goat to be so much more rational than his own, that he ceased from that time to drink liquor.[4] Rush tried to understand why a goat tended to act more rational than the master. Rush concluded that the master was afflicted with the disease of the will.

Rush believed the disease developed gradually and was progressive, ultimately producing a "loss of control" over drinking. He assumed that one's will and desire were independent of each other, and that the former became weakened and ultimately debilitated by excessive drink. Rush advocated that the first step in treatment was abstinence from alcohol.

In 1935 Alcoholics Anonymous (AA) was founded by two men, one of whom was a physician. Another physician suggested to the founders the idea that alcoholism is an allergy of the body, the result of a physiological reaction to alcohol.

At the time, the concept of alcoholism as a mark of physiological sensitivity rather than moral decay was appealing, and the allergy concept came to occupy a central, although implicit, place in AA ideology. This theory had an additional advantage over other versions of the disease concept common during the early decades of the century that suggested alcoholism was a mental illness, a notion opposed strongly by AA. The appeal of allergy rests precisely in its identity as a bona fide medical or disease condition; people with allergies are victimized by, not responsible for, their condition.[5] It appears that some of popular success of AA involved the process of removing a stigmatized label and replacing it with a socially acceptable identity, such as *sick, repentant, recovered,* or *controlled.*

According to Schneider, two themes relevant to AA's implicit disease concept are found in the first and third of the famous 12 steps to recovery. The first and most important step is: "We admitted we were powerless over alcohol—that our lives had become unmanageable." This is precisely the concept of loss of control, a key idea in the early writing on alcoholism as a disease. Step 3 is: "We have made a decision to turn our will and our lives over to the care of God as we understand him." Representatives of AA are quick to note that although this language sounds traditionally religious, such terms are to be interpreted broadly and on the basis of the individual's own biography.[6]

Mark Keller, former editor of the *Journal of Studies on Alcohol,* applied the canons of reason and medicine to the behavioral puzzle of repeated, highly consequential drinking[7]:

- If one drinks in an excessive, deviant manner, so as to bring deprivation and harm to self and others while remaining impervious to pleas and admonitions based on this obvious connection, the person is assumed not to be in control of his or her will (regardless of desire).

- Such lack of control is then explained by the medical concept disease and the medicalized concept addiction, inherent in which is the presumption of limited or diminished responsibility.

According to Keller, resting on the inference of loss of control in a cultural system in which values of rationality, personal control, science, and medicine are given prominence, the assertion that alcoholism is a disease becomes an affirmation of dominant cultural and institutional values on which empirical data are never brought to bear. Indeed, it is precisely this quality of the question that holds the key to its viability as well as its controversy: It is a statement not for scientific scrutiny, but for political debate.

Workplace Deviance

Deviance in the workplace is not generally considered a deviant subculture. It is an important subject and was inserted in this chapter as a matter of convenience. Since most of the deviance discussed in this section pertains to employee deviance, we need to define employee deviance. For the purposes of this study, *employee deviance* is defined as voluntary behavior that violates the organizational norms and threatens in some manner the well-being of the organization. For example, a police officer who accepts money from a motorist in lieu of writing the motorist a traffic ticket is committing workplace deviance. And his or her conduct, in addition to being criminal, undermines the integrity of the police department. By voluntary, it is meant that the employee voluntarily chooses to conform or not to conform to expected norm behavior.

Organizational norms may be in the form of formal or informal organizational policies, rules, and procedures. According to Robinson and Bennett, deviance must be defined in terms of the standards of a specified organization.[8] The deviant aspect of the behavior refers to the aspect that the organizational norms are broken. The term *deviant behavior* is generally reserved for those acts that violate significant organizational norms and threaten to harm the well-being of the organization.

According to Robinson and Bennett, employee deviance and delinquency produce losses in organizations amounting to billions of dollars each year. They also estimate that from 33% to 75% of all employees have engaged in some form of the following behavior: theft, computer fraud, embezzlement, vandalism, sabotage, and absenteeism. The deviance ranges from corruption among police officers to illegal activities on Wall Street.

As noted by researchers Barrie Litzky, Kimberly Eddleston, and Deborah Kidder, the definition of deviant behaviors adopted by most deviance scholars focuses on harmful behaviors from the viewpoint of managers. Under that definition, whistle-blowing would be defined as a deviant act, although many in society will disagree. Researchers discuss a situation in which an employee, against company rules, offers an unhappy customer a free product or service to regain that customer's loyalty and pleasure. Would that behavior be considered constructive and pro-organizational behavior?[9]

Litzky, Eddleston, and Kidder indicate that, aside from personality traits or environmental factors beyond managerial control, six triggers may inadvertently encourage otherwise honest employees to engage in production, property, or political deviance—and perhaps even instances of personal aggression. Experts on workplace deviance suggest that there is much that managers can do to ameliorate the triggers of workplace deviance. These managerial triggers of deviant behavior include

- The compensation/reward structure
- Social pressures to conform
- Negative and untrusting attitudes
- Ambiguity about job performance
- Unfair treatment
- Violating employee trust

Computer and Internet Addiction

Internet addiction or computer addiction is a relatively new issue. When the authors were in college, the computer was new and a novelty. One government expert predicted in the 1980s that six computers would be sufficient to serve the U.S. needs. Now, there are some homes with six or more computer type devices. For example, the iPhone or Windows cell phone of today has more computing capabilities than the computers did in the 1980s.

Computer or Internet addiction became a public issue in the late 1990s. According to the HelpGuide website, the most common of these Internet addictions are cybersex, online gambling, and cyber-relationship addiction.

Computer addiction, online addiction, or Internet addiction disorder (IAD) is used to describe a variety of impulse control problems, including[10]

- **Cybersex addiction:** This refers to an individual who compulsively uses the Internet and focuses on pornography sites, adult chat rooms, or adult fantasy role-play sites, impacting negatively on real-life intimate relationships.
- **Cyber-relationship addiction:** This refers to the individual who is addicted to social networking, chat rooms, texting, and messaging to the point where virtual, online friends become more important than real-life relationships with family and friends.

- **Net compulsions:** This label includes addictions such as compulsive online gaming, gambling, stock trading, or use of online auction sites such as eBay, often resulting in financial and job-related problems.
- **Information overload:** This describes the individual who is involved in compulsive web surfing or database searching, leading to lower work productivity and less social interaction with family and friends.
- **Computer addiction:** This label is used to describe the individual who is addicted to obsessive playing of offline computer games, such as Solitaire or Minesweeper, or obsessive computer programming.

Most of us use the Internet on a daily basis, even when we are on vacation. When does the use become an addiction? This is a difficult question in which there are no absolute answers. Spending time on the Internet becomes a problem or issue when we do it to the excess. There are many people in the world who use the Internet in their profession, and they probably spend a good deal of time on the Internet. What may be excessive for one person may not be for another.

If we use the Internet in our profession or to promote social relations and not to the excess, then we are not considered addicted to it. But if we use it to the extreme and for such reasons that include the relieving of unpleasant or overwhelming feelings, then we may be addicted. Many addicts use the Internet to manage unpleasant feelings such as stress, loneliness, depression, and anxiety. Some individuals become addicted when they turn to the computer or Internet when they have a bad day and are looking for a way to escape their problems or to quickly relieve stress or self-soothe. Losing yourself online can make you forget feelings such as loneliness, stress, anxiety, depression, and boredom. Prior to the growth of the Internet or computers, we frequently used exercising, meditating, and practicing relaxation techniques to relieve the stress and boredom.

Who Becomes Addicted?

Research indicates that for some Internet users, their use of the Internet has characteristics akin to those found with substance abusers and gambling addicts. These individuals are likely to use the Internet to modulate moods (i.e., when down or when anxious or as an escape), are preoccupied with using the Internet, have symptoms of tolerance and withdrawal, have tried unsuccessfully to cut back on use, and have serious disturbances in their lives because of their Internet use.[11]

A 2012 study examined the interrelationships among Internet literacy, Internet addiction symptoms, Internet activities, and academic performance.[12] The study used 718 children and adolescents, aged 9 to 19, in Hong Kong. The researchers concluded that adolescent Internet addicts tended to be male, in low-income families, and not confident in locating, browsing, and accessing information from multiple resources, but that they were technologically savvy and frequent users of social networking sites (SNSs) and online games for leisure. The researchers also concluded that Internet literacy, especially in publishing and technology, increases—not decreases—the likelihood of someone getting addicted to the Internet.

The researchers noted that Internet activities can be much more addictive than other applications, such as communicating by e-mail or browsing web pages. Furthermore, the higher subjects scored on tool and social-structural literacy, the better their academic performance would be; however, technical literacy skills, such as publishing and technology literacy, were not significant predictors for academic performance.

The Addiction Process

According to researcher Kimberly S. Young, the addiction process follows a general pattern of behavior as people gradually retreat into the computer.[13] They become more comfortable using the technology, they may begin to experiment with the Internet, exploring new types of websites such as pornography, or they may enter a chat room for the very first time. To the individual this is new and something tempting—and it is usually not something that he or she would have tried if he or she thought someone was watching.

Young states that the process falls into five successive and interdependent stages:

- Discovery
- Experimentation
- Escalation
- Compulsion
- Hopelessness

According to Young, the stages are interdependent and highlight how users use the Internet as a progressive means of escape as part of an addiction cycle. In the discovery phase, new users feel an excitement associated with the discovery of the Internet. The users discover that there is so much to see and do online. The second stage involving experimentation is where the users begin to explore new types of sexual behaviors. They find themselves drawn to online sex.

After the discovery and experimentation phases of becoming addicted, the individual escalates his or her use of the Internet, much like the alcoholic requires larger and larger doses of alcohol to achieve the same sensation and pleasure from the experience. The fourth phase involves compulsivity. As the behavior escalates, the online use becomes more chronic and more ingrained—and then develops into a compulsive obsession. In the final phase, hopelessness, the addict hits "rock bottom."

Diagnostic Criteria

As noted by Dr. Young, the Internet is a highly promoted technological tool, making detection and diagnosis of addiction difficult.[14] According to her, it is essential to understand the criteria that differentiate normal from pathological Internet use. Young noted that the proper diagnosis is often complicated by the fact that there is currently no accepted set of criteria for the addiction. According to Young, pathological gambling is viewed as most akin to the compulsive nature of Internet use. She defines it as an impulse control disorder that does not involve an intoxicant and developed the following criteria:

1. Does the person feel preoccupied with the Internet (think about previous online activity or anticipate his or her next online session)?
2. Does he or she feel the need to use the Internet with increasing amounts of time to achieve satisfaction?
3. Has the person repeatedly made unsuccessful efforts to control, cut back, or stop Internet use?
4. Does the individual feel restless, moody, depressed, or irritable when attempting to cut down or stop Internet use?
5. Does the person generally stay online longer than originally intended?
6. Has the person jeopardized or risked the loss of a significant relationship, job, or educational or career opportunity because of the Internet?
7. Does the individual lie to family members, therapists, or others to conceal his or her extent of involvement with the Internet?
8. Does the person use the Internet as a way of escaping from problems or relieving feelings of helplessness, guilt, anxiety, or depression?

Paranormal

Paranormal is a general term that was coined between 1910 and 1920. The term is used to define experiences that cannot readily be explained by the range of normal experience or scientific explanation. Paranormal is used to describe anything that is beyond or contrary to what is deemed scientifically possible. If we consider the world around us as normal, then anything that is beyond the normal or contrary to the normal is para. Accordingly, by definition, paranormal does not conform to conventional expectations of nature. The existence of ghosts is an example of a paranormal event.

A paranormal phenomenon is different from hypothetical concepts such as dark matter and dark energy. Unlike paranormal phenomena, these hypothetical concepts are based on empirical observation and scientific method. We often find references to paranormal phenomena in popular culture and folklore.

A famous collector of paranormal stories or incidents was Charles Fort (1874–1932). It is reported that Fort had compiled as many as 40,000 notes on unexplained paranormal experiences. These notes came from what he called the orthodox conventionality of science, which were odd events originally reported in magazines and newspapers such as the *Times* and scientific journals such as *Scientific American*, *Nature*, and *Science*. As the results of his research, Fort published several books, including *The Book of the Damned*[15] and *New Lands*.[16]

The notes that he collected were about teleportation, poltergeist events, falls of frogs, fishes, and inorganic materials of an amazing range, crop circles, unaccountable noises and explosions, spontaneous fires, levitation, ball lightning, unidentified flying objects, mysterious appearances and disappearances, giant wheels of light in the oceans, and animals found outside their normal ranges. He is credited by some as the first person to explain strange human appearances and disappearances by the hypothesis of alien abduction.

Scientific American in 1929 offered two $2,500 awards: (1) for the first authentic spirit photograph made under test conditions and (2) for the first psychic to produce a "visible psychic manifestation." The investigating committee included the world famous magician Harry Houdini. The first medium to be tested claimed that in his presence spirits would speak through a trumpet that floated around a darkened room. The individual was placed in a room, the lights were extinguished, but unbeknownst to him, his chair had been rigged to light a signal in an adjoining room if he ever left his seat. Because the light signals were tripped during his performance, he did not collect the award.[17]

Frequently, researchers try to determine if there is a connection between religion and belief in the paranormal. Individuals who belong to various religious faiths often contend that religion and paranormal are very different types of beliefs. Those who are not very religious point out that there are some important similarities that bear closer consideration. In reality, one probably does not have anything to do with the other. For example, I am sure that whether or not you believe in the existence of Big Foot has no bearing on your religious beliefs.

Abnormal Religious Practices

A very touchy issue involves the question: When do abnormal religious practices become deviant behavior? Probably an overwhelming percentage of citizens would classify an individual who commits a suicide terrorist act based on his religious belief that he will go to heaven and have

70 virgin maidens at his disposal as a deviant. That is not a close question, but what about the individual who believes that it is against God's will to take a bath on Sunday? In the latter case, no one is seriously injured and no serious social rules have been broken; as the saying goes in basketball, no harm, no foul.

The preceding two examples appear to be clear. Consider the situation where a family of five is surviving on minimum wage. The family, being religious, gives 10% of the family income to their church. Because the family is giving this money to the church, the family does not have sufficient food left to properly feed the family. Probably many individual would praise the family for their strong religious beliefs and for following through on those beliefs. Other individuals probably would condone the family for depriving the family of sufficient food. In this situation, whether you praise the family or consider their act as deviant depends on your religious beliefs. The authors assume that the readers will be conflicted on this issue. It is situations like this that make it difficult to label some actions as deviant or nondeviant.

The Kwakiutl Indians of Pacific Northwest believed that their heavily forested inland region was the home of supernatural beings. To them, the forest was an important part of their religion's spiritual beliefs and rituals. These Indians would probably consider the cutting of the trees in order to have the lumber needed to build homes in Seattle as deviant behavior. The people in Seattle, who because of the cuttings are able to buy homes, probably would not consider the cuttings as deviant behavior.

The North America Haida Indians used a power inherent from hemlock branches to scrub themselves in ritual baths. They believed that the hemlock had the power to purify and protect the Indians and enable them to attain the degree of cleanliness required during their rituals, and thus remain on good terms with their supernatural beings.

Most Christian families use a Christmas tree to help celebrate the birthday of Jesus. For them, the decorating of the tree is part of the recognition of the importance of the event. The authors considered this an important tradition when they were very young and eagerly looked forward to the act of finding a tree, cutting it, taking it home, and decorating it. A non-Christian could consider this deviant behavior and the wasteful destruction of our natural resources.

Summary

- Belief is a state of the mind, treated in various academic disciplines, especially philosophy and psychology, as well as traditional culture, in which a subject roughly regards a thing to be true.
- To a person who holds a questionable belief, it is probably unconventional to him or her. For the most part, each of us has certain

beliefs that others may not agree with, but that does not make them unconventional.

- A belief system is a set of mutually supportive beliefs. The beliefs of any such system can be classified as religious, philosophical, ideological, or a combination of these.
- Belief systems play an important role in social change. In many cases, these changes are taking place through liberation theology (whereby believers are for social reform and justice for the poor) and religious nationalism (whereby religious beliefs are merged with government institutions).
- Belief systems fulfill social needs. They can be powerful, dynamic forces in society.
- If one drinks in an excessive, deviant manner, so as to bring deprivation and harm to self and others while remaining impervious to pleas and admonitions based on this obvious connection, the person is assumed not to be in control of his or her will (regardless of desire).
- Deviance in the workplace is not generally considered a deviant subculture. It is an important subject and was inserted in this chapter as a matter of convenience.
- *Paranormal* is a general term that was coined between 1910 and 1920. The term is used to define experiences that cannot readily be explained by the range of normal experience or scientific explanation.
- A very touchy issue involves the question: When do abnormal religious practices become deviant behavior?

Questions in Review

1. What are belief systems and why are they important to us?
2. Why do workers commit deviant behavior at work?
3. How do people become addicted to the Internet?
4. What are the issues in defining abnormal religious practices?
5. Explain the research on paranormal activities.

Key Terms

Belief: A state of the mind, treated in various academic disciplines, especially philosophy and psychology, as well as traditional culture, in which a subject roughly regards a thing to be true.

Computer addiction, online addiction, or Internet addiction disorder (IAD): A term used to describe a variety of impulse control problems involving the use of the computer or Internet.

Deviant drinking behavior: Behaviors that involve repetitive, usually heavy, and always consequential drinking.

Paranormal: A general term that was coined between 1910 and 1920. The term is used to define experiences that cannot readily be explained by the range of normal experience or scientific explanation.

Endnotes

1. Eric Schwitzgebel. (2006). Belief. In Edward Zalta (Ed.), *The Stanford encyclopedia of philosophy*. Stanford, CA: Metaphysics Research Lab.
2. Jonathan Glover. (1988). *The philosophy and psychology of personal identity*. London: Allen Lane.
3. Benjamin Rush. (1784). *An inquiry of the effects of ardent spirits upon the human body and mind*. Boston: James Loring.
4. Rush, 1784, pp. 4–5.
5. Joseph W. Schneider. (1978, April). Deviant drinking as disease: Alcoholism as a social accomplishment. *Social Problems*, *25*(4), 361–372.
6. Schneider, 1978.
7. Mark Keller. (1976). The disease concept of alcoholism revisited. *Journal of Studies on Alcohol*, *37*, 1694–1717.
8. Sandra L. Robinson & Rebecca J. Bennett. (1995). A typology of deviant workplace behaviors: A multidimensional scaling study. *Academy of Management Journal*, *38*(2), 555–572.
9. Barrie E. Litzky, Kimberly A. Eddleston, & Deborah L. Kidder. (2006). The good, the bad, and the misguided: How managers inadvertently encourage deviant behaviors. *Academy of Management Perspectives*, *20*(1), 91–103.
10. Material for this section was adapted from the HelpGuide.org website. HelpGuide is a nonprofit resource that deals with addiction issues. It is located at http://www.helpguide.org/mental/internet_cybersex_addiction.htm. Retrieved August 15, 2014.
11. Janet Morahan-Martin. (2005). Internet abuse: Addiction? Disorder? Symptom? Alternative explanations? *Social Science Computer Review*, *23*(1), 39–48.
12. Louis Leung & Paul S. N. Lee. (2012). Impact of Internet literacy, Internet addiction symptoms, and Internet activities on academic performance, *Social Science Computer Review*, *30*(4), 403–418.
13. Kimberly S. Young. (2008). Internet sex addiction: Risk factors, stages of development, and treatment. *American Behavioral Scientist*, *52*(1), 21–37.
14. Kimberly S. Young. (2004). Internet addiction: A new clinical phenomenon and its consequences. *American Behavioral Scientist*, *48*(4), 402–415.
15. Charles Fort. (1919). *The book of the damned*. New York: Boni and Liveright.
16. Charles Fort. (1923). *New lands*. New York: Boni and Liveright.
17. Claus Larsen. (2003, September). Get rich quick or save the world. A Skeptic Report. http://web.archive.org/web/20070323193619/http://www.skepticreport.com/skepticism/getrichquick.htm. Retrieved August 15, 2014.

Index

D

E